Radio After the Golden Age

ALSO BY JIM COX AND FROM MCFARLAND

Radio Journalism in America: Telling the News in the Golden Age and Beyond (2013)

Musicmakers of Network Radio: 24 Entertainers, 1926–1962 (2012)

Rails Across Dixie: A History of Passenger Trains in the American South (2011)

American Radio Networks: A History (2009)

Sold on Radio: Advertisers in the Golden Age of Broadcasting (2008; paperback 2013)

This Day in Network Radio: A Daily Calendar of Births, Deaths, Debuts, Cancellations and Other Events in Broadcasting History (2008)

The Great Radio Sitcoms (2007; paperback 2012)

Radio Speakers: Narrators, News Junkies, Sports Jockeys, Tattletales, Tipsters, Toastmasters and Coffee Klatch Couples Who Verbalized the Jargon of the Aural Ether from the 1920s to the 1980s — A Biographical Dictionary (2007; paperback 2011)

The Daytime Serials of Television, 1946–1960 (2006; paperback 2010)

Music Radio: The Great Performers and Programs of the 1920s through Early 1960s (2005; paperback 2011)

Mr. Keen, Tracer of Lost Persons: A Complete History and Episode Log of Radio's Most Durable Detective (2004; paperback 2011)

Frank and Anne Hummert's Radio Factory: The Programs and Personalities of Broadcasting's Most Prolific Producers (2003)

Radio Crime Fighters: More Than 300 Programs from the Golden Age (2002; paperback 2010)

Say Goodnight, Gracie: The Last Years of Network Radio (2002)

The Great Radio Audience Participation Shows: Seventeen Programs from the 1940s and 1950s (2001; paperback 2009)

The Great Radio Soap Operas (1999; paperback 2008)

Radio After the Golden Age

The Evolution of American Broadcasting Since 1960

JIM COX

McFarland & Company, Inc., Publishers
Jefferson, North Carolina, and London

LIBRARY OF CONGRESS CATALOGUING-IN-PUBLICATION DATA

Cox, Jim, 1939–
    Radio after the golden age : the evolution of American broadcasting since 1960 / Jim Cox.
      p.   cm.
    Includes bibliographical references and index.

    ISBN 978-0-7864-7434-9
    softcover : acid free paper ∞

    1. Radio broadcasting—United States—History—20th century.
2. Radio broadcasting—United States—History—21st century.
I. Title.
PN1991.3.U6C68 2013
384.540973—dc23   2013034590

BRITISH LIBRARY CATALOGUING DATA ARE AVAILABLE

© 2013 Jim Cox. All rights reserved

No part of this book may be reproduced or transmitted in any form or by any means, electronic or mechanical, including photocopying or recording, or by any information storage and retrieval system, without permission in writing from the publisher.

Front cover: DJ photograph and background texture (iStockphoto/Thinkstock)

Manufactured in the United States of America

McFarland & Company, Inc., Publishers
  Box 611, Jefferson, North Carolina 28640
    www.mcfarlandpub.com

For John and Larry Gassman
and Walden Hughes —
Peerless Radio Broadcasters
with Extraordinary Vision

Table of Contents

Acknowledgments ix
Preface: The Nation's Soundtrack 1

1. The Best of Times 9
2. The Goose, the Egg and the Evil Eye 23
3. At Last, Wireless for Real 44
4. From Victrola to Payola 57
5. Power Shift Fuels Fine-Tuning 76
6. Escalating the Continuum 87
7. Narrowcasting: A Captive Audience 105
8. Talk Is Cheap 116
9. Theater of the Mind Déjà Vu 142
10. Satellites and Automated Dialing 159
11. Pillaging the Public Airwaves 169
12. Multicolored Radio 178
13. An Acoustical Smorgasbord 195
14. Tune in Again Tomorrow 207

Appendix: A Half-Century of Radio Evolution 215
Notes 227
Bibliography 245
Index 253

Acknowledgments

A very long time ago I figured out that no author is solely responsible for what goes out with his name attached to it. I've never produced a book manuscript without having to turn to a few knowledgeable friends for assistance. I learned way back yonder that those individuals, most of them sharing my abiding passion for radio, not only exhibit an innate brilliance about whatever subjects may be tossed their way but manifest qualities of modesty, solemnity, and availability to press ahead on whatever it takes to pursue a given task.

While there are many who have influenced these pages by demonstrating nothing short of extraordinary levels of input, I'll cite a small handful who made substantial donations in researching and clarifying some of the details recorded here. The leader of the pack is the investigator I have depended upon most heavily for years — Irene Heinstein. She possesses an uncanny ability to ferret out the most obscure facts that may never have been reported by anyone in hard copy, online, on the air, via audio transcription, videotape, or on stage, or the silver screen. We are all in her debt, and I'm pleased to express my profound appreciation to her once again.

To assist in some of these explorations, I have also leaned upon the talents and connections of pals Harry Dellinger, Martin Grams, Jr., David Schwartz, and Jim Widner. They have all played a vital part in helping expose a vast timeframe in the history of radio that has, for the most part, been bypassed in any meaningfully comprehensive way. Hopefully this text will fill in some links that have been missing in the annals of radio's legacy. And if there are errors or omissions, be assured that they are the author's and no one else's, and that they are definitely unintentional.

I'm exceedingly grateful that my lifelong partner, Sharon Cox, continues to allow me to devote many hours to these endeavors. She is the love of my life, and her willingness to share me provides some incentive to pursue the mysteries we uncover.

And thank you, dear readers, for your interest in the continuing saga of radio. My hope is that this odyssey will fulfill some of your expectations by supplying answers to questions you may have about the aural medium in America once its celebrated heyday had passed.

Preface:
The Nation's Soundtrack

> Radio is the oldest of the electronic mass media, tracing its roots back to the late nineteenth century, as well as the most ubiquitous. Most households in America still have more radio receivers than occupants. It's also the most under-appreciated, long ago relegated to third-tier status as a kind of bush league for the entertainment world, where flashier media such as movies, television, and the Internet easily overshadow it.
> It also is the most profitable of the traditional media, due to its relatively low overhead, and thus regarded as a bellwether of the media industry.[1]
> Radio is arguably the most important electronic invention of the [20th] century. Cognitively, it revolutionized the perceptual habits of the nation.... It forever blurred the boundaries between the private domestic sphere and public, commercial, and political life. It made listening to music a daily requirement for millions of Americans.... Today we have twice as many radios in America as we do people.[2]

Approbation like this from an array of spokespersons rains down on the nation's original omnipresent soundtrack. While radio may be regarded as an "also ran" among our foremost sources of knowledge and amusement today, low-tech and unglamorous to most observers, the fact that we as a nation depended upon radio for *all* our earth-shattering news flashes, opinion, and mass distraction in times past and delivered concurrently too — and that millions still steadily rely upon it — indicates that we aren't yet ready to adjust our dials or turn off our sets. With about 1,400 U.S. daily newspapers, fewer than 1,800 full-power TV outlets, and almost 15,000 full-power radio stations in this country presently, Americans still turn to radio as a pervasive force in entertainment and information, despite — and synergistically in conjunction with — the proliferation of the Internet.[3] A pilgrimage odyssey into exploring resonance technology can be mysteriously captivating.

In the beginning, there were the *hams*. That was a label that in due course was to be affixed to the incredibly enthusiastic, unrelentingly industrious fellows (and a few gals) who markedly altered the panorama of the acoustical atmosphere. Sometimes taking the din of the needle of a phonograph and intermingling spoken utterances from their own articulation alongside it, they dispatched whatever hullabaloo resulted and sent it spiraling across the ether. There it may have been seized by crystal-set owners who frequently went to the trouble of acknowledging its arrival to those who transmitted it.

In the meantime the commotion had invaded the solitude of an environmental milieu which, up to then, had gone largely undisturbed. With the signals racing through ever-increasing expanses of space, those formidable experiments in sound transmission surely qualified their originators as redoubtable clansmen set among a hardy cluster of radio's classic forbears. One of the foremost members of that tribe, commonly dubbed *wireless operators* back then, was certified to have been at work as far back as 1906. He is, in fact, considered the medium's first DJ. (In its most rudimentary construct the wireless apparatus was already dispersing its tones by 1893. Mesmerizing details are divulged in Chapter 3.)

By the 1920s, these sound engineers were joined by many of their contemporaries who ran tactical broadcasting stations of brick-and-mortar fabrication. Distinguished and separated by commercial, private capital, and public-oriented interests, the newest titans of broadcasting beamed their wares over the ether via the AM band. That's a designation that, admittedly, didn't gain notice endemically for a while. A couple of decades would pass before Americans finally started to realize that the broadcasting spectrum had been enlarged to accomplish at least two things of mounting unease: to improve the sound quality of radio transmission by virtually eliminating all static, and to accommodate — at the same time — more aspirants wanting their own turn on the air, people who had thus far been denied it. Until FM palpably broadened radio's horizons in the 1940s, some candidates simply had little chance to pursue their visionary quests of ethereal opportunity by the sole spatial limits of an overcrowded AM band. A couple of decades more actually elapsed before FM finally hit its stride and ultimately overtook AM as the aural airwaves' dominant continuum.

As most who have followed this pastime we call radio can now comprehend, the aforementioned is but a portion of the developing and persistently awesome vista that witnessed the profession's increase into a cornucopia of multidimensional provinces. Following the emergence of FM, the perennial *broadcast* arena (for which the idiom *terrestrial* is sometimes substituted) was joined by both *satellite* and *Web-based* endeavors. Myriad stations and operators are currently active, fully engaged in intensifying, escalating, and diversifying the processes by which we currently receive sound waves. This had formerly taken a more traditional routing to our ears and was, predictably, exhibited by reliably conventional platforms. But if there's one thing we've learned in all these years of intervening media history, it's that radio — like just about anything else — will hardly remain motionless. Change is inevitable.

"We are fast-entering a time when 'radio' will become a feature of other things rather than simply a destination unto itself, as it has been up until now," predicted occupational analyst Mark Ramsey.[4] In the modern epoch we've already seen some of the results of altering the listening schematic. It has been accomplished by music downloading media (e.g., MP3 digital audio players; iPod portable music players), mobile music services (e.g., iTunes, Napster, Rhapsody, and Spotify, to name a few), as well as mobile multimedia gadgets like cell phones with music downloading functions and PDAs (personal digital assistants, embracing hand-held computers, palmtops, and pocket computers). This will only increase, given the ever-expanding WiFi and WiMax universe.

Despite the multiplying mechanization of the world we live in, the myriad styles of conduction are purely extensions of the rubric we have characteristically appreciated all along as radio, pure and simple. Can a rose by any other name smell as sweet? Not so long ago an academic christened that medium as "the soundtrack of the nation."[5] He may not have been stretching the truth. As of this writing at least, radio's obituary has yet to be written.

> Broadcast radio continues to hold its own in the face of the many new competing audio technologies and the seismic shifts in its management and operational structure due to the elimination of long-standing ownership caps and the subsequent consolidation and clustering of thousands of stations....
>
> Although overall listening has declined (over 15% between 1990 and 2008 according to recent estimates and mainly among younger listeners), as has the actual time people spend tuned to broadcast radio ... due to increased competition from other audio choices and legislative changes, radio continues to be one of the most pervasive media on earth, even more so than the Internet....
>
> There is no patch of land, no piece of ocean surface untouched by the electromagnetic signals beamed from more than 40,000 radio stations worldwide.[6]

Can you handle a couple of added startling statistics? Radio remains popular even in the face of millions who are surfing the Web and large numbers who remain glued to the tube. Not long ago the national ratings service Arbitron announced that 92.7 percent of Americans age 12 and higher listen to radio every week.[7] Furthermore, that figure is higher than the numbers for television, magazines, newspapers, or the Internet, Arbitron reports. And — if you really want to be blown away — in an age in which so much technological innovation has showered us with gadgets galore for grabbing our attention and clasping it for undue periods, as recently as 2007 Americans were tuning in their radios for news, music, sports, talk, or other forms of aural amusement and enlightenment — get this — typically 18.5 hours weekly, or more than an two hours in the average day![8]

While a portion of that may have been heard directly through some device derived from the plethora of technological breakthroughs, the fact that we continue to spend so much time with the original electronic mass media clearly means our addiction requires regular feeding. Without exhibiting the glitz of the latest bells and whistles, radio remains a very relevant factor, a very powerful influence, in most Americans' lives.

Concentrating on radio in America, this text takes a broad view of the landscape that has clearly evolved in the aural medium since its Golden Age faded. While the incredibly profound epoch of radio's "heyday" will be frequently referenced, as well as the early history of the airborne mass media, you may nevertheless anticipate discovering answers within the lion's share of these pages to a single question: "What happened to radio after 1960?" That monumental time zone isn't flippantly selected by the way. It's a fairly firm line of demarcation that satisfies a plethora of vintage radio scholars who particularly celebrate all that occurred before it.

The Golden Age was dominated by a handful of transcontinental chains augmented by affiliate outlets as well as independent stations, all of which filled broadcasting's hours with a flurry of features from myriad genres. The ephemeral shifting of gears about 1960 distinguishing "all that went before" from "what came after": an era of seemingly endless experimentation and innovation that insulated America from traditional radio as if sealing off the past from what transpired from then on. From the late 1950s and 1960s, much of what we had always known radio to be literally expired or became unrecognizable. This was due to a coalescing of factors that included not merely technological breakthroughs — although that was a very large part of it, and we still witness that evolvement today — but also changes in how, where, and when we listened to radio, based on numerous ways in which we re-ordered our lives, our preferences, our interests, our leisure time, our work habits, our cultural tastes, and our need to know. All of this makes radio's story in the last half-dozen decades as compelling as the heavy emphasis many sources have given to its Golden Age. Lamentably, not a whole lot of scholarship has been provided to date in defining how radio's fortunes shifted from the 1960s until the present. This volume is an attempt to provide some justice for that regrettably enduring drought.

To properly answer "What happened to radio after 1960?" it's obligatory that we return to "those thrilling days of yesteryear" numerous times to examine radio's legacy. In so doing we can discover *how* it changed in the years hence. Although it may seem as if we are dwelling "way back yonder" too often, setting the stage for what happened by supplying some background detail from an earlier epoch seemed perfectly fitting. It will hopefully not become distracting or constricting: how otherwise could we evaluate what radio *became* and *is* without understanding what it *was*?

After unifying the country with its original means of reaching everybody in the same instant with the same sounds, radio began to gradually change in the middle of the 20th century. Within a decade it was station-oriented rather than subjugated by national networks. By then it was filling a new niche, appealing primarily to individual tastes and preferences rather than those of families and groups, while supplying background din to an increasingly mobile population. Radio did not die, of course, but began to thrive in increasingly newer manifestations. Some were painful; others were practical, beneficial, beautiful, and vibrant.

By the time you've completed reading this text you may have learned a thing or two about radio in the past half-century that you didn't know before:

- You'll encounter the knights of the turntable — the platter-and-chatter crowd that filled the airchairs coast to coast as ubiquitous giants of the airwaves, saving local radio in the process. Suddenly, the DJs were declared expendable by their employers and swiftly disappeared from the very stations they had rescued. Their banishment in an environment that increasingly dwelled on bottom lines (theirs and station owners') elicits some answers for their downfall.
- After lying dormant for a few decades, FM radio was transformed into euphoric vibrancy that unambiguously marked it as "the place to be" in ethereal transmission. FM even superseded the AM band in number of listeners and steadfast loyalty, a radical departure catching many listeners by surprise. Not only did FM supply improved sound quality but a proliferation of new formatting possibilities, targeting precisely what smaller groups wanted to hear. FM was the first of many unending technical innovations to appreciably impact the audio industry after the Golden Age.
- You'll find out what it took to reverse the fortunes of AM radio during the latter years of the 20th century. Viewed as a losing proposition most places at the start of the century's final decade, with some insiders wondering if AM could possibly survive at all, by the time the decade ended, AM was completely resuscitated — and in some markets, it was clearly sitting in the proverbial catbird seat, heard once more by millions of Americans, just like "in the good old days." Why the stunning revolution? It took a four-letter word to make an irrefutable difference. (Hint: rhymes with *walk*.)
- Some in the radio audience believed that the feds — charged with protecting the airwaves for its owners, the U.S. population — did its subjects few favors when it removed constraints on broadcasters that totally reversed some durable terms of endearment. By "selling out" to the megabucks-minded media moguls, radio — previously oriented to the communities served by it — became disoriented, distanced not only from the listeners

but situated far from their geographical district. Conversely, when some restrictions on verbal exchanges on the ether were lifted, many more of those tuning in were gratified.

It's the objective of this author to relate radio's saga over the last half-century as precisely and as comprehensively as possible. That includes warts and all, the "all" being some very high moments in its performance; the "warts" recount some weaknesses that could seriously imperil the aural medium's continued existence. In the early years of the current millennium there were a few indications that radio could be headed for serious trouble. Some will be considered and examined. Broadcast radio advertising expenditures rose a negligible 0.3 percent while the collective audience plummeted 0.8 percent to a sparse 27.4 million listeners in that era.[9] Those dual factors were recorded in 2005, turning it into radio's most lackluster year in several recent years. This kind of news generates a sinking feeling that, if left unchecked, portends a colorless future for the medium.

Not long afterward, to radio's detriment, a handful of increasingly burgeoning technologies gained a somber foothold on the nation's conscience, vying for equal or greater time and attention, and threatening to erode listeners' dependence on broadcast radio still further. Among the most promising detractors (if indeed that is the appropriate designation, depending on your particular point of view) there is Internet radio, podcasting, portable iPods, and subscription-based satellite radio. Perhaps there will always be a need for the audio medium (e.g., in our vehicles and in domiciles and other environments in which competing systems aren't preferable, present, or practical). Yet, does it seem that radio's fading influence could be destined to erode even further?

The reality is that the foremost structure of mass media communication which possesses the capability to, theoretically at least, reach everybody in the country all in the same instant — once unchallenged and all-pervasive, solitarily occupying that lofty and very prestigious and powerful pedestal — has steadily lost ground. Indications are that the medium will continue to progress down that road. But writing broadcast radio off entirely doesn't appear to be in the foreseeable future either. The nation's soundtrack has inspired several new and astonishing, even awesomely stunning, innovations.

And after intensely investigating this endeavor in as near-comprehensive a fashion as possible, exploring hundreds, and perhaps thousands, of fundamental sources among the minutiae that envelop it, I've arrived at this simple conclusion: radio is here to stay. Perhaps you will draw a similar deduction by the time your own quest is fulfilled in the text that follows.

Before I sign off and let you sign on to the main body of this tome, may I share a little personal and poignant observation with you?

In his delightful treatise *Charles Kuralt's America*, released in 1995, the wandering minstrel who spent his 37-year career in a charmed existence as a CBS news junkie (and on many a junket, we might add) recalls some of the heartrending tales of his journeys throughout the U.S.A. after his professional exploits were finished. "It was a long, happy affair, and I was faithful," he says of his esteem for his employer. To prove his love, Kuralt allows, "I took crazy chances for her, especially in the beginning, often sleeping too little, working too hard, driving too fast, risking too much in places too dangerous." Finally — just before he took off across the country with no plan, no route, and no budget in mind, acting "a little irresponsible" — he remembers, "I woke up one morning and realized I didn't love her [CBS] anymore."[10]

While *this* author was always on the outside looking in — having never had an opportunity to work for a real live radio station, or even better, for one of the few transcontinental chains that enveloped America back in the day — I nevertheless developed a relentless passion for all that radio represented. And I was just as committed to that notion as Charles Kuralt appears to have been toward CBS at one time.

Only with me, the passion *never left*. It's just as strong now as it was then.

1

The Best of Times

> It was the best of times, it was the worst of times, it was the age of wisdom, it was the age of foolishness, it was the epoch of belief, it was the epoch of incredulity, it was the season of Light, it was the season of Darkness, it was the spring of hope, it was the winter of despair, we had everything before us, we had nothing before us, we were all going direct to Heaven, we were all going direct the other way.—Charles Dickens, *A Tale of Two Cities*

The opening lines of Dickens's historical novel articulate the highs and lows that prevailed in the late 18th century. This oft-cited passage intimates that a response by the citizens of dual capitals, London and Paris, is imminent. Likewise in the United States the aphorism that Dickens adopted appears to embrace a pertinent application for the era readily dubbed by passionate enthusiasts of aural broadcasting as the Golden Age of Radio. For purposes of this discourse let us assign that label to the interval that extended from the late 1920s through the late 1950s. If you were a fan of what is currently epitomized as *old-time radio* or *vintage* radio or radio *back in the day*, this period in question was—for you—categorically *the best of times*.

> In a society of modest incomes, steam locomotives, rhyming roadside Burma Shave signs, movie double features, nationwide general-interest magazines, and touring carnivals, circuses, and dance bands, radio was a spectral world of joy, discovery, even magic that imparted the exotic glamour of worlds [that] most listeners could only imagine....
>
> Those were extraordinary times, a kind of Age of Innocence increasingly foreign to today.[1]

During that same stretch, in the meantime, our national civilization was in utter disarray, provoked by the most ruinously damaging fiscal collapse the country had ever experienced. The demoralizing phenomenon was closely followed by two absolutely devastating wars. Given enough time, Americans would awesomely rally from all three destructive episodes. Yet each circumstance was separated from the others by little more than transitory intervals which left the nation with only brief opportunities to catch its collective breath before the onset of the next calamity's intervention. Indubitably the United States was experiencing some of the worst of times it had ever encountered as a nation. Radio reflected the cultural, social, economic, political, and unification inducements of that awful period as citizens all over the place pitched in to do what they could to right the capsized ship.

The hardships of that agonizing juncture are mentioned only as an offshoot of a different type of account that is chronicled in the pages that follow. For radio lovers, the Golden Age was doubtlessly the best of all worlds. That theme will resonate again and again throughout this volume. And particularly will it be evidenced in this gateway discourse that highlights the specific point in time when a new medium was effectively symbolized in most American domiciles by an all but indispensable piece of furniture. That apparatus was a visible, abiding link to the power of auditory transmission beyond the far horizon, and one our nation had never previously encountered.

> Radio's Golden Age—[is] so described both because broadcasting was the age's sole instant home information and entertainment provider and it reflected remarkable quality, diversity, and taste. This, it is now apparent, was partly due to a unique alignment of constellations in the nation's political, cultural, and economic cosmos. These included electronics' state of development, national network structures, station ownership patterns, cultural vigor, civic activism, regulatory oversight, and the era's social cohesion.
>
> The 1920s through 1940s ... constituted a belle époque in American culture, manifest in the achievements of Broadway, Hollywood, Carnegie Hall, Tin Pan Alley, Publishers' Row, and distinctive major newspapers and magazines. Both network and local broadcasting mirrored and magnified them all. Just as the 1920s laid the foundation for Golden Age programming, the 1930s marked its maturation.[2]

While radio is as customary to us as the air that transmits the treasures it bestows, for most of global history, nonetheless, nobody was aware of it. Until the early 19th century communication over any *real* distance was literally restricted to how far people could *hear* or *see*. Bells, guns, shouts, trumpets, or whistles were commonly summoned to gain attention via sound. At the same time fires, flags, mirrors, and smoke regularly accomplished the same ends by furnishing an inventory of ready-made visual techniques. More extensive outreach meant engaging carriages, horses, runners or ships. As inconceivable as it may now occur to us in the 21st century, as recently as 1852, France sustained 500 towers visible to one another by way of telescopes. This form of signal "transmission" was also being practiced around that late in the day in Great Britain, Russia and Sweden.[3] The introduction of the Internet, satellite, smartphones, and all the other electronic paraphernalia, gadgetry, devices, and added emblems that are employed today as communicative tools in booming proportions has altered everything.

Radio, which in its earliest days was commonly referenced as the "wireless telephone" or just plain "wireless," can be dated well before the 1920s — the decade we almost always associate universally with its start. The medium developed out of the fervor of a few inventive individuals who demonstrated an infatuation with some very cool and incredibly noble concepts.[4] They were committed to the notion that there must be a whole lot more to communications than the telegraph (1844) and telephone (1876).[5] Those mechanisms undoubtedly inspired — instead of discouraged — progressive thinkers.

Inquisitive and unsatisfied investigators like James Maxwell (1831–79), Nikola Telsa (1856–1943), Heinrich Hertz (1857–94), Nathan Stubblefield (1860–1928), Reginald Fessenden (1866–1932), Lee de Forest (1873–1961), Guglielmo Marconi (1874–1937), Frank Conrad (1874–1941), Edwin Armstrong (1890–1954), and many more of their ilk figured prominently into nurturing radio's advancement. Their distinctive gifts to the evolving process make for fascinating reading. Their collective efforts were swift, extensive, effective, and played straight away to a thoroughly receptive audience. The yield from their toil, in fact, frequently became the centerpiece of many an American living room.

> By 1932, one out of three homes had a radio, some of which were the most expensive piece of furniture in people's houses — splendid domed cathedral consoles made by Stromberg-Carlson, Philco, Majestic, and Atwater Kent. The boxes themselves were wondrous instruments, known in the trade as highboys, lowboys, consoles, tombstones, and chairsides, often finished with filigree detailing. The ornate Philcos were beautifully designed by Norman Bel Geddes, Albert Mowitz, and Edward L. Combs; Combs dreamed up the famous "Model 90 Cathedral" that most people think of when they think of big fancy old-time radios.[6]

Wondrous instruments indeed!

Another wag perceived that source of awe as follows:

> The family radio was more than a piece of furniture, it was a magical link to an enchanted world of entertainment, news, and culture. By the mid–1930s the radio was the most important item in the home. It provided shared experiences to everyone, rich and poor, city dweller and farmer, black and white, educated and illiterate. The programs and the advertising created an image of an ideal America beyond the problems of poverty, war, and race. It made radio performers national heroes.[7]

One of the most riveting applications that still another segment of creative geniuses fostered — including some key individuals who were responsible for programming American radio over much of the Golden Age — was the attentiveness to humor that they employed in attracting audiences. That idea flourished and even evolved into pervasive magnitude in the early years, especially following the inception of nationwide hookups that linked people on dual coasts to one another and to those living in between. Listeners rebounded from their troubles with the levity that was ushered into their homes from distant origination points.

Many of the early features were designed to incorporate comedy into a multiplicity of formats. Even more ingeniously, the jesting proved to be a relief mechanism, one that much of the country turned to in periods of persistent distress in order to gain even momentary distraction from its times of woe. This was certainly the case during the economic upheaval that affected almost everybody in the 1930s. Radio supplied a go-to form of transient release from the pervasive adversities, suffering, and destitution of that disparaging epoch. It was also, and thankfully so, very inexpensive entertainment, when 15 or 25 cents for a movie was out of the question for most of the country's denizens.

This was a genuine hallmark of the times, enjoyed by many who benefited from the efforts of performers with an ability to create audible laughter and nourish it across the airwaves. Many of the new national *stars* had been successful in silent screen, in vaudeville and in other types of stage productions (musical revues, plays, summer stock, etc.). These were all forms of amusing distraction that had enjoyed durable runs amusing crowds in theaters, clubs, and myriad additional venues to be found throughout the land. These were now surpassed by radio's induction with its prevailing capacity for reaching millions of people instantaneously. America's funny bone was overturned with chuckles aplenty as hilarity and lightheartedness became the new norm. If initially for no other reason than that one perhaps, radio became an instant sensation. Virtually, it affected the entire country.

Among its comic entertainers who successfully vaulted from one medium into another were Fred Allen, Gracie Allen, Phil Baker, Jack Benny, Edgar Bergen, Fanny Brice, George Burns, Eddie Cantor, Charles Correll, Jimmy Durante, W.C. Fields, Freeman Gosden, Bob Hope, George Jessel, Jim Jordan, Marian Jordan, Groucho Marx, Jack Pearl, Joe Penner, Will Rogers, Red Skelton, and Ed Wynn. All of these had enjoyed enduring runs in one or more of amusement's ancillary avenues before maneuvering themselves into radio. On the air — if it hadn't happened to them already — their careers shifted into overdrive while their names became implicit household words.

A Fred Allen biographer offers some insightful landscape that helps in attaining an intuition of the environment within show business at that time as it related to a individual performer's stance.[8] These were the years in which the umbrellas of the transcontinental networks were just beginning to sprout, fusing the whole country under their wide-ranging shades. Before long all of the nation's tuned-in occupants were laughing at the very same cues at the same precise instant. It was clearly a revolutionary marvel that had transpired.

> On the eve of America's most devastating Depression winter, [Fred] Allen, an unemployed vaudeville and Broadway actor, obtained his own network radio

comedy show. Debuting on October 23, 1932, just as the Hoover–Roosevelt election campaign was drawing to a close, Allen joined a growing number of broadcast comics who injected interludes of laughter into the lives of demoralized and confused Americans. Public morale was of little concern to him, however. Of far greater immediacy was the challenge of establishing himself in a medium whose comedic potential was still undeveloped, in the wake of vaudeville's collapse and Broadway's morbidity.

The economic crisis of the early 1930s did not strike each branch of the entertainment industry with equal effect, and therein lies the explanation of radio's appeal to many performers.... During the remainder of the Depression decade "the automatic movie-going of the late 1920s was no more; theater managers had to work for their patronage" with such gimmicks as free dishes and Bank Night.[9]

The live stage, in New York and across the nation, including vaudeville, the legitimate theater, musicals and revues, suffered a precipitous audience decline beginning in 1930.... The live stage's economic difficulties translated into large-scale unemployment. Vaudeville, which had featured thousands of performers on national regional circuits at the height of its success between 1895 and 1925, experienced multiple ills even before the Depression hit. Both the sound motion picture after 1927, and radio, whose major national networks formed in 1926 and 1927, drained vaudeville of its material, its performers, and its patrons. The economic crisis merely finished what these electronic forms of mass amusement had begun.

Radio alone was Depression-proof. Among entertainment forms, only broadcasting would "emerge from 1932 with an increase of business over the previous year and show a substantial profit," *Variety* reported at the end of that year, and the medium's success continued unbroken into the post–World War II years. The opening of the National Broadcasting Company's (NBC) Radio City in the RCA Building, a part of the fourteen-structure Rockefeller Center complex in midtown Manhattan, symbolized radio's success story. That a business could celebrate growth by dedicating lavish facilities during the subdued Christmas season of 1932 was a telling fact not lost on listeners or performers.

Thus it was that scads of artists, not only comedians but actors, musicians, writers, and interlocutors as well — in fact, almost anyone with any demonstrated talent for pacifying an audience — found ways into the portals of radio theaters to exhibit their wares or, at the very least, to audition for a future recital. This newfangled medium was, as one critic put it, something "no performer could afford to be out of."

Those early comedians were often headliners for what would be widely dubbed as variety series in which more acoustically oriented entertainers might do their thing. Hence, along with the humor one might hear musical insertions of sundry persuasions, dramatic renderings, interviews, quizzes and other conversational exchanges that included scripted banter as well as freewheeling discussion. Dancing would not be seen, of course, except by a studio audience, but nearly every other drawing card could be fully subscribed by a clientele of listeners at home.

As time passed the creation of situation comedies, popularly trademarked as *sitcoms*, were added to the multiplying portfolio of auditory indulgences. A surfeit of those humorous offerings, the preponderance of which was family-oriented, ultimately flourished on the ether. Among the more unforgettable were *The Adventures of Ozzie and Harriet, The Aldrich Family, Amos 'n' Andy, Archie Andrews, Beulah, The Bickersons, Blondie, A Date with Judy, A Day in the Life of Dennis Day, Easy Aces, Ethel and Albert, Father Knows Best, Fibber McGee and Molly, The Great Gildersleeve, The Life of Riley, Lum and Abner, The Phil Harris–Alice Faye Show*, and *Vic and Sade*.

Most of those programs were the inventions of large advertising agencies which, in the early 1930s, stepped into an abyss that had extended from the inception of the major broadcasting chains.[10] They relieved the operators of the duties associated with selling a show to one or more sponsors, enlisting the talent (including the performers, musicians, announcers, directors, writers, etc.), and then rehearsing and putting a program on the air. For contractual fees these agencies took designated network time sold to them by the major chains and filled it with entertainment. The time (programming blocks or shows) was underwritten by benefactors with goods, services, ideas or goodwill to market. All of this — in theory at least — purportedly attracted large numbers of listeners to the transcontinental chains that were airing the shows that the agencies produced.

Quoted in the *Variety Radio Directory, 1937 to 1938*, Edgar A. Grunwald declared: "Currently, network commercial program production stands virtually at zero — attesting to the profit derived from radio by the advertising agencies, and indirectly indicating no compliment to the networks for their style of programming." The big hookups, of course, were highly competitive as were the agencies themselves. The burgeoning creative ad bureaus engaged time with the rival networks for their clients, sometimes doing so for contenders through their diametrically opposing commitments with various consumers in the trade. The bottom line, of course, was invariably about money changing hands, their (the agencies') *raison d'être*.

In 1937, a typical year during the heyday of network radio as a pervasive supplier of entertainment and information, the coast-to-coast broadcasters collectively earned $56,192,396 by selling their only substantive commodity: time.[11] Of that aggregate $15,962,729 was dispatched to the affiliates (member-stations) of the major networks, including some regional alliances of outlets. Another $8,428,860 went to the advertising agencies, the guys that were hypothetically, at least, performing all the creative stuff as well as the actual production and marketing tasks. The balance of the proceeds, $31,800,807, remained in the coffers of the networks themselves for — perceptually, at least — doing ostensibly very little to achieve (earn) it. At about the same time Federal Trade Commissioner George Henry Payne certified that the broadcasters were realizing an annual profit of 350 percent.[12] As the 1930s drew to a close, the ad agencies were producing more than four out of every five hours of network commercial features.[13] Those concerns were, in effect, the tail that wagged the dog. And, of course, it was the program underwriters that were instigating all of it. "A sponsor's word was law," esteemed media observer Leonard Maltin acknowledged.[14]

The voguish comedians and other shows headlined by classy humorists were supplanted in the middle of an ocean of supplementary and yet equally popular fare in further disciplines during radio's Golden Age. There were popular singers, including Rosemary Clooney, Perry Como, Connee Boswell, Bing Crosby, Morton Downey, Eddie Fisher, Dick Haymes, Al Jolson, Peggy Lee, Vaughn Monroe, Dinah Shore, Frank Sinatra, Jo Stafford, Jack Smith, Kate Smith, and Rudy Vallee.

There were plenty of big bands sounds of aggregates fronted by Ray Anthony, Les Brown, Xavier Cugat, Bob Crosby, Jimmy Dorsey, Tommy Dorsey, Duke Ellington, Benny Goodman, Glen Gray, Lionel Hampton, Woody Herman, Sammy Kaye, Wayne King, Kay Kyser, Guy Lombardo, Vincent Lopez, Freddy Martin, Glenn Miller, Artie Shaw, Orrin Tucker, Anson Weeks, Ted Weems, Paul Whiteman, and many dozens more.

There was another wave of instrumental sounds in radio's musical portfolio, a brigade of specialists that comprised the big networks' house bands. These skilled and versatile virtuosos were well prepared for their sundry responsibilities which might allow them plenty of advance warning and rehearsal prior to a broadcast — but not always so. They were subject to being summoned at a moment's notice as well to appear before the microphones to fill dead-air time when there was an equipment failure or mechanical malfunction. Or it might occur when a performer was unable to appear.

The house aggregates were responsible for many of the shows' theme songs heard on the air. They also played the bridge music between scenes as well as the background melodies during those programs. On occasions they presented an instrumental number of their own in a distinct segment of a program's bill. They were also responsible for any live advertising jingle melody accompanying the commercials.

Without the house bands there would have been lots of awkward moments in Golden Age radio. Their contributions could hardly be considered negligible, yet they were often bypassed — very possibly the literal unsung heroes and heroines of radio — or maybe they were mentioned hastily as the credits were announced near a show's end. Many of the conductors of these in-house troupes eventually fronted better-recognized orchestras or ensembles of their own. The careers of all of the following, and many more like them, at some point consisted of being impresarios for a house band for one or more of the national chains: Alfredo Antonini, Victor Arden, Robert Armbruster, Mitchell Ayers, Eddie Ballantine, Howard Barlow, Frank Black, Archie Bleyer, Al Goodman,

Morton Gould, Jerry Gray, Gus Haenschen, Wilbur Hatch, Gordon Jenkins, Abe Lyman, Muzzy Marcellino, Billy Mills, Ozzie Nelson, Ray Noble, Raymond Paige, Al Rickey, Nelson Riddle, David Rose, Walter Schumann, Harry Sosnik, Leith Stevens, Peter Van Steeden, Donald Voorhees, Paul Weston, Meredith Willson, and Victor Young.

Almost every zealot of radio music back in the day could find something that brought satisfying pleasure to his or her ears. For long hairs, there was *The Bell Telephone Hour*, *The Fred Waring Show*, the Longines' *Symphonette*, the *Metropolitan Opera*, the *NBC Symphony Orchestra*, the *New York Philharmonic*, and the *Voice of Firestone*. On the other hand, for shorter hairs there was *The Chamber Music Society of Lower Basin Street*, *The Chesterfield Supper Club*, *Club 15*, *Curt Massey and Martha Tilton*, Gene Autry's *Melody Ranch*, the *Grand Ole Opry*, the *Manhattan Merry-Go-Round*, Martin Block's *Make Believe Ballroom*, the *National Barn Dance*, *The Railroad Hour*, Robert Q. Lewis's *Waxworks*, Peter Potter's *Juke Box Jury*, and the perennial turntable-tabulating *Your Hit Parade*.

The theater of the mind, a branding that radio proudly boasted during the halcyon days for its limitless imaginative properties (and which will be explored more extensively in Chapter 9), proved to be a fabulous place for staging dramatic encounters in teeming dimensions. From *The Lone Ranger* to *The Romance of Helen Trent*, from *The Cavalcade of America* to *Mr. Keen, Tracer of Lost Persons*, from *Dr. Christian* to *Counterspy*, the medium habitually presented a veritable smorgasbord of theatrical delicacies that could be savored by playgoers any day of the week. The ether's acoustical capabilities — augmented by sound effects, choral and symphonic ensembles furnishing melodic bridges, strings, and themes — established a complete environment for artists with strong suits cloaked in the vernacular of the time.

Actors with penchants for juvenile action, mystery, science fiction, soap opera, straight drama, westerns, and other narrative fare plied their crafts from studio to studio. Sometimes they had just minutes to spare as they sped between venues for rehearsals and performances. (Sometimes they greased the palms of bellmen to hold elevators for them; they had taxi drivers waiting at a network's door to whisk them to another chain's facilities for a close call; and they paid stand-in thespians to voice their lines at rehearsals when they couldn't be there in time, just to keep themselves in harness.[15])

As noted previously, the new medium became the salvation of many an endangered performer's career. A pundit correctly professed: "Radio proved to be a mother lode for actors who had the style and the flexible vocal cords that allowed them to move from show to show, type to type, age to age, nationality to nationality, even race to race — often playing several roles at once while awaiting a movie or Broadway job. It was regular work, a lucrative living, and a godsend during the Depression."[16]

Droves of flexible thespians found work as headliners on recurring series. Many more appeared in guest shots or in supporting parts. Some of these practiced artisans were lucky enough to be appearing concurrently elsewhere. Radio required so little of a performer's time that he might be moonlighting in summer stock or in the legitimate theater or possibly in films. He might join touring circuits that slogged within the geographical proximities of some of the major broadcasting centers, including Chicago, Detroit, Los Angeles, and New York. The flexibility to do other things was one of the aural medium's hallmarks. It attracted legions of artists whose professional livelihoods were increasingly derived by escalating into complex disciplines.

In network radio's early years some of the dramatic fare presented on the airwaves can be acknowledged to have been fairly rudimentary in nature. This was certainly the case with such little-remembered entries as *America's Lost Plays, Arthur Hopkins Presents, The Black Chapel, Dangerously Yours, Police Headquarters,* and *Terror by Night.* Nonetheless as time elapsed dramatic manifestations often soared to far more sophisticate levels. Portions of these may have actually equaled some of the most commendable features screened in cinema houses at the time.

A few series embraced progressively adult-oriented fare. *Dimension X, Dragnet, Gunsmoke, The Line-Up, The Six Shooter, Suspense, Twenty-First Precinct, The Whistler,* and *Yours Truly, Johnny Dollar* consistently reached lofty plateaus to the delight of their legions of faithful followers. During the sunlit hours there were also lengthy stretches when the serials *Hilltop House, Ma Perkins, Pepper Young's Family, Perry Mason,* and *Wendy Warren and the News* reached similar literary plateaus. Unfortunately, these were exceptions.

On Monday nights, radio proffered adaptations of sterling cinematic box-office hits on the enduring hour-long *Lux Radio Theater.* That was traditionally the highest-ranked evening program in the Crossley ratings. For five consecutive years (1947–52), incidentally — of scores of continuing network series — *Lux* earned the singularly distinct honor as the topmost rated program on radio.[17] Between 1936 and 1955, major Hollywood stars reprised some of the roles on those broadcasts, emerging in person in abbreviated versions of the original screenplays.[18]

In addition to the dramatic series previously named, there were many more enduring members of that tribe that also witnessed decent followings. Their number included *The Adventures of Sam Spade, The Adventures of Superman, Big Town, Casey—Crime Photographer, The Challenge of the Yukon, City Hospital, The FBI in Peace and War, Gangbusters, Grand Central Station, I Love a Mystery, Inner Sanctum Mysteries, Jack Armstrong—the All-American Boy, Let's Pretend, Lights Out, Mr. and Mrs. North, The Mysterious Traveler, One Man's Family, The Roy Rogers Show, Sky King, Straight Arrow, True Detective Mysteries,* and *The United States Steel Hour.*

To break a stranglehold that the relatively audacious advertising agencies had held on network radio since the early 1930s, CBS majority owner-chairman William S. Paley devised a bold strategy in 1946 to retake control of his web's manifold programming responsibilities.[19] By implementing his proposal, the broadcasting mogul intended for CBS to regain a vital function over which it had lost control when it shipped that oversight out of its facilities. The function was then being handled by vets who projected track records that had long demonstrated their creative propensity. Paley believed that recovery of the phase would allow a substantial paring of the network's pecuniary expense and possibly drive the network ahead of its competition at the same time. A 15 percent commission, usually paid to the agencies for production services, plus another 15 percent raked off the top for talent fees for every sponsored show would remain thereafter at CBS. That would net a sizable financial savings even as the web's overhead increased.[20]

Rather than outsource a package that embraced production, direction, writing, and talent (including hiring actors, comedians, musicians, announcers, and whatever others a script called for), units would be added at CBS to derive all of these components. Of course, the instigation of such intrepid alterations meant that any shifts in the ratings would be a direct result of the broadcasting chain's own efforts rather than pegged to the rise-and-fall actions of another party. CBS's entry into the proceedings was to ultimately become either a windfall or a pitfall. The unknown outcome notwithstanding, a pundit suggested that the proposed option — once it was put into place — might have been "the single most important business decision that Paley made in his long career."[21]

Paley began initiating the changes with a string of personality-driven sitcoms that had been developed totally in-house. The conversion commenced with a half-dozen new comedies appearing on the network over a period of several radio seasons between 1947 and 1957. The schedule redesign introduced *Life with Luigi* (J. Carrol Naish and Alan Reed), *Meet Millie* (Audrey Totter and Elena Verdugo), *My Favorite Husband* (Lucille Ball and Richard Denning), *My Friend Irma* (Marie Wilson and Cathy Lewis), *My Little Margie* (Gale Storm and Charles Farrell), and *Our Miss Brooks* (Eve Arden and Gale Gordon). All of these quickly developed extensive followings and became part of CBS's programming mix for several years, even as the twilight of the Golden Age was approaching.

Eventually, the choice to recover the control of the programming division proved profitable to CBS as well. A landmark reassignment that established new trends in radio's engagement with the ad agencies, the alteration also figured notably into setting a pace for future handling of TV advertising. The agencies would never hold the invincible authority over TV that they had demonstrated over radio from the early 1930s to late 1940s. Paley's determined intervention nevertheless manifestly impacted a relationship between the broadcasters and agencies that — for all intents and purposes — remains in force industry-wide today.

In the meantime once he joined NBC in 1949, Sylvester (Pat) Weaver — who seemed destined to become a future president of the rival chain (in 1953) — was a fervent disciple of Paley's thinking about retaking control of the programming function. Actually, to hear him tell it, you would think it was *he*— Weaver — and not Paley who originated that brainstorm: "I was proud of the broadcasting revolution I had started — an upheaval that put the networks back in control of radio and television."[22] It wasn't long, in fact, before Weaver was stridently beating the same drum at NBC, determined to see that his employer followed CBS in that train (without an admission of doing so, of course).

Whether the chimes chain took its cue from Paley or whether it acted completely on its own, Weaver — who had arrived at NBC after many years at Young and Rubicam, one of the most prestigious and commandingly influential U.S. advertising agencies, and one he was then thwarting by his consequent actions — was a leading proponent in wresting away the duties that NBC had also handed outside in the early 1930s.[23] The two largest national broadcasting hookups were then responding in like manner on that issue, driving yet another nail into the coffin of the once-dominant ad agencies. It was to result in a new phase of work performance in the years ahead.

In addition to the comedies, musicals, and dramas that were hallmarks of network radio back in the day, some other formats could be depicted as equally enveloping. The audience-participation shows were among those manifestly admired genres encompassing radio's Golden Age. They were also so diverse in nature that they ran an extensive gamut of possibilities: at times listeners at home could literally interact with the tricks transpiring at a broadcasting site (often relating through telephone or mail links) and, on other occasions, they could respond vicariously through the enhanced curiosity, fascination, appeal, and gratification of a given performance. In the latter instance the sensibilities of the listeners were piqued by the antics of live spectators to some of the on-air antics they encountered, including (but not always limited to) studio witnesses. The fare in the audience-participation category was so wide-ranging that it encompassed a plethora of contrasting disciplines even as numerous illustrations can be offered for each track. Some of the distinct types and a few examples follow.

Contests, mental dexterity games, tests, and quizzes: *Break the Bank, Can You Top This?, Dr. I. Q., Double or Nothing, Give and Take, Grand Slam, Name That Tune, Pot o' Gold, Quick as a Flash, The Quiz Kids, The $64,000 Question, Stop the Music!, Take It or Leave It, Twenty Questions, Two for the Money,* and *Winner Take All.*

Human interest features: *The Answer Man, Breakfast at Sardi's, Bride and Groom, Dunninger the Mentalist, Emily Post, Queen for a Day, Strike It Rich, This Is Your Life, Vox Pop, We the People, Welcome Travelers,* and *What Makes You Tick?*

Performance tryouts: *The Horace Heidt Show, Live Like a Millionaire, Major Bowes'* (later *Ted Mack's*) *Original Amateur Hour, The Metropolitan Opera Auditions of the Air, National Amateur Night, National Radio Auditions, Talent Scouts,* and *Talent Search Country Style.*

Public affairs entries: *American Forum of the Air, America's Town Meeting of the Air, Face the Nation, Information Please, Meet the Press, People's Platform,* and the *University of Chicago Round Table.*

Stunt shows: *Beat the Clock, People Are Funny,* and *Truth or Consequences.*

Variety shows with headliners or hosts: Art Linkletter's *House Party,* Arthur Godfrey Time, *The Big Show* with Tallulah Bankhead, and Don McNeill's *Breakfast Club.*

Potpourri shows combining multiple elements: *County Fair, Ladies Be Seated, Thanks to the Yanks,* and *You Bet Your Life.*

Beyond all the shows to amuse us, there were endless live athletic competitions and sporting events of every imaginable type to enthuse us. The networks and the local stations offered hordes of recurring vehicles to keep us well informed at one and the same time. There were newscasts, panel discussions, public forums, town-hall meetings, and legions of useful how-to tips from a seemingly endless array of resourceful authorities. They covered topics like banking, business, child care, culinary arts, education, entertainment, environmental issues, gardening, health and exercise, hobbies, home improvement, insurance, interpersonal relationships, investing, legal matters, leisure activities, music, pets, politics, purchases, reading material, real estate, religion, safety, travel, sports, vehicle maintenance, welfare issues, and countless other themes.

There were also what might be classified as gossipmongers on the ether — a segment of the trade devoted to dispensing behind-the-scenes details that occurred in the private and professional lives of public figures from the entertainment, political, and sports arenas. These investigators toiled shamelessly and unstintingly at sniffing out little-known secrets which some fought desperately to maintain under wraps. Invariably, the members of that reportorial brigade hoped to be the first to rush a choice morsel onto the airwaves, beating out the competition not only in radio, but in print media. To break a juicy tidbit ahead of the others — one that would set the tongues of a receptive, titillated audience to wagging — gave the namedroppers some self-satisfaction. They were also earning powerful leverage within the trade, particularly evidenced by acquiring more and more prominent venues (and underwriters) for their wares.

Of nearly two dozen individuals practicing this craft on one of the networks or through syndicated hookups during radio's halcyon days, a few with incredible successes were instantly recognized in most American households. On the other hand, those with fewer jubilant exploits were not nearly as widely touted. Among the more familiar to most listeners were Jimmy Fidler, Hy Gardner, Sheilah Graham, Hedda Hopper, Dorothy Kilgallen, Louella Parsons, Ed Sullivan, and Walter Winchell. It was a dirty business but it netted multimillionaire status for several of them.

On other radio platforms there were perpetual interviews of just about *everybody*, or so it seemed. They included every available public official and politician along with pervasive throngs of sports figures, venerated entertainers, and newsmakers. Some of the neighbors just might be found within that breed. One might react on the ether to the commotion caused by setting the house on fire with the accidentally spilled contents of a greasy skillet that flared over a hot stove burner. It really didn't take a lot to gain the proverbial 15 minutes of fame, even if it was in succinctly reduced fashion. Radio's fascination with detail frequently pricked our consciences as it kindled our appetites for the responses we sought to a perennial unknown: "What happened?" It took radio to persistently and reliably fill in the gaps.

As it turned out, the aural broadcasting mechanism became not only a constant companion but an increasingly powerful wellspring of useful information and data on virtually any topic. As we sifted through its storehouse of veritable treasures we discovered gifts in abundance that constantly enlightened as well as amused us. What a supply house of so much, and right at our fingertips! As long as we had electricity or batteries (the latter from the 1950s) we could tune in and turn on!

> Considering the possibilities for glitches in a live medium, it's astonishing how word-perfect the shows sounded — especially when you realize that most of the network programs were broadcast twice, once per coast, or three times if from Detroit. Most comedy, variety, and game shows were performed before a studio audience and went on the air quiveringly live, as did most of the dramatic shows before finally, in 1948, giving into "electrical transcriptions." By 1949, taping was still rare, except for commercials. Radio had to be timed to the second, a delicate tightrope act that allowed for no fluffs or other human error; Jackson Beck says it was like being in a spaceship for thirty minutes "and you've got to get back to land safely." Radio actors needed a tightly wound internal clock to stay in step with each show's tempo, as well as in time with the clock on the wall.[24]

While they were broadcasting, of course, some of radio's most talented and most industrious luminaries were simultaneously making phonograph records, others were producing sheet music and extraneous merchandise for consumer sales, some penned books and magazine articles, and many turned up incessantly in beau coups of personal appearances (performances of many types, plus local groundbreakings, ribbon-cuttings, dedications, watercraft send-offs, and the like).

Some fans could hardly contain the idyllic worship they exhibited for favorite icons that appeared at nearby ampitheaters as well as at book-signings, city coliseums, civic ceremonies, community festivals, on college campuses, at fairs, in little theaters, music festivals, parades, rodeos, sporting events, store-openings, summer stock, supper clubs, and practically anywhere that large crowds assembled for merriment and celebrations. Radio had made many of its voices "stars" in their own right and those occasions proved to be some of their most zealous fans' chances to actually see and possibly even greet the luminaries they fawned over. Many would not be denied.

If you were passionately into radio as we knew it then, that was without any doubt *the best of times* for you. Radio was far better than anything America had experienced before it arrived. During the years of its ethereal domination the aural medium was — to the thinking of many — far superior to whatever other communications methods may have been available to the masses as entertainment venues and enlightenment resources. Included in that inventory are the permanent and touring stage shows and other live productions of many stripes, plus the cinema, phonograph records, telephone, and telegraph. Most old-time radio aficionados would likely disagree that the passing of the Golden Age was a gratifying occasion. It was anything but that. All who lived through the heyday of that unprecedented and extraordinary era would have hung on to it much longer had there been any way. And in a contemporary epoch of resurgent nostalgia, many would undoubtedly welcome its return if it suddenly reappeared. That's not realistic, of course.

Although we may be convinced beyond any shadow of doubt that the best of times is in its rearview mirror, right now — *today* — radio is a viable resource relied on by millions for determining what's going on in their world. It can stir our imaginations, generate our opinions, trouble our consciences, and persuade us to action. An interest in politics, cultural issues, and a host of contemporary topics is spellbinding to hordes of listeners who tune in for verbal exchanges over the airwaves. At the same time radio remains a viable source of marketing, music, sports, weather reports, and traffic data. It keeps us company too even at times we are oblivious to its clamor in the recesses of our environment. In an age of electronic wizardry radio has carved out a seemingly permanent niche for itself. While to so many enthusiasts the best may appear to have already been, the aural medium's demonstrated resiliency hints that its future can propel an aura of expectation, too.

2

The Goose, the Egg and the Evil Eye

Almost all of us like fairy tales.

Do you remember the one about the Little Red Hen who couldn't get any teamwork out of her mammal cronies? Those conditions festered until she baked a loaf of bread after they had watched her go about the task of producing it from seed. To repay them for their restraint, she announced, "I'll eat it myself." And she did.

Then there was the one about Chicken Little, who just may have been related to the Little Red Hen although we can't be sure. After an acorn fell on her head, this chick was convinced the sky was falling and set out to tell the king. Enroute, she convinced several of her peers on the farm that the world's demise was fast approaching. They joined her on her journey. Eventually this motley crew of mammal creatures encountered the sly Foxy Loxy, who must have been somewhat smarter than they: he didn't view the news as they did but merely as a chance to get them all into his den for a barnyard feast — his guests being the entrée. Just then the sky fell on him, saving his prospective vittles, who realized it was too late to tell the king, and returned home. The narrative hints that those who are too gullible sometimes meet with fowl ends. (Pun intended.)

There are lots of stories like these in the nursery rhymes and children's fairy tales. Do you remember The Ugly Duckling who took a while to discover that he wasn't born a duck after all but instead was a handsome swan? There was Little Red Riding Hood, a *real* (albeit mythical) girl, who had her own near-fatal crisis with yet another fox, this one sporting massive choppers. (Did you ever wonder why foxes were incredibly depraved in kids' fables? They seemed to lay incessantly in wait for a meal, maybe the most starved beasts to be found on the planet.) Lest we acquire a distorted view of the lowly species, however, it was a wolf that came after The Three Little Pigs. A couple of them lost homes of straw and wood to his antics with reference to huffing and puffing. Yet the trio of swine was triumphant over their cunning adversary within a house of bricks. In tarnished terms, the moral of these tales could be: you may have been switched at birth; big teeth can spell trouble; and applying a little common sense could save your bacon.

Did you also hear the one about the goose that laid the golden egg and the evil-eyed monster that ate it? Very likely you didn't. It's an original. Whether the other allegories are based on fact, this one definitely has some authenticity. Let's set the stage for it:

Radio — back in the day — became an astonishingly phenomenal entity that permeated the homes of average Americans coast to coast, doing so incontrovertibly, just as the populace needed it most. Radio was expansively introduced in the 1920s yet it was really transmitting in primitive mode for a couple of decades before that (recounted briefly in Chapter 1). The earliest medium of sweeping synchronized mass communications didn't attain its zenith (no quip intended) until the 1930s, however.

In that Depression-impaired decade the gems radio offered supplied a fleeting respite from the sweeping wreckage of personal tragedy resulting from the nation's economic catastrophe. To radio was attributed an ingenious, instant, inexpensive, imaginative, incessant supply of edification, enjoyment and enlightenment that never subsided (until the power was interrupted) throughout the broadcast day. It was a veritable treasure chest of bliss, contained in an electric box. On occasions it was the most sumptuous and extravagant enhancement in some listeners' homes. And it was to be found almost anywhere one went. One wag recalled that epoch like this[1]:

> *The World Almanac* for 1932 reported that at the end of that year, 16,809,562 American homes had a radio in the living room, which was where virtually every one of them was placed in those days. Your Philco or Stromberg Carlson or Majestic or Atwater Kent console was the most prominent piece of furniture in the house, and frequently the most expensive. The family would gather around it and stare at it as if it were a glowing fireplace. The 1932 U.S. radio census reported an increase of 4.5 million sets in the previous three years. The American public had spent $1.5 billion buying radios — a staggering figure for the depression days of the early 1930s. California alone boasted 1,067,705 sets; New York, 2,500,723.

Radio became the principal asset of a soon-to-be phenomenally prosperous and burgeoning industry that grew up around it. In addition to the airwaves' programming and the talent broadcast, advertising mushroomed into a highly profitable enterprise as telephone wires were leased all over the nation. And while there was soaring production in crafting and fabricating radio sets, there was also the manufacture of replacement tubes and parts, of microphones, hardware and apparatus for control booths, transmitters, and zillions of miscellaneous expenses required in maintaining it at optimum levels. All of this, of course, gave large numbers of Americans jobs at a time when many were practically destitute. If not for radio, thousands might have been unable to meet their own financial obligations. For lots of reasons the new trade could hardly have developed at a more suitable moment in the country's history.

In the mid–1940s, the world seemed to be radio's "oyster" in the United States, as we transitioned from wartime to peacetime. With almost a thousand licensed AM stations and broadcast time sales exceeding $330 million, the industry was booming. In 1945, more American residences were equipped with radios than bathtubs.[2] In 1946, almost nine out of ten U.S. households in metropolitan markets, plus an additional six million vehicles, contained radios.[3] For many people nighttime air features could be the following morning's "conversation starters" at work or leisure activity.

In this postwar epoch we were getting most of our news as well as most of our amusement from radio, far more than from anywhere else. Americans lived in 37.6 million radio-outfitted dwellings in late 1948 — the average radio tubes typically lit up for 5.1 hours per day. The number of operating sets had risen 11.6 percent over the previous year while we were listening to them a half-hour more every day.[4]

This epoch was "high tide" for the auditory medium, giving patent evidence of radio's peerless saturation in a nation that included slightly more than 42 million households at the time.[5] In practical terms, the U.S. exhibited nearly nine "radio homes" out of every ten residences. In addition to news, comedy, drama, and musical features, vast numbers of passionate fans were glued to their sets to hear consummate sporting enticements like the Kentucky Derby, the Rose Bowl, and the World Series. Radio had them all and in those days it's where America's dials were set.

In the meantime there was no shortage of cynics who could not easily be convinced that TV would ever sufficiently materialize to become a viable certainty. From the 1920s onward, video had been habitually touted by some as being "just around the corner." Yet as one pundit tersely and perhaps aptly summarized the scenario: "It seemed stuck there."[6] As early as the mid–1920s, no less a venerated wellspring of foresight as the *New York Times* brashly estimated that — within five years, by 1930 — "every home" in America would be outfitted with an apparatus providing "visuals of the programming people are hearing" (on their radios).[7] "Television Near Ready" proclaimed a headline in the entertainment trade's *Variety* on April 16, 1930. And the fact that Wheaton, Maryland-based inventor Charles Jenkins was able to transmit the first television commercial that very year, having gained the first U.S. TV broadcast license two years earlier (1928), didn't impress enough people.[8] They either failed to see his accomplishment or didn't see it as more than a passing fancy of little import to them.

The search for television over wires had started long before the search for radio. As a concept it predated the idea of wireless, being related to telegraphy over wires. Attempts to send images through space were made in many countries in the second half of the nineteenth century. Imaginative men sought at first to transmit "still" pictures and documents — what would today be called facsimile — over wires. They used whirling discs or spinning drums of many types to scan the image, converting it into a flow of electrical impulses for reassembly at the receiving end.

The inventor of the telephone, Alexander Graham Bell, was one of several persons who in 1880 took out patents for television devices. In the following decade a German and a French inventor, independently, put together systems of mechanical scanning to send and receive pictures *in motion*, which is the essence of television. Neither of them was successful — the technical tools of their time were inadequate — but they defined the character of the problems for successors.

By 1911 a British scientist, A. Campbell Swinton, established in theory that the Braun cathode ray might be adapted for electronic scanning. The same idea was conceived at about the same time by a professor at the University of St. Petersburg, Boris Rosing. Historically the Russian's experiments were especially fruitful because they kindled the imagination of a gifted student in his classes, Vladimir K. Zworykin, who eventually brought his genius and dedication to the United States.

From the 1920's forward, crude but identifiable pictures — still scanned mechanically but now conveyed by radio waves — were actually sent and received in America and Europe. In 1927 both General Electric and the American Telephone Company succeeded in flashing images in motion across impressive distances. The illusion that television was "around the corner" spread in radio circles....

...Only a few at this stage took its advent seriously and they timed it for a safely distant future. The most optimistic and voluble among them was David Sarnoff. For him the question was no longer *whether* sight would be added to sound but *when*, and he dared promise that it would not be long delayed.[9]

Still, another dozen years would pass before an infinitesimal fraction of the general public got a glimpse of what was on the way. It happened during the 1939 New York World's Fair. Several more years rolled by before TV — its pervasive inception by then postponed by the Second World War — could be declared a viable reality by sufficiently ample viewers.

Recounting an internal experimental system at a Los Angeles radio station in 1932, an insider remembered the experience: "If any of the staff wanted to see the picture being transmitted we had to climb to the roof and look at a monitor there.... Among radio people at that time, the development of television was believed to be countless years in the future. When you looked at the picture on that tiny screen, you might think it would be centuries in the future."[10] In reality, of course, in less than a couple of decades TV was coming on strong. By that time, in fact, it was starting to monopolize (and even cannibalize) the nation's broadcasting.

There were others in the industry that appeared to be biding their time, cautiously waiting to step forth when the iron seemed a lot warmer. *Billboard* added TV reviews to its insider revelations in 1939, the same year that the fanzine *Radio Mirror* confidently re-titled itself *Radio and Television Mirror*.

Following TV's well-documented roll-out at the public exhibition during the 1939 fair — an all-NBC production, incidentally — on July 1, 1941, NBC and CBS debuted the nation's earliest "permanently functioning" commercial television stations in New York: NBC's Channel 1 WNBT and CBS's Channel 2 WCBW.[11] The former aired the very first commercial after Bulova Watch Company paid $4 (you read that right) to display a clock's face while a voice announced "B-U-L-O-V-A, Bulova Watch Time." It was the same tagline Bulova customarily applied on radio for many years as the hour was identified over NBC Red's local flagship outlet WEAF in New York.

The advertising tariff increased astronomically that evening when Channel 1 emitted Lowell Thomas's Blue network radio newscast at 6:45 P.M.— broadcasting's original simulcasting audition. (Of course, without benefit of props or pictures, Thomas simply sat at a desk with a microphone on it and read from a prepared script, sans visuals, hardly playing to or bothered by the camera. There was no teleprompter then. And it would have been boring had it not been so utterly fascinating to an astounded heretofore aural-only audience.) For that quarter-hour the TV station charged the newsman's radio sponsor, Sun Motor Oil, $100. It was a tad pricey by the station's matinee tariff.

When WNBT produced its first advertising rate card in the mid–1940s, it offered prospective clients a one-minute commercial for eight dollars.[12] Radio, we may be sure, was still covering the start-up costs — and the decades of experimental technology before then — as it consistently fed the hand that would eventually bite it big time.

Then, of course, only a few thousand TV sets were disseminating those pioneering features. Even though those were bargain basement tolls when contrasted with those of today, the viewers then — most hypothetically potential consumers — were comparatively few. They didn't have long to get accustomed to video either. Five months after TV's 1941 breakthrough in New York City, Pearl Harbor changed it all. After December 7, the tube simply ground to a near halt. It wouldn't be returning in any fluent manner until sometime following the war's end in summer 1945.

At the outbreak of combat just a foursome of U.S. cities boasted a collective 10,000 TV set owners who were capable of viewing but a dozen telecast-originating stations. As the battles engaged overseas, that handful of outlets was reduced by half and transmitted their meager offerings to a presumably radically diminished audience size. Despite this course of retreat, the wartime lapse wasn't synonymous with the industry's annihilation. When peace arrived at last, so the *Wall Street Journal* forecast in 1943, Americans would be able to anticipate "large-scale production of 'popular-priced' TV sets" occurring and that would be followed by literal saturation of the market "a decade after peace." (Reflecting now on the history of TV's early widespread dispersion, just where did a newspaper acquire such a meticulously precise crystal ball?)

The skepticism of earlier times surrounding television's future quickly dissipated in the postwar era. Particularly did TV become the new norm after thousands — and very likely millions — were able to stand on sidewalks outside appliance dealers' urban showrooms and see the long-heralded fabrication for themselves. Peering through the plate-glass windows of those burgeoning emporiums, ordinary citizens gawked at the original diagonal 9- to 13-inch black-and-white TV screens that they could actually observe. Until that occasion, some could be genuinely described as harboring virtual disbelief.

Even then they pondered a sense of wonderment: How can this be? What does it mean? How will it affect *me*? A media scholar affirmed that the long-proffered query of "when and how will television establish itself?" began to drift into "what will happen to radio?"[13] Previous doubters — abruptly presented with hard evidence to the contrary — were having a change of heart. Never mind the negative sentiments that would stem from all of this. They would appear on the horizon all in good time.

"The genesis of Network Radio's decline," according to retired broadcaster Jim Ramsburg, is traceable to the evening of Friday, June 27, 1947.[14] Ramsburg points out that on that momentous (and, for a favored few, memorable) occasion NBC fed its TV viewers a three-hour block of programming that marked the medium's permanent — and ultimately pervasive — arrival. Although only citizens living in or near New York, Philadelphia, Schenectady, and Washington were hooked into the network, nevertheless that audience watched in awe as a speech, short film, variety show, and boxing match were delivered to their homes, neighborhood bars, and those infamous sidewalk showrooms. TV was here to stay, and would be having an incredible impact on a whole lot more Americans' lives in the not-too-distant future. While it wouldn't happen overnight, that inception signaled the beginning of the end for Network Radio.

In a sense, TV figured to harmonize with radio in those days. Many considered it to be something of an expansion of auditory machinery. People ascribed expressions of endearment to it like "sight radio," "radio optics," "radio moving pictures," and "radio vision." Some of the earliest visual programs were, in fact, adaptations of leading radio features or somewhat analogous to radio shows then airing. Therefore, the newer medium's experimental entries weren't totally unfamiliar to radio listeners.

An early example of TV's surprisingly astonishing impact is effortlessly traced to the incredible escalation of comic Milton Berle in Videoland. Berle was the embodiment of the classic vaudevillian slapstick clown. While he typically never really turned that many heads in radio, he burst onto TV screens in 1948 like a conquering juggernaut. "The early history of television and the story of Berle's show were close to being one and the same thing," an epoch chronicler affirmed. "The very success of Berle's show accelerated the sale of television sets; those Americans who did not yet own sets would return home after watching him at their neighbors' homes and decide that, yes, it was finally time to take the plunge."[15]

A textbook academic charged: "By 1948, radio had enjoyed the privileged status of an only child for 28 years. But in that year, a smarty pants kid, television, began to emerge as the dominant functional medium."[16] Visionary Hubbell Robinson, Jr., a CBS VP, didn't mince words when he tersely related the changing state of affairs to Custer's last stand, warning: "Television is about to do to radio what the Sioux did to Custer. There is going to be a massacre."[17]

Just how was TV to affect radio anyway?

> In 1949, with 97 TV stations operating, ... the radio networks ... suffered their first aggregate revenue drop ever.
>
> In 1950, TV homes tripled to 7.5 million.... In radio, all four networks lowered advertising rates, Mutual was put up for sale, and ABC, which also had entered TV, agreed to merge with United Paramount Theaters.
>
> In 1951, TV reached nearly one-fourth of U.S. homes and turned its first profit—which surpassed radio's and became the networks' main revenue source....
>
> With each year, average daily radio listening slipped — in 1949 by nine minutes, in 1950 by 19, and in 1951 by 36.[18]

If anyone needed further evidence to convince him which way the wind was blowing, NBC's *The Big Show*—signified by many historians as radio's final ultra-impressive exploit, and rolled out in the fall of 1950—ought to be corroboration enough. The colossal series was "mounted on a scale unprecedented in radio," according to one report.[19] *Newsweek* branded NBC's lavish disbursements at $100,000 per performance as "real television money." *The Big Show* arrived with venerated guest stars from the stage, screen, and broadcasting arenas; a generous orchestra of versatile musicians conducted by veteran impresario Meredith Willson; a live studio audience reacting to its comedy, music and drama selections; and a recurring cast headed by legendary stage and movie actress Tallulah Bankhead.

The well-promoted glitzy showcase, capturing 90 minutes of NBC's weekly primetime agenda, fizzled speedily (e.g., nobody was listening). In the nearly 13 months' aggregate that it was broadcast the program lost a million dollars for the chimes chain (and soon-to be Peacock Network). There would be no more extraordinary productions of its stupefying magnitude and quality on radio to originate before a national live studio audience every week. The series' abrupt departure prior to its scheduled second-season finale was like throwing in the towel, an epitaph of sorts to radio's inventive mind.[20]

In just nine months during 1952, the Federal Communications Commission was inundated with 700 applications for TV stations. Before the year ended, the federal panel issued licenses to 165 of those applicants and 21 new stations were already on the air. NBC opened studios in Burbank, California, as CBS inaugurated similar facilities in Hollywood. Network radio revenues fell to their lowest levels in nearly a decade, with the quartet of national webs again trimming rates while their total quantity of affiliates dwindled. "Radio's new destiny, as a medium in which networks struggled for a role, was sealed. It was now TV's Golden Age," a historian conceded.[21]

By 1954, the futuristic novelty of television was thoroughly entrenched, already residing in 56 percent of American homes (26 million of 46 million domiciles). In the previous eight years a half-dozen TV outlets had rocketed to 354.[22] How many other industries had prospered that amazingly and that speedily? Despite those impressive stats there were still two or more radios in 70 percent of American households in 1954. And a third of all U.S. households possessed three or more radios.[23] Our listening habits, still active, had been altered from communal-type reception to a more individual, personalized function.

Television had other effects on the American home entertainment environment as well.

Mounting psychological pressure that was linked to video's inception is cited as instigating a tendency away from programming dramatic offerings in network radio to less costly music and game-show manifestations.[24] A wave of those strains began to fill the bills of the quartet of transcontinental audio chains during a postwar period in which the tube burst into the nation's conscience. Among the myriad innovative audio charms debuting then was *Break the Bank* (1945–55), *Winner Take All* (1946–52), *Twenty Questions* (1946–54), *Hit the Jackpot* (1948–50), *Sing it Again* (1948–51), *Stop the Music!* (1948–55), *Take a Number* (1948–55), *Rate Your Mate* (1950–51), *Live Like a Millionaire* (1950–53), *Name That Tune* (1952–53), *The Phrase That Pays* (1953–55) and *Two for the Money* (1952–56). All were leading examples of a fad that might not have proliferated so thoroughly had TV not begun to manipulate traditional radio features.

In this same interval some of the leading local radio broadcasters invented their own program concepts that mirrored the national drift toward audience participation, talent, and quiz features. In doing so they generally shied away from any that required a flourishing entourage of artists and extraneous cast. Presumably, this would have helped ease some of the anxiety that was imposed on many by TV's enormous start-up payout. By 1952, meanwhile:

> A typical network affiliate now originated more programming than it took from the network—a reversal of the two-decades-long trend of network domination. The conviction that television would soon make all radio programming obsolete gave the radio business a general feeling of foreboding. Bright young, and not

so young, programming executives looked for opportunities to move over to the newer medium. A straw in the wind was the increase in *simulcast* programs in the 1950s, in which popular radio programs became television programs, with the audio portion carried on radio. Radio listeners reacted with annoyance to unexplained references or disconcerting studio laughter. Many of these programs gave the impression of waiting for the time when they could abandon radio completely.[25]

Would it be difficult for you to believe that some of the leading station owners were, at this same time at least, tacitly opposed to television's arrival? "They had climbed one hill and didn't want to start up another," Frank Stanton, CBS president, conjectured. Stanton's superior, Chairman William S. Paley, even argued *against* TV's advance, having been a radio emissary his entire professional broadcasting career. "He thought it would hurt radio," and speculated that it was something "we couldn't afford," Stanton disclosed.[26]

There were broadcasting personalities who disparaged the new medium, too. CBS news guru Edward R. Murrow (1908–65) cheered when a capital-based reporter wouldn't accept a transition opportunity to depart radio for television. Murrow confederate Alexander Kendrick observed that — even though his friend (Murrow) was destined to become a bona fide "star" in the new medium, "He believed, and always would, that radio was a more useful and serious means of communication."[27] CBS newsman Joseph Wershba, who moved from print to radio to eventually assisting Murrow in TV journalism, allowed that in the late 1940s and early 1950s, "Nobody wanted to go into it. None of our top people had any interest in it at all."[28] Douglas Edwards, CBS-TV News' premiering luminary, had to be boldly persuaded by Frank Stanton that he wouldn't live to regret it.[29]

After stressing to readers nearly all of his (almost) 500 pages how much Murrow — the flawless electronic journalist of *any* period — preferred radio to TV, biographer Joseph Persico speculated how Murrow might qualify the tube later.

> One imagines that Ed Murrow, as a viewer, would watch with pleasure and pride his lineal descendants on the network news, clearly the finest continuing work done on contemporary commercial television. He would no doubt beam with a paternal pleasure at CBS's *Sunday Morning* and *60 Minutes* and stay up for intelligent discourse on a program like *Nightline*. He would envy the technical resources that enable correspondents to follow stories almost instantaneously to virtually the ends of the earth. He would probably applaud the choice offered, if not always the content offered, by all-news channels. But he would likely miss the bit and idiosyncratic perspectives of that virtually vanished breed, the broadcast commentator, an Elmer Davis, a Raymond Swing, a Quincy Howe, an Eric Sevareid. One is left with a sense that when the news and public affairs ended on the commercial networks, Ed Murrow would be listening to NPR and watching PBS.[30]

There were many reports that advertisers feared the significant sums that would be required of television to make a go of it. In its early days, advertising revenues hardly made a dent in the capital needed to underwrite programming and technical outlays. "Thanks to the precedent of more than two decades of radio advertising," a couple of broadcasting scholars noted, "advertising promised from the start to become television programming's prime support."[31] Yet uncertainty abounded: When, for example, would the new medium be seen by enough substantially large metropolitan audiences to make networking viable?

In the meantime, a 1949 investigative document expressed a sinking feeling as it revealed the suspicions of some seeking to recoup TV's huge financial investment: "We seriously doubt that television will ever become a truly nationwide medium (as compared with present radio patterns and service) if it has to depend on the economics of advertising alone."[32] Calling all skeptics!

In the late 1940s, expenses for TV were frequently estimated at ten times those of radio.[33] Station construction was exorbitant by radio standards, and operating an outlet required far more technical and business personnel than the audio counterpart. Sets, lighting, costumes, makeup, cameras, and more studio equipment escalated costs appreciably. All of it required added personnel. AT&T raised its hourly charges to ten times the comparable rates for radio network lines as it laid coaxial cable or created microwave links, even in 1949–50.

Encountering time charges that were high enough to encompass all of this, advertisers moved into television quite cautiously. Some ad agencies remained aloof altogether, believing their standard commissions would never make a heavy investment of work and time in TV profitable. Soon, the agencies were abandoning any thought of program development, a field they had relinquished to the networks which had been a property they had virtually controlled since the early 1930s.

None of this seemed to faze Radio Corporation of America (RCA) Chairman David Sarnoff, television's most relentless exponent. As the man who categorically controlled all of the puppet strings that really mattered at RCA ancillary NBC, he had overseen TV's development since the 1920s, and still did. Sarnoff's lifetime obsession with the tube suitably coined for him the term of endearment *televisionary*.[34] (The term was meant pejoratively by those in the trade who viewed Sarnoff as "a gorilla wrecking the radio industry."[35]) When a report was made public in 1946 that start-up expenditures for television would run $8 million spread over a four-year time frame ($88,352,000 in 2010 figures, the most recent year's data available),[36] Sarnoff announced that TV *would be financed from radio profits*.

In like manner CBS embraced an analogous blueprint for underwriting the costs tied to its pioneering video exploits.[37] "We had to keep radio strong," CBS's Stanton confirmed, "because we had to pay for television out of radio."

That company initially divided the dual mediums for administrative and budgetary purposes. (NBC soon pursued a similar course as Pat Weaver signed to fill a newly created TV vice presidency.) Stanton elucidated: "If television wanted something that radio was doing, they had to negotiate with radio for it."[38]

Meanwhile, "A timebomb was ticking beneath network radio," historiographer Alfred Balk prudently speculated.[39] Others affirmed the opinion: "Perhaps the radio networks assisted in their own demise when they provided the initial financial support for television stations and networks, an invaluable training ground for personnel, and models for television network organization, operations, and programming."[40] Then again, when you stop and think the matter through carefully, just where else could we anticipate that the initial financing, personnel, and formatting might originate if TV was to be owned and operated by profitable radio broadcasters? Nothing in the way of an equally reasonable alternative readily comes to mind.

Some hard figures (in every sense, a literal term) validate just how the aural medium was affected in one sphere.

> While radio advertising revenue was rising, the network share of it, including O & O stations [chain owned and operated], fell from $23 million to just over $11 million — a drop of more than 50 percent in seven years. The four networks' share went from 47 percent in 1945 to 26 percent in 1952. As early as 1948, more and more programming became sustaining and networks repeatedly cut their time charges, but to no avail. Advertisers changed to local spot radio and other media, including television. Once network radio started to slip, it went fast.[41]

Beyond the problem of bankrolling TV's arrival, some of radio's biographers maintain that "the rise of television, at the expense of radio, has stunted the American imagination," further insisting: "While radio, banalities and all, expanded the imagination, its successor, television, constricted it, and we are the worse for it as individuals and as a culture."[42] Yet another observer complained: "Listeners ... relied on their imaginations to visualize the scenes. Television shattered the illusions."[43] Writing in 1960, still one more scribe, plaintively waxing over the good old days of adolescence, expressed thoughts in a few eloquent terms like this:

> Radio, for me, is part of the Lost Childhood, and those old-time radio voices ... have set up an everlasting static in some inner ear. It's the only reception left them nowadays....
> ...They demanded the very thing TV has scotched: imagination. The listener produced half the show right in his own head, taking his lead from a range of voices, a musical bridge, and a few sound effects. The viewer doesn't have to produce anything. It's all right in front of him on the "big" screen ... and only an old-time listener can tell him what a narrow, little everyday vista it is....
> ...We took Radioland for real and found in it a certain permanence that seems woefully lacking in TV programming.[44]

As this reporter pointed out in an earlier tome, a second-grader — when quizzed about whether he liked plays that aired on the radio or television more — responded, "On radio!" Petitioned to explain his sunny partiality for radio, the youngster replied: "I can see the pictures better!"[45] A mind, as the commercial chides, is a terrible thing to waste. TV removed much of our capacity for sustaining creative cognition as it dutifully supplied the whole package, leaving little to the mind's eye.

As the country hastily shifted its allegiance for entertainment and information sources from ear to eye, what were the perceived advantages of television over radio? Answering that in 1950, media scholar Charles Siepmann hypothesized:

> What television has to offer — to sponsor and viewer alike — is the incomparable appeal of sight, plus sound, plus motion. Army experiments during the war years went far to prove ... that the recall impact of sight-sound-motion stimuli is in general greater by far than either oral or visual stimuli alone. Experiments in television advertising seem to confirm the fact. A camera company that advertised a special offer received enough telephone orders by the time the program left the air to pay for the entire show. A company offering a recipe book was flooded with requests, at a cost of .8 of a cent per inquiry. A watch company offered and displayed for 14 seconds a booklet with a four-word title; 85 per cent of the requests named the book with complete accuracy. Television has, for the moment at least, the further advantage of exposing more people to its selling power.[46]

Just as they were during radio's Golden Age, in TV's similarly branded epoch the most esteemed series were telecast live. Ubiquitous advertisers pursued superior programming as choices in the public interest sector flourished. As the 1950s evolved, radio experienced a severe siphoning of its artists, audiences, and advertisers by television. Some of the noteworthy modifications by year included[47]:

1953: TV household penetration reached nearly half that of radio; *TV Guide* debuted.
1954: The number of TV outlets surpassed 400; color "spectaculars" premiered on NBC-TV.
1955: TV was in 32 million U.S. residential dwellings (two-thirds of 48 million homes) as typical viewing time rose to five hours daily; radio use shrank to 2 hours 25 minutes daily; of 2,800 U.S. AM stations, just 840 (30 percent) persisted as affiliates of a major chain.
1956: TV viewing exceeded time devoted to newspaper reading; the number of American TV stations soared beyond 500.
1957: A TV craze occurred when big money quizzes were introduced.
1958: Outrage erupted from TV quiz-rigging as fans learned they had been duped.

1959: Congress launched hearings into TV quiz-rigging; CBS and NBC slashed radio schedules by 50 percent.

1960: 46 million of 53 million U.S. domiciles (87 percent) were TV-equipped as the country watched 583 telecasters more than five hours daily; listeners spent just 1 hour 40 minutes with their radios; the Golden Age unofficially but unequivocally ended as final holdout CBS deleted decades of radio shows, leaving little more than a residue of news, commentaries, and pithy personality-driven features.

> By 1954, there were 32 million television sets throughout the country, CBS television's gross billings doubled in that single year, and CBS became *the single biggest advertising medium in the world* [italics added]. The real money, money and revenues beyond anyone's wildest dreams, was in television.... The possibilities of nationwide advertising were beyond comprehension; afternoon newspapers quickly began to atrophy; mass-circulation magazines, which up until the early fifties had been the conduit of national mass advertising — razor blades, beer, tires, cars, household goods — were suddenly in serious trouble, within little more than a decade they would be dead or dying — *Collier's, The Saturday Evening Post, Look, Life*. Television was about to alter the nature and balance of American merchandising.[48]

And along with newspapers and magazines, radio was also withering on the vine. The evil-eyed monster — possessing just one eye, mind you — had contributed mightily in sacking the goose that had laid the golden egg from which that fiendish beast had hatched. But it couldn't take *all* of the credit by itself for the barnyard pillaging that occurred in Radioland. It would require yet something else, something extraordinary, to ultimately wring that feathered fowl's neck, finally snuffing the life out of the form the golden goose had exhibited for so long. The very real prospect exists, as we shall soon see, that there was at least one more culprit in radio's retreat in the 1950s. It actually wielded far more clout than television acting all by itself.

> By the early 1950s, radio was thought to be dead, a victim, like the movies, of television.... "Within three years," proclaimed NBC's president, Niles Trammell, in 1949, "the broadcast of sound or ear radio over giant networks will be wiped out." Trammell was right: by 1954 network radio, with its primetime programming that brought national stars to a huge national audience, was all but gone.
>
> But radio was hardly dead.... Those of us who lay in bed at night listening to it, or walked around with a transistor earplug, or drove to it, or later plunged ourselves into the lush, stereophonic dimension of FM radio know different. So did the advertisers, rock 'n' roll stars, DJs, and station owners who made careers, and often fortunes, from that durable old box in the corner of the room or the dashboard of the Chevy.
>
> ...Each year in the 1950s and '60s showed increased advertising revenues from the year before, and sales of radio sets — especially portables and sets inside cars — continued to increase. Unlike during the 1930s and '40s, listeners now

tuned in to stations better known for their local, rather than national, identification. In 1948 there had been 1,621 AM stations in America; by 1960 that number had more than doubled, to 3,458. Listeners included housewives, people driving to and from work, truck drivers and cabbies trapped in their vehicles all day, and, in increasing numbers, teenagers.[49]

The song may have ended but the melody lingered on. Just because radio's Golden Age had passed didn't mean the form was to be cast aside. Radio was instead pursuing new programming structures while also maintaining some of its familiar embodiment.

When the historiographers of contemporary times sought a scapegoat on which to pin radio's shortness of breath, there was television ("eye radio" in one interpretation) wearing a sheepish grin. For a trio of decades at least radio had been at the forefront of our need to know and to be amused. All of a sudden it was overshadowed by the new kid on the block — the very offspring it had given birth to, that it had financed and nurtured to robust health and maturity. TV was plainly the most visible contender for the answer to the question, "Who killed radio?"

Pardon the brief digression for a personal reference. The reason should become clear shortly. For several decades the author researched, inquired, and recorded some of the chronological proceedings of broadcast history, arriving at a categorical conclusion that there was at least one extra mitigating circumstance instigating radio's catastrophic toppling. The outcome of that upheaval netted an unmistakable shift in allegiance from audio to video in the U.S. in the 1950s. Although it didn't precisely coincide with TV's onset, the co-conspirator played a powerful and momentous role in radio's devaluation and television's ascent.

The certainty of the second stimulus stems from the radio stations affiliated with the four transcontinental radio hookups. Speaking altogether as an individual examiner, those station owners and executives are maybe as responsible for the banishing of the national audio features back in the day as any other credible source. And maybe more. TV may have supplied the sensation and flash needed to attract the populace to its screens. But the individuals who controlled the local voices of the broadcasting industry that were related to the major chains worked in a milieu that hinted at times that they may have labored in an environment of greed. Attempting to improve their bottom lines, they relentlessly tore apart an auditory system that had placated, pleasured, and enlightened a nation for a few decades.

After years of considerable haggling with the networks to which they were tethered — some of their unions dating all the way back to the 1920s — those influential broadcasters ultimately gained the upper hand. The result of acquiescing to their demands saw radio quietly fade while TV contrarily soared, the latter doing so practically unchallenged. At that juncture there was little remaining doubt that the dual mediums wouldn't coexist as equals.

Nor was there any uncertainty about which would dominate the living room corners that the radio consoles had occupied for many years in so many millions of households; nor the spaces in workplaces and bars they had held along with occupancy in restaurants and pool halls, hotel lobbies, barber shops, hospital rooms, waiting rooms, public transport terminals, community centers, recreation halls, and other municipal venues that had been radio's singular possession. The transformation was especially validated in 1963 as it was confirmed by the assassination of President John F. Kennedy. For four days the eyes of America were glued to the nearest TV set. From that time forward we as a nation would view television with far greater respect than any of us had ever dreamed before.

> Television coverage of this national tragedy changed the country. It also changed the relationship people at home had with their television. Families sat riveted to their TVs for hours on end, almost as if sitting at a wake. Television became the medium that linked our people together in times of tragedy or disaster; it still fulfills that function today. TV coverage of the Kennedy assassination united the country in national mourning and set the stage for coverage of other catastrophes in the future.[50]

With those charismatic images emblazoned in denizens' minds forever following that horrific cataclysm, the country anticipated pictures with its pivotal news-making dispatches thereafter. If we weren't aware of it before we knew it then: *One picture is worth a thousand words.*[51]

The imbroglio that involved the radio station owners and officers, meanwhile, actually began simmering quite some years before it finally came to a head. The hassle was tame in those early days, however. A little background will be beneficial in helping to sort this out.

The coast-to-coast networks of radio's Golden Age were formed across a span of several years. In 1926 and 1927, NBC appeared with its twin Red and Blue chains (the latter of which was separated from that alliance by federal mandate in the early 1940s; the Blue net was rebranded ABC in 1945). CBS was established in 1927. MBS came along in 1934. From the earliest days the number of stations joining a hookup was inherently important to it: the more outlets carrying a show, the greater a network's chances of attracting larger and larger numbers of listeners, increasing its prestige as well as the sums that could be assessed to the advertising clients for carrying those underwriters' programming.

The battle for affiliates was approached with dogged resolve by the varied chains. They gingerly, yet persistently, courted local broadcasters, and especially so any that were perceived to be highly touted and respected within a community. The outlets that were considered to be markedly influential and powerful (particularly when measured by high wattage, which could boost their signals radically over minimal-signal operators) were valued as trophies worthy of a network's most cherished respect. At the close of 1927, NBC claimed 28 affiliates and — just a year later — an impressive 71, a rise of more than 150 percent in that brief time.[52] In 1934, that figure had grown to 88 stations. By the close of 1940, the Red and Blue were jointly transmitting to 182 local outlets. In the meantime at CBS — a singular broadcasting hookup that was launched a year after NBC's Red chain — the numbers grew from 1928's foundational 17 affiliates to a very decent 112 in 1940.

> Furthermore, by 1938, the four networks ... had affiliated with 50 of the 52 clear-channel stations in the United States. A federal inquiry in that ... epoch concluded: "By and large, the stations associated with Mutual are less desirable in frequency, power, and coverage." All of it made a huge difference in perception, in audience size, in web ties and in amounts advertisers were willing to spend in given markets. The big audiences that popular chain-fed shows drew were magnets for local advertisers, significantly boosting local affiliates' bottom lines. Consequently, NBC and CBS — including the networks and the stations they owned and operated — controlled more than half the business of the trade by the 1940s with MBS commanding just two percent of net time sales. The disparities could hardly be any more pronounced.[53]

On another front, in 1936, NBC added exclusivity provisions to the contracts it negotiated with its local outlets. As a result those stations were barred from sharing physical properties (buildings and sites) with stations that were tied to different coast-to-coast chains. From that point forward, a station's deal with the network bound it to NBC for a term of five years while NBC could opt out of the pact annually, the traditional provision (one-year intervals) that had been available previously to the affiliates.[54] We can't state unequivocally that there were grievances over this issue, but speculate that, theoretically, it could have been unsettling to some. It appears that if any feathers were ruffled by the "unfairness doctrine" it would have been those feathers of the individual affiliates rather than of the network itself. In this instance it was clear it was the chain that had the most to gain, seemingly well positioned in the proverbially venerated catbird seat.

Could such irritants, if indeed that's what they were, have festered to the point of adding to mounting dissension and discord that was quite apparent at a subsequent date? There would be some occasions down the road when those exchanges exhibited more pressing issues that were on the agendas of the local outlets, which carried greater weight as far as the stations were concerned. Just how much bearing might a litany of smaller gripes have added to the fray that had been needling the troops for a while? Under those circumstances the national chain would almost certainly be forced to play defense while it attempted to sustain a position of superiority, perceptibly so at least. We may only conjecture about any of this although the possibility of such a scenario involving an assortment of minor grumbles isn't altogether moot.

Offering 16 hours of programming per day to its affiliated stations in 1939, NBC explained in its annual report: "To help create a true democracy of the air, NBC has sought to preserve the individuality which characterizes every station's approach to its own audience." That bit of fluff from an internal publicity mill may have sounded rosy on the surface but as a contemporary observer cautioned: "Of course, affiliates had to agree to clear the best parts of their schedules for network transmissions, leaving only late night, early morning, and weekend daytime hours for expressing such individuality."[55] But, nevertheless, it *sounded* good!

As the 1950s advanced, there were some nagging allusions that the local affiliates of the major chains were at least laboring under minimal duress. Regulations, guidelines, and strategies proffered by the networks may have increasingly defied some of the stations' hopes for radically improving their bottom lines. Anything that implied greater centralized authority with edicts filtering down from on high could be suspect, of course. But there was more to it than that. Soft-spoken murmuring eventually turned into a groundswell of audible protests that were directed from the local outlets' owners and executive management levels to the varied networks' upper echelons. Some of the affiliates' anxieties as well as their ideas appeared — to them, at least — to fall on deaf ears, particularly so as the 1950s continued to progress without much in the way of tangible change.

The stations' most sensitive requests — which grew increasingly louder as the years elapsed — were focused on the argument of requesting the networks to delete more and more of their broadcast hours, vacated time to be taken over by the member outlets. Since the mid–1930s, both CBS and NBC had gotten their affiliates to sign commitments mandating that their stations carry all of their network's commercial programming. Sustained features (those without sponsorship) were viewed as another matter entirely.

In gaining the upper hand on this issue the two leading nets (in audience, impact, and revenues) could assure their prospective advertisers that their messages would be heard by people residing on both coasts and nearly everywhere in between. In this way they could propose to an advertiser a certain number of listeners that might be attracted by a given show. At the same time the chains were guaranteeing themselves a larger share of income than if they were forced to sell time to a paltry number of stations.

All of this worked satisfactorily until the various stations carrying those shows became discontent with the "trickle-down proceeds" that were being dispatched to them by their chains. In reality, the receipts they got from that source were but fractions of the normally munificent returns the national hookups received and retained for themselves. And somewhere in the midst of all of that discussion there was probably some demonstrated avarice, too. A few of the stations, at least, grumbled among themselves as they pondered:

why settle for so little when we could earn so much more? By hiring their own talent and sales personnel, these stations reasoned, individually — or in clusters of outlets working in tandem — we could market the programming we offer directly to prospective advertisers and come out financially well ahead of where we are.

Selling the only commodity they really had — time — certainly would obliterate the middleman, permitting the respective outlets to retain *all* the profits for air time which they themselves sold. It made fiscal sense to the station owners but the networks viewed it as detrimental to their health (the health of the nets, not the affiliates). From the start of such perceived nonsense — sheer murmurings then — the most prestigious chains were determined not to give an inch, to put down any talk of an uprising without retrenching even a little. It would take a while and more than a little intimidation by the affiliates before headquarters' house of cards began to collapse.

In 1954, at the time all of this was going on, CBS — soon followed by NBC — cut its advertising rates across the board between 10 and 15 percent. This was an outcome principally tied to the shift of audiences from radio to television, ominously reducing the levels of listeners available to access the sponsors' advertising messages. All of which had the ultimate effect of depressing the proceeds sent to the stations for carrying the national chains' programs even further. This action exacerbated the problem to an effective degree like adding fuel to a flame at a most inopportune moment. There was still more bad news on the way: some major radio players (payers) like Kellogg's, Pillsbury, and Standard Brands were pulling all of their marketing dollars entirely out of the aural medium to send them elsewhere — mostly to TV, but also to billboards, direct mail, point-of-purchase promotions, transit advertising, etc.

Yet another longstanding radio underwriter, General Mills, which had assigned half of its $10 million annual advertising budget to the aural medium in 1946, redirected the bulk of its allotment to Videoland just five years later.[56] Wasn't that indicative of the handwriting on the wall? Stuff like that added to the dire consternation already felt by the local (as well as the national) radio tycoons. It was to pave the way for increased covetousness among the outlets that would be exhibited in still greater numbers in the years just ahead.

Under its contract with affiliated outlets, CBS could require complete scheduling allegiance all day long. With its pact, NBC could control most of the daily schedules of its stations by informing them of its intent to implement changes 28 days in advance. The outlets had given NBC that authority in writing when they signed up to be affiliates. MBS on the other hand could compel its member-stations to clear just four hours of time daily for network programming.[57] While the member-stations had the right to omit any sustaining (unsponsored) shows that were transmitted to them — substituting locally originated features in their stead — an outlet could put itself in serious jeopardy with headquarters if it eliminated commercial shows from its lineup. That could be cause for instantly terminating a station's ties to a national hookup.

The stations were enabling their chains to sell time across the board, guaranteeing nationwide transmission of programs that had the potential of being heard by millions. That was appealing to many prospective underwriters. It could be a good deal for all parties concerned, not limited to advertisers alone but also to advertising agencies, performers, chains, and member-stations.

The disturbance over the issue of relinquishing the air time to the outlets was hardly more than a whisper in its earliest phases.[58] As the weeks, months, and years rolled by, however, there were more and more voices joining that restive chorus, swelling the tempo at last from a low guttural rumble to a surging reverberation that had grown discordantly vociferous. Eventually, it was to reach a stage of utter rebellion, but not yet. Station owners in a handful of urban markets were noticeably upset when the networks dragged their heels after their repeated calls to take action.

While the least powerful chains (MBS and ABC) were responsive fairly early to their affiliates by, in the main, acquiescing to the protests of their station owners, NBC and CBS held out longer, vigorously standing guard, defying most of the challenges. That duo — and particularly CBS — took a very hard stand against any notion of radically trimming its network schedules. It felt that giving any appreciable consent to the affiliates' requests might be to the chain's peril by diminishing its image while unacceptably reducing its revenues big time. Relinquishing some of the advantageous turf on which it had long ago planted a permanent flag was hardly an option at CBS.

NBC was the first of the holdouts to cave. By 1959, it had scrupulously scrubbed its daytime and evening offerings to leave but a modest residue of its earlier agenda. CBS had dug its heels in deep, however, determined to remain aloof, firmly entrenched in its hard-nosed position. Its inaction might suggest a conviction like this: "Why give away the store when we can throw a bone to the dog with very little meat on it?" There would be some retrenchment, gradual and slim, in the latter years of the 1950s. But not until 1959 — when NBC plainly evidenced it was running up the white flag — did CBS take prudent steps to pacify the hungry mongrels that were nipping at its heels for most of the decade. And that would come about only on the verge of mutiny, after the network's hand was ultimately forced into action.

Pushed back against the wall, at the start of 1959, CBS reluctantly reduced its broadcast schedule of 63 hours per week to a mere 30 hours.[59] Several of its strongest long-playing primetime and weekend features evaporated overnight. And the face of daytime radio was radically altered at that point, too. *Arthur Godfrey Time*, which had, since 1945, occupied up to 90 minutes of CBS's weekday agenda, was curtailed to 30 minutes. Five minutes was pared from the durable Art Linkletter's *House Party* audience-participation show, also heard since 1945.

And the soap-opera sagas — the literal backbone of daytime radio since the early 1930s — were pruned to just seven narratives (there had been 16 running on CBS in the 1940s, and more than 300 on the four national hookups through the years). The enduring *Backstage Wife*, *Our Gal Sunday*, *The Road of Life*, and *This Is Nora Drake* were suddenly missing from the schedule in early 1959. A quartet of a dying breed with open-ended story lines was still running: *Ma Perkins*, *The Right to Happiness*, *The Second Mrs. Burton*, and *Young Doctor Malone*. The foursome aired alongside a couple of dramatic anthologies, *Best Seller* and *Whispering Streets*, plus the humorous dialogue exchange *The Couple Next Door*. The rest of the day was devoid of habitual features, by then a barren landscape in marked contrast to what had existed a short time earlier.

Still, none of this Good Faith Award was enough to pacify the hungry sharks in the Affiliate Sea that had tasted blood by this time and desired lots more. Standing united in their quest, they weren't going to be mollified any longer with just a portion of what they demanded. This time they threatened *real* upheaval: if CBS didn't meet their stipulation (by relinquishing more broadcast time to the point of leaving but a negligible trace from the network) they would pick up their marbles and go home.[60] A handful of the more respected, celebrated, and highly prized AM stations in their respective markets which carried enduring identities with CBS gave notice that "you either meet our demands or we'll become independents or join a rival network." Ultimately, with that irreversible taunt, CBS saw no give and take any longer.

That's when the cries of the affiliates apparently sunk in for the first time on CBS czar William S. Paley. At that juncture he realized his network was in critical jeopardy, possibly even of folding altogether. It was either to accept the mandate proffered by the member-stations and to persevere with a remnant of former glory days, or maybe lose it all. Paley chose the former. He had been a radio man since the first day he got there, in 1928. But realizing that if he didn't act his beloved audio network could be reduced to a minuscule component among the players in the national arena, Paley finally gave the order, albeit reluctantly.

It set into motion what allegedly marked the end of the Golden Age of radio. TV may have carried a big stick but it was the insistence of the affiliates that ultimately sealed radio's fate. Had those owners/managers not been as strident in their approach, the effects of the Golden Age might have lingered in greater proportion beyond 1960. New directions would take hold now and the marvelous lineage endowed by network radio would be virtually eradicated.

Let us make no mistake about one thing, meanwhile: Paley valiantly persevered to the very end. To his interminable credit, only in the face of insurmountable odds did he finally succumb to the mounting pressures around him. Radiophiles had to be in his everlasting debt, grateful to him whether they recognized it or not. Otherwise, the Golden Age literally might have disappeared five years sooner, as other chains played "follow the leader." He held out until the other shoe dropped.

In mid–August 1960, Arthur Hull Hayes (1904–86), then president of CBS Radio, appeared before the news media to make the official announcement. He proclaimed that radio "must shift from entertainment forms which can be presented more effectively by other media." Hayes revealed that the remnants of much of CBS's existing radio schedule would disappear from the airwaves in the three-day period of November 25–27, 1960. The early notice gave scriptwriters time to bring meaningful conclusions to running story lines that, in some cases, had been airing for multiple decades. It also gave the casts and other personnel a little lead time before the ax fell on most of their ethereal pursuits. (As the final major holdout, with few exceptions CBS Radio was employing almost every actor still working in the profession by then.)

All seven of radio's remaining soap operas were scrubbed on that fateful weekend along with *The Amos 'n' Andy Music Hall*; *Have Gun, Will Travel*; and *Suspense*.[61] While a few five-minute matinee personality-driven features were added to help flesh out CBS's programming, about 45 minutes of every hour was completely open to local stations to originate their own programming. And they had much more freedom to choose which New York-based entries they aired in the future. They also decided whether to run them on a delayed basis, something heretofore restricted. As Ed Bliss, who chronicled radio's history, ascribed the situation evolving from that shift: "With all their news sources and other programming available to them, the affiliates no longer live by the networks. The networks live by them. And both know it."[62]

And without stating the obvious earlier, the entire aural broadcasting panorama was being revolutionized through the transfer taking place right then.

> Listeners made a transition that the prophets of doom had not anticipated. They began listening to radio differently. They listened to stations rather than programs, and they tuned in at more times during the day.[63]

Whatever one's age, it clearly wasn't your father's — nor even your grandfather's — radio any more.

3

At Last, Wireless for Real

As has been observed already, in its earliest days radio was persistently certified as the "wireless telephone" and sometimes as "the wireless" and just plain "wireless," too. (Chapter 1 introduces this topic.) Some of the original practitioners of the method dated their use of it quite early, in fact. An electronic marvel in its day under its varying designations, when viewed by modern standards the operating wireless would have been something far less than sophisticated — characterized by comparatively restricted and primitive demonstrations.

The introductory, since-heralded exploitation of the apparatus is believed to have occurred on December 24, 1906. To the surprise of many, this date is chronologically much earlier than most people probably think that it was. On that auspicious Christmas Eve, inventor Reginald Fessenden (1866–1932) — employing the high-frequency alternator he fabricated — dispersed the sound of his voice across the ether from his home on Massachusetts Bay's southern shoreline at Brant Rock (now part of Marshfield, Massachusetts). Some accoutrements added variety to Fessenden's debut.

Erik Barnouw, a most scholarly and comprehensive radio historiographer — reviewing the conditions of that occasion a half-dozen decades after it happened — pontificated that the christening of the genre of the disc jockey (DJ) must have occurred at that time and in that place.[1] We aren't exactly certain of the physical distance involved for that "broadcast" (only that "over a wide area ship operators, with earphones to head, alert to the crackle of distant messages, were snapped to attention"[2]). Suddenly, Fessenden's nocturnal maritime audience must have been taken aback to hear out of the great beyond:

> A human voice coming from their instruments — someone speaking! Then a woman's voice rose in song. It was uncanny! Many of them called their officers to come and listen; soon the wireless rooms were crowded. Next someone was heard reading a poem. Then there was a violin solo; then a man made a speech, and they could catch most of the words.[3]

Fessenden himself played the violin solo — Charles Gounod's *O Holy Night*—and he sang a few bars, too, plus he read some verses from the book of Luke recounting the holy nativity of that sacred night. The woman's voice, an unknown contralto, emanated from a phonograph recording of George Frideric Handel's *Largo* from the opera *Xerses* (thereby achieving the earliest DJ designation).[4] At the close of his inaugural program, Fessenden wished his listeners a Merry Christmas and alerted them to a projected subsequent aircast one week later, on New Year's Eve (the first urging to "tune in again next week" perhaps?).

It certainly may have been the birth of the DJ as a profession, as Barnouw intimated. But was it not also (and absolutely no disrespect is intended by this) the very first variety hour of the airwaves? Think of it! Fessenden had staffed his showcase with an announcer, a vocalist, instrumentalist, speaker, recording, and even had extended felicitations at the close. All of the ingredients for a diverse variety act! Why, did Allen, Bankhead, Bergen, Cantor, Crosby, Durante, Godfrey, Jolson, Smith, or Vallee ever preside over a better exhibition? Or air from a more imposing venue? We think not. What a performance!

Fessenden's follow-up exploit on December 31, by the way, was savored by ship crews as distant as the West Indies (nearly 2,000 miles from Massachusetts, mind you) that included some banana boats of the United Fruit Company (UFC). Actually, in advance a little judicious marketing by code had tipped the UFC brigade to expect some auditory surprises on given dates.[5] (Maybe the original tease to listeners to "stay tuned"?) Wearing their headphones at the appropriate hour, those wireless operators — while doubtlessly overwhelmed by the magnitude of their experiences — were also anticipating something unusual as Fessenden's articulation poured across the atmosphere. It was good to have a ready-made audience, too. The crew later substantiated their reception of those exploits by code or by mail.[6] All of it was truly a remarkable breakthrough. Fessenden's efforts had earned for him the distinction of conducting what is traditionally earmarked (no quip intended) as "the first actual scratchy broadcasts."

His timing was impeccable, too. This dramatic audio activity transpired just in advance of a successive consequential feat by communications leviathan Lee de Forest (1873–1961).[7] In 1907, shortly after Fessenden's triumphant dual feats, De Forest manipulated his own contrivance known as the Audion tube in order to dispatch — over a distance of 14 miles — an eyewitness portrayal of a yachting race. Wireless operators at the Brooklyn Navy Yard thought at first they might be hearing the voices of angels through their headphones.[8] We really don't know who or how many people could have been in De Forest's audience for that episode.

Nevertheless, wouldn't that scenario have made him, at least hypothetically anyhow, broadcasting's first sportscaster? (Fessenden, the first DJ; De Forest, the first to report on athletic matches: So what's next?) And from the top floor of the Parker Building in New York, he (De Forest), too — perhaps not to be outdone by his illustrious ethereal precursor — pressed a gramophone into service, broadcasting the *William Tell Overture* across the atmosphere. That one would be heard a time or two in the ensuing century!

The history of the wireless extends even a little further back than these magnificent machinations, however. In its most basic primitive form, in 1893, the wireless joined a band of other communications inventions, including the telegraph, telephone, loudspeaker, microphone, phonograph, and tape recorder, all of which were already in existence in primeval models. Radio signals were to emerge just two years after the wireless (1895). In the meantime, the newest member of this tribe was experiencing a colorful inauguration.

In 1887, German physicist Heinrich Rudolf Hertz (1857–94) found that invisible radio waves were equivalent to light waves; radio waves, too, were moving at the speed of light.[9] Hertz also made the discovery that electricity is conducted on these waves.[10] Imprints were implemented to measure radio and electrical frequencies and their names were inspired by the physicist: *kilohertz* and *megahertz*. Although Hertz failed to grasp the communications capabilities of radio waves, nonetheless there were successor experimenters who did.

In the following decade Italian engineer Guglielmo Marconi (1874–1937) effectively dispatched and received radio-wave transmissions over a geographical breadth of 1.5 miles.[11] Keep in mind that this was several years prior to Fessenden's sterling Christmas and New Year's broadcasts that could be heard practically 2,000 miles away. Yet when authorities in Marconi's native land would not agree to underwrite his conception with the financial backing he needed to proceed, Marconi himself — in 1897 — instigated the Wireless Telegraph and Signal Company to develop his expanding ideas much further.

> Now came a small and momentous event. In 1898, through facilities provided by Marconi's newly founded wireless company, the *Dublin Daily Express* received minute-by-minute coverage of the Kingstown Regatta. This was wireless telegraphy — no sportscaster's voice was heard over the air. And the name for news heard over the air is broadcast journalism. Because of this success, the *New York Herald* the next year commissioned Marconi to provide wireless coverage of the America's Cup races. With these two yachting events at the close of the nineteenth century, news and radio were joined. Broadcast journalism, in dots and dashes, was born.[12]

In 1901, Marconi dispatched a signal across the Atlantic Ocean that traveled some 2,140 miles. Achieving that, the "wireless telegraph" (his name for the instrument he had given birth to — which applied Morse code minus a direct connection) confirmed the device's competence forever.[13] Wireless telegraphy thereafter was found everywhere. It was especially useful in dispatching warnings from ships in trouble at sea. (Remember the *Titanic* and its belated attempts to attract other vessels via telegraphic distress calls?)

Radio (another name for the wireless) was on the way!

Unlike some other inventors of that time, Marconi determined not to limit wireless telegraphy totally to military applications and ocean-liner catastrophes. He was convinced that this newfangled phenomenon could just as easily transmit music and speech, readily broadening its appeal as it contributed to the edification, enlightenment, and entertainment of vast numbers of people.[14] Such alternative functions swirling about in his mind would ultimately prove prophetic. Once the microphone became commonplace in 1912, Marconi's appliance would be much more practical, and from then on radio (by whatever its designation) showed signs of becoming "a done deal."

As early as 1904, the United States Navy had no less than 20 wireless stations in operation. References to copious supplementary applications of Marconi's marvelous fabrication appear in abundance, both online and in myriad hard-copy references. While it's not our intent here to recount what is so reliably reported elsewhere, the fact that wireless was operating so pervasively for diverse types of communication is a vital factor in the medium's early history. It's unequivocally a contributing part of the legacy of broadcasting's incubatory years.

Once it was fully developed, some of the radio gear that we are most familiar with began to appear in people's homes. Would you believe that some of it still remains in service and working condition now — certain examples of which are seven, eight, or possibly closer to nine decades old? That includes some well-preserved antique (*prehistoric* may seem to be a more apropos term) table models as well as those tall console relics that required considerable space.

A modern sports zealot, Josh Pahigian, recalling how baseball addicts huddled around monstrous-sized floor models as they hung on for every pitch and hit, reminded readers of the era "when your grandfather used to listen to games on a radio the size of a coffee table."[15] He wasn't all that far off the mark. With its insides sporting orange-lit tubes that still brighten today, those units may persist in pulling in the din of distant broadcasts now, albeit very possibly still accompanied by the crackle of static popping and hissing in irregular reverberations.

Back in the day such fanciful symbols commanded hallowed spots within American domiciles and workplaces. Table models in particular could be found lodged on book cases, end tables, nightstands, windowsills, and occupying racks and shelving in basements and unattached garages. There they spent their working lives engaging the ears and hearts and minds of eavesdroppers to the endless collection of amusing and edifying contents that they proffered at the flick of a knob, incessantly acknowledged by an unremitting, lighted dial.

Those devices evolved from some earlier radio headgear and crystal-set manifestations that belie anything we might consider adequate in contemporary times. Yet such primitive contraptions quite capably (in a manner of speaking) delivered the words and music of their day to a limited audience.[16] Those sets were primarily restricted by the fact that only one listener could successfully hear what was on the air at a time, unless, of course, the headphones were held up to two or more people's ears simultaneously.

> In 1920, at the beginning of radio broadcasting stations, factory-made radios were expensive and in short supply. As a result, people were urged to either get a simple crystal set or build their own. No batteries were required to pick up signals, and the device could be put together with a few hand-made parts.... A metallic mineral such as galena could pick up signals. A fine pointed wire was used to tune in a selected station by making contact with the crystal. This wire detector came to be known as a "cat's whisker"....[17]
>
> Until late 1920, just before [Pittsburgh's] KDKA's first broadcast, all receivers were homemade. Some, like the crystal set, were cheap and simple — all it took was some wire and an oatmeal box to wind it on, a purchased piece of galena or other crystal and cat's whisker to probe it with, and a pair of earphones. More complicated sets were more expensive — the price of tubes, like many weekly wages, started at $6 — though not beyond the capabilities of experienced amateurs or the thousands of ex-servicemen trained in radio.[18]

Radio's regard by a generation of grassroots hobbyists need not be underrated, nor dismissed unhesitatingly. The members of this crowd could be classified as fraternizing with like-minded individuals comprising a couple of marked alliances: (1) amateur fanatics who built their own broadcast receivers and transmitters and thereby became wireless hams, literally as broadcasters on the airwaves, and (2) crystal-set owners whose homemade creations or store-bought substance let them pick up transmissions through archaic (to us today) headphones.[19] We know that they date so far back as to nearly startle us by the point in time of their commencement as well as the frenetic levels of commotion that were occurring in that nascent period.

> As radiotelegraphy and radiotelephony became increasingly prominent, thousands of amateurs from coast to coast became involved in this new hobby. The barriers to entry were low; all one needed was a relatively inexpensive and easy-to-build radio set.... Radio amateurs had been active in the United States since before 1910, and they were a devoted, ever-growing group of private citizens ... who spent countless hours sending and receiving signals. There were radio clubs in high schools and colleges, and associations sprang up to support these hobbyists. It was a terrific activity for young boys, many of whom would later in the decade use their skills to help the military during World War I.
>
> The earliest devotees communicated with one another using the dot-and-dash code....
>
> But as quickly as the radio technology emerged, so did the fight to control it.... On August 13, 1912, Congress approved the Act to Regulate Radio Communication. Rather than banning ham operator transmissions though, ... Congress decided to limit amateur broadcasts to a wavelength of 200 meters, or 1,500 kilohertz.

...The government had ostensibly stepped in to organize what was becoming a crowded field, but the net result was that corporations with large investments in the business and technology of radio had found a protector in the government, with its ability to control individuals who wanted to fill the air with their own messages.[20]

The gadgets these enthusiasts employed in *surfing the airwaves* (one of the earliest uses of that idiom) could be diverse. The contrivances were frequently fabricated entirely at home by industrious scientific hobby addicts who had been caught up in a wave of experimentation that was considered a sporting challenge in the 1920s. All of the parts might be gathered by the owner himself or the finished product might be the result of the builder's efforts in assembling the contents of a radio kit which shopkeepers sold with unadorned instruction guides. Either way, the final assembly of the multiple parts of those early radios was generally left to the ultimate user. It could be quite commonplace in those days to visit someone's home and encounter pieces of odd-looking trappings strewn all over the living-room floor and spread out on the kitchen table before the widget was fashioned into its finished functional construction.

Several of the early experimenters in wireless productions lived to see some of the further advancements that resulted from their inspiring efforts. De Forest, Fessenden and Marconi were among them. While many scientists added to the eventual results, it must have been extremely satisfying to those emerging contributors to be recognized for possessing a major hand in advancing the universally applied communication tools in practical ways. At their earliest stages, who knew that they would be put into pervasive action by diffusing sound so thoroughly among mankind — and transferring it over such vast distances to virtually everywhere on earth?

> In fall 1920, commercially manufactured radios became available, principally in large department stores. The Westinghouse "Aeriola Jr." was a crystal set that cost $25, and the "Aeroila Sr." was a tube set for $60. By 1922 there were hundreds of manufacturing companies.... RCA, as sales agent for sets made by Westinghouse and GE, was the foremost distributor, but Crosley, Grebe, and Atwater Kent also became familiar brands. Fortunately for the companies competing with RCA, ... the long lead-time needed for this intercompany ordering made its "Radiola" sets obsolete by the time they hit the market. The public soon realized that inexpensive sets were no bargain due to their lack of quality and performance, and the average price per set climbed well above $100.
> ...
> In 1926, "battery-eliminator" or plug-in models reached the market to the delight of everyone except the battery manufacturers and households with no electricity, a rapidly shrinking proportion. A simple connection to a house current eliminated 40 to 50 pounds of batteries and a maze of wiring.[21]

Improvements continued to be made in radio sets as the years rolled by, and radio's popularity grew by leaps and bounds. Sales skyrocketed.[22] With better quality in making parts inside newer units, better sound arrived. More pleasing designs made the table and floor-model sets even more attractive pieces of furniture that often harmonized with existing home furnishings — mahogany cases blended, for instance. Nevertheless, the one fixed irreversible that all of these newer radios exhibited — which was seldom altered very much — was the cord that connected a receiver with a 120-volt electrical outlet. This gave the unit power: without electricity, there was no sound. Without the wire coupled to the radio it would have been like an automobile attempting to run without gasoline. Now, of course, today some vehicles are manufactured that don't require gas; at least not all the time. Something similar happened to radios. The wireless literally went wireless!

The onset of the changeover is dated from the latter years of the fourth decade of the 20th century. Between 1949 and 1960, radio experienced more than one metamorphosis. Not only was it losing incredible ground to television, at the same time — along with its deficit of advertisers, affiliates, alliances (those previously robust transcontinental chains), artists, and audiences — something else was transpiring: in those very same years radio was being disconnected from its wall sockets and accompanying listeners wherever they went. A 1950s institutional commercial repeatedly aired over CBS typified what was happening with a tagline that urged: "Wherever you go, go with radio." In that 11-year epoch (1949–60) the number of portable radio sets made by American manufacturers quadrupled. And at the same time, the sum of Japanese-fabricated transistor units imported into the United States vaulted by sevenfold.[23]

> No invention was more essential to radio's survival in the age of television than the transistor. Developed by John Bardeen, Walter Brattain, and William Shockley of Bell Labs in 1947, the transistor performed most of the functions of the electron tube but was much smaller and required a fraction of the power to operate.[24] It was about the size of a kernel of corn, and using tiny crystals of germanium or silicon it rectified and amplified radio signals when placed in an electrical circuit....
>
> By the end of the war few scientists talked about crystals. Instead, there was a new field, solid-state physics, and a class of solids called semiconductors.... When these semiconductors were used in radio receivers, they did what crystals couldn't: amplified the incoming signals enormously. After years of dealing with expensive, fragile, short-lived tubes that consumed a great deal of power, the transistor was an improvement in almost every way.[25]

Among the transistor's numerous advantages over the vacuum tube found in table- and floor-model receivers were that it required less power and generated less heat, was sturdy and had a longer life, was less costly, and was diminutive. Electronic gadgets could now be miniaturized thanks to the transistor (the label, by the way, is a contraction of *transfer resistor*).

While military applications of the transistor were examined, news of the breakthrough was suppressed until June 30, 1948. It was refined for several years and then tested in consumer equipment. The first commercial transistor radio, the Regency, made by Texas Instruments and priced at $40, went on sale in 1953. At first it was marketed — and perceived by the public — as a novelty. "The world's smallest radio — small enough to fit in the palm of the hand — was demonstrated yesterday afternoon in Times Square," Jack Gould wrote in *The New York Times*. "The populace took the coming of the 'Dick Tracy Age' with disconcerting calmness." But consumers quickly grew excited about the transistor radio, and sales took off.[26]

Nielsen ratings released late in 1955 confirmed that radio had lost its audience and — if it was to persist in a viable form to any degree whatsoever — it had to adapt to the new environment in which it found itself. Radio network offerings were by then purely auxiliary in nature, irrefutably presenting a far less extensive panorama of matchless entertainment than listeners had been accustomed to since the early 1930s. Fred MacDonald, an observant academic, pontificated: "To survive, it [radio] had to do better those things which television could not do."[27] The assessment seemed to be right on the money. Radio absolutely had to find some methods of attracting an audience and advertisers to its niche market if it seriously intended to remain in business.

As the 1950s progressed, the proliferation of the medium's portability reassured apprehensive listeners that yes, there was indeed a need for radio to subsist. For the first time it was offering those individuals a practical solution for the times that there were gaps in their personal broadcasting quests. At the same time radio was gaining a shot in the arm in coping with the financial losses that resulted from its displacement by TV. The increasing mobility that radio offered became an attractive marketing bonus to local radio station sales forces and correspondingly lucrative for a station's bottom line.

The aural medium's recognition of the portability and mobility factors, its potential and response appeared to be impeccably timed. A little background is necessary to grasp the scenario in which portability began to flourish. At the middle of the 20th century there was a gradual but rising perception among broadcasters that people were done with being tied to their radios in a single spot for undue, protracted periods of time. The nation's release from years of poverty resulting from the Great Depression followed by an era of pronounced restrictiveness: the unavailability of many goods during the war years had now ushered in a distinct reversal of fortunes for many Americans in the 1950s.

Instead of holding back from spending any longer, millions were at last doing just the opposite. National prosperity was suddenly evident in legions of middle-class homes. Production soared as U.S. factories turned out more and more commodities for people with good-paying jobs and in a free-wheeling buying frame of mind. Citizens were acquiring homes, vehicles, new kitchen appliances, washers and dryers, television sets, air conditioners, and other modern conveniences they had either been denied or denied themselves. In addition, they were starting families as well as private business enterprises and remodeling jobs and at the same time sending sons and daughters away to college — all of which they may have been reluctant to do and unable to afford in the two preceding decades.

Americans were also spending on leisure-time activities, including entertainment, vacations, sports equipment, travel, and even vacation cottages at a pace the country had never witnessed. Their pent-up inhibitions about money were seemingly being reversed overnight. While many moved cautiously, recalling the Great Depression in the not-too-distant past, purchasing on layaway and credit was gaining a substantial foothold. They wanted what they wanted, and they wanted it now.

All of this signified an avowed restlessness among the population that could easily be seen in their independent thinking characterizing the movements of many denizens. In that environment radio's portability began to thrive, ideally suited for the demonstrated impatience that Americans displayed in a novel and seemingly incessant quest for something not yet acquired, or as they proceeded to be somewhere else in their living standards. It was a new day for the United States, and radio adapted to what was transpiring in people's lives.

The portability factor prompted a rapidly discernible revolution in the radio listening habits of large numbers of Americans. The behavior that had been demonstrated since the medium's enveloping presence emerged three decades before — which had withstood virtually every interceding modernization that had transpired — started to noticeably adjust. How, who, and where Americans heard their radios was being altered pervasively. Instead of a crowd of listeners gathered around the set as the prevailing custom had been in a great many homes in the 1920s, 1930s, and 1940s, from the 1950s on radio was frequently enjoyed by an audience of just one. That reversal of a longstanding practice was a direct result of the technological advancements that introduced the TV to living rooms and permitted a radio receiving set to go on the road. Now the aural medium could be transported virtually anywhere at any time, rewarding the single bearer it accompanied with a box of informative and amusing features, without the owner seeking a power outlet. This could be focused on intently by a solitary listener or merely offer companionship by supplying unrelenting background din. The perceptions of the individual and the conditions by which he tuned in to radio were to be adjusted forever in the wake of that watershed transformation.

From the nation's original "boom boxes" the sounds of voices and music abruptly poured forth in backyards everywhere. The same occurred at local swimming pools and alongside sandy surfs; at ballparks, stadiums, and more sports and athletic complexes; at municipal parks, playgrounds, picnic shelters, and recreation halls; in transit on buses, subways, trains, ferries, and in taxis. In fact, wherever people were to be found — by themselves and in small and large groups — there was radio. Transistors allowed sound to redefine public space. The electric cords that had tethered an audience to a stationary spot for decades in order to listen in were now — out of the blue — instantly old-fashioned and out-of-sync in many places.

There was another segment of the shift to mobility in radio that has not yet been addressed but which progressively modified the conditions by which Americans were listening to radio. It's the inclusion of receivers in cars and trucks casually identified in the trade under the varied labels *auto radio, automotive radio, car radio, motor car radio,* and *motor radio.*[28] Beginning in 1927, sound systems for vehicles emerged, with Philco Corporation (a name derived from Philadelphia Storage Battery Company) ultimately taking the lead in producing those units.[29]

Statistics on how many radios were included in personal transit conveyances started to surface in the 1936 edition of the industry periodical *Automobile Facts and Figures*. That year 1.1 million receivers were reported for 1935 car models. With an aggregate of 5.5 million radios of every persuasion that were sold in this country that year, one in five was permanently affixed to individual modes of transit at the diverse vehicle manufacturing plants.[30] It was an added expense that a portion of new car buyers was willing to shell out for, even at a time they continued to cope with the financial fallout of the Great Depression.

By mid-century, meanwhile, no less than 64 percent of all American cars (including old and new) were equipped with radios, a proportion that improved to three-fourths of their total within four years (1954). Between 1953 and 1957, the number of American vehicles with radios jumped from 25 million to 35 million.[31] Only a few years later, 62 percent of new cars exhibited factory-installed radios as they rolled from the assembly lines of U.S. car-making plants in 1963. That figure soared to 85 percent within a quadrennial (1967), the same year that tape-player installations were initially reported in *Automotive Industries*, yet another trade paper. Chilton Company supplied 138,000 of the latter units to carmakers then representing 2 percent of new autos being manufactured.[32]

The Federal-Aid Highway Act of 1956, creating the interstate highway construction program, prompted millions of drivers to take to the open road for long-distance trips. That resulted in many more families, couples and single drivers spending more and more time in their vehicles than ever. It was a natural impetus, too, for stimulating even greater sales of new autos which displayed radios as standard (not optional) equipment. The profusion in radio-installed vehicles underscored the fact that the mobility dynamic was in lock-step with the growing trend toward portability. All of this exhorted listeners to travel with radio wherever they went. A few more statistics are worth noting that suggest how pervasive people's emerging preferences were becoming as innovative technology continually resulted in more and more ungraded (and enviable?) sound systems.

Pulse, Incorporated noted in 1974 that something above 85 percent of cars in America had radios mounted inside. About one-fourth of these proffered FM station reception by this time.[33] In 1986, 46 percent of all new U.S.-manufactured cars came equipped with dual AM-FM stereo systems. That year only 5 percent of new automobiles had AM-only factory-installed units in them; it was a diminishing reporting zone that became so negligible by 1990, it was deleted altogether by *Ward's Automotive Yearbook*. In the meantime, AM-FM stereo with cassette players proliferated: in 1983, U.S. car models, some 1.6 million of those sound units (26 percent of all sales) appeared; in 1986, 3.5 million (42 percent); in 1990, 4.6 million (66 percent); and in 1993, 5.2 million (76 percent). The latter year witnessed a profusion of systems sporting sophisticated selections that included AM stereo, compact-disc players, amplifiers, equalizers, and specially designed speakers.

A subsequent advancement, nationwide reception of a single station by way of satellite delivery (think *USA Today* on the ether, for comparison), has put accessibility to commercial radio stations within easy reach almost anywhere a traveler might be. And all of it stems from the nation's growing predilection for portability and mobility in radio that began to manifest itself during the middle of the 20th century.

Starting with that point in time, from those automotive sound systems a colorful history emanated for at least one sector of the population. Vehicular radiomania stoked profound fantasies for several successive generations of older adolescents.[34]

> A potent synthesis of cars, young people, rock 'n' roll, and the radio meant that teenagers could — and did — use broadcast music to become unlawful occupants: they staked out terrain that wasn't theirs by enveloping a geographical district with rock 'n' roll. They did so while driving around undersized hamlets, gliding up and down specific strips, discharging their radios in laundromats and sweet-treat emporiums, and capturing wedges of parks and slices of beach. After sundown and particularly on weekends they claimed public facilities earmarked for their elders and diverse business enterprises, performing manifold types of trade, applying the din of their radios and cars to rebel against whatever neatness and obedience to regulations they found. The cars and radios had a strong impact on a culture that wasn't quite ready for adulthood but was well past puberty.

Some of this trend toward mobility began to have an effect on the programming available to listeners in the 1950s as well as it did on the hardware that was used to receive it. Beginning in October 1953, NBC added a dual-hour Sunday afternoon entry titled *Weekend*. The series provided a primarily news-and-documentary feature to its lineup, allowing listeners to tune in to snippets they were interested in without necessarily hanging around for both full hours. Three months after it bowed, in January 1954, the same web began relinquishing much of its Saturday matinee programming to the *Road Show*. This smorgasbord of news, weather reports, traffic information, interviews, recorded music, interactive games, sports scores, and sundry features hosted by well-known broadcasting luminaries Bill Cullen and Dave Garroway, expanded a short time later into most of the matinee hours on Saturday.

Those two programs became prerequisites of the most strikingly enduring example of the magazine format that lay just ahead. Arriving in June 1955, the debuting phase of NBC's *Monitor* was a 40-hour weekend marathon "radio service" (as opposed to a defined "show"). In theory, at least, it traveled on-location wherever newsworthy events were occurring throughout the planet. It sort of eavesdropped on big- and small-time events, often procuring reports through NBC's ability to reach vast, even desolate territory, with pick-up transmissions through the network's extensive long-line capabilities. (There were of course, no satellites in those years.)

Monitor aired news reports at the top and bottom of each hour; there was some recorded music; there were interviews with eons of icons from political, entertainment, and sports arenas; some comedy snippets; a profusion of handy tips and advice segments from authorities on myriad topics like finances, gardening, interpersonal relations, health, home maintenance, major purchases, vehicle upkeep, and the like. *Monitor* usually appeared to try to "cover the world" and whatever seemed of pressing interest or newsworthy to Americans at a given moment.

Contributing significantly to its distinctiveness was its stunning disregard for the clock. Instead of following broadcasting's etched-in-stone addiction to split-second timing so that every feature reached its denouement within enduringly prescribed 5-, 15-, 30-, or 60-minute intervals, *Monitor* threw out the time-honored model (wisecrack intended). With the exception of its scheduled newscasts, the balance of *Monitor*'s fare aired on an uncertain blueprint: each interview, pick-up of a live event, piece of music, how-to tip, humorous dialogue (or whatever else it offered) was allowed as little or as much time as it required. An insert might run for a few seconds or a few minutes. All of this was breaking new turf in broadcasting: the form (or absence of it, perhaps?) is quite commonplace today in radio and television (typical illustrations: NPR and cable TV news channels). But in the period of its introduction to America's listeners it was extraordinarily irreplaceable. It was a weighty split with the customary patterns of the past.

Monitor capitalized on a new epoch in auditory aircasting that matched the "come and go" lifestyles of escalating numbers of Americans. In many ways its arrival signified a trend that has burgeoned with the passing of time. And, although the model it fostered was copied and tweaked scads of times by multiple innovators who attempted to improve upon it, none may have done it so with the fervor, pizzazz, and sizzle that the original displayed.[35] Pat Weaver (1908–2002), NBC president then, who credits himself with bringing *Monitor* to radio, immodestly hinted that the innovation spared his chain in some perilous times, as radio audiences disintegrated and TV's rose: "*Monitor* lasted for two decades on NBC and saved the radio network from disaster."[36] And indeed in its day *Monitor* had no comparable rivals.

Overruled by portability and the profuse accessibility advantages to news and amusement that accompanied that mobility, the radio table models and consoles began to almost fade in some quarters. While the majority of sets still in use required current, the aural medium had added a futuristic dimension to its mix that gave it fresh appeal, particularly among teenagers. This segment of the listening audience rapidly discovered radio all over again, falling in love with the epoch that was presided over by the disc jockey and typified by the sounds of rock 'n' roll.[37] Despite television's omnipresence across the land, radio increasingly and incessantly developed new reasons for being.

By the end of the 20th century and before the advent of an avalanche of hand-held computerized gadgets offering a spectacle of platforms that sent radio sound waves cascading down everywhere, the Nielsen people reported this affirmation: seven out of 10 radio listeners in America tuned in outside their residences — mainly in their vehicles or at their worksites.[38] Mobility and portability were in good health (and are undoubtedly in even better shape today as the country truly has gone absolutely crazy for wireless).

Integrated circuitry would be required in the late 1960s, as it turned out, to ultimately surpass the transistors in portable receivers and to institute a new standard in radio's fabrication.[39] For a couple of decades (the 1950s and 1960s), nevertheless, the transistor had become the "permanent" first-generation replacement for the vacuum tube, a remarkable improvement over its predecessor. More importantly, the transistor ushered in widespread mobility and portability in radio as well as other devices. This breakthrough established still greater opportunities for relying upon — and even a preference for, among some aficionados — an audio diversion during a period when radio's future effectiveness could have been considered to be in serious jeopardy.

All of which set the stage for monumental programming modifications that were just beyond the horizon. Radio might be "going places and doing things," to cite NBC Radio's *Monitor* familiar tagline, but — even with the availability of such welcome conveniences notwithstanding — for many people, the new sounds coming out of its integrated circuitry and transistorized receivers, it was still going to take some getting used to.

4

From Victrola to Payola

More than anyone with a continuing presence on the ether, the disc jockey (DJ) is a transitional figure in Radioland. He (or she — 31 percent of DJs in the U.S. were a *she* in a recent year[1]) originated before there was much more than experimentation with pint-sized transmitters and plainly primitive sound reception. The DJ was there before any permanent radio stations existed ... before there were aural networks ... and long before radio's Golden Age became a resplendent expression to depict an era.

For anyone who hasn't yet reached at least his 107th birthday, the DJ has been practicing his craft all of your life. Throughout the industry's most awesomely celebrated decades of the 20th century, the DJ was a fundamental symbol of aural broadcasting. As recently as four decades back he engendered so much respect among radio listeners that he commanded four-fifths of the aural broadcasting time in this country.[2] And long before then, as stations aired a mixture of programming breeds, whenever there was an unpredictable lapse in the schedule a DJ could be summoned in a split second to fill the void as nimbly in a protracted time period as he could in a pithy moment.

Most broadcasting operations maintained large music libraries. Recorded tunes were the most frequently employed solution when dead air time arose unexpectedly. And as if that wasn't enough, "The real language of radio during the early golden years was music," affirmed a media historian. "Beginning with the mid–1920s nearly two-thirds of all air time was dominated by music."[3]

> The effect of free music on radio not only brought opera and concerts to the masses but sparked the recording industry, which for years feared radio would destroy it when sales fell in the phonograph, sheet music, piano roll, and piano businesses; meanwhile, saxophone, mandolin, and banjo sales boomed. But Victor and Brunswick, the two leading phonograph companies, soon recognized the promotional value of radio programs, which were, in essence, hour-long singing commercials for record players.[4]

All of this, of course, gave rise to the DJ, the "scourge of postwar radio," in one critic's opinion: "Small stations began clandestinely interspersing live music with records (despite the label warning 'Not licensed for radio broadcast') or playing old records after it was ruled in 1940 that if a broadcaster bought a record, he was free to play it without paying royalties."[5] The profession of the disc-spinner proliferated and by the prewar epoch, it was generally viewed as a respectable occupation — one offering a service that gave pleasure and growing satisfaction to a tuned-in, turned-on crowd. Some of that professional breed was more prominent than some other sectors.

> The morning man was, and is, a reflection of the culture and social mores outside the radio studio. It was no coincidence that the most popular morning deejays in virtually every American city in the 1940s were gracious, articulate, and reserved. After all, that was the way people were expected to behave in public. In fact, the morning man could reinforce this behavior by inspiring listeners with flawless diction and impeccable manners, just as Clark Gable or Ronald Colman did with movie-goers. It would probably astonish a lot of youngsters to learn that many morning men dressed for work in suits and ties, even though no one could see them. It behooved a station to seek out a warm, well-known individual to open the broadcast day to build an audience not only for the day, but in some cases for decades.[6]

Around the midpoint of the last century — as the period of the disparate network-originated features started to ebb and ultimately fade from the dial — the stature of the DJ as an ethereal showman genuinely prospered. Not only did DJs continue to be vital to the core programming at many outlets, in beau coups of places a DJ's hours on the air perceptibly intensified. His value was increasingly viewed as more indispensable than at any time in radio's history. Local stations advertised widely through the trade press, seeking to fill their airchairs with individuals on whom their whole operations were to rest, practically speaking. The following published solicitations were typical.[7]

> **Early Morning man.** Minimum two years experience. Southerner preferred. No drunks or drifters. Send picture, audition tape and references....
> **Experienced Radio** pitchman who can pull mail for all-night trick by large midwest station....
> **Zany DJ-glib.** Ad lib. Humor. Actor background. Do character voices: "life of the party." ...
> **Experienced Hillbilly** and gospel DJ for live-wire 1000-watt daytimer.... No drifters....
> **Top Hillbilly Disk Jockey** ... that certain touch which appeals to the common folk. Must be able to hit a commercial hard and sell it....
> **Somewhere West of Erie** and east of Laramie there is a man who is still old-fashioned and likes to work. He doesn't have long hair and he isn't theatrical. He is a sound program man who builds his programming to the needs of his audience.... Give full information in first letter.
> **Experienced Staff** announcer for music, news station. Family man preferred....
> **Colored Disk Jockey.** Must be good southerner. Humorous. Good ad-lib....

In many markets it was the DJ who grew occupationally to inhabit the catbird seat all by himself. A new designation with the DJ at its core — marking some scattered outlets that at first were primarily of FM community and college orientations — was branded *freeform radio*.[8] In that modus operandi the outlet's owners and management literally handed over absolute control of program substance to the DJs. Under the rubric of freeform, the only real restrictions on the DJ pertained to operating within FCC guideline directives like stipulating station IDs and avoiding offensive speech.

With the halcyon days of freeform occurring in the late 1960s and early 1970s, its implied free-spirit ethic and negligible rules reverberated with an immense youth counterculture at work in that epoch. Because the style has a perceived status for rocking the boat, advocates and cynics alike agree that it has seldom charmed commercial sponsors. Freeform radio found a more welcoming home on the reserved noncommercial FM band, therefore.

In 1967 — when an FCC-mandated FM "non-duplication rule" kicked in and numerous commercial FM outlets consequentially altered their formats — some of them instituted freeform programming because teens and young adults were responding well to it at noncommercial operations. For a while outlets like Baltimore's WHFS, New York's WNEW and WPLJ, San Francisco's KMPX, and a few more of their standing prospered by employing freeform. Eventually, however, the management at each of these reinstated prescribed playlists and instituted greater manipulation over DJs.

One of the few freeform stations that continues to prosper in contemporary America is the Pacifica Radio chain's non-commercial listener-supported siren in the Big Apple, WBAI-FM. With a leftist-progressive bent for political news and opinion and eclectic styles of music, the outlet offers some relatively far-out features that embrace Muslims, queers (WBAI jargon), feminists, aboriginals, interculturalists, and Asian-Americans.[9] It rebroadcasts radio serials from back in the day and limited original narratives, just as if the fare of vintage radio was still in business. The station's history has been depicted as "long and contentious," referenced by a *New York Times Magazine* piece as "an anarchist's circus." However, WBAI was on the cutting edge when freeform radio was advanced and remains at the forefront of both it and counterculture today.

Radio Unnameable, hosted by WBAI air personality Bob Fass, stimulated the creation, exploration, and defining of freeform's potential.[10] Fass's late-night DJ show has been suitably designated as "*de rigueur* for Gotham's bohemians."[11] Its transmitter placed atop the Empire State Building and sticking 1,454 feet into the air, with only 4,300 watts of power, WABI-FM is able to extend its reach more than 70 miles from its broadcasting base at 120 Wall Street in downtown Manhattan.[12] It remains one of the more powerful and influential freeform stations in the modern era.

Despite this success, in the present age there aren't very many places where freeform programming survives. At the time of this writing (early 2013), a website identifies almost 100 U.S. radio stations at which the freeform model is presumably still booming.[13] In fairness, it must be noted that the overwhelming preponderance of these outlets is operated by colleges and universities, places where one might more readily anticipate discovering freedom and youth culture prospering. By comparison, only a handful of freeform stations appear to be situated in major metropolitan centers while unrelated to a specific educational institution (e.g., KCMP, St. Paul; KDHX, St. Louis; WBCN, Boston; WEVL, Memphis; WEXP and WKDU, Philadelphia). (Note: There is no hint at the website that any of these should be linked to academia.)

Before leaving this topic, what should not be missed here — and this will become abundantly clear in time — is that the DJ was in a unique spot for determining what went out over the airwaves as he conducted his business in the freeform construct. That would not always be the case. There would come a time in the not-too-distant future in which virtually all of the decision-making processes would be snatched from his (in a few instances, *her*) grubby little clutches and placed securely elsewhere. His day in the sun would soon pass. From that standpoint, if he enjoyed the power, he need not become enamored with it nor accustomed to it as if it would be there forever. For most DJs, the 1950s, 1960s, and early 1970s offered him the best his profession was ever going to be in the role of decider at the majority of stations.

In essence, the DJ represented the only broadcasting species then still on the air at copious stations (certainly so beyond the newscasters and announcers, all of their functions being rolled into lone individuals at some outlets). The DJ was there when the house of cards that *was* network radio collapsed. On some local stations he persisted for many years as a permanent fixture. He is active today at more than 700 outlets where he contributes a kind of tuneful oasis within a veritable sea of commercialism. And in the current radio environment that is almost overwhelmed by nonstop conversation, his music can be a refreshing interlude to many listeners seeking to spell relief in some other way.[14]

> The DJ-oriented phase would prevail in radio for a decade or so before losing ground to mounting competitors hankering for equal opportunity on the ether.... When the golden age of radio passed — the DJs were waiting in the wings to occupy the time the multiplicity of shows had vacated. The DJs weren't the instigators causing network radio to pass from the scene. Rather, they were the beneficiaries, the professionals who inherited the "space," filling it with their style of entertainment. They can't be accused of killing old-time radio, only of filling the void it had occupied.[15]

Despite the euphoria surrounding the DJ and his manifest contributions to saving the station, his profession cultivated detractors anyway, just as one would possibly anticipate. A modern historiographer, Alfred Balk, disparaged that era of audio broadcasting as unseemly, signifying that some outlets became little more than "commercialized jukeboxes" with formats tilting totally toward "fast-conscious, free-spending youth." The recording industry, abetted by radio, switched from "an adult base to an adolescent base," proclaimed the scholar. Electronic sound effects and "screamer" DJs were supplemented by news fragments and unremitting commercials.[16] In some quarters it was all more than irresponsible; it was patently reprehensible to a mortified (and perhaps relatively large) segment of the mature audience in particular.

In any regard, the DJ unequivocally became the aural medium's sparklingly effervescent personality of ups and downs. More than any other achiever, he represents the Alpha and the Omega of the Golden Age, steady as a rock on the scene from its foundation to its finish (from its incubation to its annihilation, perhaps). His legacy is vital to any account of the Postgolden Age, for he was in full bloom at its inception and indisputably flourished for years — even to the present decade in many markets. In this chapter we'll attempt to commemorate his and her manifold accomplishments.

A DJ is a performer who selects and plays recorded music for the listeners. A showbiz trade journal didn't coin the term *disc jockey* until 1941.[17] Until then a slightly more cumbersome taxonomy, *record jockey*, had been in vogue dubbing the guys and gals at the turntables. The origin of the permanently accepted banner under which the designee would spin tunes, however, actually emanated from the previous century. All of this stemmed from the culmination of an idea conceived by native German engineer Emile Berliner (1851–1929).[18]

After migrating to America, he patented a sound recording system on November 8, 1887, using flat discs (records). He was the first to do so after Thomas Edison (1847–1931) and Alexander Graham Bell (1847–1922) experimented with recording cylinders a few years earlier that proved deficient. Berliner's gramophone utilized glass discs, then later zinc, and, finally, plastic. A spiral groove with sound information was etched into the disc as it rotated on the apparatus. By vibrating, a needle-bearing arm read grooves in the disc and sent it to a speaker. Sound familiar?

The disc established inexpensive mass duplication of recorded material for the first time. In the 1890s, Berliner formed the Gramophone Company to mass produce his sound discs and devices to play them. Ingeniously, he engaged then-popular singers to record, using his system (Enrico Caruso and Dame Nellie Melba were among them). In 1908, Berliner adopted Francis Barraud's painting *His Master's Voice* as the firm's insignia. You may have encountered it in advertising. Do you remember that it features the dog Nipper listening to sounds pouring out of a gramophone?

Berliner later sold the licensing rights to his gramophone patent, plus his method of making records, and that logo along with it to the Victor Talking Machine Company (RCA). Interestingly, the inventor also shared in early prototypes for helicopters and automobiles. And although Berliner was never a DJ, he created an industry by making what they did relevant and practical.

"The disc jockey isn't an artist," insisted one wag. "He is a vicarious exploiter of other people's talents. He's a selective exploiter."[19] Originally *disc* (also *disk*) *jockey* referenced playing phonograph recordings, not the Compact Discs that succeeded them. That label now embraces every form of music playback, regardless of the medium. And unlike the past with its radio DJs, myriad types of disc jockeys have since emerged. A radio DJ or a radio personality — our precise absorption here — introduces and plays music that's aired on radio stations of several stripes: AM, FM, shortwave, digital, and Internet. There are a few categories that exist beyond the aural broadcasters, however, as a parade of newer technology and shifting venues has evolved persistently.[20]

> Because of radio's uniquely seductive nature, the disc jockey quickly gained adoration, fortune and notoriety. The power of someone playing records across the airwaves was soon noticed and immediately questioned. It was seen as a great threat to employment by musicians and viewed with suspicion by those responsible for society's cohesion. It was even perceived as an economic threat by the record companies, who thought it would replace rather than promote their products.
>
> And the radio DJ was undoubtedly powerful, almost from his inception. His promotional muscle was the major factor in the creation of the modern music industry (and the broadcast advertising industry, too). He was instrumental in founding new genres of music, by bringing together unconnected stylistic strands and by creating pride and ambition in the local folk musicians who played them. In a similar way, the early disc jockeys were key in fostering understanding between different races and cultures.
>
> The disc jockey's influence was soon so strong that it attracted more than just envy and suspicion. America's musicians went on strike for a full year in protest over the rise of the DJ. And before his profession was very old, a radio DJ would be targeted, investigated and eventually hounded to death by the U.S. government, largely because he was perceived as enjoying too much power.[21]

The first of a long line of representatives of the professional breed of radio disc jockeys in America emerged with the embodiment of Massachusetts audio experimenter Reginald A. Fessenden (1866–1932). On December 24, 1906, as alluded to in the previous chapter, he was at the forefront of that genre's stimulating tradition: it underscored the fact that the form dates back considerably farther than most of us realized. The simple beaming of a recording of an unidentified soloist emanating from Fessenden's antediluvian gramophone to an unseen wireless audience tuning in hundreds and maybe thousands of miles away clearly puts him at the vanguard of a parade of impending spinmeisters.

Fessenden is believed to be the very first individual to occupy the hallowed perch before a broadcast turntable of any type and thus attract listeners to a classic melody (or to any other kind of song, for that matter). In his unique circumstance, that crowd was more than a little mesmerized by his exploits, and with good reason. Fessenden's startling escapade was momentous if for no other grounds than that those affixed to his transmitter by headphones had never in their whole lives heard anything to equal it. That episode is believed to have encompassed casting the human voice onto the ether without benefit of wires for the very first time. Reginald Fessenden was the man securely fastened to the right place at the right moment as that momentous historic spectacle transpired.

He was closely followed in the strain by Lee de Forest (whose celebrated heritage has been cited earlier, too). When Rossini's *William Tell Overture* wafted onto the ether early in 1907, no one had any inkling that Kemosaby — aka *The Lone Ranger*— and his Indian pal Tonto were on the way (arriving in 1933 at a radio near them). That brilliantly memorable fanfare ricocheting along the Eastern seaboard a few weeks after Fessenden cranked up his gramophone signaled a notion that canned music was probably gonna be a biggie on the air (though nobody knew it at the time). And apparently without any shame De Forest declared that *his* efforts gave him the right to crow: "I was the first disc jockey."[22] As legendary comic Jimmy Durante consequently exclaimed about a whole lot of subjects: "Evvvvvreeebody wans ta git inta da ack!"

Some historiographers — this author sheepishly discloses that he is among the culpable — mistakenly believed that the heritage of the radio disc jockey probably stemmed from an auspiciously modest initiation in western Pennsylvania. As it turns out, that research was flawed. Our suspicions rested with Westinghouse engineer Frank Conrad (1874–1941). His name rings a bell with old-time radio aficionados for he's the gent who turned an experimental broadcasting test model (station 8XK) into what eventually became Pittsburgh's pioneering outlet, the legendary and revered KDKA. Conrad's exploits earned for him the duly accorded trademark of "father of radio broadcasting."[23] Many old-time radio buffs seem to think it was probably legit.

More than anyone else, Conrad and his experiments led to the spectacularly illustrious "beginning of radio" that is unequivocally acknowledged by nearly all media scholars: the airing of the famed Harding-Cox presidential election returns on November 2, 1920, were mainly responsible for the citation. A crowd estimated at only about 100 persons residing in a trio of adjacent states (Ohio, Pennsylvania, and West Virginia) was lucky enough to hear the progressively updated numbers that evening. KDKA's 100-watt transmitter was the earliest sanctioned U.S. commercial outlet operating on the occasion of that noble quest.[24] Human ears had never heard such factual statistics ferried through the atmosphere over protracted distances. It was truly a watershed moment in the annals of broadcasting.

Beginning October 17, 1919, just the same — more than a year before that election's propitious occurrence — Frank Conrad had applied the modest transmitting apparatus tucked in his garage in nearby Wilkinsburg to become what had (until we all knew better) appeared to be the country's first DJ.[25] (Reginald Fessenden and Lee de Forest, as we know, had proclivities that researchers, regrettably, missed.) After spinning all the records he owned on his little gramophone on a twice-weekly airtime odyssey, Conrad worked a deal with the owner of his hometown's Hamilton Music Store to supply newly released celluloid discs without charge to him. As he played them for his listeners, the DJ — who obviously was among the nation's early pitchmen of the airwaves — hawked Hamilton's retail emporium for its goods and services. (A fair exchange, perhaps?) Come to think of it, that could be the foundational model of payola for the Victrola.

At some point those "broadcasts" gained detection by Pittsburgh's Joseph Horne mercantile retailer. The outfit stocked radio receivers priced at $10 and higher. Horne bought an ad plugging Conrad's ethereal amusement, juxtaposed with its radio receivers, in the September 29, 1920 issue of the *Pittsburgh Sun*.

As it turns out nevertheless, Conrad, whom far more than one historian has certified as the world's first DJ — since proven wrong — wasn't even *second* in that extraordinary line! Nor apparently was he the third, fourth, or fifth among that illustrious troupe. He fell in line somewhere after that. His donations to the legacy, as crucial as they were, are diminished by yet several more prodigies of the form who appeared on the scene after Fessenden and before Conrad, an unmistakable imprint that cannot be ignored. Most of those interceding in that train (that we know about for certain) are related to the Herrold College of Engineering and Wireless at San Jose, California.

As early as 1909, that institute conducted experiments in aural transmission under the call signs of SJN, 6XF and 6XE. These were actual *broadcasts* as opposed to *point-to-point* wireless communications that were the focus of many other trial efforts of that period.[26] Founder Charles David "Doc" Herrold (1875–1947) and company boosted their signal's reception to a range of 20 miles.[27] "I had to make my own audience," Herrold recounted years later. "I went out through the valley and installed crystal sets so that people could listen to my music. There is not the slightest evidence to show that ... any of the early experimenters had in mind the use of their experimental radio telephone for entertainment purposes."[28]

> Once Herrold realized he had an audience of eager radio experimenters, he began to entertain them. He would discuss news items and read clippings from the newspaper, or play records from his phonograph. This got to be a more and more important part of the school's operations, and regular programs were heard from the station as early as 1910.
>
> Herrold's wife Sybil later got into the act. Using many techniques of the modern disk jockey, she regularly aired what she called her "Little Ham Program." ...

She would borrow records from a local music store "just for the sake of advertising the records to these young operators with their little galena sets.... They would run down the next day to be sure to buy the one they heard on the radio the night before." And she encouraged regular listeners by running contests. "We would ask them to come in and sign their names, where they lived, and where they had their little receiving sets ... and we would give away a prize each week."[29]

One of Herrold's students, Ray Newby, of Stockton, California, appeared on the CBS-TV panel game show *I've Got a Secret* in 1965, purportedly as "the world's first radio disc jockey."[30] Newby was 16 in 1909, and he remembered his experience like this:

We used popular records at that time, mainly [Italian tenor Enrico] Caruso records, because they were very good and loud; we needed a boost.... We started on an experimental basis and then, because this is novel, we stayed on schedule continually without leaving the air at any time from that time on except for a very short time during World War I, when the government required us to remove the antenna.... Most of our programming was records, I'll admit, but of course we gave out news as we could obtain it.[31]

At about the same time that Herrold's disciples were conducting their landmark broadcasts in San Jose, Detroit's Thomas E. Clark was also amusing listeners with *his* phonograph records.[32] Clark had constructed transmitters in a handful of metropolitan ports along the Great Lakes. He piped his melodies to some Lake Erie steamers in which he had installed telephone receivers. His radio pursuits actually dated as far back as the turn of the century. Clark became one of the driving forces that turned test model experimental outlet 8MK into WWJ, *The Detroit News* station, in October 1921.[33]

Another petitioner for the tribute of "first disc jockey" is Elman B. Myers. While we don't know the specific designation of his transmission signal, multiple sources state that, by 1911, he was spinning records on a wireless transmitter 18 hours daily in New York City.[34]

The Jesuits also make a claim to airing the first disc jockey. Their St. Louis University WEW Radio founding Brother George Rueppel played phonograph records. In between plays he offered his listeners a little tête-à-tête as that station debuted in 1921.[35] But who's on first? It couldn't have been George Rueppel, no matter who says it.

Then there was Ted Husing (1901–62), whose footprint in radio is quite large although it is better remembered in the arena of sports rather than music. He discounts other claimants' abilities when he attests to his brief 1927 DJ stint over New York's WHN. In a *Variety* piece, Husing implies that his innovative contributions may have topped what those who practiced the craft for long-term periods were able to achieve: "We tried placing mikes in front of the speakers, but with charts supplied us by two physicists at MIT, we cut through the amplifier into our control amplifier and began popping recorded music into the air. I wonder who of today's disc jockeys can match the fact that when it comes to spinning platters the kid [Husing] was out in front."[36]

These trailblazers — Fessenden, Herrold, Sybil Herrold, Newby, very possibly other unknown Herrold apprentices, Clark, Myers, Conrad, Rueppel, Husing, and surely many more — were, as far as we are now able to confirm, at the forefront of ethereal waxworks innovation. Some of the most unforgettable broadcasting activities in which they figured was separated by no fewer than 15 years (Fessenden, 1906, to Rueppel, 1921) and at least 3,000 miles of geographical terrain between them.

Separately, they created a model that many others may have been stirred to replicate. Fessenden and Conrad received fan mail — assurances that they had connected with their listeners. And Conrad even began taking mailed-in requests for the songs that he played. (Parenthetically, was this jockey maybe a rhinestone cowboy — "getting cards and letters from people I don't even know"?) The transaction is indicative of a pattern that, more than a century after its initiation, not only persists but still thrives.

The history of the American radio DJ continues. The trade looked as if it might be doomed when the U.S. Department of Commerce banned the use of "mechanically operated musical instruments" on certain high-powered stations serving wide areas in 1923.[37] The Federal Radio Commission, organized in 1927, relaxed that rule by making it mandatory for recorded programs to be so identified.[38] The rendering eased stress on the DJs as well as other areas of broadcasting.

While the DJ was a permanent fixture at many independent stations after the organization of the national hookups, at the chain-linked outlets the spinmeisters competed with the network fare for airtime. At most of those, the DJ was restricted to not much more than early-morning and late-night gigs plus some occasional hours that were limited to periods sandwiched between a station's network commitments. You'll recall that, in the 1950s, the affiliate outlet owners eventually persuaded their networks to pare back national programming to allow them (the locals) to more equitably compete for revenues with the independents operating in their markets.

Selling the bulk of their greatest asset (time) themselves allowed the chain-tethered outlets to fill their coffers self-confidently. As a result the DJ was the guy or gal that predominantly got the nod to fill the air chairs at most of those stations once the network agendas were almost emptied, with many programming hours left to fill. For anybody beyond the national hookups and those who especially loved the surfeit of the quality features they provided (including millions of listeners), the revision was netting a win-win conclusion. Especially was this true for the affiliates and their DJs. The "golden knights of the turntable," as historiographer Tom DeLong identified them, were suddenly purely "money-making machines."[39] And it was all cost-effective, too.

> Deejay shows required no orchestras and no writers. Gone were actors and actresses, directors, and most of the support staff. One critic contemptuously labeled the deejays' product "gypsy radio" and noted: "It is ludicrously cheap ... only a license, a transmitter, and a subscription to *Billboard* [for its charts of best-selling records] are essential."[40]

The DJ had risen to the forefront at many stations during the Second World War, when economics propelled him there. He became "the music phenomenon of the 1940s,"[41] and increasingly the new linchpin of the aural ether. For a few years, at a great many stations from the mid–1950s through the 1960s, he dominated the ether. The platter-and-patter format he commenced synchronized perfectly with the nation's shift to mobility and portability in fans' radio-listening habits. The glut of radio receivers being added to new vehicles increasingly as standard equipment coupled with the pervasiveness of newer lightweight portable transistor models (both innovations highlighted in Chapter 3) fit the music-and-comments style of the DJ.

Many listeners no longer wanted to be tied down to their radios for lengthy periods when they had to concentrate on programming demanding rapt attention until reaching its conclusion. Music, along with a DJ's chatty banter, appealed to a younger tune-in/tune-out crowd that seemed to be discovering radio all over again. Or maybe for many it was for the very first time.

The aural medium in that period was indeed a new source of leisure distraction for lots of listeners. On quite a few stations the DJs became the instantly recognized celebrities of local radio. In many communities, large and small, it was often the radio DJs whose luminary standing saw them readily filling off-hours with all sorts of activities that appeared to boost a station's visibility as well as increasing the personalities' own notoriety.

Hence a DJ might be found doing any or all of the following in the metropolitan area in which he broadcast: introducing the performers and program participants at local civic functions and at amusement venues; riding in convertibles and on floats at street parades during local festivals; entertaining at high school assemblies and at half-time shows during basketball and football games pitting high school or college teams against one another; raising money to add a wing to the city hospital, build a new fire station, or helping someone displaced by flooding or other natural disaster; shoveling a few spades of dirt at groundbreaking ceremonies for a new park, school, or library facility; presiding at new store opening ribbon-cuttings; and promoting every worthy cause that did not infringe upon any relationships with the station or a sponsor.

In the 1950s and 1960s, the DJ was a VIP in many geographical territories. The denizens regarded him with something of the same awe they reserved for prominent statesmen, historians, visionaries, business leaders, clergymen, academicians, entertainers, athletes, artists of multiple persuasions, and high-society mavens. He was "somebody" in a community, even if he was viewed as primarily appealing to a younger-oriented crowd.

An impressive segment of radio DJs became established well enough on the air to gain a berth on network radio before its voice was radically diminished. In that way, DJs became known to millions of listeners residing all over the United States, adding substantially to their fame as well as their fortune. Among those spinning records on the quartet of national chains were Martin Block (*Make Believe Ballroom*), Leonard Feather (*Platterbrains*), Eddie Gallaher (*On a Sunday Afternoon*), Freeman Gosden and Charles Correll (*The Amos 'n' Andy Music Hall*), Robert Q. Lewis (*Waxworks*), Howard Miller (*The Howard Miller Show*), Bob Poole (*Poole's Paradise*), and Peter Potter (*Juke Box Jury*). For many years Andre Baruch hosted *Your Hit Parade* on both radio and television. Top sellers in record stores and the tunes played most often on jukeboxes and requested of radio DJs were performed by live vocalists and an orchestra.

Martin Block (1903–67) was considered the first superstar among the nationwide DJs.[42] A salesman at heart, Block's career was launched as he pitched goods and services from a truck outfitted with a loudspeaker. He drove up and down New York's Broadway, hawking his wares, interspersing the announcements with phonograph records until irate merchants blew up and prompted the cops to intervene. Block found work announcing at WNEW in 1934. He bought records — the station didn't own any — and played one singer's myriad vocals back-to-back, intimating that he was broadcasting from a dance hall. Listener approbation arrived in boatloads. Block was soon on his way to filling two-and-a-half hours of daily airtime, plus gaining a contract with ABC Radio (which touted him in newspaper ads as "that old Block magic"). At the same time he was reaping millions of dollars by syndicating his show nationally. Others copied his formula but none came close to superseding his coup. Block even taught classroom sessions for visiting DJs in how to exploit his system!

The venerated list of renowned spinmeisters on the ether doesn't end with those already named by any stretch of the imagination. Among personalities on local stations, in syndication, or on nationwide hookups, were Steve Allen, Sandy Becker, Dick Clark, Del Courtney, Bill Cullen, Tommy Dorsey, Hugh Downs, Duke Ellington, Art Ford, Dave Garroway, Arthur Godfrey, Benny Goodman, Al Jarvis, Kasey Kasem, Durward Kirby, Jack Lescoulie, Vincent Lopez, Jim Lowe, Tony Marvin, Gene Rayburn, Joe Reichman, Lanny Ross, Soupy Sales, Robert "Wolfman Jack" Smith, Jo Stafford, Jack Sterling, Jack Teagarden, Rudy Vallee, Mike Wallace, Ted Weems, and Paul Whiteman.

Unfortunately, before the heyday of the professional radio DJ had passed, the trade was sullied by greed. Some who filled those air chairs at local stations fell victim to temptations that were largely inspired by people outside their ranks. The outsiders found a way to make big bucks by taking advantage of the DJ's strategic slot. Eyebrows began to arch when a handful of trade journals revealed that some in the business were courted heavily by allied industry reps that stood to gain by manipulating the DJs through tangential ventures.

The trouble reportedly began with some producers of rhythm and blues (R&B) recordings ("race music," in colloquial parlance).[43] R&B was a soulful forbear of the rock 'n' roll fad that operated at full throttle by the mid–1950s and held a commanding presence for ten or 15 years.[44] (Rock 'n' roll is still around today in reprise, of course, commonly referred to as "oldies" by contemporary outlets. In 2012, there were 706 AM or FM stations in North America programming oldies music.[45] Many of that number, but definitely not all, were situated in smaller cities and rural areas.)

Some unsettling concerns began to mount in 1954: "The public did not determine its own preference in music," an unidentified DJ intimated, "but instead was almost completely influenced to accept the music played for them by the nation's disc jockeys."[46] Worse, there were growing indications that the palms of some DJs were being salaciously greased by recording company agents. Those outfits had rightly determined that the more air plays a specific tune received could transform a disc into phenomenal financial proceeds: hence the greater the exposure, the greater the prospect for mind-blowing pecuniary returns.

Soon branded *payola*, the phenomenon was delineated by NBC-TV newsman David Brinkley as "the practice of paying a disc jockey to play a record so often that listeners thought it was a hit and went out and bought it, whether they liked it or not."[47] In 1959, to spotlight a single year, nearly 2,000 U.S. record producers were releasing up to 250 just-cut vinyl discs every week.[48] Not all of them could get their entries on the air, of course. Some practitioners within the trade in the meantime — casting aside whatever moral, ethical, and legal considerations might be cited — conjectured that payola was thereby justified. DJs in L.A., for instance, were gaining an extra $300 to $500 per week beyond their $25,000 to $50,000 annual salaries, boosting a few into the $75,000-per-year category.[49] According to one conversion table, that figure in 1959 could translate into $590,673 in 2012, certainly better than most station managers were making and probably a whole lot better than many station owners![50]

With a few perks unobtrusively supplied to strategically situated spinmeisters, some obscure artists suddenly burst into stardom. Personal appearances, tour dates, events that they sponsored, records, sheet music, associated merchandise like photographs and apparel, radio and TV shows, movies, commercial enterprises in which they had a hand, product endorsements, and whatever else they touched to generate profits received massive boosts when their music was frequently reprised on celebrated stations. Without regular airplay a new song or artist would never make the charts. The results could literally make a vocalist's professional career, assure that a recording reached staggering sales figures, and guarantee a publisher's future at the same time. The prospect of that imposing outcome was absolutely intoxicating to some unscrupulous distributors and eventually became an obsession with them.

> The subject got much additional publicity as time went along, with the climax coming in 1959. Investigation of the quiz shows on television gathered radio and the disc jockeys up in the momentum, and shook them around, too. "Payola," a word with far-reaching connotations, but actually coined many years earlier, was now in standard usage by the public in general. Yet the same public sat back and looked on with only lukewarm interest as attempts were made to prove that many of the nation's top disc jockeys had a good thing going for themselves with an under-the-table arrangement to see that the right discs were programmed....
> Not a great deal came of the "payola" investigation except to cast a reflection on the innocent along with those who may have been guilty.[51]

Oh, really?

With all due respect, some of the nation's most venerated platter-and-patter guys were found out and were instantly removed from the air. "In the end, no deejays were packed off to prison," a critic noted, "but the broad brush wielded by the investigators ruined the careers of dozens and dozens of radio disc jockeys." A pall of gloom may have spilled over payola's innocent victims who either refused or who weren't offered bribes. But the loss of duty, salary, status, and character was probably deeply injurious to those who had participated and were found out. Some may have sacrificed whole careers in the process.

Pundits cited Alan "Moondog" Freed (1922–65) as payola's most visible poster boy. He's even credited with originating rock 'n' roll after applying the phrase to the music he played in the early 1950s. A classical announcer in 1951, Freed was persuaded by a local record store merchant to add black-inspired rhythm and blues to his playlist. The transformation became the cradle of the rock revolution. Freed continued to program R&B on his gig at Cleveland's WJW. In 1954, he shifted to New York's WINS, where his enveloping influence rose prolifically. He expanded into nationwide syndication in 1957, and was also heard in Great Britain.

Still heavily invested in R&B along with rock 'n' roll, Freed catapulted into a trade figure that was widely imitated by others. By the late 1950s, he presided over a couple of superlative Big Apple radio DJ and TV dance party stints while reforming the local listening habits of 60 other markets. Despite it all, in November 1959 he was dumped by not one but both of his then-Gotham employers, WABC Radio and WNEW-TV. Freed refused to sign a statement at the former "on principle" that he had never accepted anything for promoting records; the latter let him go "by mutual consent" two days after that.[52]

> The scandal broke on 19 May 1960 when indictments were handed down against five deejays as well as some record librarians and program directors. The air personalities included Alan Freed..., Peter Tripp of WMGM, Tommy Smalls of WWRL, WLIB's Hal Jackson, and Jack Walker of WOV.... They were charged with "commercial bribery," a misdemeanor punishable by two years in prison. Twenty-three companies had admitted the practice to prosecutors.
> None of those caught up in the payola scandal ever served jail time.[53]

Little more than five years beyond his dual firings in New York, on January 20, 1965, Freed was dead at 42, a victim of alcohol abuse. He never effectively recovered from his downfall, passing virtually penniless and in professional ignominy.[54] He had "taken the fall for the industry," in the theory of one pundit.[55] Another historiographer summarized: "Freed was heir to all the 'evils' of the pop music business — the cut-ins, angles, and gimmicks that are the ambiguous practice of 'payola.' There is no way to gauge how much money he was responsible for during the fifties — and its material accumulation meant little to him."[56] Yet another source believed his insistence on bringing music that white listeners previously had little exposure to sent the establishment into utter turmoil and set him up for reprisals while others escaped.

> Because of his love of black music, Freed was a far more appealing target. Congress wanted a scapegoat and if they could discredit rock 'n' roll at the same time, so much the better.
>
> ...
> ...Before Alan Freed, rhythm and blues was unknown to the vast majority of white people. Rock 'n' roll not only affected music ... black artists no longer had to water down their style to achieve widespread success — it also had a profound social impact, bringing many their first experience of black culture.
> For having such influence, Freed paid dearly. He was a clear example of how much power a DJ can wield, and an even clearer example of the lengths to which the establishment will sometimes go to curb that power.[57]

In the meantime the black music itself became a sensation in radio, binding the dual arts together in an unparalleled cultural enrichment never previously encountered. Considerably more will be said about racial undertones and their implications upon broadcasting in the United States in Chapter 12. Yet radio's powerful stimulus on the music popularized in the 1950s and 1960s gives plenty of credence for an ephemeral reflection now. The mixture, as examined by one observer, even went beyond radio and records to impact the society at large.

> Clearly, blacks had experienced by 1955 a tremendous alteration in their relationship to American radio.... Liberal politics, a declining radio audience, and the lure of the multi-billion dollar black economy after World War II ... produced a

significant change of attitude on all levels of broadcasting.... The most significant development was the appearance in the mid–1950s of rhythm and blues as a national musical phenomenon relying upon radio for ... mass dissemination through scores of radio disk jockeys.

Rhythm and blues was nothing more than ... race music —...since the 1920s ... the blues and jazz recordings performed by, and produced for, black consumers....

The importance of rhythm and blues music on radio was that it was heard by integrated audiences.... White teenagers who purchased these records helped to change the course of American cultural and social development.

Between 1948 and 1955, dozens of radio stations ... developed a new breed of disk jockey to play and promote this new black music....

...

...The new black music ... introduced almost totally through radio [let] a generation of white youngsters, protected from black realities by ... segregation and bigotry, learn ... to appreciate Afro-American attitudes and realities. Dancing, working, relaxing, and singing to rhythm and blues, white listeners of radio in the 1950s came to know better than their parents the illogical nature of racism. Within a few years it would be this generation that would join with youthful blacks to form the idealistic vanguard of the civil rights movement of the 1960s.[58]

In the late 1950s, Top 40 formatting emerged and started to penetrate and then saturate many quarters of a disc jockey's province. The Top 40 incursion came about after Todd Storz (1924–64), owner of Omaha's KOWH, observed patrons dropping coins into jukeboxes in diners one day.[59] According to his own account, he was intrigued that they seldom gave any impression that they soon tired of hearing the same songs over and over again. Storz pondered: Could that principle also work in radio? He decided to give it a try. "The gospel in radio in those days was that no tune ought to be repeated within twenty-four hours of its broadcast — surely listeners would resent having to hear the same song twice in one day," a critic observed.[60]

Storz's converse hypothesis — which he branded *Top 40*— spelled out the limited number of records his station would air. Market research hardly existed at the time. To justify their selections, station officials swapped with local music emporiums, offering an advertising spot gratis every week for the names of their best-selling discs.[61] It didn't take the Storz people long to figure out that they could increase the size of their audience still more without extra fanfare by simply reducing the playlist from 40 to 30 or even 25 tunes. In fact, it seldom failed to work.[62]

Some of the most requested hits would be repeated at least once an hour. The idea caught on with KOWH listeners in a flash. Within a matter of months in that first year (1951) the station's share of the Omaha audience escalated dramatically from a mere 4 percent to 45 percent.[63] Word of Storz's success infiltrated at other stations, spreading across the country like wildfire. Soon, a second exponent of the Top 40 supposition, Gordon McLendon (1921–86), a

Texas multiple station owner, put the paradigm to work at his stations, with similar jubilant results.⁶⁴ After New York's WABC adopted the same modus operandi nine years later (1960) it left its rivals in the dust by 1962 in the world's largest radio market, ascending to the coveted first spot among the plethora of Big Apple broadcasters.⁶⁵

Meanwhile, Storz's blueprint was simultaneously pursued by hundreds of other local broadcasters across the country seeking to attract more listeners, higher ratings, increased advertising, and greater profits. Numerous markets fell under the spell of raucous, razzle-dazzle, rocking Top 40 stations. Nearly fanatical, mostly pubescent audiences pushed those outlets to the top of audience-ratings charts wherever they surfaced. In the 1960s, notions like Storz's were carried to excess.⁶⁶ Playlists were trimmed to 25 hit tunes and the trendiest songs were aired frequently. Radio stations were "formatted," restricted by individual choice to compactly defined species: Adult Contemporary, Album-Oriented Rock, Top 40, Urban, and so forth. New records were added to playlists only after scrupulous market research had been conducted.

And when payola came to light, the Top 40 figured notably in the revelations. Ex-DJ Norman Prescott of Boston's prestigious WBZ said he quit the station when he became "contaminated" by the scandal and no longer had the stomach for it.

> The main fraud that Prescott detailed was the one that hit hardest for most Americans: those Top 40 or Top 20 charts that deejays were forever yapping about were a complete fiction. They had little or nothing to do with popular taste and everything to do with payola. Other witnesses backed up Prescott. Deejay Bob Clayton of Boston's WHDH told the [investigating Congressional] committee that the weekly Top 10 list he provided for publication in the *Boston Traveler* newspaper was based on no poll of any kind. "I make them up and send them in," he said. "It doesn't say 'Boston's Official Top 10,' it says 'Bob Clayton's Official Top 10.'"⁶⁷

The DJ's influence in determining what was aired was sharply curtailed, possibly as a consequence. No longer the "Czar of the World's Entertainment" as the trade paper *Billboard* earlier dubbed him, in the evolution the DJ lost one of his prime duties to someone else. Selecting the music was assumed by the program director (PD) at many medium-sized and larger stations. The PD was, practically speaking, hardly more than a market researcher by that time, in reality an extension of the outlet's commercial sales department. He was a cog in the wheel — like the on-air talent — with both jobs resting on driving the station to first place in its region and maintaining its presence there, whatever might be legally required in achieving that end.

Despite all the aforementioned obsequious tributes, accolades, and bouquets to the DJ already cited, there is little doubt that his reputation languishes in many cities — his halo now tarnished. "It should be obvious to any radio listener over the age of 30 that the prevailing style of … deejays has been changing since the mid–1950s," a biographer of local U.S. radio candidly observed not long ago.⁶⁸

> The public generally has become less folksy, faster paced, and more specialized in its demands.… This trend … has been exacerbated by radio station takeovers and by conglomerate managers who are more interested in the bottom line than in providing a quality entertainment package. Someone can be hired to spin records or read news copy for a considerably lower salary than that of a comedian like Gene Rayburn or a musical scholar like Jonathan Schwartz.⁶⁹

The reference to Rayburn and Schwartz pertains to individuals with inherent abilities to amuse and enlighten merely beyond sitting in front of a turntable and spinning wax between commercial timeouts. In prevailing practice, much of the time the DJ has been physically removed altogether. One wag branded "robot DJs" as "characterless," dubbing their syndicated formats as "the worst of all possible musical worlds."⁷⁰ The emphasis on quality performance is missing in action as absentee broadcasters relentlessly pursue cost-cutting provisions and bottom-line revenues.

The DJs that are left and the other personalities of the local airwaves are now means of achieving those ends and are often devalued as expendable options. Not that the DJ himself has prospered all that well either. Aside from having a steady job to report to in the midst of an anemic contemporary economy, plus whatever tinges of glamour and exhilaration may be squeezed out of his occupation, the DJ today isn't part of any get-rich-quick schemes. According to 2010 PayScale data the income range for DJs was $20,677 to $38,116. Bonuses and commissions typically added another $1,197 to $15,750 in take home pay.⁷¹ It wasn't an especially handsome reward for being a "star," particularly if the DJ supports a family with his remuneration. Gone are the days when he alone was able to adequately provide for a whole family's needs.

In the modern age, the DJ himself seems to be a missing factor in the mélange that has taken over at some radio stations.

> Increasingly, program directors have been using computers to choose the records their stations will play. The most popular such program is Selector, made by Radio Computing Services. Once a catalog of the music library has been entered … the director gives Selector a series of instructions and the program produces a playlist. Those parameters might be broad genre restrictions ("no rap"), general patterns ("two upbeat songs, followed by one ballad, then repeat"), or more narrow rules ("no more than three songs with female vocalists per hour"). Selector then chooses which songs will be played, and in what order, for the next 24 hours, seven days, or whatever horizon the programmer prefers.
> …Selector has spawned several offspring.… Master Control NT doesn't just choose which songs to play. It actually plays them, along with all the appropriate ads, promos, and prerecorded DJ bits. Welcome to the completely automated radio station.⁷²

As far as the professional duty goes, beyond the Internet and satellite operations, rare are the radio stations controlled by long-distance owners which are concerned with broadcasting excellence now — the needs, interests, and expectations of a nearby audience driving the businesses' core values. While there are some exceptions to every rule, for the most part the public isn't being well served by those opportunists.

> The local DJ in many places was banished forever. In his place was a single distant voice speaking simultaneously in hundreds of markets as he championed the "one size fits all" model. The DJ frittered away time with idle chatter between discs, serving up that all-encompassing brand of "amusement" to millions of listeners. The inane patter linked the tunes and endless commercial segments, another "worst of times" scenario for listeners....
>
> Today ... radio is "stuck on a relentless treadmill of news-music-sports, interrupted for warmed-over weather, commute, and stock updates every ten minutes." Not so in the halcyon days of the DJ. While that epoch was never as extraordinary as the golden age that preceded it, the phase was indubitably far better than the "babble of opinion, most of it mindless and mean-spirited, whipped on by shrill talk-show hosts" available to radio audiences today.
>
> The interval of the local DJ appears to be history in many quarters. Americans may not have realized just how well off they were until the spinmeisters disappeared from the scene — and those syndicated hookup, often vitriolic, never-at-a-loss-for-an-opinion talk show hosts arrived.[73]

Very little has altered the quotations there since they were penned in the 1990s. Except ... now ... there are more commercials, more frequently than there were. From the listener's point of view, is radio headed in a more desirable direction?

Simply put, the "quality entertainment package" that many in the audience took for granted during the Golden Age — and which may have persisted into the early 1980s, incidentally — isn't in vogue any longer in very many places. In their haste to remove whatever oversight obligations that once existed, the feds (as delineated in greater detail in Chapter 11) have virtually given away the store. Although the music still being played may sound familiar, to most of our ears the automated environment in which we hear it today probably isn't nearly as good as the guys who used to play it.

It's just another reason for wishing we could return to "those thrilling days of yesteryear," including the days not long after the Golden Age bit the dust.

5

Power Shift Fuels Fine-Tuning

When the nationwide radio networks retrenched by radically economizing their programming agendas, effectively marking a defined watershed terminus for the Golden Age, the big four — including ABC, CBS, MBS, and NBC — didn't entirely fade from the radio dials. While their presence was irrefutably diminished and would never rebound to anything approximating their previously elevated status, they were all still open for business. And instead of providing a bevy of mysteries, sitcoms, juvenile adventures, soap operas, musical features, and quiz shows, those continental broadcasters served up a smorgasbord of novel scenarios.

Although news and public affairs were interlaced throughout their daily and weekly schedules, the transcontinental chains persisted in supplying the local affiliates with a maze of special events that they were better able to cover than the pack of local stations. Among the wares that inhabited their stash were the quadrennial political conventions and presidential inaugurations; myriad special occasion holiday and commemorative observances; breaking news of national and international import that frequently exhibited the networks' ability to deliver details directly from the sites of commotion as it occurred; and key competitive athletic contests (the various bowl games, Final Four, Indianapolis 500, Kentucky Derby, Masters Tournament, Super Bowl, World Series, et al.).

In general, a single station fielding multiple staffers couldn't normally handle these occasions as effectively as a countrywide chain. Meriting greater exposure, coverage like this was inevitably directed to coast-to-coast broadcasters with extensive technological capabilities, commensurate talent, and the accompanying resources of availability and readiness. That isn't to suggest that the chains were wielding the powerfully big stick that they brandished before the mid–1950s, and to a far lesser extent to about 1960. But they were well equipped and capable as various needs arose.

By then radio's epicenter in the United States had transitioned to the local stations, including the affiliates of the networks as well as the independent outlets (which were unaffiliated with any chain). Discounting the potent influences of satellite, automated programming, and Internet broadcasting which emerged in successive decades of the 20th century, the local station became the epitome of radio broadcasting in America from the late 1950s forward. It remained so in many communities, profoundly so, at least until distant forces outside those local havens assumed virtual control of many local programming operations once again.

A large number of key outlets relinquished their affiliation altogether with a given network in order to program their own substance full time. For instance, in August 1956, Westinghouse Broadcasting Corporation — a major group owner of radio stations — pulled a quartet of its outlets out of NBC.[1] Many other operations that still remained tethered to a specific hookup did so only for the news programs and whatever additional matinee features a network supplied that possessed ample audience appeal to make it financially worthwhile.

Selecting 1960 as the pivotal demarcation boundary for the transformation of the big four national radio chains, let's recognize that it did occur earlier under some scenarios. For that foursome, however, that era was The Land of Beginning Again. With apologies to poet Louisa Fletcher, it signaled the promise of "some wonderful place" where "all our heartaches" loitering in the glories of soaring past ethereal highs "could be dropped ... at the door and never ... put on again."[2] The programming that legions of listeners had more or less wistfully sanctioned — for some, from the very inception of commercial broadcasting — had practically ground to a screeching halt. In its place the national hookups attempted to keep America satisfied with just enough substance to impress upon the listening audience that they were still in business. To those for which radio was a daily companion, at that apex the sharp contrasts resulting from the cutbacks were a chronic reminder that the medium had experienced a metamorphosis of landmark proportions. Starting over was, hypothetically so it seemed, radio's tangible Land of Beginning Again.

Some of the historiographers conceptualizing that epoch hardly saw it as one of much promise, nonetheless. One scholarly resource insisted that, by 1960, the national chains were "little more than AM news outlets."[3] Another well-versed intellect was equally dismissive: "Radio by this date was reflective of a mobile, affluent, and commercialized America, solidly committed to television for its creative amusement, but still requiring radio for music and instantaneous information. Radio in the 1960s would be the realm of the disk jockey and the newscaster."[4] Still another estimate by that time branded the aural medium as nothing more than utilitarian in nature, ostensibly "something you had on in the background of life" for which there was little compelling logic for its continued existence.[5]

Well perhaps in reality, yes maybe to all of those evaluations. Yet there were still some obvious remnants of good times past, including a minuscule quantity of durable programming that remained credible even by continuing to offer some of it in diminutive doses for a while. (This will be delineated in more precise detail later.) The schedulers at the quartet of transcontinental chains fashioned an assortment of fare to fill tidbits of time that was suddenly up for grabs, without overextending their reach. Those billboards were crafted to retain the residue of the national radio audience while concurrently seeking to maintain listeners' loyalty for a particular hookup and its local affiliate.

The smorgasbord of offerings included a wide range of personality-driven features; how-to hints for household applications; self-improvement help in finances, relationships, communications, health, personal appearance and intellect; politics; commentary on the passing scene; leisure-time activities, sports, hobbies, and travel interests; and a multiplicity of supplementary topics that could appeal to diverse segments of those who tuned in. Almost all of this programming was furnished in pithy daily doses, usually of one to five minutes' duration throughout the weekday. Some of it encouraged listener response with mailed-in questions or replies that were shared on the air.

The most prominent continuing ingredient in the schedules of all four of the transcontinental chains was news. This became even more obvious with the passing of the Golden Age. The brief one-minute bulletins that many are currently accustomed to, frequently broadcast randomly close to the half-hour mark throughout the weekday, hadn't yet originated. But a handful of respected news commentators still pontificated on the current events of the world every weekday evening in ten- or 15-minute analyses.

This was a practice that millions of Americans had been tuning in to as far back as the late 1930s or maybe early 1940s when Elmer Davis, Hans V. Kaltenborn, Lowell Thomas, Walter Winchell, and a few more observers did their thing. In a brief while, Cedric Foster, Gabriel Heatter, Fulton Lewis, Jr., Edward R. Murrow, Raymond Gram Swing, and a few others joined them. They also put their own spins on developing situations of international consequence. And with the most notable exceptions of CBS's Harry Reasoner and Eric Sevareid in television newscasting during subsequent decades, TV really had very little to offer in the way of news analysis within its daily key evening reports. Although TV anchors now chat with guest authorities during brief exchanges that allow them to interpret issues more substantially, broadcast TV (*not* including cable TV networks) doesn't generally encourage its reporters to express their personal opinions on controversial matters as was regularly done in radio.

In the aural medium, legions relied on those interpretations even well beyond the Golden Age. Lowell Thomas, the last of the breed who figured prominently in that style during radio's formative years, continued to air his observations into 1976. That technique partially laid the groundwork for the cable news nets that air many seemingly trifling harangues today. Maybe it was better then: there was only one voice in radio giving an opinion at the moment, not several "sides" spouting simultaneously. In the heyday of audio-only broadcasters, a listener could almost surely find one to his liking: left-leaning, right-leaning, or fairly objective analysts who merely presented the issues and cited their perceived strengths and weaknesses.

By the late 1950s, on the other hand, news throughout the day was reflective of the networks' newly adopted scheduling patterns. While we can't be entirely certain when and where the practice of radio news on the hour came into vogue, one theory suggests it may have originated as early at 1926 at a Manitowoc, Michigan, station.[6] We know that, in 1954, ABC Radio launched a weekend, five-minute, hourly news update, commonly recognized as the initial attempt by a transcontinental chain to pursue the style. ABC alleged that its epigrammatic news bulletins were in harmony with the shift by many local outlets to schedule patterns with greater elasticity. ABC's competitors, closely watching the experiment from the sidelines, concluded that it was a positive stroke. Within a few years most followed suit.

In attempts to discriminate their unique news products from those of their rivals while seeking to gain greater penetration and thereby superior market share, the chains implemented a range of individuality to achieve a leg up on the competition. Although airing news at the top of the hour was the most common model adopted by the coast-to-coast broadcasters, ABC tried to gain audience margin by spinning its newscasts at five minutes prior to the hour. More than one chain furnished a second newscast during some hours at 25 or 30 minutes past the hour. And NBC's epic weekend marathon, *Monitor* (1955–75), ultimately settled into five-minute newscasts at the top and bottom of every broadcast hour. As CBS wiped away most of its slate of durable programming in late 1960, the network boasted that it was expanding hourly newscasts to ten minutes ("CBS goes double for you on the hour" chortled gleeful announcers in repetitious plugs touting the changeover). That blueprint didn't last long but created enough stir to distinguish its current events reporting from what the others were doing. Mutual, which customarily had scheduled more daily quarter-hour newscasts than any of its competitors, persisted in that vein.

On April 2, 1973, CBS earned credibility for airing its then-five-minute on-the-hour newscast 24 hours a day by becoming the first transcontinental hookup to do so. Until then, it had provided those capsules from 6 A.M. to 1 A.M. weekdays, 7 A.M. to 1 A.M. Saturdays, and 8 A.M. to 1 A.M. Sundays. Suddenly, it seemed that radio was recognizing that news was happening around the globe at every hour, whether the majority of Americans were awake or not. Not to be vanquished by its chief opposition, NBC — on January 1, 1974, nine months after CBS's lead into virgin territory—expanded its five-minute top-of-the-hour newscasts to be heard at every hour throughout the day and night. A source noted:

> In a changing and frightening world, special news events were to remain radio's forte, as it could deliver flash or bulletin stories faster than television or any other medium.... Radio networks became vestigial. Stations without network affiliations offered a minimum of "rip 'n' read" or "yank 'n' yell newscasts, composed of wire services" five-minute summaries read by a disc jockey. However, in times of great stress or national disaster the networks often allowed independent stations free use of their coverage.[7]

Beyond the news, which formed the backbone of every national chain's scheduling framework from the late 1950s and early 1960s forward, a handful of crowd-pleasers that endured from the good old days were permitted to linger a little while longer, albeit at times in diminished manifestations. (These are explored in greater depth in Chapter 9.)

A milestone occurred in 1965 when all four transcontinental radio chains made money for the first time in 11 years. It was an indication that not only had they trimmed whatever fat might have slipped into their budgets but further suggested that they maintained a resolve to persevere even during their inability to turn a profit.

During the 1960s, the major radio networks sprinkled their weekday agendas with a glut of five-minute topical vignettes. Each chain labeled its portion of that surfeit of daily conversational exchanges with nomenclature peculiar to it. ABC gathered its informative bits under the *Flair Reports* banner, chatty inserts on wardrobe and epicurean quests that broke the music's continuity.[8] The taxonomy emerged after a daily 55-minute DJ feature, *Flair*—running since October 1960 with Dick Van Dyke in the air chair—ceased operations in July 1963. By then, two of the other chains already had a few years of practice transmitting pithy contemporary entries several times daily. CBS gathered its features under the *Dimension* nomenclature. NBC catalogued its food for thought under the *Emphasis* brand.

In actuality, there really wasn't a whole lot of difference in subject matter between the allotments proffered by the trio of broadcasters. Many times, only the personalities who delivered the expositions signified any genuine distinctions at all. This is beyond the fact that somebody might try to put a spin on a controversial theme, or tweak some other concept, and perhaps only slightly so. Otherwise, except for the nomenclature, you could think you were hearing *Flair Reports* or *Dimension* when you were listening to *Emphasis*. In spite of that fact, their subject matter was timely and generally caused Americans to think in rational terms about a wide range of information. Topics might pertain to international relations or, just as well, the calamities experienced in repairing a leaky faucet at home.

One of the big differences in this new radio era — for the affiliated stations, at least — was that, among the new rules of the game, they adopted a cafeteria approach to programming network offerings. The stringent rules of the network-dominant epoch were relaxed and, sometimes, abandoned. This allowed the individual members of a broadcasting clan to pick and choose what they wanted to air from the hookups' originations without a compulsory mandate to air everything (or even most) of what was provided. The new rules were in sharp contrast to the requirements that stations experienced there in the past. The entire landscape shifted in the implementation of newer station-friendly policies. Theoretically at least, this netted more amicable relations between local outlets and their chains. The transfer of power from the networks to the stations was demonstrated through myriad observable outcomes.

Here's a rundown on some of the network offerings that filled the ether after the Golden Age ended, in chronological order of their starting dates.

- Ex–New York Yankees shortstop-turned-broadcaster Phil Rizzuto (1917–2007) hosted *It's Sports Time* over CBS for a 19-year run, 1957–76. That series was preceded by a few years of Rizzuto's *Sports Caravan* over NBC from 1952. The sportscaster's durable aural run was one of the most spectacular in that discipline to be carried by the transcontinental chains.
- In that same arena CBS offered its listeners a weeknight quarter-hour rundown of scores, highlights, sidelights, and observations titled *World Wide Sports* starting May 28, 1962. Chris Schenkel (1923–2005) was the debuting host; when he joined ABC in late 1964, Frank Gifford (1930–) inherited that daunting duty.
- Syndicated newspaper advice columnist Abigail Van Buren (1918–2013) joined CBS's daily lineup on December 31, 1963, signaling more novel starts in an innovative period in national audio broadcasting. For 11 years, through December 27, 1974, she meddled in the personal affairs of her listeners, dispensing sage counsel.
- *Mike Wallace at Large*, a weekly 25-minute feature focused on interviews conducted by the investigative reporter with current and past newsmakers, premiered over CBS in the fall of 1965. Persisting for many years, in the early 1970s Wallace (1918–2012) and his show was reordered into five-minute installments and aired every weekday. In 1979, it shifted again, that time into dual broadcasts on both Saturdays and Sundays.
- On November 19, 1965, ABC became the first major chain to focus exclusively on the nation's then-current war when it began airing newsworthy reports under the banner *Vietnam Update*. While that's old hat on TV today and has been for decades, it was innovative in broadcasting at that time.
- NBC proffered a 55-minute documentary entry, *Second Sunday*, in October 1966. The series aired monthly on the Sunday in its title through December

1982, an enduring run for a feature that launched well after radio's Golden Age had passed.
- *Perspective*, a two-part 50-minute commentary on public-affairs issues in the news — interrupted in mid-broadcast by five minutes of genuine news — premiered over ABC in 1967. ABC's attempt at flexibility seemed to backfire, however: it tendered the dual portions to its affiliates with the option of taking less than the complete package, and thereby some stations were airing just a single 25-minute portion instead of the whole shebang. The concept was short-lived as references to the preceding or successive analyses that some listeners weren't hearing left them feeling more or less disenfranchised.
- *The Osgood File*, featuring CBS's resident poet laureate Charles Osgood (1933–) has been airing incessantly since 1971. In a fifth decade in late 2012, his three-minute droll perspectives on current events are broadcast four times daily Monday through Friday. A prolific author of books, magazine articles, and a syndicated newspaper column, Osgood is an award-winning English "protectorate" (i.e., heralded guardian of the Mother Tongue) whose ballyhooed career on the national airwaves was launched as an ABC News reporter in 1963.
- The personality-driven features were still arriving in spades on nationwide hookups as late as the fourth quarter of the 20th century, sometimes in syndicated form. Comedienne Lucille Ball's actress-daughter Lucie (1951–) hosted the consortium-based *Tune In with Lucie Arnaz*, bowing in 1978. That interview entry may have paved the way for similar fare headlined by more second-tier luminaries in a disappearing epoch for radio. It occurred prior to television's usurping of most broadcast interviews, where such exchanges have been permanent residents for decades.
- In early 1981, Dan Rather (1931–) segued into the anchor chair of video's *CBS Evening News*. After replacing retiring newscaster Walter Cronkite (1916–2009), similar action transpired in their respective CBS radio series. One of the popular succinct, personality-driven, analytical series, *Walter Cronkite Reporting*, was re-dubbed *Dan Rather Reporting*. Rather's aural observations persisted through 2005.

In the late 1960s, upon discovering that it could do so legally and inexpensively by following certain rigorous stipulations, ABC Radio announced that it was spinning its single chain into multiple affiliates in the markets it served. The alteration was an attempt to make serious inroads on its competitors by gaining margin in numbers of listeners, by appreciably increasing profits, and by diminishing the frequency of interruptions in local stations' music cycles to present fixed network features. That meant abandoning the few vestiges of traditional fare that ABC was still carrying, such as *The Breakfast Club*, a daytime staple that had been running since 1933. The big switch came at the close of 1968. The solitary chain expanded into a quartet of derivatives. With some tinkering in the intervening years, this "new direction" has perpetuated to this writing (early 2013). ABC continues to maintain specific format-oriented outlets in localities all over the United States. A historian who was on the scene at the time recounts how it transpired.

> The group vice president for radio, Ralph Beaudin, not yet having a satellite to work with, had figured out that if ABC abandoned all long network radio programs, four networks could share the time on the one network line, and share the cost as well. Different networks would use the distribution line at different times during the hour. At the beginning of the hour the ABC Information Network would offer a newscast designed for talk-, information-, and all-news-formatted radio stations. At a quarter past the hour the ABC-FM Network would present news specifically written for so-called beautiful music stations. The newscast at half past the hour would be designed for middle-of-the-road stations and country stations and would be on the ABC Entertainment Network. Five minutes before the hour, the ABC Contemporary Network would present news for rock music stations. Headline and newsbrief services would also be given to those stations that wanted shorter newscasts.... ABC would have to have up to four affiliated stations in each city. Since the stations delivered different types of audiences who used different products and services, advertisers would love the concept — targeted delivery of demographic audience groups. For ABC's part, the network would quadruple the number of commercials it could sell. All they needed was government permission to have multiple affiliates in each market. Because network radio had been a bust as a business, the government saw nothing wrong with scrapping the old anti-monopoly rules.... For [New York flagship] WABC it meant the lines that tethered our airship had been cut. We were free.... We would carry a brief network newscast five minutes before the hour, and that was all.[9]

Perhaps you can sense the elation that that one station executive had. The euphoria was similarly catching at ABC outlets all over the county. It was a watershed moment in the life of the affiliates of that chain while realigning the programming that was available to listeners on some stations.

A defining moment in the life of NBC Radio occurred on December 31, 1982, when the news-and-features blueprint it had pursued since the late 1950s was erased on a single day. Virtually all of the network's public affairs programming and personality-driven features were scrubbed. Encompassing the disappearing act marking that day was *Ask Dr. Brothers* with psychologist Joyce Brothers, *Here and Now* with newsman Roger Mudd, *The Jensen Report* with financier Mike Jensen, *Man about Anything* with entertainment reporter Gene Shalit, *Willard's Weather* with weatherman Willard Scott, plus the award-winning *Second Sunday* documentary. At the start of 1983, in fact, all that was left of NBC Radio was the hourly news, a handful of two-minute inserts titled *Comment on the News*, and *Meet the Press*, an audio extension (to 1986) of the weekly TV dialogue exchange.

Did that ostensibly heartless massacre at NBC signal there was more — and even greater adversity — to come? As a matter of fact, in just five years and nine months more, NBC Radio was so severely abridged that its flagship outlet in the New York market (WNBC) completely vanished from the ether — sold along with seven other prime NBC-owned properties piecemeal, a few of them auctioned off to Emmis Broadcasting Corporation. The final vestiges of traditional NBC programming, with the exception of compacted news capsules, disappeared as well. On October 7, 1988, WNBC itself switched to all-sports programming. Redubbed WFAN Radio, it was relocated to a new spot on the dial. This was indeed a sad epitaph for a foremost principal among the aural broadcasters. And not much more than a decade beyond this tumultuous debacle, the continental chain itself all but arrived at a calamitous end — kept alive only by some near-silent articulation and whatever legal licensing and branding existed.

> NBC had vanished from most people's radar after Westwood One — which bought the chain's audio division for $50 million in 1987 — gradually pared down those operations to 1999. That year the net practically went away altogether. Only some weekday morning programming survived, and then only to 2000. While GE continued to license NBC nomenclature to Westwood One early in this century, according to an Internet source, the brand was "not promoted heavily." Nevertheless Westwood One still offered radio stations a service it labeled NBC *News Radio*, advertised as "the only radio network with newscasts fully anchored by top television news talent" despite its limited accessibility. One-minute newscasts were aired hourly throughout the day at 10 minutes before the hour with a transcription of that played back on the hour, diminishing still further any valid semblance that it might be dispatching breaking news.[10]

In 2012, NBC took a few strides to make a tenuous comeback even though the chain is still but a microscopic figment of its former self.[11] There are no guarantees that it will rise from its deathbed for resuscitation yet another time, should its owners come to the conclusion that it's time to administer final rites.

Mutual, incidentally, disappeared from the radar screens at midnight on April 17, 1999.[12] Although its name is still in lawfully accepted inventory and could be withdrawn from the isolation booth and reintroduced wholly at a future date, the likelihood of it at this juncture looks remote. For all intents and purposes, so it would seem, MBS entered the Valhalla of Fading Broadcasters in 1999 and ostensibly appears to have been lodged in Siberia evermore.

Returning to the latter decades of the 20th century, while ABC, CBS, and NBC were demonstrating that they were still running viable radio hookups, it was nonetheless quite obvious that most of their stock was concentrated in television as their dependent bread-and-butter source. (The shoe from earlier times, so it seems, was then being worn on the other foot.) And that's where everything was to rest for the foreseeable future. Perhaps as an appeasement to the perennial crowd that had always been there for them — yet which had never wholeheartedly embraced the tube, at least not yet — the networks tipped their collective hats to the aural broadcasting medium.

Their rather oblique acknowledgment underscored the unmistakable fact that the local stations were dominating radio's landscape. New York, Chicago, Hollywood and other metropolises that had previously determined what the majority of listeners would be exposed to through the aural ether paled. Suddenly the little guy in the *uncommon* municipalities, albeit mere hamlets when compared with the megalopolises, determined what was happening in broadcasting — perhaps so for the very first time. Akron, Brisbane, Des Moines, Galveston, Montpelier, Santa Fe, Savannah, Walla Walla, and legions of smaller burgs were clearly sitting in the drivers' seat.

In many markets of varying dimensions, for a while at least the DJ rode the crest of that newfound occupancy. The Golden Age had passed into the sphere of national folklore and listeners were taking note of the trending closer to home in learning who was filling the air chairs during most of the hours of every day. On most dials it wasn't someone speaking from either coast or hundreds or even thousands of miles away. The boys from the local community were finally having a shot at making good during most of radio broadcasting's airtime hours.

One of the characteristic innovations that predated this new sound wave occurred on April 13, 1953. Disc jockey Bob Hall launched a calming six-hour nocturnal reverie over New York's WCBS titled *Music Till Dawn*. Originating on CBS's flagship outlet, the upstart not only caught on with listeners who were fortunate enough to tap into its weeknight forays; it also persisted for 17 years, to 1970. And picking up American Airlines as longtime sponsor, the feature spread to CBS owned-and-operated stations in such megalopolises as Chicago, Dallas, and Los Angeles.

That durable entry reflected how a group of stations could share satisfactory good fortune without committing all of the affiliated outlets in a chain. It was reflective of countless regional hookups that emerged within that epoch during which radio experimented with substitute and alternative methods of reaching more listeners. Replicas on lesser and larger scales materialized in the period. Most of the time the innovations didn't involve the flagship stations and former points of origination: for so long, they had determined what America heard on their Emersons and Philcos, but no more. Newer configurations of programming imitation, origination, and duplication had surfaced in their stead.

There were still further attempts to modify traditional longstanding models that had been functioning across the years. Sometimes they were tweaked, sometimes circumvented altogether as power shifted from the national chains to operations conducted at home. All of it took some getting used to as fresher developments, programs, and personalities appeared on the scene and as the broadcast days and times of continuing features were altered.

Radio had turned a corner by the 1960s. More than a half-century later, we can say with pretty fair assurance, along with novelist Thomas Wolfe, "You can't go home again." Radio never tried. The roles of ABC, CBS, MBS, and NBC transitioned into something they had never been. The power shift to the American hamlets and villages and towns and metropolitan centers instigated new forces in radio's command. And millions of denizens were attempting to make the adjustments to programming, patterns, and formats that they had never heard before.

6

Escalating the Continuum

A half-dozen years back a couple of venerated media historians, Christopher Sterling and Michael Keith, recounted some minutiae that characterized the environment currently prevailing within aural broadcasting in the United States. In reference to the frequency modulation (FM) spectrum, that pair attested:

> FM is the predominant American radio service in ... both audience and advertising. Three-quarters of all radio listening is to FM outlets. American public radio is almost entirely FM based and serves a growing audience.... By the early twenty-first century, there were far more FM than AM stations and the gap continues to widen.[1]

Of course, writing in *this* millennium, the authors had the facts to support their claims. An antecedent among their number in media observers, on the other hand, basically relied on his own instincts to ferret out where all of this was leading during FM's embryonic era. As he held forth in the mid–1940s, Charles Siepmann assertively pontificated:

> Frequency modulation is a new technique for the transmission of sound over the air. Most people are persuaded that, except perhaps in rural areas, FM, as it is called, is destined within a few years to replace Amplitude Modulation (or AM), our present method of transmission, altogether. Within ten years, in other words, we shall all have FM receivers and none, or few, will have AM receivers.[2]

What a difference a day makes!

The advantage of hindsight is that reality sets in during the interval that elapses and one can surely see things much clearer (if indeed, he is still around). Author Siepmann (1899–1985) mentioned television only fleetingly in the text from which he is quoted, as if radio was going to dominate broadcasting's horizon for all the foreseeable future. Of course, TV was then but a year or two from bursting into the living rooms of America and, for the majority of the nation's populace, virtually replacing aural broadcasting altogether. Certainly so as the dominant medium for a while at least. Although FM would transform radio listening more than two decades later, it hardly became the definitive method of mass communications that had been implied by at least some segments of forecasting in the 1940s.

To reach such a lofty plateau, FM not only had to muster formidable resiliency as well as patience but even, on occasion, it had to trounce a few relatively intimidating obstacles that were persistently blocking its path. Long before reaching its widely touted zenith, however, the frequency modulation band was speedily charging in the *opposite* direction while looking — at that very cagey moment — as if it might flame out.

The fact that FM exists at all is a tribute to the tenacious perseverance of a technical wizard whose ceaseless faith was centered in its potential for prosperity: not only convinced that it offered a better method for listening to the radio, its most stalwart champion was committed to making others see it, too. His perseverance eventually persuaded larger and larger portions of the audio audience to be similarly convinced once they had sampled the focus of his life.

The extraordinarily imposing FM innovation that left its mark on radio's lineage can be traced to the postwar era.[3] That period was a transitory interval in personal leisure amusement in which acoustical testing was fostered by a wave of ambiguity and instability in professional entertainment. Stagnation, regulation, counterculture, hi-tech innovation, and a craving for more diverse music — particularly among the younger listenership — were some of the precipitating causes of this movement.[4] Yet at its core the rise of FM could be measured by a quest for enhanced gradation in ear candy which could exhibit finer distinction and provide a deeper, richer tone. At the outset in that epoch, engineers focused on the aesthetics of sound that emanated from the phonograph. But this was soon joined by the appeal of enriching radio resonance as well. One of the outcomes of the quest was a technological revolution that, in due course, redefined radio design and function.

Some observers have enumerated the dynamics which prompted a heightened desire for greater fidelity in sound. They arrived at a potpourri of multifaceted answers. Part of it lies in the baby boomers' coming of age. Research suggests that our hearing skills become more acute with the passage of time.[5] In general, as listeners mature they tend to appreciate intricate types of music that they would not have enjoyed at an earlier age. In the late 1960s, for instance — a couple of decades *after* the inception of FM — a rather sizable throng arose made up of individuals who jubilantly shifted their fascination with "Big John" recorded by Jimmy Dean to "A Day in the Life" recorded by The Beatles. The big difference? It wasn't the artists alone persuading them to favor the latter. Dean's disc was airing over monaural AM radio stations while The Beatles' number was being beamed from stereo FM radio outlets.

The hankering for modifying sensory impulses didn't surface overnight, however. Dating to the late 1940s, the introduction of FM gradually altered the physical apparatus of both radio and record player. Not only that, it transformed the flair and façade that characterized the disc jockeys of the period. For a while they were the predominant "entertainers" of the ether.[6] At the same time, FM implemented significant adjustments in broadcasting formats and even the technology applied to diffuse the programming. The hardware for all of this conversion had been developed in the 1930s through the labors of a solitary scientific engineer, Edwin Howard Armstrong (1890–1954), a technical genius that at least one informant attributes as "the most prolific inventor in radio's history."[7] His intrepid pursuits are worthy of keen exploration.

Dubbed "the Major" for his martial services during the Great (First) World War, he was born December 18, 1890, at Yonkers, New York. Armstrong determined at 14 that he would devote his life to scientific experimentation. Reading of Guglielmo Marconi (1874–1937) and gaining a passion for the precepts surrounding wireless radio conduction, before celebrating his 20th birthday the Major built his own transmitter and broadcast radio signals. Enrolling at New York's Columbia University, he earned a degree in electrical engineering at 22 in 1913.

By then he had already cultivated one of a trio of key innovations that would be credited to his experimentation. In 1912, Armstrong established the regenerative circuit. Working with the audion vacuum tube invented earlier by Lee de Forest (1873–1961) — it detected radio signals — Armstrong learned that feeding the device's electrical current back into itself radically enhanced its sensitivity. In doing so he eliminated a need for headphones that had been required to sharpen distant radio signals.

Seeking a patent to officially sanction his find, the Major was rapidly plunged into a four-way legal quagmire. This was the first of several multiple conflicts that saw him devote "as much time in court fighting lawsuits as he did in the laboratory," in the affirmation of one modern source.[8] Claiming priority in the issue, De Forest, Irving Langmuir of General Electric Company, and German scientist Armstrong Meissner were separate parties sparring with one another. After Langmuir and Meissner were finally dismissed from the convoluted litigation, the impasse with De Forest dragged on for a full score of years.[9]

Actually, De Forest had invented a telephone circuit with the *potential* for radio amplification while Armstrong invented the circuit *specifically* for radio. Although the latter's patent was at first upheld by the legal system, eventually — with AT&T's powerful weight behind him — De Forest persuaded the U.S. Supreme Court to overturn a lower court's ruling that had favored Armstrong. "Technically knowledgeable scientists continued to credit Armstrong for the discovery [anyway] and gave him numerous awards," a reporter allowed.[10]

The war intervened before Armstrong's technique had created much of a stir. That was to come later. For a while the experimenter was an officer in the U.S. Signal Corps. In a gust of munificence, Armstrong made some FM patents (on which he obviously had been laboring already) royalty free for armed forces' use. FM was the idyllic and lone remedy for solving the need for contact over long distances during mechanized warfare. Every U.S. tank, Jeep, and command car brandished FM gear not long afterward.[11] FM had literally gone to war.

Sought out frequently by military leaders while in the Signal Corps, Armstrong was dispatched to Paris, where the second of his most weighty inventions emerged. In 1917, he improved the heterodyne technology already in use that had been developed by Reginald A. Fessenden (1866–1932). Armstrong anticipated that his discovery might be applied to ferreting out enemy aircraft. While that didn't happen, eventually his circuitry became the core for 98 percent of all radio and television receivers: it furnished them with the ability to be tuned to multiple stations with the simple twist of a dial.

Following the war, Armstrong returned to Columbia University. Although he taught no courses and was paid $1 annually, his status as professor of electrical engineering advanced his investment in scientific discoveries and development which were conclusively the absorption of his life. In 1920, at Columbia, Armstrong created a super-generative circuit that was widely applied in aircraft, in amateur, and in police radio models. It also made him a millionaire. RCA paid him $200,000 plus 60,000 shares of stock, then subsequently added 20,000 more shares to his aggregate.[12] Armstrong became RCA's largest-single stockholder overnight.

At that juncture he was ready to turn his attention more wholly to what was destined to be his optimum exploit. Fessenden had facilitated the reality of amplitude modulation (AM) of radio waves in 1906, thereby making the synchronized diffusion of voice and music possible. Despite that accomplishment—taking nothing from it, and as magnificent as it was—electromagnetic interference created by lightning storms continued to result in bursts of static that broke up the signal. Inserting himself into the process once more, Armstrong was at first intrigued and, finally, fixated with the notion of possibly boosting the bandwidth of the radio signal. He was fairly well convinced that at least the option abounded for eliminating whatever interference from other energy waves might exist. If there was a way, he insisted, he intended to discover how to correct it.

> After devoting two years to frequency-modulated radio waves, Armstrong arrived in late 1930 at the key to successful FM broadcasting: the FM broadcast channel had to be many times wider than the standard AM channel of 10 kHz. Using a channel 200 kHz wide, with low power, Armstrong got excellent audio frequency response with FM—and virtually no static, even in electrical storms. (Actually, the swing of the modulated FM signal occupied only 75 kHz, but the additional

bandwidth protected against interference from adjacent channels due to the instability of receiving equipment on the very high frequencies employed.) Armstrong applied for the first four patents on his FM system in 1930 and received them just after Christmas in 1933.[13]

Until his discovery, in fact, most engineers believed that noise reduction and its elimination was virtually hopeless. Electrical engineer-transmission theorist-mathematician John Renshaw Carson (1886–1940) testified: "Static, like the poor, will always be with us."[14] Yet frequency modulation, Armstrong's third foremost discovery — and unambiguously, his most impressive — produced exceptionally natural sound quality that was immune to electromagnetic interference. The only valid deterrent linked to his discovery was that FM signals were limited to a broadcast distance of roughly 50 miles. FM signals don't bounce off the ionosphere like AM signals and, therefore, fall off the Earth due to the global curvature.[15]

Yet FM's widespread acceptance was anything but easy.

It arrived just as America was suffering through the very depths of the Great Depression. An impediment stemming from the epoch was that major investments in new technology simply couldn't be encouraged. It took seven years for Armstrong to receive the green light he absolutely had to have in order to fully implement his by-then compulsive mission to establish FM as a viable option in commercial broadcasting. In March 1940, the Federal Communications Commission (FCC) embarked on eight days of hearings surrounding FM's standing.

Twenty-something experimental FM stations were already operational at the time, with more projected to join their fraternity in the near future. Most of the trial ventures were linked to an AM outlet in the same city.[16] The commissioners heard a divergent litany of opinions on the subject of FM. One of the surprises of those hearings was that RCA, which was heavily invested in TV development, offered no objections to FM.

On May 20, 1940, the FCC authorized commercial FM in this country to become operational effective January 1, 1941.[17] Forty channels were to be reserved for FM in a new and wider band of 42–50 MHz, with the five lowest channels designated for educational broadcasters. Experimental television relinquished one channel while governmental agencies gave up seven MHz of spectrum (also known as continuum) space to secure FM.[18]

In March 1941, the first commercial FM station with FCC authorization went on the air, identified by the call letters W47NV.[19] It grew out of W4XA, a 1,000-watt shortwave outlet that Nashville's 50,000-watt powerhouse WSM-AM. That's the very same WSM that originated the *Grand Ole Opry* broadcasts on Saturday night in the autumn of 1925, and still does to this day. WSM had conducted shortwave experimentations for years. From atop the station's impressive 878-foot tower, the one from which four dipole FM transmitter antennas were attached, one's view "stretched nearly from Kentucky to Alabama," a station biographer noted. Impressive, indeed.

Because their audiences were too small and their broadcasting hours too few, the handful of commercial FM stations were airing almost no advertising.[20] Sponsors held off, preferring to continue to concentrate on bigger fish in the sea at the AM band. In the meantime, Edwin Armstrong's attempts to bring FM's implementation to a satisfactory level were short-lived. A few months after FM was beginning to make a few waves, the exploit was torpedoed by the outbreak of the Second World War. It only survived the war by the profits of co-owned AM outlets or out of the deep pockets of some station owners. Broadcasters limited their overhead by programming recorded music or duplicating network shows on both sides of the spectrum.

Following the war, the process of instigating FM radio was frustrated yet again, this time as the major radio networks interjected further delaying tactics. As an industry they viewed the FM technology that Armstrong offered as a threat to their own long-running AM broadcasting schemes. Moreover, they were mindful of TV's looming financial potential for them. TV was a fast-approaching commodity that segments of the trade — including some of the big chains — had invested years and titanic sums in by underwriting experimentation and development phases. Those transcontinental hookups had plenty of reason to be fearful of upstarts that might tread on "their" turf. Anything that threatened to drain public interest as well as commercial resources from their recovery of spent sums and projected expansion could be anathema to their plans.

Radio Corporation of America's (RCA's) David Sarnoff became a resolute obstructionist, vigorously protesting that — as FM receivers would initially cost buyers more than AM receivers — listeners wouldn't be willing to pay more to acquire superior fidelity in sound. And Sarnoff knew that if buyers did shell out more for improved radio reception they just might be unwilling to purchase TV sets. A perceptive sage explained: "Committed to television as the broadcast medium with a big future, Sarnoff bank-rolled its development with profits from NBC's two AM radio networks; an industry-wide shift to FM broadcasting and consequent revenue reductions did not at all fit with his agenda."[21] RCA, the parent firm of NBC Radio and TV, was destined to become the leading manufacturer of television receivers and related picture transmission apparatus at the forefront of the visually oriented breakthrough. Another historiographer surmised:

> Given that RCA was an empire built on patent monopolies, he [Sarnoff] was wary of investing in a technology that wasn't his company's intellectual property, especially since it would be competing with an older broadcast system that largely was — and particularly if he could instead be pushing television, a technology he hoped RCA *would* develop and own.

6. Escalating the Continuum

...The big broadcasters dominated the FCC as thoroughly as they had the Federal Radio Commission before it, and juicy jobs at RCA were available for powerful bureaucrats willing to toe the company's line. Federal regulators threw a series of obstacles in FM's way, using any argument, no matter how nakedly false, to justify themselves. Meanwhile, RCA's patent attorneys set to work trying to appropriate the Major's rights to his creation.[22]

Intriguingly, while NBC was fervently pushing its radio affiliates in the early– to mid–1940s to apply for television licenses as soon as the feds authorized the go-ahead, CBS was precisely heading in the opposite direction.[23] Believing that TV would arrive later than sooner, CBS implored its stations to resist applying for video licenses and instead to seek FM certification. Some CBS outlets even surrendered their TV channel allocations, persuaded that there was no cause for rush. An imbroglio between the two chains over dual-color telecasting methods added to CBS's laid-back stance, hinting that no urgency existed since the big question was far from being settled.

The FCC was illogically used in the meantime, influenced to alter the frequencies assigned to FM and to limit FM signal power.

> Sarnoff and RCA, still out to hold control of their radio empire, pressured the FCC to change all of the FM radio frequencies — a move they knew would instantly obsolete all the exiting FM radios, and cause Armstrong to lose his personal investment in FM radio....
>
> Years of costly legal battles ensued that RCA could afford and Armstrong couldn't....
>
> Although Armstrong tried to fight for his superior radio system, RCA continued to tie him up with years of legal battles. These both sapped his creative energies and drained his financial resources.[24]

In the meantime, listeners were justifiably angered when their radios were turned into something totally worthless. Having been scorched once, they were hesitant to purchase replacement FM receivers instantly. When the major broadcasting companies were ultimately persuaded to embrace FM, they plainly assumed Armstrong's patents as their own. As a consequence, the inventor sued RCA and its subsidiaries for infringing upon his lawful rights. That turn of events resulted in a demoralizing outcome for the inexorable entrepreneur. Although Armstrong's legacy was to outlive him, it would do so at great personal peril and sacrifice.

As FM began arriving initially in limited public notice, its pioneering developer was quietly underwriting the bills of a fledgling regional FM-only radio hookup that went on the air in 1947. A station he owned with call letters W2XMN at Alpine, New Jersey, was a key spoke in the wheel of the Continental Radio Network. (Within range of New York City, the town of Alpine is situated on the Hudson River Palisades.) The hookup optimally reached a handful of affiliates along the upper Eastern seaboard and a few Midwestern locales. The pioneering Continental system was buttressed by a Yankee Network based in New England, which had been operating since 1933.²⁵ Yankee applied for permission to construct a 50 kw FM outlet at Paxton, Massachusetts, to test long-range and relay broadcasting. In 1939, Yankee launched a couple of FM stations. General Electric subsequently opened stations at Albany and Schenectady, New York, testing FM reception while exploring plans to build FM receivers for sale.

By the end of 1939, FM outlets were also airing at several sites in Connecticut and Massachusetts as well as New York City and Washington, D.C. In early 1940, three more experimental FM stations, including two in Wisconsin and one owned by NBC, went on the air. That trio programmed no commercials but beamed various tests that were supplemented by boatloads of music. In the meantime, a number of New England outlets were experimenting with relay broadcasting. In doing so, one station aired a program and others rebroadcast it by picking it up with sensitive antennas. This gave them better sound quality than AM and shunned the considerable charges that AT&T proffered for connection to and conduction over its lines. Minus the static and with an audio-frequency response up to 15 kHz, relaying was viable on the FM band, although it wasn't on the AM continuum.

The direct-line connection or relay technique wasn't cost-effective or geographically possible for a few of the Continental Radio Network's most distant Midwestern outlets, however. In their case, it was more practical to mail tapes of programs to them for broadcast following the original airing. This rather unusual and unwieldy (although not unique) experiment ceased altogether upon the sudden death of Edwin Armstrong, Continental's chief instigator and financier.²⁶ By 1952, FM's future was depressing, looking desolate to all but a pithy number of independent station owners that were programming classical or other music for a minuscule crowd of hi-fi fans.²⁷ FM had deteriorated into little more than a "class benefit" in what had been anticipated would be a mass medium. The 616 FM stations on the air in America in 1952 shrank to 530 in 1957.²⁸

Concurrently, Edwin Armstrong was, by the early 1950s, visibly in failing health, pecuniary shambles, and incredibly emotional turmoil. Much of it stemmed from the enduring machinations which had spent his energy and resources while dominating much of his time across the years. As a result, he finally gave in to the distress that had so weakened him. He had had enough of the railing against the establishment (including the FCC and, particularly, his taxing battles with Sarnoff and RCA). It didn't seem to matter to the capitalists that they could bring about the inventor's ultimate trouncing. On January 31, 1954, at 63, Armstrong threw in the towel.

After scribbling a note to his wife in which he expressed contrition for what he was about to do, he removed the air conditioner from a window in his Manhattan suite. Crawling through the aperture he leaped to his death on a third-floor extension some ten stories below.[29] To his detractors, however, perhaps quite surprisingly, Armstrong's widow — who had once upon a time been David Sarnoff's secretary at RCA — proved to be of similar resolute mettle that had typified her late spouse's indomitable spirit.[30] In similar manner, she subsequently pressed forward with 21 lawsuits that sought to protect her late husband's rights. Eventually winning every single case, she ultimately pocketed $10 million from the courtroom verdicts.[31] Edwin Armstrong's name was to be permanently inscribed with the fatherhood of FM radio — a heritage that he surely earned and that has remained unchallenged to modern times.

The tide noticeably began to turn for FM in 1957. That year — for the first time since the previous decade — applications for new FM stations outnumbered those going off the air, so the trade weekly *Broadcasting* reported in an April issue. Several station group owners revealed intents to establish separate programming for their FM outlets, and there was talk of the possibility of a new FM chain. By 1960, nearly 750 commercial FM broadcasters were on the ether, an all-time high (it had been just 530 three years earlier, you'll remember).[32] Something was definitely relighting FM's fire. RCA, meanwhile, had immediately begun pushing FM's expansion while earning millions of dollars from its sales of FM transmitters and equipment.[33]

> The two most controversial social movements of the 1960s, the counterculture-antiwar movement and the Black Power movement, also contributed to FM's rise to prominence. The first FM stations to identify with those movements did so by experimenting with "underground radio" formats, as they were initially called by their listeners. The counterculture outlets were located in urban centers with large college-student populations, for instance, Boston (WBCN-FM); New York City (WOR-FM, WNEW-FM); Washington, D.C. (WHFS-FM); Los Angeles (KPPC-FM); and San Francisco (KMPX-FM, KSAN-FM). Soon after their appearance, the music and broadcasting trade magazines began to call them "progressive FM" stations. Several characteristics set them apart from AM Top Forty. The progressive FM outlets played albums instead of 45s and broadcast in stereo; they supported their local counterculture, especially its music scene; and they returned control over the playlist to the disc jockey.
>
> A boom-and-bust cycle plagued most of the progressive FM operations and eventually wiped them out.[34]

In major cities, the teeming AM spectrum was having a colossal effect in aural broadcasting. By the late 1950s, there was almost no room for additional AM stations in cities of any appreciable size in America. The only way to get a new radio signal on the air — and particularly at night — was via an FM channel. At about the same time the original growth spurt for television was reduced in intensity, thereby freeing up investment capital as well as labor for FM wannabes. As listeners' cultural identifications also shifted toward broadcasters that were programming their specific wants, needs, and tastes — a hallmark of many FM outlets — production of lower-cost FM receivers began saturating the market. Sets on local dealers' shelves were initially imported from Germany, followed in even more abundant supply from the Far East. At last, too, transistor AM-FM radios had made the scene, highly desirable for their built-in Automatic Frequency Control, preventing annoying drift that had always been common with tube-type receivers.

> All these factors helped break the vicious circle of no audience/no advertisers/no money for stations/no stations/no programs/no audience and finally produced the growth in FM which had been expected when it was approved for commercial operation in 1941. FM radio was still a secondary radio service, but the increasing number of stations on the air and growing audience suggested that it was here to stay.[35]

In late 1958 and 1959, more than a million FM receivers were sold in the U.S. That figure nearly doubled in 1960, and 20 percent of the sets were German and Japanese imports.[36] In both foreign nations war-devastated electronics industries had reawakened stunningly, propelled into progressive technologists overnight, and prospering into highly efficient enterprises. This was merely the tip of the iceberg of what was coming from both distant outposts.

In the postwar era, 1946–48, small table-model AM radios placed in bedrooms and kitchens (in addition to most households' large living-room consoles) sold for about $15. In the same era, FM receivers sold for $50 or more.[37] A decade afterward, a typical combination AM-FM apparatus was available for about $30, while AM-only radios could be purchased for $15–$20. (In 2013, the $30 of 1958 would equate to $244.[38] That's hardly cheap by most comparable standards for an AM-FM radio — even in a flourishing U.S. economy.)

Despite the newer FM band's exposure and gradual ascendency, its availability certainly could not be declared universal overnight. For a while (to the late 1950s or early 1960s, no less) FM was ostensibly pigeonholed into a fairly limited, quite distinct echelon. The common man hadn't hastened to the other side in great numbers in spite of FM's appeal by the absence of "drift" made possible by transistors and innovative circuitry. (Maybe $30 was a tad pricey? RCA was making a mint off the 90 percent of trade in American-made color TVs it was then selling at $500–$800 per unit, or $4069–$6511 in 2013 dollars.[39] For many buyers, a lot had to be weighed carefully. Some residents may have compromised, retaining older, smaller, black-and-white TVs to invest in AM-FM radio receivers.) Public awareness about FM quality was getting out, the result of word-of-mouth publicity as well as heavy advertising by both the manufacturers and the retail emporiums.

> In the early 1960s, FM remained the province of the privileged, appealing primarily to educated and affluent pockets in places such as New York, Washington, Boston, and San Francisco. FM meant the classics and Broadway show tunes —

1961's top five bestselling LPs included two Broadway cast albums, *Camelot* and *The Sound of Music*, as well as the soundtrack to the movie *Never on Sunday*—which were rarely played on AM radio. AM listeners bought 45 rpm singles—period. FM also served up "beautiful music," the purportedly inoffensive background sounds designed to fill the silences in elevators and dental offices. In Houston, this was marketed as "The Velvet Touch" from KODA; in New York, as "The Sound of the Good Life" from WPIX's PIX Penthouse. None of this required much effort or any significant spending on talent. FM was a music service and that was that.

...The mass media offered hardly any outlet for the alienation and tough questions that were pushing their way to the surface. But the assassination of John Kennedy, the first battles of the civil rights movement, the initial cries of campus protest, the acid commentaries of comedians such as Lenny Bruce and Dick Gregory, and the sudden popularity of politically charged folk music called out for a place in the popular media.

FM radio stood empty and waiting.[40]

Edwin Armstrong's unparalleled feat imparted more innovations. FM opened the way not only for multiplex and stereo broadcasting but for microwave relay links, too. Multiplexing in radio, by the way, is transmitting two or more signals concurrently on a carrier wave within a station's designated bandwidth. As a consequence, FM stations are able to offer their listeners programming in stereo (separate left and right channels). Starting in the early 1960s, multiplexing allowed FM outlets to become more competitive with their AM peers, extracting more and more of the audience share.[41]

The march of progress finally accomplished what Armstrong had not: the introduction of stereo records in 1957 fed a growing popular appetite for "hi-fi," top-quality sound systems that took advantage of the new 33-1/3 rpm, long-playing discs, which generated much less noise and achieved finer reproduction than the old 78s. Veterans coming home from the military brought with them a new penchant for things technical. Magazines such as *Popular Mechanics* and *High Fidelity* won huge audiences; the popular press commiserated with female readers in articles such as "I Am a Hi-Fi Widow" and "The High Fidelity Wife, or a Fate Worse than Deaf."[42]

Granted, there were some stumbling blocks that almost appeared to purposely dispatch those people that were out of the loop in this hi-fi fraternity, preventing them from fully appreciating and joining the leisure-time pursuit.[43] For one thing, a contrived lingo (with "common" terms like *equalizer, preamp, tweeter,* and *woofer*) tended to detach the conversant from the uninitiated. (Think how *apps, bluetooth, e-reader, streaming,* and *tablet* in their most replete treatments may be beyond the grasp of various denizens in contemporary America.) The verbal and written exchanges between mechanically savvy proponents often had the affect of alienating those who were on the outside looking in. Yet the end product that drew all of their attention simply thrust recorded music that exhibited sound resonance vastly improved over anything they had heard that preceded it. The result was a rewarding appeal to millions of purchasers of amplification devices and the vinyl tracks that supplied those sterling sounds.

A historiographer of the FM revolution, Marc Fisher, summarized the welcome effect of the realization upon twin disciplines.

> FM radio, and the new stereo systems that showcased it, represented at that time the ultimate use of technology to magnify, extend, and deepen the capabilities of the human ear. The new technology separated sounds, highlighted how they were layered, made the components of music more distinct and pure. When young people tuned in to certain FM stations in the late 1960s, they entered a brand-new auditory, political, and cultural world. And they went there specifically to indulge in a newly heightened, much more concentrated mode of listening, fidelity listening.
>
> Gone were the AM jocks with their rapid-fire delivery who called listeners "baby" and "cousin," hyped H.I.S. pants and station contests, and played the same twenty songs every hour. Instead the lush, stereophonic sound made possible by the new transmitters and receivers allowed listeners to concentrate on the layering of instruments, voices, and sound effects in a song like the Chambers Brothers' "Time Has Come Today," which stations ... played in its full nine-minute version.... Sadly, much of this audio revolution has been lost or destroyed [in the years since].
>
> The long-delayed success of FM built, in part, on the success of the transistor, and also on the postwar hi-fi craze, which eventually led to the unpacking—and enlarging—of radio and the phonograph into stereo components. And it was the interaction between these inventions and the baby boom generation that played a major role in redefining how radio would be used in the late 1960s and early 1970s.[44]

The FCC approved stereo broadcasting on FM, incidentally, in 1961, seven years after Edwin Armstrong's death. In 1963, FM car radios were making the scene pervasively. A year beyond (1964) the FCC declared that AM stations owning FM outlets in metropolises must air fresh, separate programming on the FM continuum no less than 50 percent of their broadcast day.[45] Although station owners had until 1967 to comply with the order, there was no mistaking the edict's meaning. By then AM was crowded while FM was poised for an exploding surfeit of outlets.[46]

The statute was extended to smaller markets in the 1970s, netting an almost inevitable consequence: FM drifted into specialism as much as AM had and FM was soon concentrated into format orientations, programming beautiful music or classical, country and western, progressive jazz, rock, or any of dozens of divergent yet narrowly defined themes. A couple of academicians, Christopher Sterling and John Kittross, noted, "By the late 1960s, the specialization had changed the decades-old idea that 'FM is special' to the view that 'FM is radio.'"[47]

The appeal to audiences, nevertheless, could be witnessed in increasing numbers of sets equipped for receiving FM. Gradually, manufacturers were shipping combination AM-FM table radios and hi-fi sets complete with stereo speakers and FM receivers to distributors to be funneled into appliance retailers' showrooms. Specialization was having some observable positive effects.

Listeners began to examine this new dimension in sound for themselves and plainly liked what they were hearing. Within a five-year period beginning in 1960, Americans' fascination with FM quintupled, skyrocketing from six million sets in use in 1960 to 30 million in 1965. In the next five-year period, the numbers tuning in to FM escalated astoundingly, to 93 million sets by 1970.[48] Industry analysts estimate that by 1972, in metropolitan Boston and Chicago, 95 percent of their residents were in domiciles equipped with at least one FM receiver. Within a few years, that percentage could be exhibited in many additional places throughout the United States.

A few more figures, while clearly skimming the surface of the FM insurgency in this nation, reflect what was transpiring as Americans developed a magnetic predilection for higher-quality broadcasting sound than they have been accustomed to.[49] The FCC reported that 983 commercial FM stations were operating in 1962. In 1972, that number had climbed to 2,328, an increase of 137 percent in a decade. In 1976, about 3,700 FM stations were broadcasting in the U.S., a 59 percent rise across that quadrennial and a 276 percent hike in 14 years. In 1964, meanwhile, total net FM revenues were $19.7 million. In 1974, the cumulative had jumped 12.6 times, to $248.2 million.

In the mid–1970s, FM stations — the majority of which were broadcasting in stereo — approached the AM stations in geographical territory accessed as well as in number of listeners.[50] Not only was the perception of FM on the rise, but sometimes the actual physical value of those outlets. In 1968, an FM outlet sold for a million dollars, the first of its kind to do so. In a short while, the bulk of FM-licensing cases resulted in comparative examinations before the FCC as prospective broadcasters vied for channel authority.

How, in some markets, had FM finally overtaken AM in drawing the bulk of radio listeners in the nation to the latent, sometimes overlooked upstart? Several reasons contributed. There were some fundamentally sophisticated mechanical enhancements that had made it feasible in the first place. There was also an excess of broadcasters occupying the AM band, which resulted in a glut attempting to do business there. Alterations in federal oversight of the industry ran counter to the wishes of some radio buffs as well.

But the detail most often credited with the pervasive shift among U.S. radio listeners from the AM to FM continuum — which came about in the 1960s, when the transition was so overt — was just this: the advent of a flagrantly stunning anti-commercial, anti-corporate mindset that had become almost omnipresent. Some scholars said the exhibition of this brazenly deliberate attitude hinged on contempt for what had generally come to be referred to as "mass culture."[51] Pundits pictured the phenomenon as "disdain for the 'vast wasteland' of television and for the formulaic, overly commercialized offerings of radio." Supplementing their belief, they opined that it incorporated utter scorn "on the part of older intellectuals and later on the part of the counter-culture" toward mainstream popular music for its "predictability and mindlessness."

> The quest for fidelity, in other words, was not only a technical quest driving the improvements in FM transmitting and receiving. It was also a cultural and political quest for an alternative medium marked by fidelity to musical creativity and cultural authenticity. The quest for fidelity meant the reduction of noise not just from static but from the hucksterism of America's consumer culture.[52]

All these factors coalesced during a period in which renewed passion for fidelity in sound and, indeed, listening itself escalated into vogue. While the zeal for all of this had been gradually building since the late 1940s, by the 1970s, the combination of annoyance, promise, and pent-up emotions permitted frequency modulation to burst onto the scene as a wholly venerable craze. It has continued to supply Americans with a major source of auditory resonance as well as persisted in educating and informing them to this point in the present millennium.

In the late 1960s, the FM band was largely populated by a multifaceted cadre of broadcaster types: with collegiate operations of the nonprofit variety, with autonomous alternative outfits, with still more outlets of an independent nature that were controlled by capitalists who sought profitability and little else, and by the transcontinental hookups with "a bottom-line mentality and stockholders to please," as one wag put it. Collectively, they confronted worrisome economic and cultural strains. FM's scarcity of commercials drew many people to tune in, of course, yet its broadcasting sector was missing precisely what could make that wedge stable and sustainable. Therein lay a tightrope that had to be negotiated circumspectly. Even in the midst of the following decade (the 1970s), while FM attracted a third of all radio listeners, just 14 percent of the industry's revenues were being earned there.[53] And the listeners were being divvied up to an even greater degree as hundreds of new FM outlets had taken to the ether in the early 1970s. What then?

The booming audience for many FM stations had been fittingly recognized as youthful and financially flourishing, two factors that were highly alluring to marketers. Ad agencies advanced strategies to reach this demographic segment that extended the promise of greatest potential rewards. The substantial, well-heeled youth market had discretionary funds that it needed for purchasing alcohol, food, jeans, records, stereos, T-shirts, and toiletries, and it didn't demonstrate any intention of holding back on buying what it wanted. As advertisers and FM station owners fully comprehended this, the broadcasting outlets were increasingly rehabilitated. From pioneering classical music formats or another design, they were altered to rock stations which would haul in the older teens and twenty- to thirty-somethings. Between 1963 and 1973, the nation's number of classical-themed FM stations was cut by half.[54]

Nothing lasts forever, we are well aware, and as the mid–1970s approached, there were signs that the freeform application so prevalent across FM might have run its course. By 1974, the tighter playlist, one of the identifying symbols of the AM stations, surfaced at numerous progressive rock outlets. It was an early hint that things were transitioning dramatically. "We're seeing a nationalization of tastes," proclaimed an FM staffer. A citadel of early FM, albums out of the conventional weren't showing up any longer on very many playlists. And those lists, by the way, were set either by station program managers or a panel of judges just as they were in the heyday of AM DJ operations in many places in the 1950s and 1960s. The matter of settling what to play was no longer the discretionary province of the guy or gal who was actually spinning the discs at many FM outlets.[55]

One reporter acknowledged "the assembly line had come to FM." It broke down freeform programming into sundry elements, stripped the disc jockey of autonomy, and made the varied programs (or airtime shifts) far more consistent and obvious than ever before. Programming decisions were centralized. An insider referred to instituting "the format" as symbolizing "the antithesis of everything FM radio stood for." The blueprint set by the program director or an outside consultant became a framework for what tunes were to be played and when that would occur. Sales figures, telephone surveys, demographics, and focus groups determined everything. The DJ merely came to work and picked up a playlist, proceeding through it as his on-air agenda for the day. Creativity and inspiration were substances of the past. Susan Douglas, a modern chronicler, characterized what was transpiring in the trade.

> Just as the 1950s witnessed the invention of the disc jockey, the 1970s saw the invention of his behind-the-scenes successor, the radio consultant. Mention this term to most disc jockeys, especially those who were on progressive rock stations, and the revulsion is palpable.... Consultants routinized, standardized, and codified what DJs felt they did by instinct, and they returned FM to many of the conventions of AM that progressive rock had cast itself against.... Consultants relied on demographic data, purchasing habits, and ratings, and linked these to specific formats, depending on the demographic the station was going after. So many of these consultants also became de factor programmers, and they especially emphasized the importance of repetition of tunes, and music that was not too threatening or unfamiliar.... They took the feeling out of FM programming, made it bloodless and allegedly scientific. Music, once so sacred to FM DJs, was now called "product."[56]

Are you familiar with the axiom, "The more things change, the more they stay the same"? FM had invested wholeheartedly in freeform FM radio programming on many stations. Eventually, it made a U-turn and ended up back at the place it had initially abhorred.

Stations and advertisers were clearly pointed toward a specific fragment of what had heretofore been a "mass" audience. One of the respected bibles of its industry, *Advertising Age*, published in 1978: "With the increased emphasis on specific demographics, stations are finding it imperative to implement tight format control to ensure that the target audience is being reached. The day of the disc jockey who controls his individual program is quickly becoming a dinosaur." Whereas in excess of 300 progressive rock outlets existed in the U.S. in the late 1960s and early 1970s, their number had dwindled to roughly 25 around 1975.[57]

That notwithstanding, the systematic research and prescribed programming designs resulted in significantly increased advertising revenues which was, of course, the underlying goal in its implementation. In 1976, FM maintained about 40 percent of the radio audience and maybe 20 percent of the income. By 1986, FM controlled 70 percent of both audience and revenue shares.[58] Between 1976 and 1977 alone, FM stations' income had leaped nearly 30 percent, to $543.1 million.[59] Meanwhile, a new business model was in full swing — automated-programming services selling syndicated formats to FM stations. A more meticulous depiction of this enveloping innovation will be extensively delineated in Chapter 10.

By 1979, FM was outstripping stations in popularity in such pivotal markets as Boston, Chicago, Dallas, Detroit, Los Angeles, and New York. Nationwide, more than half the outlets occupying the top 10 ranks in the country's 50 leading metropolitan centers were broadcasting on the FM band.[60] Almost all new portable or vehicle radios were of the AM-FM variety. With free choice, listeners were inclined to be drawn to the superior-sounding medium. At length, FM was starting to outpace AM. The medium Edwin Armstrong had pioneered was at last coming into its own, albeit a quarter-century following his untimely death. A trade weekly proclaimed:

> FM audiences led AM for first time in ... radio usage report for spring 1979. Overall Monday–Sunday figures show 24-hour FM share at 50.5 percent, 42 percent for 6 A.M. to 10 A.M. and 58 percent for 7 P.M. to midnight. Teen-agers and young adults (18–24) devote 59 percent and 65 percent of their listening to FM, respectively, while the figure for persons above 50 is 37 percent.[61]

By 1992, FM accounted for three-quarters of all radio listeners.[62] Meanwhile, three years earlier (1989), AM stations were scurrying to replace current formats with new programming designs which would help them draw many defectors back from FM, so they were betting the rent.[63] All-talk was the pick of many.

Dwelling in the realm of formatting a tad longer: a few comments on those programming designs in the 1980s and 1990s seem to almost unintentionally, yet unmistakably, let it drop that FM had transitioned into some concepts that it (and the majority of its listeners) disdained and even shunned in the preceding couple of decades.

First, while stations continued to emphasize music and their low-fidelity AM brothers concentrated more on various talk ... formats this division was not always observed. Music remained on many AMs, while talk increasingly appeared on FM. Second, though music formats continued to splinter, reflecting changing musical tastes, more than a few critics argued that stations were beginning to sound increasingly alike. Third, and more seriously, it seemed ... that FM's growing audience appeal — and thus financial success — was creating growing caution and less innovation. Increasingly, stations took the safe approach of imitating successful formats rather than developing new directions.... Some critics claimed FM was declining to the bland and prosaic — albeit with growing profits — just as had AM before it.

A causal relationship seemed apparent between the loss of the cultural ferment characterizing the two previous decades and the decline of innovation in FM programming. The medium in the 1980s and 1990s seemed rudderless and uninspired.... Passions that typified earlier social and political protest movements had been supplanted by ennui and self-absorption.... With the exception of the anti-industry micro-radio crusaders and the altruistic sensibilities of many noncommercial program schedules, FM was drifting onto the shoals of stagnation. Observed underground-radio pioneer Larry Miller: "The hopefulness for something extraordinary and far-reaching had faded.... The 'spirit' had been abandoned by the medium as the consequence of its acute corporatization. FM became a business model rather than a model of invention and freshness like it once was."[64]

At the start of this millennium, one partisan, Jesse Walker, cited more than 11,000 AM and FM radio stations operating in this country tendering beau coups of formats for listeners to dawdle over. "For the most part," he lamented, "this is diversity without depth: an ether carved into a thousand niches, each only an inch deep."[65] He went on:

The freedom to create is being withheld by an alliance of policymakers and professionals. Since the mid–1980s, the technical cost of starting a low-power FM radio station has been within most Americans' reach — a couple hundred dollars plus the monthly power bill, which for low-watt stations isn't very high. The *legal* cost, however, is much higher: almost $3,000 for a license, plus $100,000 or more in startup costs. With very few exceptions, the FCC won't issue licenses to noncommercial stations of less than one hundred watts. Class A commercial stations require at least *six thousand watts of power*.[66]

The possibilities seem endless, and the splintering is commensurate.

For now, suffice it to say that the birth of FM — once it got past its protracted infancy — introduced considerable change to the airwaves. In addition to ushering in a vastly improved means of capitalizing on pure and nearly unblemished quality sound fidelity that wafted across the ether, one's programming choices were significantly enlarged. Perhaps not until some in the industry found methods of becoming avaricious did the immense potential for pleasure in a box return to precisely what had given it incentive for many to try something else in the first place. As the line that separated FM from AM became muddled and blurred, without direct knowledge, many times one could hardly distinguish just which band he was hearing any longer. Though radio universally would persist in entertaining, informing, educating, and amusing its American audiences, by the final quarter of the 20th century some of the promise that FM's early efforts had extended in so many quarters was muted at best.

In the 1980s and 1990s, as media corporations swept most FM stations into their already bulging portfolios, illegal (pirate) low-power FM (micro) outlets appeared as surrogates for the ensuing decay in local service and programming variety, ushering in Low Power FM. Now, digital satellite and terrestrial services (as well as the Internet) are threatening to become viable substitutes for FM. For several years the youthful radio crowd has been scurrying away from analog radio, preferring in its place a wave of commercial-free digital audio music exponents. More and more MP3 gear (iPods, etc.), satellite radio services, and supplementary hi-tech options are "sowing the seeds of FM's eventual disappearance," according to some seemingly well-versed radio authorities.[67]

> Looking ahead, the ultimate demise of analog FM broadcasting is already visible. While we cannot venture exactly when this will take place since there is no mandated deadline, our best guess is sometime during the second decade of the twenty-first century. [That's anytime now, folks, if you haven't figured that out.] FM will ultimately imitate AM again in this final stage of disappearing from the scene. Both are based on analog technology and are thus outflanked by the vastly sharper sound of digital transmission. The FCC will eventually close both analog services in favor of the more efficient digital operations. Millions of Americans enjoy satellite digital service as this is written, with more subscribing all the time. Terrestrial digital or HD radio service is not far behind. Just as FM radio was a marked improvement over AM, so these digital services mark a huge advance over FM.[68]

The message seems copiously clear: if you like FM, enjoy it now; one day soon you might wish you had.

7

Narrowcasting: A Captive Audience

A large number of Internet sites compellingly implore their viewers that the label given narrowcasting is an invention of comparatively modern happening. Most of those Web spots, in fact, restrict the classification to no earlier than the epoch surrounding the widespread unveiling of television. Some exhibitions, however, disregard TV altogether in resolving the origin, bringing it even closer to contemporary times. A few samples make the point:

The [TV] networks maintained their stronghold until competition emerged through the addition of many independent stations, the proliferation of cable channels and the popularity of videocassettes. These competitors provided television audiences with many more viewing options. Consequently, the large numbers previously achieved through mass-oriented programming dwindled and "narrowcasting" took hold.[1]

> Narrowcast — to send data to a specific list of recipients. Cable television is an example of narrowcasting since the cable TV signals are sent only to homes that have subscribed to the cable service. In contrast, network TV uses a broadcast model in which the signals are transmitted everywhere and anyone with an antenna can receive them. The Internet uses both a broadcast and a narrowcast model. Most websites use a broadcast model since anyone with Internet access can view the sites. However, sites that require you to log-in before viewing content are based more on the narrowcast model. The various push technologies [Webcasting enabling websites to deliver content directly to users' desktop computers] are another form of narrowcasting. Perhaps the best example of narrowcasting is e-mail lists where messages are sent only to individuals who subscribe to the list.[2]

> Narrowcasting — transmit a television program ... to a comparatively small audience defined by special interest or geographical location.[3]

> Narrowcasting is directed to a particular audience via proprietary equipment and encryption, or by some other discriminatory means. One of the most common

examples of narrowcasting is cable TV.... Another example is satellite radio. Satellite radio is commercial-free radio, requiring a proprietary receiver or tuner.... Because narrowcasting is directed towards a limited pool, it is associated with target and niche marketing.[4]

Narrowcasting can be described as the digital delivery of information to a select audience. The most mainstream form of narrowcasting is using LCD [liquid crystal display], TFT [thin film transistor LCD] and LED [light-emitting diode] displays to deliver promotional and/or informational messages. Narrowcasting has conquered a dominant position as [a] relatively new advertising medium.... In the United States it is common to use the term "Digital Signage" rather than Narrowcasting. The term "Narrowcasting" and "Digital Signage" do mean the same.[5]

Yet another application of narrowcasting — this one in very early radio — was advanced by two of the medium's foremost historiographers.[6] Their reference is to the era of the second and third decades of the 20th century, during which more than 8,500 licensed amateurs constructed their own sending "stations" (sometimes built from kits). Such operations exhibited transmitters capable of dispatching sound (the human voice, music, signals, and other din) across terrain of varied distances. The product of these stalwarts' ambitions was generally captured from the air by receivers of the homemade variety too, belonging to other "radio people" (buffs, aficionados, hobbyists, plus the leading electrical and wireless firms of that day). The historians' use of the idiom related to *point-to-point communication*. The majority of their number was absolutely convinced that the future of radio lay in *this* function of narrowcasting. Certainly, it gave an atypical meaning to how people would comprehend the term in the late decades of the 20th century and into the 21st century.

Even though some pacesetters may be convinced that narrowcasting initially appeared on the horizon some two to four decades *after it did*, according to Merriam-Webster, the metaphor was coined in 1928. Webster demarcated it as *radio or television transmission aimed at a narrowly defined area or audience* [italics added]. Of course, since that release (2001), the expression's use has been unremittingly expanded as evidenced in the preceding illustrations. In earlier days one of its principal applications was in scrupulously circumscribing individuals who could be meticulously segmented into precise fragments of the general population (or mass audience). The genuine article it launched in the pre-television era is of paramount importance to us in this chapter's premise.

An instance from the Golden Age of radio will surely suffice. Actors in this little drama include four CBS staffers: Frank Stanton, researcher and the chain's future president; Edward Klauber, second-in-command; Paul Kesten, promotion director; and Bill Paley, CEO.

> In the network's earliest days ... its programming schedule was a hodgepodge. A quarter hour of poetry reading would be followed by organ music, fifteen

minutes of vespers, a fifteen-minute soap opera, a talk broadcast, and a little dramatic sketch. The cycle would be repeated throughout the day. Not long after his arrival, Stanton noticed that CBS's ratings were higher in one [unidentified] city than in all the others.

The station in that city ... had taken similar shows and grouped them back to back. Stanton thought the idea ingenious and proposed that the network try the same tactic. The sales department was offended, the program department outraged. So Stanton did what he called some "missionary work." He told advertisers of soap operas that if they asked CBS to cluster their programs together, higher ratings would result. They followed his suggestion, and block programming, one of the most sacred scheduling techniques, was born.

Bolstered by that success, Stanton urged that news programs be similarly grouped. The idea outraged Klauber. "He thought I was an idiot," Stanton recalled. "People had to have their news separated. You couldn't put [H.V.] Kaltenborn back to back with [Edwin C.] Hill. It was a crime you shouldn't commit." Stanton went to Kesten, who persuaded Paley it was worth trying. It worked. Henceforth, the hour from 6:00 P.M. to 7:00 P.M. was given over to news and analysis.[7]

Stanton's clever discovery occurred in the early 1930s. It turned out that scheduling a handful of similarly themed radio series back to back encouraged the listener to remain with a particular station or network once a show reached its conclusion. The hypothesis was based on the assumption, "If he liked program A, he will probably like B which follows it, and won't turn the dial to something else." The concept caught on throughout the industry once primitive radio surveys of what people were following confirmed it. As a result, numerous soap operas were grouped one after another during the weekday matinee hours when the housewives — presumably their greatest fans — were fervently engaged in their washboard weepers. On the other hand, the late afternoons on weekdays became prime-time for juvenile adventure serials, airing after the adolescents returned home from school. And nights and weekends were earmarked for more general fare that could interest a broad range of family members from different generations. Those hours were reserved for comedy, drama, games, music, mystery, news, public affairs, sports, variety, and other amusement paradigms.

By arranging the schedule in a pattern of analogous shows within a customized timeframe, radio often drew more people who were interested in hearing more than a single series within a genus that they especially liked. This could easily have been termed narrowcasting, although in those days it was most often referenced as *block programming* by the pundits. The crowd was factionalized just as well: the broadcasters had drawn a target on the backs of splinter groups of listeners whether that audience realized it or not.

Through radio's Golden Age, the idea that "one size fits all" had often dominated the airwaves. The objective of local stations and of the regional and national hookups was to attract as many listeners as possible by whatever legal, ethical, and moral means were at their disposal. Jack Benny and Bing Crosby, therefore, as well as *Amos 'n' Andy, Dragnet, Gunsmoke, Fibber McGee & Molly, Kate Smith, The U.S. Steel Hour,* and *The Voice of Firestone* and all their peers lived and died by the numbers. The series named were fortunate enough to bask in inordinately high stats most of the time — figures gathered and released by multiple ratings services. The numbers were absolutely critical to sponsors and networks. Higher numbers than the competition usually meant that a feature wasn't in danger of being removed from the air for low ratings. (It works the same way in television now, with some new shows yanked after only a telecast or two.)

Mass appeal finally went by the wayside, however, especially after the Golden Age passed. Whereas the programmers had tried all those years to draw the *biggest* crowd, a new blueprint subsequently came into fashion. In a marketing volume, Art Weinstein, a scribe in that academic discipline, allowed: "*Segmentation* is the process of partitioning markets into groups of potential customers with similar needs and/or characteristics who are likely to exhibit similar purchase behavior."[8] Transferred to radio, they are people with similar interests and needs that may be satisfied by tuning in to a type of feature or genre that programmers have focused their stations on to suit the individuals' specific preferences. Segmentation, or narrowcasting, was to be the chief gambit of most aural broadcasters of the future — at least up to the present time.

> By the late 1940s, recorded music had become more prevalent on radio stations. Recorded music programs ... were common on independent stations that could not depend on network programming. As network radio stations began to lose programming to television, they turned to recorded music to fill the gaps....
> Some station owners held on to the notion that they could still attract mass audiences but most recognized that they would do better attracting segments of the radio audience with a particular style of music. This was the philosophy of radio formats or formulas: People watch television programs, but they listen to radio stations.
> It was not until the advent of a new music style that format radio really emerged as a major programming force.... Rock 'n' roll appeared on radio in the form of the first format: top 40. [For more on this, see Chapter 4.]
> By 1960, it was clear the radio would survive — but not as a network-dominated medium serving mass audiences. Radio's future was in formats geared to localized target audiences. With the development of transistors, radio receivers had become more mobile and personalized. This was something that television could not offer.... With the success of the top-40 format, station owners were inspired to experiment with other formats designed for special segments of the population.[9]

Not until the Golden Age faded did the audience start to appreciate the fuller implications of narrowcasting — and perhaps catch a glimpse of its outcome tucked in the programming methods that were being applied in heavy doses. Not that it mattered, of course, for the then-splintered audience aggregate was actually receiving more of what it desired in well-defined structures.

Marketing author Weinstein again offered this advice: "*Recognize that everyone is not a prospect for every good or service offered.*"[10]

In that regard, stations were proceeding in the tradition fostered by NBC's *Monitor* (1955–75), much of which was programmed quite literally for people on the go. (At its inception, for 40 hours on the weekend *Monitor* was heavily touted for "going places and doing things" with few beginning/ending starts and stops.) This initiated an industry pattern for the future, one evident on most U.S. commercial radio stations, AM and FM, as well as cable TV news channels today. You can tune in and out almost any time without missing a great deal that went before or will arrive after you switch stations or turn it off. In our fast-paced environment we barely have time for unlimited minutiae, nor are our powers of concentration what they once were. We've been conditioned to accept things in condensed amounts instead.

In the meantime, radio began to go off in tangents. The homogenization resulted in stations becoming bound to a specific restrictive programming configuration.

> As the "baby boomer" generation began aging, they were not interested in hearing "beautiful music" renditions of their favorite songs. Beautiful music formats that had dominated their markets began to lose listeners.
>
> Almost overnight, the format went from being one of the biggest to one of the least listened-to. Stations were dropping the format and replacing it with soft hit records from the actual artists, not the instrumental versions. This was the beginning of adult contemporary or, as it was first called, "chicken rock."
>
> Adult contemporary opened eyes to new forms of targeted programming. Before long, there were many variations of adult contemporary. Some leaned soft, while others were almost Top 40-sounding. Some even mixed country music in with their hits. These hybrids of radio were popping up everywhere. There were variations in country and also in black music.[11]

Parenthetically, "beautiful music" alternately dubbed "easy-listening," "good-music," "soft music," and "elevator music" had originated in the late 1960s when Jim Schulke's Stereo Radio Productions began shipping the program service to FM outlets.[12] The mellow-sounding instrumental and choral recordings it featured in the main (think Ray Conniff, Percy Faith, Bert Kaempfert, Andre Kostelanetz, Henry Mancini, Mantovani, Robert Shaw, Lawrence Welk, and that ilk) initially drew well-heeled older audience members who were disenchanted with other broadcast strains. These listeners had become a disregarded silent majority of the audience.

In due course those stations pioneered unremitting music sweeps and bunched commercials in small doses to keep an audience in the 34–50 age range happy. Eight to ten minutes of music between three or four clusters of two-minute spot advertising sets were incorporated. Announcers with polished voices read brief music notes and were rarely engaged in loquacious "morning-zoo" conversational styles.[13] News was always less consequential to music. The typical aficionado of this sound out in Radioland was college educated, devoted, and seeking a relaxed, satisfying music environment with almost no chatter whatsoever.[14]

As it topped the summit of its popularity, the broadcast form inundated waiting rooms, elevators, mercantile emporiums, medical facilities, and lots of other public spaces with its offerings. Multiple syndicated easy-listening music services without commercials (Muzak is an example) were transmitted on FM subcarriers that needed adaptors for reception. The breed was marketed to commercial enterprises as a method of relieving stress in the workplace, increasing sales, and combating fatigue. The beautiful music/easy-listening segment reached its zenith in 1979, when Arbitron revealed that it was the nation's most listened-to radio format. But in the following decade the audience and the advertisers dwindled steadily, preferring programming targeted to the baby-boomer bracket almost entirely. By the late 1990s, beautiful music curried favor with just 1 percent of the U.S. radio market.

In contemporary times a single website has identified no fewer than 70-something radio format possibilities.[15] (Recently, a veteran media journalist, Michael Keith, claimed that U.S. radio's formats, or sub-formats — to put it more precisely perhaps — have already exceeded 100 in number.[16]) Roughly half of the original 70 have labels like Adult standards/nostalgia (pre-rock), Album rock/album-oriented rock (AOR), Beautiful music, Big band, Bluegrass, Classic rock, Classical, Comedy, Contemporary Christian (CCM), Classic country, Educational, Folk music, Hot adult contemporary (Hot AC), Hispanic rhythmic, Jazz, Lite adult contemporary (Lite AC), Middle of the road (MOR, aka Full-service adult radio), All-news radio, Oldies (primarily 1955 through early–1980s pop music), Progressive rock, Psychedelic rock, Radio documentary, Radio drama, Regional Mexican (banda, corridos, ranchera, conjunto, mariachi, norteño, et al.), Soft rock, Soul, Sports, Talk radio (conservative), Talk radio (progressive), Talk radio (public), Talk radio (hot talk/shock jocks), Traditional pop, Tropical (salsa, meringue, cumbia, etc.), Urban contemporary (mostly rap, hip hop, soul, rhythm & blues), Urban adult contemporary (rhythm & blues, soul, and sometimes gospel, without rap), Variety, and World music. There's not a lot of intersecting of musical styles on most of these tightly formatted stations, however.

Robert Finney, an academician at California State University, Long Beach, provides some stimulating detail into how formats are presently determined and implemented in radio:

> Following in-depth analysis of the characteristics of a particular radio market, including competing stations and other competing media, a station's management selects a specific format such as all-news, all-talk, or a particular music genre. The final selection is usually determined by which format is likely to attract the

largest target audience, thereby ensuring top dollar for commercial time sold, which ultimately turns into higher profits. Most commercial radio stations adopt popular music formats.... Programmers build the schedule horizontally (weekly) by scheduling station breaks, news, commercials, and songs at the same time, Monday through Sunday. They build it vertically (daily) by scheduling the program elements consistently throughout the day, and with a hot clock (hourly), which places different program elements, minute by minute, within each hour in the same consistent pattern with the hours that precede and follow it.[17]

Hand in hand with the absorption in formatting a commercial radio station is target marketing. That's an attempt by advertisers to attract an identified cluster of listeners that has the interest, the desire, the need, and the ability to purchase their product or service, or — if touting an idea or cause — to embrace it and support it. Beauty products, for instance, may be pitched to a troupe that's composed largely of feminine members. On the other hand, sports cars may be plugged on features known to draw a heavy male bloc. At the same time, narrowcasting or target marketing doesn't eliminate noncommercial broadcasters. Those operators attempt to reach precise factions of the audience that are most likely to pay membership fees or provide additional support for their "free" service. Radio also utilizes "segmentation" to define exceedingly constricted subsets that may be drawn from demographic (gender, race, age, mobility, geography, etc.) and/or psychographic (personality, values, attitude, interest, lifestyle, etc.) dimensions.

Narrowcasting goes far beyond merely programming all-talk or all-news or all-music of one style or another. It's an entire package geared toward a certain type of individual with programming, advertising, public-service announcements, and other data and information geared to that clearly defined mark.[18] And all of this began to predominate in American radio in the years following the medium's Golden Age. Actually, the age of radio specialization goes back much further than most of us ever dreamed — to 1921, in fact, before there were any networks or what could be loosely defined as "full-time stations" in the majority of American cities.

That year, Chicago's KYW, founded by the Westinghouse Electric and Manufacturing Company, literally invented programming and audience fragmentation.[19] KYW aired opera and nothing else six days every week. After the opera season ended, however, the station proceeded with more conventional fare: pop and classical records interspersed with sporting events, lectures, fictional narratives, newscasts, weathercasts, market reports, and political commentary. Westinghouse came to the conclusion that, although it had been successful in airing a previously untried format, it might be best to roll with the punches by diversifying the schedule to retain practicality in the market. KYW thus became one of a growing number of Windy City outlets offering similar features.

Yet while the idea of narrowcasting to a limited quantity of listeners might have been dormant for a while, it never completely went away. Some time following the Golden Age it returned with a vengeance — and remains to dominate the aural ether today. Yet it hardly seems thinkable that somebody would have been applying it more than 90 years ago!

According to one informant, more radio broadcasters in the United States presently focus their operations on country music than any other niche. Most of these are situated in rural zones. Conversely, while the number of news-talk outlets is dwarfed by the sheer quantity of country music stations, the news-talkers — predominantly located in urbanized metropolitan settings — gain much greater penetration by reaching far larger listener accumulations. Thus, while there are more country music outlets, more people hear stations of with news-talk strain than any other.[20] (For much more on this breed, see Chapter 8.)

One pair of analysts (Peter Fornatale and Joshua Mills) perceives shortcomings in the formatting phenomenon. Radio's attempts to deliver listeners to commercial underwriters are called into question on the premise of serving everybody. Pointing out that not all listeners are being treated equally, a monkey wrench appears in the mix.

> These desirable segments of the audience do not mirror the public. Systematically excluded are those substantial elements of society that advertisers are not interested in reaching, most notably the poor and the elderly. Stations tend to ignore programming for children and minorities — until the minorities can demonstrate middle-class economic clout.[21]

A leading American broadcasting educator, author, and contributor to professional journals on telecommunications topics, Christopher H. Sterling, is a listener who has felt the pangs of being disenfranchised in the world of modern radio. As the system focused elsewhere and perceptibly passed him by, Sterling related:

> Like many older Americans, I used to listen to radio, especially in the car ... but ... here in Washington, the medium has left me in the lurch. I used to listen to three stations ... but all have dumped friendly formats to slave after programming already available on other outlets in this market. The main public radio station dropped a decades-long classical music and talk format to rely totally on the latter — including British talk shows that keep giving me numbers I can call in London.... The remaining commercial classical music station got caught in a shift of Clear Channel station frequencies and now uses a fringe transmitter that can't put a decent signal into downtown.... The oldies station that had played music from the 60s and 70s "moved ahead" and now focuses on the late 70s and the 80s. Why do programmers presume nobody of 55 matters? Thank heaven for satellite radio where genuine choice thrives. I almost never turn on a radio anymore.[22]

Obviously, there are issues in which some patrons of the aural arts are being passed over, as if they don't matter much any longer. In limiting the choices that will appeal to them by not responsibly adhering to their predilections, radio justly earns a black mark in that customer-service arena.

Before dispensing with the subject of formatting and programming, a brief overview of a few basics of the packaging of elements encompassing what is heard over the ether could be intriguing. This may be new information to some and its revelation not only may be stimulating but perhaps a little startling. In the modern age, as has been noted already, very few programmers hand to DJs and announcers the arbitrary selection and scheduling of music and other resonant elements. Too much is at risk, with too many internal and external variables impinging on those very consequential decisions. A whole lot is riding on it and the slightest deviation from a predetermined format could cause an outlet to miss reaching some of its desired goals.

Without belaboring the point, careful plans are laid in advance to achieve maximum effectiveness once a show or personality is on the air. This is the result of years of studies and research by the broadcasting industry netting a wealth of data pertaining to carrying out given aims. Preventing dial switching, effectively selling products and services, and keeping the listener gratified are among the primary intents. This is a far cry from having a DJ sit before a microphone and a turntable with a stack of discs of currently requested tunes nearby and having him haphazardly spin them between aimless chit-chat and commercials. Think 1950s.

Nothing is left to chance now, according to well-versed broadcasting authorities. The effective presentation of all of the on-air ingredients follows a meticulous blueprint that a station's program director (PD) lays out beforehand. The design is classified under several labels, all referring to the same documents: program wheels, sound hours, hot clocks, and format discs. These advise the broadcast talent and engineering staff what is to air and at precisely which minute of an hour each component is to occur.

In the talk format, meanwhile, two-way conversation and interviews may fill time that would be allotted to songs in the music format. There are multiple variations adapted by some stations so that not all of them do any of this alike. And, although not every outlet in contemporary times follows such a plan, the overwhelming majority do. Radio programming has become an "exacting science," confirmed one wag. Eliminating the chances of mistakes is a paramount issue.

A succinctly curious explanation of those clocks (wheels, hours, and discs) will be, to some readers, particularly compelling. Ed Shane of Houston, chief of his own media consulting agency, has shared how format clock hours are structured. Shane includes the detail in talks given to college classes under the banner "Clock Construction 101":

Arbitron entries show that the first quarter hour (00:00–00:15) gets the largest number of new entries, that is, when the radio is turned on for the first time or switched to a new station. The third quarter hour (00:00–30:45) gets the second largest number. The second quarter hour (00:00–15:30) gets the third largest number, and the fourth quarter hour (00:00–45:00) gets the fewest new tune-ins. That pattern is why many stations load their commercial content in the final or fourth quarter hour — trying to prevent a new listener from hearing a commercial as the first thing when tuning. Since the first quarter hour is so valuable in terms of new tune-ins, the most valuable programming elements should be placed in that segment.[23]

If this author might take a point of privilege, please allow a reflection on a tangible method of applying those clocks to some personal listening habits. For a couple of decades we've intermittently tuned to a prominent syndicated radio financial guru whose name is widely recognized. While his daily three-hour performance proffers what seems to be fairly sound economic sense, an unsettling distraction invariably has been that every hour is packed with about 20 minutes of commercials and other nonessentials in addition to a five-minute news insert at the top of every hour. The host is left with no more than 35 minutes per hour to help his listeners, his reason for being there. America's broadcast airwaves are top-heavy with advertising, a fact addressed more thoroughly in Chapter 11. While the bills of radio must be paid, a preponderance of ads can make their presence more than a little annoying.

More than a dozen years ago, yours truly figured out that the aural financier was pursuing a constant timing pattern in every hour, every day. Without exception, he ceased his contributions (the meat of the show) for a trio of five- to six-minute commercial breaks (during which a dozen or more commodities are plugged). All the breaks occur at precisely the same time in every hour: 15, 29, and 45 minutes past the hour. There are also briefer promos in the last 90 seconds of an hour, just before the news, and following the news before the next "hour" launches.

The secret is now revealed: turning the radio off or the dial to another station at 15, 29, and 45 minutes past the hour has reduced a boatload of stress for this listener. In this situation the novelty of the hot clock outline is applied in reverse. Of course, the broadcasters undoubtedly hoped none of us would ever discover it. But it works — as long as you remember to return to your show at the designated time the commercial breaks conclude. If the long stretches of advertising pitches are more than a little irritating, try it and see. (Note: The reverse application can also work with some TV series, especially dramas and sitcoms. Experiment and see.)

In contrast to narrowcasting and formatting, let us not overlook *underground radio*. For a little while at least — in a handful of locations — listeners could still hear a hodgepodge of elements blended together and blasting from their radios beyond the passing of the Golden Age. Perhaps they had been accustomed to that style during the halcyon days of the medium. It may have come as a surprise that anybody was still airing it nonetheless when most weren't in the 1960s and 1970s. A concept of practically "no structure" was just about radical in American broadcasting then. Had those behind it failed to get the message about shifting to focused subsets of listeners with limited and very specific preferences? Maybe they hadn't.

> Underground, commercial radio ... debuted in 1966 on station WOR-FM in New York City. It offered listeners an eclectic mix of rock, folk, jazz, classical, and blues. By broadcasting such a unique blend of recordings, it defied the conventional approach to radio programming, which invariably prescribed a single or primary music genre, such as that featured by top 40, beautiful music, country, and other popular formats....
>
> Although WOR-FM's underground presentation was short-lived (lasting but a few months), another station soon undertook the challenge of countering the established norm.... KMPX-FM in San Francisco went on the air with its freewheeling, unstructured sound in 1967.
>
> Many of the individuals who played a central role in developing the commercial underground format were from mainstream stations, which strictly adhered to rigid programming guidelines. These individuals were eager to break from the predictable playlists in order to provide audiences with music that commercial radio seldom aired. The discontent resonated with the rebellious nature of an era that gave rise to significant counterculture behavior, especially among young people....
>
> ...Other early commercial underground stations include WNEW-FM (New York), KSAN-FM (San Francisco), WBCN-FM (Boston), WABX-FM (Detroit), WEBN-FM (Cincinnati), and KSHE-FM (St. Louis).
>
> The format came to a premature end in the 1970s as big business and owners reasserted their control and re-imposed strictures that proved antithetical to the nature of the underground programming approach.[24]

Narrowcasting introduced the concept of trimming the number of listeners to a much smaller size — targeting a specific demographic who maintained common characteristics or interests or goals, a segment that advertisers also wished to reach. It was a trend diametrically opposed to reaching "everybody," a model that had prevailed for decades. And it revolutionized the way we have listened to radio ever since.

8

Talk Is Cheap

The repeal of the bedrock Fairness Doctrine by a 4–0 vote of the Federal Communications Commission (FCC) in August 1987 had sweeping and incontrovertible repercussions in broadcasting. An astute media historiographer observed quite properly that its abolishment initiated a constructive chance "to change radio forever."[1] And an astute opportunist summarily seized upon that occasion to turn it into a monumental revolution of the auditory airwaves. The adjustment instigated, then radically altered, what we hear pouring forth from our radio speakers every day, now more than a quarter-century after the fact. More enlightenment will be shared on that topic momentarily. Before that, however, just what was the Fairness Doctrine anyway, and why was its abolition so historic in reshaping radio's history?

First, it's important not to confuse this with the Equal Time Rule. The Fairness Doctrine pertained to the presentation of and response to contentious subjects while the Equal Time Rule referenced candidates for elective office. Moreover, in August 2011, the FCC formally removed the language that implemented the Fairness Doctrine.[2]

The chief concern of the dogma enacted by the FCC in 1949—almost four decades prior to its retraction—was to make certain that members of a broadcast audience were exposed to a variety of perspectives on any given issue. A couple of fundamental components were highlighted by the canon: (1) the measure mandated that broadcasters set aside some air time for discussion of discordant matters of public interest. Furthermore, (2) the act required them to furnish time for contrasting opinions.[3] News segments, public affairs forums, editorials, or rebuttals of another type perhaps could make "the other side" of an issue apparent on which harmony was clearly lacking. The policy invoked by the FCC in 1949 didn't demand equal time for differing viewpoints, but it did insist that they be offered as a matter of public service.[4]

The first signs that the dogma was being targeted for obliteration surfaced in 1985. That year, the FCC declared that the Fairness Doctrine shortchanged the public by violating the free speech rights that had been assured in the First Amendment to the U.S. Constitution.[5] At the time the FCC chairman was a Reagan Administration appointee, Mark S. Fowler (1941–). A communications barrister by trade, Fowler had served Ronald Reagan on his presidential campaign staffs in 1976 and 1980. Two years after the Fairness Doctrine business was brought into question, the FCC revoked the order.[6]

A couple of corollary statutes of the Doctrine remained in force until 2000, nevertheless. Included were both "personal attack" and "political editorial" directives.[7] The former applied when an individual or limited party (in number) was subject during a broadcast to a verbal assault. It was necessary in those instances for stations to inform those affected of it within a week, then ship transcripts of the incident(s) to them, and to give them a chance to refute what was said on the air. The latter tenet applied only when an outlet aired editorials that sanctioned or dissented against aspirants for public office and specified that the unendorsed candidates were to be alerted and permitted a practical occasion for response.

Having devoted a brief overview to defining the basic concepts of the Fairness Doctrine, let us turn attention to the effects of its purge on broadcasting and, in particular, to radio. It may be plainly stated that, in the mid– to late 1980s, AM radio was in solemn trouble. It had fought a valiant fight against a rising FM continuum, but had come out on the short end of the stick. AM's enduringly powerful image of the past was tarnished as audiences gravitated to the attractive programming mix that FM offered. As listenership mounted on the FM side of the bandwidth, not only did AM lose in audience and advertising share but in long-heralded esteem. An estimated 70 percent of radio's listeners and revenues were invested in the FM band in 1986, an illuminating figure.[8]

With some few notable exceptions, especially in the mammoth metropolitan markets, that era was not a particularly blissful time to own an AM-only radio outlet. (This is delineated with some appraisal in Chapter 6. A few of the circumstances surrounding FM's astonishing rise in popularity, beginning in the latter 1960s, are given and a few of the myriad reasons that prompted it. While FM suffered some substantial lapses in the intervening time, by the 1980s, the newer band was clearly enjoying much more than modest prosperity.) FM talk would also become a permanent resting place for the irreverent "shock jocks" of aural broadcasting, a circumstance that will be broached later in this chapter.

The origins of all-talk radio have been contemplated from manifold perspectives. One common hypothesis purports that the novel format stems all the way back to the early telephone-quiz shows.[9] Those features earned status during radio's Golden Age from the late 1930s to the 1950s (e.g., *Pot o' Gold*, *Truth or Consequences*, et al., ultimately reaching their zenith in *Stop the Music!*

in 1948).[10] Masters of ceremonies called listeners in the home audience to ponder questions. Only the host's portion of the exchanges could be heard at first. Eventually, both sides of the conversations were aired, with a periodic high-pitched "beep" tone signifying that listeners were hearing a telephone dialogue on a tape-delay basis. Some vintage radio analysts are convinced that the two-way exchanges were the historic beginnings of talk radio in America. Admittedly that could be a stretch for some purists who seek a more literal representation.

From another point of view, "the father of talk radio," according to Leonard Goldenson (1905–99), late chairman of the merged American Broadcasting Company and Paramount Theaters, was Ben Hoberman. Hoberman earned the label in 1960. He was station manager at KABC in Los Angeles at the time, a city Goldenson identified as "the most competitive radio market in the world." Although Hoberman was able to turn KABC's sinking fortunes around — from the earliest days after instituting talk, in fact — he himself admitted it took until 1974 until "it [talk] really started to take off." That was the year the outlet finally acquired broadcasting rights for the L.A. Dodgers baseball club.[11]

In the meantime, some other sources have maintained that St. Louis's KMOX shares no less than equal billing with KABC for originating the all-talk show format in 1960. Station manager Robert Hyland contended that his outlet was actually the first on the air with the programming model. Salt Lake City's KSXX (now KTKK) professed that it was third in the all-talk field, five years behind the others in 1965.[12] By the 1970s and early 1980s, numerous key AM outlets across America with less-than-stellar histories in playing recorded music abruptly dumped that programming replica. They, too, hoped to curb the outflow of listeners to more attractive music niches at competing FM stations in their markets. They intended to do so by switching to all-talk orientations. Among the more respected outlets making this transition were KFI, Los Angeles; KLIF, Dallas; WABC, New York; WHAM, Rochester; WHAS, Louisville; WKBW, Buffalo; WLS, Chicago; WLW, Cincinnati; and WRKO, Boston.

Back in the day, however, entered Edward F. McLaughlin (1926–). A broadcasting prodigy, McLaughlin had invested his whole career in radio. He had launched his occupational quest as a salesman at an Oakland, California, station in 1958. By 1964, he joined the staff of ABC as general sales manager for its network-owned KGO Radio in San Francisco. Two years earlier, KGO had become the Bay Area's original news-talk outlet.[13] McLaughlin would soon demonstrate that he was on a fast track of ascent in ABC's organization. His next move, to New York in 1972, found him occupying the presidential suite of the firm's multiple radio networks. During his 14-year tenure there, he amplified the number of ABC affiliates while purchasing Watermark, the radio syndication outfit that produced the massively popular *Casey Kasem's American Top 40*.

But it was after leaving ABC in 1987 to create EFM Radio that McLaughlin was to modify the audio medium in what (so far) appears to be "forever."

EFM was a production venture specializing in talk radio. Once the FCC banished the Fairness Doctrine, McLaughlin categorically smelled the mind-blowing prospects of a bona fide killing in AM radio while at the same time experiencing the possibility of putting his indelible imprint upon it. No more rebuttals to inhibit or obstruct anything said on the air within limits of common decency, he fully ascertained. This was just the ticket he needed to return AM to a flourishing profitability status once more. With just the right stroke of genius, the audiences and advertisers who had vacated AM's premises for the greener pastures on the other side of the meadow (i.e., spectrum) just might be attracted to rethink their devotion all over again.

McLaughlin crafted his plan carefully. At "the start of something gig" he engaged flamboyant Sacramento broadcaster Rush Limbaugh (1951–) to lend his voice to the initiative.[14] Beginning in August 1988, the highly opinionated commentator on local radio abruptly streaked onto the national panorama, his daily rants rapidly drawing a partisan crowd from everywhere. Out of the gate, Limbaugh not only gained a devoted following but enough media hype to turn his name into a well-recognized moniker in many households across America. Within two years *The Rush Limbaugh Show* had mushroomed; it was then heard weekdays on more than 200 stations, most of them AM.[15] A few years hence his series would exceed 600 outlets.[16]

At one point, Limbaugh's daily audience trumped 20 million listeners; it was a pinnacle never before accessed by any radio voice on a sustained basis— more listeners than the combined number of viewers for television's evening network newscasts![17] And despite the fact that National Public Radio recently exceeded 28 million listeners, that peak includes all of its weekly programs combined.[18] What one gets with Limbaugh — like it or not (and obviously, his fans do) — is unadulterated Limbaugh.

Writing in 2012, another radio talk-show host, Fred Lucas, affirmed: "All of us in the business owe our jobs to Rush Limbaugh. Without him, there was no resurgence of AM Radio or the movement to FM Talk that's happening today."[19] Still another wag, Eric Rhoads, corroborated: "AM radio has seen a huge resurgence, primarily as a result of Rush Limbaugh's popularity."[20] The plaudits seem warranted. An anecdote appearing in a text revealing the magnitude of the right wing's dominance of talk radio underscores the venerated regard his followers maintain for the broadcaster leading the parade: A man in his mid thirties on a cramped commuter flight into Atlanta was overheard saying, "I don't have time for a newspaper. I listen to radio for the news and to Rush Limbaugh to find out what's going on."[21] Millions of like-minded chums, characterized by a "white, baby boom-aged, male audience," acquire their "knowledge" from the same dispensary. The flattering, enveloping accolades attest to the hold at times that the man appears to have over a whole nation.

Limbaugh (and several more who have followed in his wake) supplied the substance that Edward McLaughlin originally envisioned. Almost overnight the talk-radio genre received the shot in the arm that was critical to its sudden profusion on the airwaves. McLaughlin would eventually be named to the Radio Hall of Fame (1995) and would subsequently accept the chairmanship of the board at Broadcasters Foundation (1998), a body assisting the needy members in the trade.

In the meantime, and perhaps surprisingly, a couple of prognosticators referencing "the coming assault on talk radio" sounded an alarm prior to the national election of 2008.[22] They were confident that the Fairness Doctrine would make a swift resurgence if only a Democrat was elected to the White House that year. Their pronouncement unmistakably disclosed that one side of the political scale in this country had already wildly benefited by the repeal of the doctrine, and that side hoped to continue doing so. They more than hinted it would be to that base's harm if the measure's exile should be overturned. The political commentators averred:

> One of their [the Democrats'] first priorities will be to reinstate the Fairness Doctrine. They won't be happy until they destroy talk radio by requiring a liberal response to every conservative program....
>
> ...
>
> Suddenly, any radio station that wished to broadcast three hours of Rush Limbaugh or Sean Hannity every day would have to find time for three hours of a left-leaning commentator to offset the time Rush and Sean have on the right. The Fairness Doctrine ... would force stations to hire liberals every where they might not draw an economically viable audience.
>
> ...
>
> If stations were forced to give liberal talk show hosts equal time, they would lose money — and before long you can bet that most of them would abandon talk radio altogether in favor of top forty music.
>
> ...
>
> If liberals win the White House and Congress in 2008, they plan to kill conservative talk radio by requiring stations to balance their content by broadcasting extreme liberal opinions and forcing stations to install liberals in top management positions.[23]

Earth to reporters: Didn't happen; didn't come close. While that singular issue figures decidedly into our discussion, their dire forewarning reveals a number of missed cues along the way. There was an unrelated caution, for instance, that — if Barack Obama was elected president in 2008 — "he would raise taxes immediately and substantially: increasing the top bracket to at least 40 percent."[24] Unfortunately, such faulty predictions only multiplied from that point onward rather than receding into the woodwork. In hindsight, there's still a lot of egg on the face of those soothsayers.

Other conservatives lent their voices to express similar opinions. Upon the election of Obama to the presidency in 2008, speaking strictly of the Fairness Doctrine, U.S. Congressman Greg Walden (R-Ore.) forewarned: "An Obama administration will eventually control a majority on the FCC, and they could reinstate it without a vote of Congress."[25] "The Fairness Doctrine is coming," advised conservative broadcaster Glenn Beck in a December 2008 speech as if it was a fait accompli. "They are going to do everything they can to silence our voices.... What the hell happened to America? Do we need an alarm clock?"[26] A colleague, Michael Graham, deeply concerned about the possibility of the Doctrine's return, penned a whole volume about its potential impact, cautioning: "Radio program content must be free from government regulation, or we are at risk of becoming puppets of the state."[27] Still another spokesman, Michael Harrison, *Talkers* magazine editor, pooh-poohed the doctrine's return, yet pled for watchfulness in any regard.

> Personally, I do not think there was a chance in hell the Fairness Doctrine would be reinstated. But having said that, I don't think we should ever drop our vigilance to protect freedom of speech in America and to protect radio from a regulation that is so outdated and so half baked that it would really hurt radio.... It could actually put talk radio out of business.... I don't think that the reinstatement of the Fairness Doctrine was ever a real threat. But then again, just like terrorism, you can't discount any threat.... Anytime the word Fairness Doctrine comes up you've got to fight it.[28]

As a matter of full disclosure, there had been a couple of feeble Congressional attempts to reinstate the Fairness Doctrine three years earlier (2005). They went nowhere. This followed a similarly failed attempt in 1993 by some Democratic politicians to restore it. Limbaugh termed it the "Hush Rush Bill," explaining: "I am equal time. Within a free market environment I have flourished. I am being blamed for the fact that far more American listeners, exercising their free market rights to choose their hosts and programs, choose me."[29]

Occasionally, a handful of Democratic lawmakers have voiced personal opinions that bringing the law back would be a good thing, but they never have backed up the notion with any more proposals. It now appears that the Fairness Doctrine is a thing of the past and that the literal "war of words" of every persuasion unleashed on the nation's airwaves (and, therefore, the public) which have been rightly or wrongly engendered by the doctrine's removal is unambiguously here to stay.

There are some other logical grounds beyond the repeal of the Fairness Doctrine that have contributed mightily to talk radio's proliferation — on both AM and FM bands. One that has markedly added to the rise of the national talk personalities is an economical means of acquiring national satellite distribution.

Those aural celebs, by the way, have included in recent years the likes of Glenn Beck, Bill Bennett, Neal Boortz, Blanquita Cullum, Lou Dobbs, Barry

Farber, Mike Gallagher, John Gibson, Sean Hannity, Hugh Hewitt, Laura Ingraham, Mark Levin, G. Gordon Liddy, Rush Limbaugh, Michael Medved, Dennis Miller, Michael Reagan, Bill O'Reilly, Dennis Prager, Michael Savage, Joe Scarborough, Fred Thompson, and their counterparts at one political extreme; and Alan Colmes, Al Franken, Norman Goldman, Thom Hartmann, Mike Malloy, Stephanie Miller, Bill Press, Ron Reagan, Randi Rhoads, Ed Schultz, Al Sharpton, and the rest of a contingent at the other side of the spectrum.

One source, left-leaning author Bill Press, identifies Limbaugh, Hannity, Beck, and Savage as the big talkers of the aural airwaves today. That formidable quartet, in that order, so Press asserts, commands larger crowds of listeners than anybody else on the air. Certainly at the moment they are the undisputed leaders in conservative radio.[30]

Parenthetically, in a recent survey, six of the top ten radio talk-show hosts were conservatives (Limbaugh, Hannity, Beck, Savage, Ingraham, and Levin). The source noted that seven conservatives were among the top ten if indeed Dave Ramsey's persuasion is included (his right-wing proclivities are seldom in doubt on his daily financial-advice series).[31] Hannity, appearing on nearly 500 stations in 2010 and heard by nearly 2.5 million per outing, is — in an auxiliary clarification by Bill Press — second only to Limbaugh among the high-numbers stakes.[32]

Some 35 percent of radio talk show hosts labeled themselves conservatives in one mid–1990s exploration while 45 percent claimed to be moderate and just 13 percent identified their personal viewpoints as liberal.[33] Yet another survey, conducted about the same time among patrons at the National Association of Radio Talk Show Hosts in annual session, found that 70 percent believed themselves to be conservatives.[34] Not so long ago conservative talkers were reaching an audience of 87 million vs. 24.5 million for progressives (liberals), including National Public Radio (NPR) in the latter confederation.[35]

Despite the apparent disappointments for leftists, on a typical day both Schultz and Hartmann played to three million listeners each while Miller drew more than two million, some unstinting numbers by progressive standards, according to conservative Fred Lucas.[36]

(Author's comment: If you've been following along closely, you may have perceived what appears to be a discrepancy in the numbers. If Hannity plays to 2.5 million daily and Schultz and Hartmann play to 3 million each, the two progressives may be running ahead of the second-place conservative — following Limbaugh — on at least some [if not all] occasions. However, be aware that the assertion that Hannity is America's second-leading talker [in audience draw] first appeared in print in 2010. The figures for Schultz and Hartmann were published in 2012. While the latter two talkers could be on a roll in recent years, that doesn't establish that Hannity hasn't surpassed them by now, nor does it insinuate that he has reached their present lofty perch. The best we can argue is that all of these men are unequivocally among the upper echelon of current talk-show hosts in America and thereby wield big sticks from their strategic vantage points. Nothing more — nothing less.)

In passing, NPR is traditionally distinguished by fundamentalist pundits and others as being properly situated under the progressive umbrella, although some insiders question whether it can possibly qualify for that extreme. "What you will *never* hear on NPR is what you hear all day long on conservative or progressive talk," allowed Bill Press, "a host spending three hours bashing leaders of one political party or the other."[37] He elucidated still further that — as NPR is funded by taxpayers, foundations, and individual listeners within the public at large — it maintains objectives, programming, and oversight sharply contrasting with that of commercially backed talk radio.

Press noted that, on commercial talk radio, there are frequently acerbic speakers who hurl rancorous darts at one another in a distinct environment that *is* clearly callous and biased. At the same time, NPR can boast that it produces the singular radio series that attracts more A.M. listeners than any of its airwaves rivals.[38] In truth, with the exception of Limbaugh's daily feature, NPR's *Morning Edition* outdraws its competition all day long, besting everybody else on the aural ether. That's an undisputed "win" for the ostensibly non-partisan NPR. (Note: A more comprehensive exploration of the operation of National Public Radio turns up later in this chapter.)

The Pew Foundation pointed out that — with the inception of syndicated programming — outlets no longer had to develop and pay for locally derived broadcast talent. For far less financial outlay they could air national voices that had already proven themselves worthy in other markets. The national voices, quite naturally, belonged to the most successful talk show hosts, several of whom have been named already.

> Radio is primarily an entertainment medium, always in the state of flux. A station's bottom line relies on audience ratings, which translate to time billings, and on the cost of talent. Thus, if a station can switch from local to network talent without affecting ratings, the switch will likely occur; or, should conservatism be more popular than liberalism, or sports more popular than politics, hosts and programs may be changed.[39]

A downside of the shift away from homegrown talent, of course, has been in fostering a genuine disconnect with the station's listeners. (But who's counting anything but dollars here?) Interestingly by the way, at one point it happened that — in those opinionated political diatribes — among the national celebrities on the airwaves the conservatives held a distinct 9–1 advantage over their more liberal equivalents.[40] Reasons have been cited for that, none of which are particularly germane to our line of discussion. It might be added in passing nonetheless that — a half-dozen years or so back — a couple of media scholars prophesied: "The future of liberal radio, if there is one, may be on FM."

The "if" in that declaration may be the operative word for, in the elapsed time (as of this writing), it doesn't appear that progressive radio has left very many appreciable marks on broadcasting — on either band, and certainly not so when weighed against its diametrical opposition. Unless the vast audience of conservatives turns its seemingly unquenchable thirst for reinforcement elsewhere, the station, network, and satellite owners are going to continue focusing their product on the faithful following they long ago began to cultivate. Peter Laufer, a broadcasting professional, added: "The preponderance of successful shows promulgating right-wing content gives the lie to the continuing myth of a left-leaning media."[41] Some left-wing commentators remain adamant about how the media is being "misused."

> Radio and, more recently, the Internet have had enormous impact on the political and social actions, mores, and progress of our society.... Talk show hosts, and Web-site operators who represent the right-wing political spectrum, ... have the talent, ability, and opportunity to appeal to the large number of people who are dissatisfied with one or more aspects of the world they are living in....
> ...They have not done so subtly or, in most instances, with sensitivity. They have done so, by and large, with anger, falsehoods, and vituperation. They have used the media to transmit waves of rancor.[42]

Ill-will, despite the vast lobby group it can draw, doesn't come without penalties. Not long after the national election of 2008, a left-wing broadcaster ruminated: "The hatred and intolerance oozing from conservative talk radio energizes and reinforces the party's hard-core base. But at the same time, it alienates more and more moderates and independents — the very people the Republican Party is going to need if it's ever to fight its way back from the political wilderness."[43] The sage, Bill Press, might just as easily have penned his lines following the 2012 national election.

The stalwarts behind conservative talk radio evidently weren't getting the message, having led an obedient constituency — and probably many independent followers — into the wilderness once more. Will they get it in time for the national election of 2016, revamping their radio talk into something less mean-spirited and more inclusive? There's little doubt that what they say makes an incredible impression on their infinite listening audience.

Press, an industry insider, advanced a theory on what progressives need to help them level the playing field in radio as it now stands. While the answer is simple, getting there — so far, at least — hasn't been:

> For progressive talk to really take off there is one thing necessary. Not restoration of the Fairness Doctrine. Not any edict of the FCC. Not even putting Rush Limbaugh in jail. The one thing necessary is a change in ownership of radio stations. And that's something that only liberals can do for themselves.
> ...
> Ownership! Until wealthy donors step up to the plate and start buying and

building their own network of progressive talk stations, no matter what lip service they might give to media reform, they are only kidding themselves.

Ownership! Until liberals ... buy their own radio stations, progressive talk radio will always be the poor, neglected stepsister of right-wing talk.

If wealthy liberals were really serious about building long-term political power ... they would forget about giving money to individual candidates — and put all their money into building a progressive media empire.[44]

And the beat goes on. There is, thus far, no end in sight to the political bickering on all sides. It's a trademark of radio in the present epoch, one that is deeply entrenched.

We may state without any hesitation that satellite syndication contributed to talk radio's recognized success in gargantuan terms. According to one wag, "The only level playing field in talk radio is satellite." He's referencing Sirius XM, the commercial-free satellite radio distributor that offers subscribers a choice of channels favoring conservative or progressive talking advocates.

Meanwhile, the operations of commercial radio satellite syndicators revolve almost entirely around economics. It was, is, and always will be, of course, that the overriding factor in radio broadcasting is to deliver the largest possible persuadable buying audience to the advertisers for the lowest possible common denominator in capital outlay. On that score the programming and the personalities are merely incidental to the cause and definitely expendable when deemed necessary. Nothing else actually matters (certainly not emotionally, ethically, or morally) to those charged with keeping their eyes peeled on the bottom line.

A conservative talker on the air, for example, will do quite nicely if he/she can draw more listeners — and thereby, more advertising dollars — than a progressive, liberal-leaning host. Or if the progressive will net more lucrative results than a conservative, hire the former. Who really cares? It doesn't matter to most owners when the revenues alone figuratively (and literally) steer the ship.

It may be worth noting that those who comprise the talk radio audience are, according to Michael Graham, generally better educated and better informed than readers of the daily newspapers.[45] Also, as radio journalist Randall Bloomquist observed, "The talk radio audience is *not* representative of America. It's more affluent and mature than the nation as a whole. Roughly three-quarters of talk listeners have at least some college. Nearly 50 percent make more than $75,000 a year."[46]

Talk isn't completely limited to the well-known political arena, however. Arbitron alleged that, in 2008, America boasted more than 1,500 talk-obsessed radio outlets. Something in excess of 100 of the total was utterly focused on sports talk.[47] Meanwhile, dozens more had splintered and compartmentalized into news-information niches like business, computers, entertainment, food, health, tourism, and vehicles. There have been plenty of tongue-wagging broadcasters doing their thing in myriad realms, some of them mostly or wholly beyond the specter of politics. Some even pushed the envelope on decency on the airwaves. Way back at the dawn of the 1980s, for instance...

> America was loosening up, and the need for good personalities was more evident, but few existed outside of the morning slots. Radio sex therapist Dr. Ruth Westheimer went national after a stint on [New York's] WNBC in the early '80s. She became one of the most listened-to personalities in America.
> Meanwhile, irreverent WNBC personality Don Imus was more popular than ever. It appeared that listeners were craving personality after a serious personality drought from an industry full of "more music" deejays.
> In Detroit, then Washington, then New York, Howard Stern was elevated by his listeners as the greatest [pre–Limbaugh] radio personality of all time. Stern was irreverent, willing to take on anyone and not afraid to say anything on the air. He brought common culture's street language to the airwaves and broke the "forbidden unwritten rules of broadcasting." His audience loved it. Stern stood as the hero for their culture as he broke every taboo.[48]

Imus, for one, possesses the ability to cross swords with just about anybody, and has taken special delight in skewering some of his talk show guests. On one occasion country music superstar Vince Gill shared a microphone with Imus as the host brought up the name of Gill's wife, Christian songstress Amy Grant. According to Gill, once the pair wed, "Imus really turned on me. He really liked me before that. On his show he was just ragging us every day for getting married. He just started hammering us."

When Grant's name was introduced into the exchange on the radio, Gill informed him: "You know, I heard you said some things about my wife. I've got to be real honest. That's the reason I came up here. I didn't really come up here to promote my record. I came up here to tell you we need to straighten this thing out. Because we're either going to straighten this out, or I'm going to come across this desk, and I'm gonna whip your butt."[49] It was (is?) that kind of threat that earned Imus a reputation as one of contemporary radio's "bad boys"—that he appears to dote on. Indubitably, he has earned the reputation and continues to revel in it, wearing it proudly as a badge of honor.

Gerald Nachman, in a radio chronicle, explained: "Howard Stern, Don Imus, and their copycat trash-talkers across the land bend humor to their own perverse purposes, zinging celebrities in a volley of innuendo lobbed with raunchy bravado."[50]

Another informant, researcher Annie Brewer, defines the auditory chitchat in sweeping terms:

> A radio talk show is considered one where conversation occurs between host and guest, host and listener, or guest and listener—or in any combination of these. The vast majority of the programs offer listeners the opportunity to call in. Programs which occasionally ask listeners to call in answers to quiz questions have not been considered talk shows.[51]

If this author may be permitted, he is bold enough to add one more deviating component to the talkathon concoction: talk shows sometimes have hosts that *do not interact with anybody except the listener en masse* and then, of course, only vicariously. In such cases the host may address his audience directly as if a response would be forthcoming whereas, in absolute terms, perceptibly there is none. The website for one of radio's current talk show principals (Diane Rehm) applies a sentiment that would appear to satisfy the matter in quite responsible panache: "One of her guests is always you."[52]

Of course, such programs may be only thinly disguised openings for a particular host to vent his or her beliefs and offer little more (think political harangues as one offshoot). There are some exhibitions in which there is little or no conversation whatsoever beyond that offered by an opinionated subject proffering a dynamic demeanor. He's provided a platform to expound his personal beliefs and to possibly persuade a mighty army of silent followers to become as engaged (translation: riled up) as he over issues and circumstances. Stirring up controversy and moving people to action is one of his chief goals.

"The power to influence is not with the content of the talk show," claimed one published source, "it's with the moderator."[53] A Houston newspaperwoman, Donella Meadow, elucidated even more circumspectly: "He or she establishes the rules, decides who to call on, changes the subject, cuts people off.... Some call-in moderators are neutral. Then there's Rush Limbaugh, who is funny and pompous and a scapegoater and hatemonger.... Limbaugh's show is pure put-down humor."[54]

The talk show listeners may relay the disturbed, vulgar feelings they hear from the moderator to colleagues, family, friends, and acquaintances. In such instances the broadcaster has accomplished what he (or she) set out to do. Clearly there are circumstances in which interaction (conversation between two or more individuals) may be in absentia while a talking head is on the air. (Think of a minister addressing his flock as one example; conversational, without human *exchange* in the literal sense at the point of impact.)

A veteran of the local talk show ambit, Peter Laufer, who devoted a generation to officiating over ethereal gabfests in myriad metropolitan markets, conceived a classification system for the men and women who sit behind the microphones every day.[55] One cluster — having done sufficient homework before going on the air — strives for credibility while conveying "accurate information" to the listeners. A second faction makes no effort at all to achieve a semblance of equality, never fazed by the very real likelihood of submitting "misinformation and misrepresentations" to the crowd tuning in. A third deputation is composed of presiding officers who actively exploit radio for their own "propagandistic purposes," intentionally "misleading the audience" through "distortion of facts" in order to "further a specific cause."

The broadcaster applies his sorting technique to step on toes where he feels it's warranted. Citing Adolf Hitler's *Mein Kampf*, he quotes the tyrannical madman of the 20th century: "With the help of clever persistent propaganda, even heaven can be represented to the people as hell, and the most wretched life as paradise."

> Whether or not through study of the use Hitler made of radio [is employed], successful talk show hosts such as Rush Limbaugh have been able to convince huge segments of the population to believe as they themselves believe about politics and culture.... Excerpts from *Mein Kampf* read as if they were written as a talk radio textbook. "Propaganda must not engage in an objective search for the truth.... Rather, it must unceasingly serve its own truth."
>
> Rush Limbaugh and his peers are not Hitler but the techniques being used by the strident, politically motivated talk show hosts mirror the skill Hitler and [German minister of propaganda Paul Joseph] Goebbels used to build national socialism: merciless clever repetition of misinformation and disinformation to a captive audience. American talk show hosts keep the audience captive by successfully combining entertainment with the delivery of information.[56]

Of course, confined solely to the issues themselves, your point of view may be completely converse to that one. This author has no ax to grind and no dog in this fight. We're purely captivated by the intriguing notion that one who walked adeptly in those moccasins is letting us in to his perspectives, throwing a trace of light into darkened corners. (This is admittedly one man's opinion. And while it may to some, on the surface at least, seem to be a jaundiced analysis, who is to say it's not right on the money? Given the tirades that audiences in the modern world fall victim to at the hands of a few radio voice zealots, there could be legitimacy in this introspective.) Several specific instances are cited that tend to make the point relevant, by the way.

By the 1990s, talk radio was unmistakably becoming a national fixation. Interaction between on-air personalities and their audiences through telephone calls, e-mail, and postal exchanges not only underscored but notably increased the listeners' connection with their electronic idols. Talk radio became the new address of the town hall meeting with every opinion solicited and, usually, evenly valued by neutral hosts. Boutique chains appeared on the scene: outlets that were filling their hours with talk generated locally were sometimes uplinking their media-magnetized personalities to share them with the listeners to distant stations. It was a transformation in radio with emerging technologies allowing a whole new way of doing lots of things.

Talk radio came into vogue after some earlier broadcasters realized that the boast "talk is cheap" could be applied to radio. When local outlets let most of those occupying their airchairs go except for the DJs, they had little overhead expense, save for the salaries of the talent, engineers, salesmen, and support staff; equipment and record library maintenance; utilities; royalty payments where necessary; advertising; and taxes and licenses. (The discs were usually available gratis from hungry distributors eager to get them on the air.)

Then somebody figured out that even some of the actual out-of-pocket expenses could be reduced. One wouldn't need to maintain most of the equipment or libraries, for instance, with a host chatting with telephone callers or interviewing guests in the studio. What a novel approach, and possibly even more entertaining and cost-effective! Of course, this was long before syndicated speakers almost altogether replaced the local conversationalists on the ether emanating from many stations. Owners were on a seek-and-find, search-and-destroy mission to trim operating expenses to the bone. If the product going out over the airwaves suffered as a result, so be it — so long as the audience and advertisers remained.

Talk began coming on strong in the 1970s, particularly at outlets in medium- and larger-sized municipalities.

> Seeking alternatives, some stations in virtually every major urban market ditched the news-music format in favor of all talk. Such outlets boasted programming schedules that were characterized by call-in programs, public affairs, interviews, panel discussions, and the like. While brief news updates were retained, they were no longer the centerpiece of each hour's broadcast day.[57]

For almost a decade the politics and social turbulence surrounding America's involvement in the Vietnam War offered a copious mix of spirited themes despite one's own personal contentions. But as time elapsed, the design seemed to be turning hackneyed. Statistical research disclosed that the more loyal listeners were aging and becoming less alluring to advertisers. The all-talk format was desperately in need of renovation. In 1971, it got it at Los Angeles's Storer Broadcasting outlet KGBS-AM, and it eventually raised eyebrows for having done so.

> In an attempt to reach women in the 18–34 age demographic during midday, Storer programmers brought over their all-night disc jockey from KGBS-FM to host the newly created *Feminine Forum*. Bill Balance invited female listeners to call the station and share their most intimate secrets, desires, and fantasies. The response was overwhelming, as the daytime audience doubled within a single ratings period. The program was soon syndicated, and a new all-talk subformat was born "topless" or "sex-talk" radio. As the number of stations that adopted the sex-talk format increased, so did the number of complaints to the FCC. On April 11, 1973, the commission issued a notice of apparent liability to Sonderling Broadcasting, licensee of WGLD in Oak Park, Illinois. The radio industry took the FCC's notice as a strong warning and moved to tone down the incidents of obscene, indecent, or profane language, but audience ratings had given clear evidence of what many listeners wanted to hear.[58]

Even before this, the transcontinental networks were showing unmistakable signs of embracing a hardier concentration of news, investigative journalism, and manifold byproducts, as well as a growing trend toward all-talk orientations. Included in the mix were *Second Sunday* (a monthly 55-minute

NBC documentary series that won multiple iconic awards, 1966–82), *Perspective* (a ABC public affairs commentary feature in dual 25-minute segments separated by a five-minute newscast, 1960s); Mutual Progressive Network (a MBS news service tied to rock-centered outlets going head to head with one of ABC's similarly themed chains, from 1973); NBC's News and Information Service (a financial boondoggle, with 500 staffers producing 47 minutes of national and international news per hour 24/7, but underestimating low recompense and aggressive wire-service competition, 1975–77); *Larry King* (an MBS interview series launched in 1978 that ultimately took the venerable host to cable TV); *Nighttalk* (boosting the careers of personalities Dean Edell, Sally Jessy Raphael, Harvey Ruben, and Bruce Williams upon its overnight NBC inception in 1981); *Talkradio* (ABC's attempt to copy NBC's nocturnal hit in 1982, with Ira Fistell and Ray Briem hosting multi-hour interview and call-in segments); *RadioRadio* (a CBS news slant targeting young adults, sans correspondents, with anchors reporting in two-minute summaries, plus music, features, lifestyle trends, and health updates, from April 1982); CNN Radio (a 24-hour news service updating stories in half-hour cycles, mostly airing the audio of TV's CNN Headline News, 1982 to mid–1983, when it began developing long-form news); *Byline Magazine* (a package of news features syndicated by CBS, from late 1982); *Newsmark* (a CBS documentary series, from late 1982); CBS Spectrum Radio Network (a merged CBS Radio Network and *RadioRadio*, 1990); ABC News & Talk Radio (an expansion of *Talkradio* with conversational dialoguing prevailing to 2007).[59]

These examples reflect a categorical transition from the DJ-dominated formats to those focused on interviews, telephone callers, and ideologically oriented personalities. The talk shows have been running for about four decades in many communities and for about five decades in a handful. Thus, if music in its manifold expressions may be satisfactorily exempted, talk on radio has not only existed but also thrived for a longer interlude than any other programming element.

One published resource by researcher Annie Brewer divided the nearly 1,600 talk show hosts it found on the air by subject matter, discovering 57 varieties (which sounds like a well-known foodstuff processor's advertising slogan).[60] The selections include many that may be grouped in a predictably traditional mixture:

Auto fix-it/Racing
Business/Finance/Money
Community affairs
Consumer affairs
Human relations
Lawns/Gardens

Home fix-it
Medical/Health
Politics
Religion
Sports
Travel

On the other hand, there are some categories that may be somewhat surprising, especially if you're unfamiliar with the ethereal features. For instance:

Astrology	New age
Computers/Online	Nostalgia/Reminiscence
Drugs/Addiction	Pets
Environment	Real estate
Farm/Agribusiness	Science/Technology
Hunting/Guns/Fishing	Senior issues
Legal/Law	Women's issues
Love/Matchmaking/Sex	Youth issues

Among talk radio's celebrated figures in recent decades, generally beyond the political harangues that characterized certain rudiments of the form, were these personalities with established national chain or syndicated followings: Jim Bohannon, Ray Briem, Joyce Brothers, Joy Browne, James Dobson, Ken and Daria Dolan, Tom Donahue, Dean Edell, Ira Fistell, Arthur Frommer, Gil Gross, Clark Howard, Don Imus, Herb Jepko, Tom Joyner, Larry King, Scott Muni, Deborah Norville, Charles Osgood, Dave Ramsey, Sally Jessy Raphael, Diane Rehm, Harvey Ruben, Laura Schlessinger, Tom Snyder, Howard Stern, Abigail Van Buren, Mike Walker, Ruth Westheimer, and Bruce Williams. They are only representative of the fraternity, of course; there are many, many more speaking without overt political undertones.

> Common threads seem to bind the fabric of most talk hosts, especially those who host eclectic rather than single-dimension programs. Among these attributes are a high IQ with quick recall and instant responsive wit; a voracious appetite for facts, and a boundless curiosity fed by heavy reading. Often, these hosts are driven by out-sized ids characteristic of entertainers. One can detect a certain theatricality among some hosts, hear stertorous breathing, and grave voices as from professional mourners. Columnist Russell Baker once termed talk hosts "yakmeisters."
>
> But to view radio talk shows solely as entertainment and the hosts as entertainers is to ignore their force in the national communications community. Radio talk in most cases is in distinct contrast to titillating TV talk. Most radio talk is spontaneous; most TV talk is not. TV talk is usually pre-planned, highly structured, bordering the sensational.[61]

The outbursts of Goldman, Imus, Limbaugh, O'Reilly, Schultz, Stern, and a few more invite exemptions, however. Their personal habits appear to belie any semblance of spontaneity. The series they headline almost invariably insinuate profound tactics in pre-planning, structuralism, sensationalism, and even a fair amount of titillation. But we know, do we not, that there are exceptions to every rule? Biographer of the talk show specter Peter Laufer recognized that any who fill this specialized spot may be considered a "radio god."

Radio god is often the role most talk show hosts place themselves in on the air. It is bizarre that so many listeners and callers bow and pray to that self-proclaimed deity. "Thank you for taking my call!" they say, setting up their encounter with subservience. "I'm a first-time caller, longtime listener," comes out like a chant to an almighty. While the talk show host uses the callers as free actors in the ongoing and extemporaneous radio play that constitutes a talk show, a dynamic is successfully created to convince the callers that the radio god is actually indulging the callers by allowing them the opportunity to fill some air time between the advertisements that the radio station needs to pay its bills. What the callers rarely realize is that most talk show hosts exist in abject fear that there will be no calls, a sign most feel means the show is a failure. While the callers wait for communion with the radio god, the host is praying for calls so that he or she is not forced into an hours-long monologue and an uncomfortable after-the-show meeting with the boss.[62]

It's a point of view that most callers seldom (and maybe never) would think about. At the same time, many of those hosts are egging their callers on. The host knows that the livelier the call, the more attachment for the silent audience tuning in. Talk host Michael Graham confirmed: "One of the mottos of my radio show is, 'If you can't say something nice — call me!'"[63] With some it seems to be a hallmark of their broadcasting directive.

Much has been said about the intense relationship of talk and AM radio and the weighty influence the format had on "saving" the original side of the continuum. It's an indisputable fact that talk turned AM's fortunes around, particularly so in the last decade of the 20th century when that band had almost been given up for dead by the trade. With the exception of some historic big-league broadcasters often typified by 50,000-watt transmitters — operators usually signified by deep pockets that had always found a way to survive in the middle-to-major metropolitan markets — AM was otherwise severely stressed. Talk — locally generated or transmitted by satellite — became the antidote that allowed some of those rival outlets then on life support to be able to survive and possibly to even turn healthy again. Just as talk may have saved AM at perhaps its most critical juncture, in the present millennium the breed has had an incredibly profound effect on the other side of the spectrum.

In this century, sports and other talk manifestations grew more prominently on FM stations. A trade periodical revealed that "talk on FM is the most profitable format in radio."[64] It further acknowledged that FM's successful concentration on verbal exchanges was kindled by a response to "the questionable future of music programming." The realization of satellite radio and other high-tech developments fueled some of these misgivings, providing more wallop for music customers coupled with "less dependency on the tastes and timidity of playlists controlled by bean counters and consultants."[65]

Quoted in late 2005, industry spokesman Jack Swanson forecast some changes in radio format-oriented configurations: "Talk and sports are going to

FM. Music is going to iPod, PDAs, websites, and WiFi, and religious and foreign are going to AM."[66] A couple of reporters acknowledged that by 2007 or 2008, thriving FM talk-oriented outlets were airing from Boston, Chicago, Dallas, Nashville, Seattle, and other metropolitan centers. Furthermore, with Howard Stern's departure from a New York station's staff, that outlet soon converted to an all-talk premise.[67]

A derivative of all of this emphasis on talk and one that has profited enormously in some markets is the all-news station. Five-watt KJBS in San Francisco premiered the classification way back in 1925. Although the little outfit's news-only orientation soon gave ear to a mixture of other untried temptations, at 50,000 watts of power in 1960, KJBS's owners at that time determined to revive its once-solitary all-news format. Applying new call letters KFAX to the revamped programming, within four months the station was $250,000 in the hole — unwilling (and unable) to press its noble gesture any further. Each hour had begun with 25 minutes of hard news, updated as the day proceeded. The rest of the hour was assigned to business news, features, and sports. Trying to be a "newspaper of the air," without enough advertisers, KFAX's formula spelled gloom and doom.[68]

In the meantime a few other broadcasters had been inspired by the West Coast outlet's trial-and-failure effort, enough to audition it for themselves anyway. Some of the early triumphs in this new venture, and the year they converted to *full-time* news operations (in parentheses), included XETRA, Tijuana, Mexico, with a 50,000-watt transmitter reaching the metropolitan San Diego and Los Angeles markets (1961); WNUS, Chicago (1965); WINS, New York (1965); KYW, Philadelphia (1965); KFWB, Los Angeles (1968); KCBS, San Francisco (1968); and WCBS, New York (1970).

New York University's Joshua Mills, a scholar of all-news broadcasting, observed that XETRA (formerly rock 'n' roller XEAK) and its owner, innovative entrepreneur Gordon McLendon, had gone out of the way to disguise its actual site of origin just over the Mexican border, preferring to "sound like" an L.A. outlet instead.

> XETRA's jingles would say, "The world's first and only all-news radio station, in the air everywhere over Los Angeles," or "at 690 on your Los Angeles radio dial." The only address ever announced was the Los Angeles sales office. The station was required by law to give its call letters and location every hour. McLendon handled this by having them done in Spanish in a soft, feminine voice, backed by Mexican music and followed by a description in English of Mexico's tourist attractions. He made it all too easy for listeners to assume that they were hearing an ad for Mexico, rather than the call letters of a Mexican station.[69]

You'll note that two early all-news markets, Los Angeles and New York, were served by competing dual operations. The reactions to that might have been expected but didn't necessarily translate into a drawback. When WINS successfully led the way in the Manhattan market in converting its programming to news altogether, CBS mogul William S. Paley suggested that the net's flagship station might contemplate doing the same, even though it wouldn't be the first there to do it. Some of Paley's executives predictably responded nonetheless, "But WINS is already doing that." Paley, often the optimist, replied as he did on a number of comparable occasions: "So what, we'll do it better."[70] In the modern era, Chicago and New York are served by multiple full-time news outlets; of New York's three, WCBS and WINS are currently under the CBS umbrella. It wasn't usually a particularly smart idea to bet against Paley.

Although there have been many more outlets that have had a crack at news-only operations and ultimately withdrew from the fray, by 2012, a grand total of 13 full-time U.S. commercial stations were generating most or all of their news product 24/7. Four additional stations originated a *preponderance* of their news at designated times in every 24-hour cycle. That latter quartet also presented one or more supplementary varieties of programming to their listening mix (public affairs forums, personality-driven telephone call-in features, sporting events, syndicated shows, etc.). One other news outlet didn't originate its own news material but piped it in from other sources instead, simulcasting that news to its aural audience.

Early in the present millennium the five leading commercial station owners in the U.S. operated 257 outlets with a news-talk orientation.[71] Many of those were running 24 hours daily. Most were heavily invested in talk, with only concise news reports except when extraordinary stories broke. You might also be interested in knowing that the audience of news-talk-information stations in America, according to Arbitron, is typically comprised of individuals age 18 and above. No particular surprise there, perhaps. An estimated 60 percent are men; 40 percent are women.[72]

The programming of a few of the 13 full-time news outlets generating most of their own news product was simulcast on one or more sister stations within an outlet's primary listening zone. A majority of the 13 provided a cadre of locally celebrated broadcasters with specifically assigned disciplines, such as anchors, news correspondents, newsfeature correspondents, weathercasters, traffic reporters, business reporters, and sportscasters. The total of 18 clearly identified commercial news operations in America in 2012 included: WUAM-AM, Albany, N.Y.; WBZ-AM, Boston; WBBM-AM, Chicago; WIQI-FM, Chicago; KRLD-AM, Dallas; WWJ-AM, Detroit; WINK-AM, Fort Myers, Fla.; KROI-FM, Houston; KNX-AM, Los Angeles; WCBS-AM, New York; WBBR-AM, New York; WINS-AM, New York; KYW-AM, Philadelphia; KQV-AM, Pittsburgh; KCBS-AM/FM, San Francisco; KLIV-AM, San Jose, Calif.; KOMO-AM/FM, Seattle; and WTOP-FM, Washington, D.C. The Albany outlet simulcasts news from other sources while stations in Boston,

Fort Myers, Pittsburgh, and San Jose are exclusively news-oriented in certain hours, and news-talk or sports-talk in some other hours.

> The financial commitment to round-the-clock news operations with numerous full- or part-time staff members is — as could be expected — quite expensive. If the proof is in the pudding (product), nevertheless, those journalists appear to be accomplishing the intent of their efforts in awesome style. Tuning them in for a while online can be not only mesmerizing but convincing. It hints that they well may be on to something worthwhile. Furthermore, it suggests that it may not be so long before we are witnessing an infusion of all news-oriented aural broadcast formatting in metropolitan centers in many other markets in this country....
> You might check out those now engaged in performing in that arena. Then render your own verdict after engaging sufficient time to hear a healthy sample. The professionalism, you may well think, could rival almost anything you have become accustomed to on the nation's transcontinental radio chains across the years.[73]

As a sidebar to the aforementioned, one station-owning behemoth attempted a novel approach to increase revenues in a couple of markets. The plan surfaced at least one questionable outcome of its own that was troubling to some members of its audience.

> Clear Channel stations in Madison and Milwaukee, Wisconsin, both sold "naming rights" for their news departments to commercial sponsors. News over WIBA (AM and FM) in Madison, for example, as of early 2006 was being touted as coming from the "Amcore Bank News Center." The potential ethical issues this raised (at the very least suggesting to listeners that the bank in question might have some say in which news was broadcast) were widely debated as news of the naming spread.[74]

Not many places seem ready quite yet to dub their stations' newsrooms with monikers that are so readily applied to stadiums and more athletic arenas, parks, playgrounds, schools, courthouses, libraries, detention centers, roads and bridges, and similar public facilities. It may be a way to increase the bottom line, but at what cost?

Yet another derivative of the radio talkathon — in this case, more accurately a forebear — was the first all-night network telephone call-in feature. It was actually the original nationwide talk show, too. (Larry King was fond of reminding *his* audience that his was the first coast-to-coast show. "Most had no reference point for disbelieving him." As it turned out, he had predecessors.[75]) Herb Jepko christened the province of talk as a genre with a nocturnal feature debuting in 1964 on Salt Lake City's KSL. By 1968, and then labeled as *The Other Side of the Day*, Jepko's overnight conversation had attracted national syndication.[76]

That led to shaping a subculture with its own nomenclature: listeners were labeled "Nightcaps"; they formed clubs known as "Nightstands"; and an ongoing periodical titled *The Wick* was spawned along with loads of promotional stuff (e.g., lapel pins, record albums, etc.). Service products like life insurance, travel packages, and membership cruises followed. There were also conventions drawing hundreds of constituents to their confabs. It was definitely a clubby affair, and affiliation had its privileges.

Renamed *The Herb Jepko Nightcap Show* by November 1974, that's when it truly became the inaugural nationwide talk feature, carried coast-to-coast by the Mutual Broadcasting System. Within a year, Arbitron estimated an audience of ten million insomniacs, working Americans, travelers, and whatever else people do overnight that didn't fit into one of the aforementioned categories. By then, some 300,000 were card-carrying members of the still-thriving "Nightcaps."[77] After MBS began tampering with the content, however, hoping to refocus it from primarily stay-awakes to a more upbeat, affluent, and younger crowd, the wheels fell off the Jepkomobile. As listeners and revenues dwindled in 1977, Jepko was fired. He was briefly replaced by Long John Nebel, who was assisted by his spouse, Candy Jones—but Nebel died a short time after taking over the microphone.

That's when MBS tapped Larry King to become the *third*—and best recalled—personality to occupy an airchair in the progression of moonlight talk show hosts. King arrived from Miami's WIOD. Pretty quickly he became a known quantity after assuming the reins of the five-and-a-half-hour post-midnight marathon on January 30, 1978. Within two years his celebratory status had seen its following increase from a handful of MBS affiliates carrying the overnight feature to more than 200 stations.[78] Eventually it launched King into his own weeknight interview series over CNN television, a show that was to persist until King retired from it during the latter weeks of 2010.

In the meantime, another semi-regular call-in series that premiered over CBS on March 5, 1977, drew nine million listeners who attempted to get through to the host. Only 42 of them actually did so on that occasion, but it obviously wasn't for lack of trying.[79] The host was President Jimmy Carter, who revived Franklin Delano Roosevelt's famous Fireside Chats in a modernized format. Carter took comments and questions from ordinary citizens and responded to them. Rush Limbaugh absolutely would have been blown away by Carter's numbers!

There is another potent segment of talk radio that frequently draws monumental audiences size-wise, including devoted listeners who are capable of exhibiting unstinting fervor for the cause. The vociferous engagement of fans uncompromisingly addicted to sports talk radio is little short of a broadcasting phenomenon.[80] Cultivated in the last half-century, on occasion the resulting fever pitch can—and often does—put reactions to other formats to absolute bewilderment. The sports jocks it draws may not comprise a perpetual audience that is as appreciably large as that of the political talk, music, and news-oriented enthusiasts in many megalopolises. Yet a cult-like fanaticism that characterizes the sports talk buffs is nevertheless as boisterous and animated as many of its counterparts, and frequently more so. (Think in terms of Super Bowl in modern America.)

Typically, the most rabid adherents are men ages 18 to 29. By 2009, the All Sports sub-segment of the radio conversational audience attracted more than 14 million listeners every week. Arbitron identified those comrades as a predominantly male crowd past 25 years of age. The group's demographics further indicate that the listeners are well educated and are high-achievers, comprising a well-heeled income block.[81] "The element of 'guy talk' is an important factor and one of the central ingredients that gives this [All Sports] format its special appeal," affirms Shane Media President Ed Shane of Houston.[82]

Any attempt to under-represent this faction in a spotlight on talk radio would be a clear miscarriage of justice. The wedge it embodies never peaks forever but rises to agitated, euphoric crescendos while subsiding between highs to lesser and more normal (tolerable) levels of discourse. Political commentary may be missing altogether from these discussions; if it's there it's usually tied to some issues affecting athletics which may impinge on kindred personnel (owners, managers, athletic directors, coaches, players, recruiters, trainers, marketers, broadcasters, vendors, etc.). As a part of their usual programming, many sports talk outlets offer play-by-play coverage of local and regional athletic teams in addition to that transmitted by the networks and syndicators.

> In the 1960s, talk radio began across the country, using a telephone and making the audience a part of the show.... Soon, special programs for talk radio were created around sports. On-air personalities fielded questions and engaged in discussion of sports with the public ... on the telephone. On given days, a topic will be established for the discussions. Other times, it is anything goes, with the caller able to choose the topic and ask the question.
>
> The listener is rarely allowed much time to give opinions.... The format is structured to allow the on-air person to display his or her knowledge and background in sports history, records, anecdotes, and so on. Occasional guests from the world of sports frequently sit in, joining in the talk, usually on their sport.
>
> ...The format consists of a producer who fields calls, screening out the nonacceptable callers, and the specialist who performs in the studio, on air. It is a relatively inexpensive form of programming, and the dialogue is at once interesting, and compelling, attracting listeners in large numbers.[83]

"The A-Maz-In" Bill Mazer (1920–), a sports trivia genius, purportedly introduced listeners to sports talk on the radio over New York's WNBC-AM in March 1964.[84] He was airing via the flagship outlet of the National Broadcasting Company. Mazer's arrival in the Big Apple after a seven-year stint on Buffalo, New York, radio coincided with WNBC's conversion to all-talk formatting (1964). But when six decades of heavily impacting the NBC programming legacy was abruptly interrupted, the hallowed patrician spot of 660 on the radio dial occupied by WNBC-AM was dramatically remolded. That founding sports conversation station was suddenly turned into a sports-only broadcaster. The last vestiges of the once-proud network audio flagship and — in addition — a handful of NBC owned-and-operated outlets, were taken apart piecemeal.[85]

> At 5:30 P.M. on 7 October 1988, WNBC signed off forever. WFAN would move down from 1050kHz to air its all-sports programming (and Don Imus) at the superior 660 spot. The Radio City studios had been dismantled, old equipment and memorabilia picked clean by staff and visitors. At its last sign-off, WNBC had been reduced to two model RE-20 microphones. As Alan Colmes delivered the final farewell, in the background a little xylophone rang three times.[86]

And for a while there, starting in 1999, it appeared that NBC itself as a viable brand name had disappeared almost completely, its familiar transcontinental chimes being somewhat difficult to locate any longer.[87] A seemingly serious attempt at resuscitation was made in 2012. As of this writing the jury is still out on that effort.

The first all-sports network, meanwhile, didn't fare as well as NBC. Enterprise Radio (ER) based in Avon, Connecticut, prevailed from New Year's Day 1981 through late September 1981. It boasted a pair of channels, one reserved for talk, the other for updates and play-by-play. ER's talking heads included Ed Coleman, Bill Denehy, and John Sterling — all veterans (possibly legends) of sports broadcasting.

Major syndicators of sports talk radio in early 2013 include the distributors ESPN Radio, Fox Sports Radio, Sports Byline USA, and Yahoo Sports Radio. Programming from these suppliers and others are augmented on some stations with local commentary, discussion, interviews, and call-in shows conducted by hosts living closer to their listeners. Champions of the airwaves are derived as personalities emerge in the communities served. Some are viewed as icons in one or more sports by fans of high school, college, and regional pro league teams. In the broadcast arena they represent, many have risen to the top like cream, referenced as highly prized, well-versed authorities on their sports.

Yet another corps illustrating radio's focused concentration on verbiage is the fraternity that includes public broadcast media. Dual examples are formidable in commanding pervasive followings in the United States — National Public Radio (NPR), mentioned earlier, and its most competitive yet smaller rival for the same audience, American Public Media (APM). Because of the extensive influence that the pair casts on American radio listeners, both will be presented in the summaries to follow. Of this duo APM is the slightly senior service having been organized in 1967, and based at Minneapolis-St. Paul, Minnesota. NPR was formed in 1970 at Washington, D.C.

APM is a nonprofit corporation.[88] It is the largest owner and operator of public radio stations in America and a foremost producer and distributor of public radio programming. Premiering with one classical music station at St. John's University, Collegeville, Minnesota, today APM operates a chain of 43 outlets with a trio of radio services: classical music, news/talk, and entertainment features. The organization purports to stay connected to its listeners through "breakthrough journalism" that taps into its audience's experiences via a newsgathering component, Public Insight Network.

APM is the parent concern of Classical South Florida Radio situated in Miami, of Minnesota Public Radio at the home office, and of Southern California Public Radio in Pasadena. In early 2013, APM was running 49 public radio stations and 41 translators in nine states: California, Florida, Idaho, Iowa, Michigan, Minnesota, North Dakota, South Dakota, and Wisconsin. [89]

That isn't all of its operation, however. Under a rather broad and diverse umbrella, APM owns and operates St. Paul's downtown Fitzgerald Theater (where *A Prairie Home Companion* shows originate each week before live audiences). In addition there is the for-profit Greenspring Media Group based in Minneapolis, a regional and national periodical publisher and event management venture. APM is also a co-founder and key partner of the social networking website Gather.com, which encourages radio listeners to share their responses with others of similar persuasions.

APM is the largest U.S. enterprise currently producing and distributing classical music programming. Its programs are diffused each week by in excess of 800 U.S. radio stations, with a combined reach extending beyond 17 million listeners. The broadcast programming is complemented by a spectrum of new media content and platforms that embrace online Web streaming, podcasts, video, RSS feeds, interactive Web elements, and extensive audio archives. Included among APM's inventory of more than a score of popular aural features are the *British Broadcasting Company (BBC) World Service, Marketplace, Marketplace Money, On Being, Performance Today, A Prairie Home Companion, The Splendid Table, The Story, Wits*, and unique summaries molded by the outfit's national documentary unit, *American Radio Works*. Nearly half of APM's offerings are daily or weekly shows of an all-talk persuasion, underscoring heavy involvement in a field in which contemporary radio chains are prominently engaged.

Funding for APM's operations is derived from a diverse lot of sources. The organization relies heavily on underwriters whose organizations provide much of the revenues that keep APM in business. Foundations run by a range of commercial outfits (e.g., Cargill, General Mills, IBM, W.K. Kellogg, Lilly, 3M, UBS, Wells Fargo, et al.) as well as privately run foundations (e.g., Bill and Melinda Gates, John and James Knight, John and Catherine MacArthur, and many more) have contributed to APM's support. In addition, more than 100,000 individuals are labeled "contributing members" of an enduring APM fan society. The organization further sells merchandise (books, DVDs, electronics, housewares, kitchen gadgets, music, and so forth) and media-related services as a portion of its fund-raising endeavors.

Turning to National Public Radio, after President Lyndon B. Johnson signed the Public Broadcasting Act in 1967, the Corporation for Public Broadcasting (CPB) was born.[90] "Growth and development of non-commercial radio" and programming "responsive to the interests" of U.S. citizens were cited by Congress as CPB's reasons for existence. Although public radio outlets had been airing since the 1920s, principally on college and university campuses, CPB and those independent broadcasters recognized a need for a unified radio service if Johnson's and Congress's thinking was to reach their ultimate potential.[91] CPB instituted technical and professional principles to upgrade what was transpiring at those relatively undersized public outlets. To sustain a national news delivery system, on February 26, 1970, a total of 90 charter outlets incorporated NPR.

In May 1971, *All Things Considered*, one of two daily NPR newsfeature series now routinely heralded around the globe, made its debut in a late-afternoon time period. The second of those inimitable inserts, the newsmagazine *Morning Edition*, arrived on the ether in 1979. Both persist in attracting new listeners as they continue to retain loyalists who have been there for years, some of those staying on for decades. In the meantime, NPR member stations steadily increased — to 190 during the 1970s — while asking NPR in 1977 to be their collective voice in bargaining with Congress. With about 250 affiliates to service in the 1980s, NPR launched the first transcontinental radio distribution chain served by satellite. Also during that decade an explosion of new public programming cascaded onto the airwaves.

NPR's first conversational dialogue series, *Talk of the Nation*, bowed in 1991. Not long afterward the broadcaster spearheaded the public radio newstalk format. Both of these events were outgrowths of the 1991 Gulf War and the reality that people wanted to discuss current issues on the public radio system. With the premiere of NPR Worldwide in 1993, significant expansion of program features and — for the first time — distribution of shows beyond the U.S. borders transpired. In recent years, NPR.org has been created to afford even more extensive reach of the outfit's services. Mobile sites, apps, and other digital platforms have also increased NPR's audience share. A publicist allowed, "Today we are experiencing another era of innovation, not unlike the earliest days of radio, though much faster, and more chaotic and dynamic."

NPR is a privately and publicly funded non-profit membership media cluster that serves as a national syndicator to a present network of 900 or more U.S. public radio stations. Individual outlets don't have a mandate to air all of NPR's programming. Most public radio stations, in fact, offer their listeners a blend of features from NPR, APM, other distributors like Public Radio International and Public Radio Exchange, and locally produced entries. NPR also manages the Public Radio Satellite System that ships NPR programs as well as those from other producers and networks.

Programming fees, grants from foundations and business entities, contributions, and sponsorships provide the bulk of NPR's revenues, which reached $180 million in 2010. About half of that came from the sums assessed to member stations for programming and distribution. Those affiliates typically receive their funding from on-air pledge drives, corporate underwriting, state and local governments, educational institutions, and the federally funded CPB. While NPR doesn't receive any direct federal subsidies, a handful of competitive grants from CPB and federal agencies like the U.S. departments of Commerce and Education go into NPR's coffers. This represents about 2 percent of its operating budget.

Although NPR doesn't carry any genuine radio commercials, brief statements from major donors ("underwriting spots") appear on its shows. These are restricted from advocating specific commodities or any "calls to action." NPR also proffers a wide variety of merchandise to the buying public. That includes books, apparel, electronics, food, music, and trinkets of myriad types.

In addition to the programs previously cited, some of NPR's leading features include *All Songs Considered, Ask Me Another, Cabinet of Wonders, Car Talk, The Diane Rehm Show, Fresh Air, Hearing Voices, On Point, Snap Judgment, Tell Me More, Weekend Edition,* and *World Café*. Most of these indulge profusely in dialogue, interviews, and other garrulous exchanges.

The genuine possibility exists that talk radio in its multifaceted dimensions is going to be with us convincingly, compellingly, and considerably for a long time. Broadcasters are inevitably seeking ways to extract more audience and advertising revenues in order to gain the greatest bang for their bucks. Obviously they haven't run up on anything better or — if they have — they may have run into obstacles that impede their path to whatever else might be an improvement. Securing an alternative could take a while. Success still has a tendency to inspire a whole lot more of the same. For the present and foreseeable future, it looks as if talk in some of its copious expressions, at least, may be with us a while.

As we contemplate hearing more of the same, the mantra of Charles Osgood — who spent his entire professional life addressing people who listened to him on the air — may be ringing in our ears.[92] Talk beckons now at a gadget, device, apparatus, or set near you. Tune in for it today, tomorrow, and possibly forever. *See you on the radio.*

9

Theater of the Mind Déjà Vu

Note: *We interrupt this program to carry you to a wave of nostalgia that swept into radio long after such addictive notions had been put to bed. (Or so we thought.)*

When the last unremitting vestiges of what could be reliably depicted as old-time radio faded from the airwaves in the late 1950s and early 1960s, it was like a wake to legions of American reactionaries who, years earlier, had experienced the genuine article in real time. They were there for some or all of an inimitable period to which they had assigned transcendent status. In its Golden Age, the aural medium — vying for people's attention with very little mass competition — had been a veritable treasure box of gratifying amusement, treating millions incessantly, flourishing at times to astonishing proportions.

When that interval passed at the start of the 1960s, only a few scraps of the epoch's once-proud grasp of a vast audience persisted.[1] But those leftovers were illustrious too, not-to-be-missed by many aficionados who remained steadfastly devoted to "what had been." And after an all-too-brief respite, even those features were bowing out. Zealots who appreciated vintage radio's perseverant gifts were losing their very last literal *earmarks* of that exalted cycle, and irrevocably so. The lingering remnants of a bygone era were — just like a passenger train — departing from the station (albeit an ethereal one) one last time for their final destinations. While many hoped they would return, few sagacious believers felt there was much chance of a real revival. Nevertheless, that epoch had offered an extended and incredibly rewarding run. Among the final ruins of radio's heartwarming tradition, a small handful of weekday features was continuing to entertain and inform the multitudes five days a week.

On CBS, inquisitive host Art Linkletter (1912–2010) was still peeking into ladies' purses and dangling their contents before ecstatic studio audiences on *House Party*. ("Why on earth would you have one of these in there?" he'd innocently pose as he held up a ladies' bra, a set of dentures, or a flask of rum, fully witnessed by a crowd of howling onlookers who were by then practically in hysterical convulsions.) He'd occasionally play "What's in the House?" with a contestant who was given clues to an object in the doll house that announcer Jack Slattery (1917–79) was holding. Getting it right sometimes meant a grand prize of a new dishwasher, a refrigerator, range, or comparable kitchen or laundry appliance.

The most memorable feature of the show, however, was invariably Linkletter's talks with kids. Every day he interviewed a quartet of some of the most precocious preschoolers in Southern California, the kind that—with a little prompting by him—would easily spill all a family's secrets to the nation as the studio audience roared. ("My mom used to be the most beautiful woman in the world but now that she's 35, that's all finished," exclaimed one.) A durable *House Party* entered the aural airlanes on January 15, 1945 and departed on October 13, 1967, although the irrepressibly amiable Linkletter persisted on daytime TV for another couple of years. From 1952 onward *House Party* was simulcast every day on both CBS Radio and TV.

Then there was the 35-year run of Don McNeill's *Breakfast Club*, ABC Radio's hour-long marathon of animated antics in which the venerated host bantered back and forth with singers, comics, announcers, music directors, studio audience members, and special guests. Nobody in daytime radio topped that record. McNeill (1907–96) launched the *Club* on June 23, 1933 (originally as *The Pepper Pot*) and was there for its final broadcast on December 27, 1968. Across the years the showcase for budding stars gave rise to the careers of vocalists Curley Bradley, Janette Davis, Johnny Desmond, Betty Johnson, Alice Lon, Dick Noel, and Ilene Woods, as well as comedians Fran Allison, Sam Cowling, Homer and Jethro, Jim and Marian Jordan, Bill Thompson, and many more.

A snooze alarm that roused millions on weekday mornings, McNeill's brainchild was ushered onto the airwaves from Chicago. It quickly became an authentic and acquired taste of Middle America. For many listeners, the *Club's* silly gags, vocal and instrumental tunes, stirring poetry and prose, witty skits, contests, drives for common causes, interaction with visitors, and a volley of mail read aloud from fans across the nation fostered a milieu for routinely loosening up before taking on the day. The sparkling personalities and the laid-back style suited a diverse crowd that just never seemed to get enough of its barnyard behavior.

CBS's answer to McNeill's shenanigans was, to be sure, *Arthur Godfrey Time*, which influenced many people's routines in the mid-to-late mornings, also for decades. The sometimes unpredictable emcee-humorist-singer—who occupied more hours of network time than any other individual during radio's heyday—was unleashed on an unsuspecting national audience on April 30, 1945, headlining a variety half-hour with live artists. Steadily increasing his power and pervasive grip on the nation's radio listeners, at his peak in the early

1950s Godfrey's matinee exposure swelled to one-and-a-half hours daily, five days a week (several hours of which was simulcast over CBS-TV).

Together with the weekly half-hour simulcast of his *Talent Scouts* program, plus a weekly hour of TV prime time for *Arthur Godfrey and His Friends*, and an extra hour of edited and taped radio highlights of the daily morning show each week under the banner *Arthur Godfrey Digest*, the master entertainer filled about 15 hours of CBS's radio-TV schedule every week. In so doing, with advertisers standing in line to get on his various shows as hard-to-come-by slots opened, he also paid a large percentage of the network's bills.

But it was the morning series that led the way, providing a platform for a string of first-rate musicians who grew legendary reputations in that gifted family (sometimes to Godfrey's chagrin). Among them: Archie Bleyer and His Orchestra, Pat Boone, The Chordettes, Janette Davis, Haleloke (Kahauolopue), Julius La Rosa, Bill Lawrence, Robert Q. Lewis (his summer substitute), The Mariners, Marion Marlowe, The McGuire Sisters, Frank Parker, Carmel Quinn, Lu Ann Simms, plus announcer Tony Marvin. All went well until some of those ascending entertainers grew larger than Godfrey (1903–83) anticipated — or hoped. He dismantled his own empire by firing first one and then another until nearly all of his stunningly accomplished musical staff had departed from their traditional perches.

For his high jinks, a great deal of the public which had doted on Godfrey and his showcase simply fled, leaving him with a greatly reduced venue in wholly evident proportions. As the Golden Age passed — with just one perpetual artist then remaining in Godfrey's stable of stars (Lawrence) — the big man pared down his series to a single daytime half-hour (equal to his early years as a national figure). He persisted to April 30, 1972, the 27th observance of his show's launch. His tarnished image had never fully recovered after Humpty Dumpty had suffered a great fall.

Aside from these few protracted hits from radio's entertainment portfolio for a few years beyond the Golden Age's expiration, newsman Morgan Beatty (1902–75) was still presiding over one of weeknights' calculated domestic and international current-events roundups. After an ephemeral turn as an overseas correspondent and three years as NBC's captain in the nation's capital, Beatty had devoted more than a couple of decades to anchoring his chain's premier evening quarter-hour *News of the World*. While he wouldn't be the last to speak into that series' coveted microphone, he would nevertheless maintain a near monopoly on it, one never equaled by anyone in NBC's imposing stable of radio news voices.[2]

News of the World evolved under Beatty's oversight and possibly under his tutelage. Before he arrived, the network's evening news quarter-hour appeared to languish from a rather oafish, less-than-stunning start. Detracting from it, there seemed to be a lack of a readily identifiable moniker for a while. The series launched on April 11, 1940, with the respected broadcast journalist H.V. Kaltenborn (1878–1965) sitting in the anchor chair. He had only recently defected from CBS in a quest for more editorial freedom at NBC. (He didn't find it, but that's another story.[3])

News of the World also followed in the train of CBS's pacesetting which, in 1938, had captured a strong following for its roundup reporting format direct from multiple far-flung sites — a pattern that NBC fully intended to mimic and mine. NBC appeared to jockey with its newspaper log listings between "News," "News and Comments," "War News" and other fairly evasive and ambiguous labels, frequently with Kaltenborn's name attached to them. He was assigned the 15-minute zone at 7:15 P.M. Eastern Time, a quarter-hour period that would eventually be regarded as something of a "sacred trust" by the tiny handful of commentators who were privileged to fill it.

Kaltenborn's successor at *News of the World* was globetrotting journalist John W. Vandercook (1902–63), an Englishman by birth who stepped onto that pivotal stage on October 21, 1940. (Kaltenborn later gained an exclusive quarter-hour commentary at 7:45 P.M. ET.) Sometime after Vandercook's arrival, the *News of the World* branding was adopted. Vandercook remained at the helm for a half-dozen years, although ultimately he was given a partner to share that invincible microphone.

On July 23, 1945, NBC assigned New York newsman Leif Eid (1902–76) to co-anchor *News of the World*. After only a couple of months into the arrangement the chain tapped its Washington bureau chief, Morgan Beatty, for the co-anchor slot instead while moving Eid elsewhere. The practice persisted for another year, from September 24, 1945 through September 20, 1946. Three days later Beatty slid into the "sacred trust" anchor chair by himself. Vandercook was out the door, accepting a post at MBS to be followed by one at ABC down the line before leaving broadcasting altogether.

Beatty soldiered on solo until he finally reached NBC's mandatory retirement age, departing on September 27, 1967, giving him 22 years as NBC's chieftain on *News of the World*. He moved to a stint with the Associated Press (Beatty had been there before joining NBC in 1941, thereby turning the wire service into bookends on his lengthy broadcast tenure). He was succeeded at his news desk by Bill Ryan (1926–97), the last to hold the reins over that strategic, prestigious evening quarter-hour at NBC. (The following year the series shifted to 7:45 P.M. ET.) Ryan joined the chain's New York broadcasting roster in 1952. He was a familiar voice to NBC's audience via several daily matinee news-headline inserts between longer programs.

Particularly was he recognized by viewers at the Big Apple's WNBC-TV when he and Gabe Pressman co-anchored a 6 P.M. weekday newscast starting in 1963, *The Pressman-Ryan Report*. Ryan had been especially commended by NBC-TV viewers for his impressive reportage at the time of the assassinations of John F. Kennedy (1963) and Martin Luther King (1968).[4] The electronic journalist held a few more posts after leaving NBC in 1970: as a newscaster on New York's WOR-TV; as co-host of a morning show, *Ralph & Ryan*, over Gotham's WMCA Radio; as news director at a Frederick, Maryland, radio outlet; and as senior producer and reporter at public station WNPB-TV, Morgantown, West Virginia.

In the meantime, in mid–1969 — after nearly three decades of current events roundup reporting — NBC finally threw in the towel on *News of the World*. The occasion signaled wiping the slate clean of all hard news on a sustained basis of more than five minutes' duration after dark. An institution that had extended for three decades — all the way from the recovery of the Great Depression and the immediate prewar period — was irretrievably broken with that action. In the halcyon days of radio that noble chain had proudly boasted three quarter-hour newscasts every weeknight: Lowell Thomas at 6:45 P.M. ET; Morgan Beatty at 7:15; and H.V. Kaltenborn at 7:45.

And in the intervening time NBC had given air to copious reporters, correspondents, and analysts on a plethora of news-based audio platforms: Kenneth Banghart, H.R. Baukhage, Morgan Beatty, Leif Eid, Pauline Frederick, Richard C. Harkness, Max Jordan, H.V. Kaltenborn, Herbert Kaplow, David Lawrence, Irving R. Levine, John MacVane, Robert McCormick, Merrill Mueller, Edwin Newman, Henry J. Taylor, Lowell Thomas, John W. Vandercook, and many, many more.

About the only inventory then left in informational programming at NBC after *News of the World* was scrubbed were the top-of-the-hour bulletins, a weekly simulcast of *Meet the Press*, monthly documentaries of *Second Sunday*, and the weekend newsmagazine *Monitor*. Listeners would turn to CBS Radio (*World News Roundup, The World Tonight*) or to television thereafter for extensive domestic and international accounting. In some crucial way the cancellation of *News of the World* indelibly stamped an unmistakable label of "Finished" on yet another fundamental component of radio history — one that had been a powerful and reliable service for millions for many years in its prime.

Finally, on December 18, 1971, CBS pulled the plug on one of its most enduring connections to the Golden Age. That day it suspended a formerly trendy musical staple: remote broadcasts once all the rage, airing from bandstands in hotel grills, clubs, terraces, and showrooms, and fronted by impresarios with celebrated surnames like Dorsey, Ellington, Goodman, Herman, Kaye, Kenton, King, Lombardo, Lopez, Miller, Shaw, and Whiteman. Long before recorded music was considered to be appropriate for radio, the major chains and local outlets filled a great deal of their schedules with pickups of live musical entourages performing at sundry locations throughout the nation. They debuted to excess in the mid– to late 1930s. And although most of those broadcasts ceased in the 1950s, CBS persisted in feeding them by request to a diminishing handful of affiliates. Just 40 outlets were still carrying those Saturday morning gigs when they were finally eliminated.

If we hadn't realized it before then, when American radio listeners heard the last of *House Party, The Breakfast Club, Arthur Godfrey Time, News of the World*, and the big band remote broadcasts, they could pretty well put some closure on a stretch that had originated in the mid–1920s. For all intents and purposes network radio's bubbling fountain of perpetual gifting was approaching its end at last. Only an infinitesimal handful of veritable features were still beamed to the nation via the transcontinental chains.[5] No later than the early 1970s and maybe much earlier, nearly everybody acknowledged that the airwaves had changed forever.

Poet-novelist-scriptwriter Stephen Vincent Benet (1898–1943) dubbed radio the *theater of the mind*.[6] His depiction was coined during the heyday of the mass medium from the 1930s to the 1950s. It was an era in which a plethora of innovative text and rhyme was carried by the transcontinental hookups as dramatic productions, for which Benet penned some of his wares. One wag cited brilliant playwright Norman Corwin (1910–2011) as "the foremost radiowright of the time." Indeed, Corwin was a venerated professional whose creative talents seemed to know few bounds. As his output proliferated, his works soared to literary heights and were turned into presentations that drew legions to their audio receivers in the halcyon era of radio drama.

Taking nothing from the quality accomplishments that abounded on the air in those days, all of it provided incentive to still other imaginative individuals to leave their own marks on the medium. They would do so through dramatic anthologies, gripping narratives, tales meted out in intervallic plotting, and more. The floodgates figuratively opened and America was treated to scores of hours of dramatic absorption every week. Adventure, comedy, drama, mystery, serials, storytelling, and other descriptive metaphors embraced a glut of storyline styles. Until then, Americans had never heard anything like it, and when the Golden Age ended, many believed they would never hear anything like it again.

With the exception of a few rare dramatic efforts, such as those put on by college or high school students, or maybe a repertory company passing through town — including some with unpaid speaking roles — there has been little effort in the years since the 1950s to renew the dramatic scene that prevailed en masse before and during that decade. The networks, as we know, were pressured into dispensing with most of their long-heralded programming with the principal exceptions of news, sporting events, national citations, and an occasional unique feature. And preserving drama on an on-going basis by single stations would be, for most, far too costly to undertake — certainly so on any sustained basis.

Media sage Michael Keith provides some further insights on this genre, casting light on why theatrical productions haven't re-emerged. Following the radio stations' programming explosion into formatted segmentation from the 1960s onward, Keith clarifies, it hasn't happened in any serious extent in modern times: "The radio drama was and continues to be of only passing interest to an audience with a rapidly diminishing attention span and visual orientation. In recent years, Public radio has become engaged in Radio Theater, and it is there that the medium's greatest artistic rendering makes occasional appearances."[7] Of course, a current search for "radio dramas" on the Internet will produce plenty of fodder for anyone seeking it from the past — from *The First Nighter* to *Jack Armstrong, the All-American Boy* to *Lux Radio Theater* to *Ma Perkins* to *Mr. Keen, Tracer of Lost Persons*, and so much, much more. The Web has been a boon to safeguarding a great deal of the historical narratives that once flooded the U.S. airwaves.

Nevertheless, in the 1970s, some of the major networks as well as syndicators decided to test the waters again to see if there still might be an audience for radio drama. They would drag out some of the old transcribed shows from the Golden Age, dust them off, and see what kind of mileage they might achieve with a mostly new generation of listeners who had never been exposed to such on their radios. At the same time, some of those broadcasters would actually proffer a few original shows with freshly penned scripts and a mix of new and veteran retreading thespians. The results, perhaps in both old and new shows, may have been a surprise. It was unmistakably authentic déjà vu and it began to draw a crowd.

During the decade of the 1970s, the radio syndicators acquired for distribution *Heartbeat Theater*, *Lights Out* (which they rebranded *The Devil and Mr. O* in syndication), *The National Lampoon Radio Hour*, *The Lone Ranger*, *The Shadow*, and a few scattered sitcoms and comedy features.[8] And on the major chains there were at least five entries debuting in that same decade, only one of which wasn't original material to any listener. With their networks and start dates identified in chronological order, the five premiering series were:

- *X Minus One* (NBC, June 24, 1973)
- *The Zero Hour* (MBS, October 15, 1973)
- *The CBS Radio Mystery Theater* (CBS, January 6, 1974)
- *The General Mills Radio Adventure Theater* (CBS, February 5, 1977)
- *The Sears Radio Theater* (CBS, February 5, 1979)

During its instigation on the ether on April 8, 1950 over NBC, *X Minus One* attracted a deep-seated, fiercely loyal contingent of followers. Bowing under the flag *Dimension X*, the series' gripping plotlines stirred a passionate faction of the radio audience brandishing a fixation with popular culture. Particularly was this true in the midst of the 20th century when a pervasive curiosity with all things science fiction emerged in the United States. (1951's *The Day the Earth Stood Still,* 1953's *It Came from Outer Space* and *The War of the Worlds,* 1954's *20,000 Leagues Under the Sea,* 1955's *It Came from Beneath the Sea,* and 1959's *Journey to the Center of the Earth* were but a half-dozen of 178 celluloid releases in that decade shrouded in mystery with science fiction at their core, most "coming to a theater near you."[9] This was in addition to burgeoning radio and television series, books, magazines, comics, and newspaper features targeted to that subject.)

Dimension X lasted 18 months. In that manifestation, legendary media critic Leonard Maltin qualified it as a "landmark science fiction series," a value that — due to the perpetuity status it eventually attained — may be very well on target.[10] It wasn't the first of its breed on the audible ether: acknowledging the country's fascination with sci-fi, MBS had already initiated the genre with a rather plain anthology labeled *Two Thousand Plus* less than a month before (March 15, 1950) *X's* debut.

MBS's exploit was good enough to persist nearly a couple of years, however, to January 2, 1952, with narrative titles like "The Green Thing," "The Men from Mars," "The Robot Killer," "When the Machines Went Bad," and "When the Worlds Met."[11] The Mutual entry ushered in a wave of technologically sensitive fare. While that assortment's arrival came fairly late in the Golden Age of radio — just as television was siphoning off large hunks of the medium's rapidly declining audience — nevertheless, *Two Thousand Plus* can be accredited with instituting one of radio's most potent audience enticements.

Historiographer John Dunning, who chronicled much of radio programming in a couple of consummate volumes, discussed science fiction (he terms it S-F in one treatise) as part of a relevant progression of proceedings in audio history. In so doing, he supports the theory of radio purists who believe the theater of the mind is far too intricate to be limited to a wired picture-box.

> The vast and fertile S-F field had been curiously neglected for the entire 25-year history [to 1950] of the medium. Fantasy had been relegated to such kiddie epics as *Flash Gordon* and *Buck Rogers,* with such occasional hybrids as NBC's *Latitude Zero* (1941). Occasionally an S-F story might appear on the mainstream series *Escape* or *Suspense....* But until *Dimension X* arrived, radio left the deeper reaches of the universe unexplored.
>
> The appearance of *Destination Moon* in movie houses helped make 1950 the year of S-F on radio. *Dimension X* rose to the task, proving that radio and science fiction were ideally compatible. The series demonstrated ... that adding a picture to a story of vision, illustration, or myth does not automatically enhance things. The tube is too small, the props too artificial (no matter how ingenious or technologically advanced) to compete with the landscape of the mind. For its time, *Dimension X* was a wonder.[12]

A wonder? Indeed! The substance of that innovative entry frequently pertained to interplanetary movement, although that wasn't its exclusive playpen. The program's narrator-host, Norman Rose (1917–2004), opened the tale totally cold: "Adventures in time and space ... told in future tense! Dimension X ... X ... x ... x ... x ... x ...." The organ came up with an inflating beat merged with drum thumping and cymbals and combined with the theremin, an electronic music gadget with a striking pitch and tone that cordoned the storylines into a rather troubling panache.[13]

Dimension X sported a deputation of cosmological wordsmiths whose accomplishments were already familiar to readers of astrophysical pulp fiction in myriad formats. Among the recurring practiced scribes whose work turned up on the drama were Isaac Asimov, Robert Bloch, Ray Bradbury, Fredric Brown, Robert Heinlein, Ernest Kinoy, George Lefferts, Kurt Vonnegut, and more. Pundit Leonard Maltin allowed: "As network radio headed into its final decade, the caliber of writing not only got sharper, and bolder, but in many ways more adult. [*Dimension X*] ... provided more consistently intelligent science fiction than Hollywood movies did."[14]

Many of its fables were, in fact, adaptations of works in *Astounding Science Fiction*, a foremost journal of the period that reveled in all things linked to the universal unknown — terra firma and its relationships with far-flung astrological entities especially included. Titles, some of which would appear in reincarnations in future exhibitions, were stimulating.[15] Among them: "Almost Human," "And the Moon Be Still and Bright," "Destination Moon," "Dr. Grimshaw's Sanitarium," "The Lost Race," "The Man in the Moon," "The Martian Chronicles," "Nightfall," "Nightmare," and "The Outer Limit."

Superior writing wasn't the only ingredient that urged listeners to find this intrepid ethereal endeavor utterly alluring. The casting of seasoned East Coast thespians added substantial impetus to the soaring heights the series attained.[16] Among some contemporary broadcasting thespians of that era could be found a roster of practiced audio stalwarts like Joan Alexander, Jackson Beck, Ralph Bell, Art Carney, Joyce Gordon, Jack Grimes, Larry Haines, Evie Juster, Mandel Kramer, Joan Lazer, Jack Lemmon, Ronald Liss, Jan Miner, Claudia Morgan, Santos Ortega, Bryna Raeburn, and Everett Sloane.

Beyond their proficient voice contributions, *Dimension X* offered skillfully crafted "futuristic" musical scores while as many as a trio of capable sound-effects techs added bucketloads of credible din to each show to convince the audience that their illusions might be totally believable. Superlative echo effects, for instance, were the result of airing portions of the series from a colossal broadcasting studio that was two stories high. Imagination was literally running wild among its imaginative innovators.

For its first 13 weeks *Dimension X* was carried live, after which it reverted to tape. Sustained (without sponsorship) for most of its run, the feature was withdrawn on September 29, 1951. It had encountered the difficulties that arise from inconsistent scheduling, a precedent that was still to haunt the entry under its amended nomenclature a couple of decades down the road. The show was often transitioned between Friday and Sunday timeslots and frequently interrupted, temporarily scrubbed from the schedule for enduring periods including one 19-week absence during the first few months of 1951. All of it overtaxed any concept of lasting continuity in broadcasting and had to have markedly figured in the series' seemingly abrupt cancellation when it came. Once again the inconsistency evidenced a premonition of things to come. In retrospect, such slipshod treatment was hardly worthy of the high torch that *Dimension X* had brought to the airwaves.

Fortunately for a host of fans who, by then, had become enthralled with radio science fiction, the same show returned under new taxonomy at the midpoint of the 1950s. There, as NBC's renamed *X Minus One*, it squeezed out another three years of astral interplanetary plotting — replete with Martians, spaceships, asteroids, cosmos, overpowering insects, machines that went haywire, humanoids that did so too — the whole bit. It was fascinating stuff and extremely rewarding to a faction of listeners with insatiable appetites for the unexplainable, the future world beyond our own, caught up in the midst of a craze that had swept through sophisticated American popular culture.

Dubbing it a "space opera," historian John Dunning linked *X Minus One* with the corresponding brilliance of *Gunsmoke* of a detached genus, both series debuting in the year 1955 (*X Minus One* on April 24). Dunning lauded the duo as "the most interesting dramatic radio of the 1955 season." *X Minus One*, affirmed the audio chronologist, successfully "blew through NBC like a breath of fresh air [offering] some of the most creative melodrama the medium had yet heard."[17] Referencing a single installment titled "Tunnel Under the World," Dunning cited its machinations about "a public relations experiment so monstrous that it could be done only on radio" as typically ingenious.[18] The reviews of pundits generally proved that if the science fiction classic had accomplished anything since its introductory model had left the air a few years before, it had patently improved with age.

Competent writing, acting, music, sound effects, and directing attested to the faith NBC officials put into renewing the series for a reprise. Titles of a few of its episodes give some hints of the perceptual attention-grabbing engagement that listeners would find awaiting them (and a few will be familiar already):[19] "Almost Human," "And the Moon Be Still and Bright," "Death Wish," "Dr. Grimshaw's Sanitarium," "Honeymoon in Hell," "The Last Martian," "The Man in the Moon," "Mars is Heaven," "Martian Sam," "The Merchants of Venus," "The Outer Limit," "Tunnel Under the World," "Venus is a Man's World," and "Whatever You May Be."

Once again a practiced troupe of veteran broadcast thespians turned up for those intriguing narratives:[20] Mason Adams, Joan Alexander, Joan Allison, Joseph Bell, Ralph Bell, Donald Buka, Ralph Camargo, Staats Cotsworth, Les Damon, Joe Di Santis, Robert Dryden, John Gibson, Jack Grimes, Larry

Haines, Bob Hastings, Wendell Holmes, Arthur Hughes, Leon Janney, Raymond Edward Johnson, Joseph Julian, Teri Keane, Mandel Kramer, John Larkin, Bill Lipton, Jan Miner, Santos Ortega, Ted Osborne, Karl Swenson, Reese Taylor, Guy Repp, Luis Van Rooten, Lawson Zerbe, and scores of other familiar radio players' names.

X Minus One was to persist until January 9, 1958, which was quite late in the auditory medium's Golden Age. That was an eon in which most of NBC's long-playing dramatic fare had already vanished from the ether; only some limited and unfinished business was yet to depart, principally including a few long-suffering daytime serial sagas (*One Man's Family, Pepper Young's Family*, and *The Woman in My House*).[21]

But never say die. At least, don't say it quite yet. Fifteen years past *X Minus One*'s exodus from the airwaves, it was to make a comeback by replaying some of its charmingly fetching transcriptions of the 1950s for the radio listeners of the 1970s. For many in that audience, such dramatic action would be an altogether novel experience, particularly so for those not yet born in the 1950s or who were still too young to have taken overt notice at the time. Many who were older could have heard it all before, of course, but likely didn't recollect any specific storylines. It would be a re-acquaintance for them, a time of reverie and renewal through some pleasant connections with the past.

Moreover, many people who have since demonstrated an interest in old-time radio through attendance at vintage radio conventions, acquiring recordings and published materials, joining old-time radio clubs, exchanging information electronically with like-minded individuals, and purchasing peripheral memorabilia, have attributed their initial influence to the reprise of radio shows aired in the 1970s. Yet another generation of radio buffs has been produced following on the heels of those who, in fact, experienced the Golden Age firsthand. Their numbers, incidentally, seem to be surprisingly substantial, as they have come out of the woodwork to volunteer when they "got hooked" on vintage radio awareness.

The replay of *X Minus One* was stimulated by a joint effort between *Galaxy Science Fiction*, a digest-sized periodical branded "the leading science fiction magazine of its time" (1950–80), and broadcast program syndicator Renaissance Radio Productions (RRP).[22] The pair combined their efforts to revive *X Minus One* for a single performance for the aural audience at New York City's WRVR.[23] On that occasion, on January 17, 1973, a new play — *The Iron Chancellor* adapted from a short story by Robert Silverberg — emerged, featuring actors Jackson Beck, Donald Buka, Leon Janney, and Evelyn Juster. Had it been the intent of those behind the project to intersperse some newly written scripts and modern casting with a reprise of some vintage taped chestnuts and to carry it considerably further beyond the one-night stand? That uncertainty was posed to Jim Widner, a researcher familiar with some pursuits of that nature.

It appears NBC pulled the plug on their attempts most likely when they saw opportunity to syndicate the original broadcasts without much additional cost of production. Doing so, they did not want any competition from organizations using material to which NBC owned the rights. So I think it was all just a request to step away from it. I can't find any legal type cease and desist order, which again reinforces it was all mutual.[24]

What might have been a grandiose scheme in the making — if indeed RRP was looking ahead toward syndicating *X Minus One*— became NBC's own long-term strategy. Obviously inspired, NBC executives gave a green light for its exposure to its affiliates on its coast-to-coast hookup. On June 24, 1973 — just over five months following the performance for the Gotham listeners — NBC returned the show to the air by transcription and fed it across the country, then available to all its outlets. *X Minus One* would persist on a monthly basis to March 22, 1975, a run of just under two years.

Almost immediately the project encountered a huge obstruction that was never acceptably conquered: the chain made some colossal blunders in scheduling. With little, if any, advance notice, NBC kept the repeats of *X Minus One* in a fluid state, moving the show frequently into and out of sundry timeslots. Airing it only monthly, *X Minus One* appeared sometimes on Saturday afternoons or evenings and, at other times, on Sunday, in similar periods. Often, it ran following a baseball, football, or basketball game, seemingly a kind of "catch-all" before regular network programming fare resumed or local shows kicked in. Of course, for those fans not tuned in to the games, they might miss the start of what they had been waiting for. It was a scenario targeted for disaster.

In spite of the fact that series interlocutor Fred Collins (1925–2006) used the last few broadcasts to plead with the public to register its loyalty to the show by writing NBC, the response was insufficient numbers.[25] Most aficionados may not have heard him say it because tuning in consistently so often dissolved into pure frustration. Published radio logs in newspapers listing the program's start time weren't much help when that depended on an athletic competition's unpredictable finish. That was often followed by game evaluations and summaries, too. In a medium where timing was everything, it seemed like NBC was violating every rule.

Hence, it was hardly a surprise when the chain pulled the plug after 22 months. Sterling shows with superlative casts and strong direction in a field that had drawn so much interest just two decades earlier had failed to generate audiences and advertisers alike in the 1970s. The chief culprit was most likely the inconsistency issue. In the midst of a decade that witnessed an almost unflinching nostalgia obsession in America, the competing transcontinental chains learned a valuable lesson from NBC's blunder.

Two-and-a-half months after NBC's premiere of *X Minus One* and that attempt to renew dramatic radio, an unnamed syndicator followed the introduction with its own dramatic series. *The Zero Hour*, a suspenseful anthology produced by the renowned Himan Brown, about whom much more will be said presently, debuted on September 10, 1973, at stations around the country. For 13 weeks its five-part tales were proffered on the ether each weekday evening for a total of 65 episodes. Rod Serling (1924–75) was the narrative's host. Before *The Zero Hour*'s initial run ended on December 7, 1973, the MBS network had acquired rights to broadcast the same half-hour series and was already repeating it daily (October 15, 1973–February 8, 1974, and again April 29, 1974–July 26, 1974).[26]

Unmistakably, however, the most memorable of all the auditory innovations that cropped up in the 1970s was *The CBS Radio Mystery Theater*. Every other network show surfacing in that decade — whether originating then or being a reprise from an earlier time — absolutely paled when compared on almost any level of dynamics to that one. *Mystery Theater*'s commanding lead over a tiny handful of rival entries attempting to return the listeners to those days of yesteryear was never at any time gravely in doubt. Surely an observant Gerald Nachman, who took a lighthearted approach to reviewing many coast-to-coast programs, realized far more than he alluded to when he encapsulated *Mystery Theater* into "a nightly mix of original and classic creep shows."[27] Numerous pundits saw the series as a far more pervasive accomplishment than his conclusion.

The innovative drama was the inspiration of the indefatigable Himan Brown (1910–2010), who had given birth to numerous audio legends over the course of the medium's Golden Age. Brown eventually claimed he had personally labored on more than 30,000 radio shows by the time he was done.[28] Most of those exploited a cache of beguiling sound effects: *The Adventures of the Thin Man*, *Bulldog Drummond*, *Dick Tracy*, *Flash Gordon*, *Grand Central Station*, *The NBC Radio Theater*, and *Inner Sanctum Mysteries* being among their number. It was the latter series, meanwhile, that singularly seemed to influence the venerated producer-director-writer-actor in pushing forward during the mid–1970s on a project that culminated in the unforgettable *The CBS Radio Mystery Theater*.

"Brown's classic mystery and detective shows kept families huddled around their radio sets during the Depression and World War II, hooked on tales spun through actors' voices and the inventive use of organ music, foghorns and other mood-making sounds," suggested newspaperwoman Emma Brown.[29]

The son of Jewish immigrant tailors from the Ukraine, Hi Brown earned undergraduate and law degrees from schools in Brooklyn, the town in which he grew up and where he resided most of his life. Years later he played on the infamous creaking door of the *Inner Sanctum* by reviving it for his incomparable aural hit two decades beyond the intriguing opening's inaugural invitation.

"I'm gonna make that door a star," he wistfully declared. Brown blissfully noted, "There are only two sounds in radio that are trademarked — the creaking door and the NBC chimes."[30] Spiritedly he added: "When that door creaks open, I'm in business!"[31]

Brown had been one of the audio broadcasting industry's true believers in its heyday and was loathe to relinquish the dream he harbored that there was still a prominent spot for radio in the lives of most Americans — even long after television's commencement.

> "I am firmly convinced that nothing visual can touch audio," Mr. Brown said in a 2003 interview, his eyes sparkling. "I don't need 200 orchestra players doing the 'Ride of the Valkyries.' I don't need car chases. I don't need mayhem. All I need to do is creak the door open, and visually your head begins to go. The magic word is imagination."[32]

On *Grand Central Station*, for instance, one of Brown's first hits and an anthology with an ominous opening proclaiming its celebrated depot as "the crossroads of a million private lives, a gigantic stage on which are played a thousand dramas daily," some listeners complained that the chugging sounds of a steam engine weren't typical of the electric-motorized locomotives arriving at that terminal. Brown answered: "You have your own Grand Central Station."[33] His was undeniably swayed of the theater of the mind's utter ability to supersede any man-made alternative.

The CBS Radio Mystery Theater, in the meantime, triumphed while some similar attempts with extended runs in the 1970s didn't perform nearly as well. There are a number of plausible explanations for this. In addition to scripting that at times, admittedly, could be mediocre but was more often exceptional, the show boasted strong direction, an authoritative storytelling voice in the hosting by E.G. Marshall (1914–98), matchless acting that was normally supplied by one or more practiced veterans of the Golden Age sound stage, and abundant additional factors. The series was favored with the consistency of broadcasting five-to-seven nights per week at the same hour in most places. It was also aired in many parts of the country — an attribute that could especially be appreciated by travelers. Those properties combined to grant the feature a leg up on its competition.

Unfortunately, that shouldn't indicate that every little thing was hunky-dory all the time. Audio medium biographer John Dunning decried: "It was still a poor man's version of what radio once was, an echo of its unfilled promise. CBS gave the time but precious little money, and the affiliates felt free to tape-delay or drop it from the schedule at will."[34] (Ah, but for those who didn't give in to those more perverse base instincts, what an awesome indulgence!)

Also, there were times when the scripting lagged and the budget constraints resulted in trimming the number of original dramas to add more and more repeats to the mix. Despite that, *Mystery Theater* was rated by most inveterate fanatics as a genuine success. The fact that the fare it offered had been virtually absent from the airwaves for nearly a dozen years — and almost two decades in any really prolific prime-time fabrication — made it a welcome treat to vintage radio buffs. For years they wallowed in their memories of the delicacies of the past, but experienced a long dry spell since their last sip of wine. It was a happy homecoming for legions among that contingent of dispossessed.

The titles of the self-contained narratives alone were intentional grabbers. A score of them were: "After the Verdict," "Dead Ringer," "Deadly Honeymoon," "Don't Play with Matches," "A Dream of Death," "Dressed to Kill," "Enough Rope," "Frankenstein Revisited," "A Lady Never Loses Her Head," "License to Kill," "A Long Time to Die," "A Matter of Love and Death," "Murder One," "The Night Shift," "The Old Ones Are Hard to Kill," "The Shock of His Life," "Thicker Than Water," "This Will Kill You," "Time Killer," and "Too Many Women Can Kill You."

The various characters were also played by skilled professionals of their craft, many of them returning to the microphones after an absence of two decades or more. Among them: Mason Adams, Jackson Beck, Ralph Bell, Court Benson, Roger De Koven, Robert Dryden, Robert Dryfus, Elspeth Eric, Morgan Fairchild, William Griffis, Jack Grimes, Larry Haines, Mary Jane Higby, Leon Janney, William Johnstone, Evie Juster, Teri Keane, Mandel Kramer, Joan Lorring, Ian Martin, Grace Matthews, Paul McGrath, Agnes Moorehead, Arnold Moss, Santos Ortega, William Petrie, Bryna Raeburn, William Redfield, Tony Roberts, Marian Seldes, and Guy Sorel.

Many of the show's writers could also be heralded with bona fide "cream of the crop" status. Included in their number were: Mason Adams, James Agate, Jr., Murray Burnett, Sam Dann, Elspeth Eric, Frederick Lewis, George Lowther, Ian Martin, Henry Slesar, Sidney Slon, and Roy Winsor.

Premiering on January 6, 1974, the 55-minute nightly odyssey provided a return to the dramatic form that could be exemplified by sheer terror, often a critical ingredient of America's aural addiction in the 1930s, 1940s, and 1950s. Running through December 31, 1982 — much longer than most industry observers would have fathomed — *Mystery Theater* brought chilling tales of greed, envy, murder, subterfuge, rivalry, hate, suspicion, turmoil, covetousness, disenchantment, dysfunction, immorality, lying, cheating, stealing, and other abnormalities.

Those ghoulish narratives were well received by many critics notwithstanding and won for the show a prestigious George Foster Peabody Award for exceptional drama. After CBS pulled the plug on its enduring experiment, producer Himan Brown lamented, "There is no reason that radio can't accommodate drama now"; he also insisted that the medium was "a still-vibrant form."[35] As one of the old guard, then in his late eighties, he was surely one of the few entrepreneurial dramatists who would have been capable of pulling off such an accomplishment. He was as perseverant as well as he was creative and focused.

Chronologically, the next feature to air within the same decade among the major chains' dramatic wares was *The General Mills Radio Adventure Theater*. Premiering on CBS February 5, 1977, it was heard twice weekly, on Saturdays and Sundays. It demonstrated a few traits beyond the tie it shared with its illustrious predecessor as a member of the CBS family. While *Adventure Theater*'s narratives could be characterized as daring, bold, and brave as its graphic title hinted — sans a heavy crime theme as its equivalent *Mystery Theater* proffered — the new series was also 55 minutes in length and was produced by Himan Brown.

After its underwriter dropped out six months into the endeavor, on August 6, 1977 the show was re-titled *The CBS Radio Adventure Theater*. It persisted under that banner to January 29, 1978. Once again, a repertory company of East Coast thespians was pressed into service with *Adventure Theater*, many regulars on the roster being regulars of *Mystery Theater* casting as well.

The last entry among the aggregate of network radio dramas introduced in the 1970s was *The Sears Radio Theater*, which debuted on February 5, 1979 over CBS. Through August 3 of that year it aired 55-minute original narratives five times weekly. Produced by Elliott Lewis (1917–90), another of the first-rate personalities from radio's halcyon days, it was accompanied by the music of Nelson Riddle's (1921–85) Orchestra.

Those narratives were repeated between August 6, 1979 and February 11, 1980. Shifting to MBS at that point, the weeknight anthology persisted as *The Mutual Radio Theater*, running from February 14 to December 19, 1980, after which it disappeared from the transcontinental chains.

This *Radio Theater* pursued an absorbing concept in its delivery of charming fictional yarns. Each night of the week featured a particular host introducing and narrating its acts on a given hypothesis. Monday night brought listeners Lorne Greene (1915–87) with a western-themed tale. On Tuesday night, Andy Griffith (1926–2012) turned up with a humorous plot. Wednesday, there was Vincent Price (1911–93) presenting a melodrama. On Thursday evenings, Cicely Tyson (1933–) bore a love-hate saga. And Friday ushered in Richard Widmark (1914–2008) with an adventure-filled fable. Variety was among the *Radio Theater*'s sparkling attributes.

These five series—*X Minus One* (1973–75), *The Zero Hour* (1973–74), *The CBS Radio Mystery Theater* (1974–82), *The General Mills Radio Adventure Theater*, a.k.a. *The CBS Radio Adventure Theater* (1977–78), and *The Sears Radio Theater*, a.k.a. *The Mutual Radio Theater* (1979–80)—were the major hookups' last-ditch crack at reviving radio drama coast to coast.

It was a synchronous epoch in which the big chains were able to capitalize on a groundswell of reminiscence wafting throughout the nation in that decade.

For many of those in the radio audience, it was their initial (and perhaps only) exposure to that type of amusement supplied by the ether. And for many more, it was a transitory connection in recapturing an infinitesimal part of what had been some of their comfort zone many years before.

"Radiophiles," said author Gerald Nachman, "remain convinced of the inherent superiority of a medium whose full-bodied return we await like members of some cult huddled in remote mountain outposts watching for signs of the true messiah, listening for the sound of NBC's welcoming door chimes — *bing! bang! bong!*— that ushered America into radio's home within a home."[36]

The fact that the 1970s experimentation didn't draw sufficient numbers of listeners, advertisers, and affiliates to sustain its narratives — though a keen disappointment to many, including some in the industry who were wholly committed to that innovative concept — requires no apology. They had hoped that the auditions might open doors to still more chain-fed entertainment as in the days of yore. Although it wasn't to be, the effort was worth doing anyhow: its execution could be termed little short of valiant. The reality that it got as far as it did is a testament, in fact, to the perseverance of a few hardy advocates and a tribute to what they achieved. Without them, millions in the listening audience would have missed hundreds of hours of enthralling theatrical fare.

> In a 1979 speech, Norman Corwin ["the poet laureate of radio"] said with feeling that radio drama could be revived within a week. "It's no great trick. It could be done tomorrow if radio was willing to do it. Golden Age II could be back tomorrow! There's no great mystery to it.... You don't *need* the set! You don't *need* the lighting! You don't *need* the wardrobe!"[37]

Pulling it off is, nonetheless, an opportunity that's still awaiting somebody's attention.

Note: *We now return you to your local station.*

10

Satellites and Automated Dialing

The 1960s introduced some significant technological innovations to the sounds that people heard emanating from their transistors, their vehicles and their table model radios. The advancements were there to stay, apparently to affect the stuff pouring out of listeners' receivers forever. The authorization and implementation of stereophonic FM (highlighted in Chapter 6) is one of the watershed improvements occurring in that pivotal decade. But there were some others which impacted the industry just as strikingly and probably with even greater benefit.

The creation of radio automation and the launch of satellites remain at the forefront of these novel achievements, although the use of satellite would not come into its own in radio for a couple of decades. Eventually its revolutionary effects would make their way into broadcasting where they were to have incredibly enduring consequences.

Taken together, this impressive trio of powerful innovations — stereophonic FM, automation, and satellite — signaled the start of a new wave of upgrades in broadcasting modernization. Ultimately, many Americans would realize that all of this was but the tip of the proverbial iceberg, the launch of an abiding parade of startling, steadily forthcoming advancements that — as those of us living in the present age can gamely affirm — appear to know no conclusion whatever.

An authoritative-sounding disclosure simplified the concept of automated programming to its lowest common denominator. Be forewarned, however: it could prove to shatter a few myths that have been long-held by scads of radio dialers.

> With a computer and a package of sophisticated equipment, a station can remain on the air indefinitely without human participation. Automated stations can easily broadcast music, with a computer switching to recorded commercials at

appropriate times. Prerecorded comments from disc jockeys can be interspersed and the computer can be programmed to give the correct time. It can pick up network news services and other "live" feeds. (A typical package at an automated station might include a computer with memory; four or more open-reel tape recorders for music; two or more tape-cartridge players for commercials — jingles and spot announcements — and an interface with other audio sources for news, network feeds, and so on.) Add to this a consultant who provides the tapes, and you have a local radio operation whose staff might consist of a general manager, sales personnel, an engineer, and a janitor.

...Some stations use the automated equipment to play music then have the computer turn on the deejay's mike for 15 seconds so he or she can identify the songs. At these stations, news is usually done live. But others prefer to have the deejay prerecorded. A disc jockey can record all the material for a four-hour shift in about 15 minutes....

Although early experiments with automated equipment involved Top 40 formats, they have achieved their widest use at Beautiful Music stations, the very purpose of which is to provide "wall-to-wall" music with as little interruption as possible. But automation has been tried with virtually every format.[1]

Another reliable source revealed even more, paring down a station's operations to still less:

For a modest initial investment, outlets could put their facilities on a kind of autopilot, and many did so with alacrity, as was described in *Business Week* in September 1966: "So-called station automation [is] a set of [audio] tapes, featuring bland, middle-of-the-road popular music, coded for automatic switching and broadcast. The object, of course, is to economize on live engineering and announcing staff. A single staff announcer ... can easily operate a station all day." These systems used carefully timed tapes and "silent tones" (below the level of human hearing) that triggered electronic switching devices. Often one tape would contain music from a syndication firm and another the announcements, with tape cartridges providing commercials. All of this was interleaved using the timed switching device.... These early systems were not foolproof, however, and stories arose of embarrassing moments when the mechanisms ran amok before a human could intervene.[2]

Whatever preconceived notions you may have held about the man or woman behind the microphone, revelations like this spark new images of radio broadcasting today, do they not? Armed with such information, will you now be able to listen to such programming from the apparatus you depend upon to deliver your radio features in precisely the same way you have in the past? There may be a rather disconcerting counterfeit quality about some of it if you have believed all along that someone is sitting there continuously uttering the words you are hearing at exactly the moment in which you receive them.

The same is true if you didn't realize that computers had virtually usurped the tasks of the personnel that used to handle most of the mechanical responsibilities at the local stations. Even if a station doesn't offer local news (and thereby has no need for a news staff), most outlets will keep an engineer around to make sure all of it is working as it's supposed to — that the feed is indeed going to the transmitter. But clearly, even that isn't always necessary and it hasn't been for decades.

In its most sophisticated form, automated programming maintains the capacity for an outlet to be running literally without anybody onsite 24/7! It's not quite like having a pitchman such as the Golden Age's renowned salesman par excellence Arthur Godfrey talking *directly to you*— live and in person — in a one-on-one tête-à-tête as if you are the *only one* listening to him, is it? Franklin Roosevelt addressed his national audience as if they were also *one listener* in his legendary series of Fireside Chats. Gone are the days of the close encounters of the intimate appeal!

The introduction of satellites is one of the most stupefying high-tech developments to find its way onto the stage. The original communication satellite, Telstar I, was boosted into orbit in July 1962. It could relay every variety of dispensing contact with the masses, television included. "The event was thus comparable to the laying of the first Atlantic cable or the sending of the first radio signal across the Atlantic," wrote historiographer Erik Barnouw.[3] NBC-TV newsman David Brinkley, passionately exalting the feat with a telecast from Paris, indulged his playful wit by soberly announcing, "via Telstar," that there was no weighty news to dispatch. But the prospect of conveying actions "live" to and from all parts of the planet marked a true defining moment in the history of communication.

Today, of course, satellite transmission is patently familiar to and commonly accepted by almost everybody living in industrialized nations. At its inception, nonetheless, few of us knew what to anticipate and how it would dramatically alter the way we were to receive information and entertainment in the future. Satellites are electronic retransmission contrivances boosted by rockets or transported on National Aeronautics and Space Administration shuttle craft to geosynchronous orbital positions 22,300 miles above the Earth's equator.

A satellite's transponders receive signals from uplink stations on Earth and retransmit those signals to downlink receivers. The satellite itself has a fairly long life due to the fact it uses solar energy to recharge its batteries. Originally, satellites provided wide coverage for radio chains by overcoming barriers that limited terrestrial wireless signals. They also superseded the higher costs and lower quality that wired networks typically manifest. All of this cost-effective retransmission and diffusion by satellite generated a profusion of dedicated radio hookups and programming services.

Be aware that in practical applications, satellites have obstacles that intervene intermittently, deterring even their powerful signals.[4] On occasions like these one is reminded that there are not yet any utterly perfect transmission systems that can be depended upon to operate successfully 100 percent of the time. Although satellite doesn't suffer from many of the reception hurdles that terrestrial AM and FM radio broadcasting operations routinely encounter, nevertheless, they can be temporarily thwarted by heavy rain, thick trees with high moisture content, snow, sleet, ice, tunnels (the latter encountered with vehicle-equipped satellite receivers), and the like.

All of these barriers momentarily obstruct the satellite signal from reaching its intended receptors. (As a practical example, you may have a satellite dish for TV reception that occasionally must be cleared of wind-swept debris or other incapacitating weather-related conditions. The impediments briefly suspend the signal from reaching the dish, leaving the TV screen black. The author has been there and done that on myriad occasions, thus he knows firsthand whereof he speaks.)

Although FM was confirmed as the place for music of all types, many format experiments were attempted to rejuvenate AM radio in the late 1970s and 1980s. AM had reached crisis mode by then.

A renaissance occurred for AM stations with the premier of the Satellite Music Network (SMN) in 1981. Originating at Mokena, Illinois, it subsequently transferred its operation to Dallas, Texas. SMN was the first satellite-delivered chain offering local stations live, 24-hour music programming under myriad formats. With affiliate status, a SMN station could run virtually unmanned with not much more than a computer and a satellite hookup. For stations situated in small to medium markets — and that was the bulk of SMN's member affiliates — all of a sudden big name talent from major markets was being sent to listeners that those isolated outlets otherwise never could have hired.

The formats were widely flexible, enough to permit stations to select from two-, three-, and five-minute newscasts on the hour. At the same time, holes for local commercials or news input were available for filling by partner members. The programming was conducted live and the "national" DJ hosts avoided references to anything that didn't satisfy listeners living in multiple time zones, things that included weather, traffic conditions, sports scores, and local landmarks and events. An 800 telephone line was ultimately provided for spicing up the chit-chat in between tunes. This "personalized" the operation to some extent by allowing the live DJs to receive live or taped musical requests from listeners all over the country pretty much in real time.

It was a new wave of radio programming and underscored a trend in the medium that was clearly distancing those generating what was being heard further and further geographically (and most likely apathetically) from those who were tuning in. At a majority of stations, the heyday of the local (literally *local*) disc jockey had plainly passed. By the mid 1980s, most stations (nine out of 10) — AM and FM — were making extensive use of satellite program delivery.[5]

After six decades, the transcontinental radio chains dissolved their pacts with American Telephone & Telegraph Company for transmission interconnections, replacing wire with lower-cost and more pliable satellite linkages. Almost three score of program services (syndication hookups for multi purposes) became accessible to stations, including 10 digital, 40 analog, and seven that used both. Storecasting soon converted to direct satellite reception, too, thereby evading FM-station FCC Subsidiary Communication Authorization rules (in place since 1955) that embraced functional-music services. By 1986, about 3,000 broadcasters had made the switch to satellite and a tenfold jump was believed possible within five years.[6]

Satellite offered still more advantages. Engineers had correctly ascertained that the higher a transmitting tower, the greater the territory a station's signal could cover. Transmitting from hundreds of miles in space above the Earth, therefore, would extend that exposure exponentially when compared to a mere antenna situated on Earth, no matter how tall it might be or upon how high a mountaintop it might be placed. Very definitely the potential for a transmitter orbiting the earth could be just absolutely unfathomable in its reach.

With satellite's cost-savings, someone who knew nothing about the audience and physical parameters of the communities in which he or she was entertaining might be holding down the fort. For that matter he/she could have been 3,000 miles distant. The good times that many took for granted as the DJs called out the names of multiple listeners living within a few miles of his/her broadcast voice were past. AM radio had taken a major turn, and not necessarily one for the better.

In reality, the only guy actually at the station might be an engineer who made sure that the mechanics of the system were working properly, that the feed from the supplier was going out across the ether, and that the local commercials were inserted in the holes left for them at the proper time. If there was a local news item to be read, the engineer could even perform that task. Once all of this innovation was refined, meanwhile, there would actually be stations in smaller markets running without anybody present at the site on a round-the-clock basis. Why pay for something you didn't need once computer technology reached that high level of refinement? For traditionalists, within the trade as well as those in the audience, it was nevertheless quite a tough act to swallow.

Is there a chance that this situation might be reversed some time — that local stations being programmed from afar might revert to features originated much closer to home once more? Certainly no blanket statement may be made that encompasses every case. As technologies, goals, finances, regulations, owners, competition, and other factors adjust in the future, it's not without precedent that stations could reposition their focus again on the hometown audience almost entirely. Having clarified that, let us not count our chickens too early.

There are voices within the industry that don't give such notions much credibility — and therefore, not a lot of chance for becoming reality, and certainly not anytime soon. "I doubt local radio will ever get back to the so-called 'community,'" allowed ex-XM satellite radio programmer Lee Abrams. "They're going the other way by cutting costs and taking on more remote voice track and syndicated programming."[7] Others have expressed similar sentiments, and logic — for the foreseeable future anyway — appears to be on their side.

SMN, by the way, signed on with dual formats for its affiliates in 1981: AC (adult contemporary) and Country. By the latter part of that decade, the outfit was reaching more than 600 outlets across the U.S. and in the Caribbean. Late in 1989, SMN merged into ABC Radio (later renamed Citadel Media). That's when it transferred from Mokena, Illinois to Dallas, Texas. At this writing the division is labeled *ABC Music Radio*.

Bonneville Broadcasting appeared on the ether the same year as SMN, and ran out of the same Illinois facility. This second satellite service moved out into separate quarters in June 1984. It currently operates under the nomenclature Bonneville International Corporation (BIC) from headquarters in Salt Lake City, Utah. As of late 2012, BIC focuses on radio and TV properties in a quartet of Western U.S. markets. Beyond those, it concentrates on brand strategy, media syndication, and satellite. BIC's Web site is typical of some other satellite programming suppliers, illuminating some highlights that possibly distinguish it from the pack.

> It begins with our stations' intrinsic sense of caring. Blending that with the attentive cultivation of close relationships and the generous use of their broadcasting assets, our stations are so comprehensively integrated and in touch with their communities, they're able to feel a need, define its scope, and then bring their professional resources and facilities into play to respond with a solution. Therein lies our abiding belief in the power and effectiveness of broadcasting localism.
>
> Whether it's producing responsive public affairs programming, creating a local PSA campaign, engineering an on-site live broadcast in support of a charity, or utilizing the incomparable local news-gathering capabilities of our news/talk properties, we foster localism. Our Bonneville stations are as proud as they are pleased to respond meaningfully to local issues and to support our friends and neighbors in their worthy efforts to make life a little better for someone else.
>
> Our program directors, producers, on-air personalities and support staffs take great pride in their responsiveness to the issues and events impacting the lives of our audiences.[8]

It's a sales letter pure and simple, of course, but hints that not every member of the satellite fraternity may be classified as purely plain vanilla. There are operators in the business that — on the surface, at least — appear to take a less caring approach to the communities they serve. If true, the bottom line professes to be of paramount importance to them with not a lot of regard for the listeners who make up their constituencies. That tactic is invariably laced with skepticism among discriminating audience members and leaves satellite broadcasting in general with the proverbial — and seemingly deserved — black eye.

In 2008, an investigative reporter, sharing some of his findings, determined not to mince words with readers about how he envisaged one of the nation's media behemoths, which he references again and again as "the Evil Empire." In spite of Clear Channel Communication's role as the pivotal architect of America's radio, concert, and billboard advertising industries for more than a couple of decades, he pondered, "How did the company once proclaimed the radio industry's white knight come to be held responsible for radio's decline?"[9]

> Clear Channel ... didn't invent classic-rock radio. But ... the company perfected it, whittling a familiar playlist of thirty- to forty-year-old rock songs into what sometimes feels like the same hour-and-a-half mix played over and over ad infinitum. Then they saturated the nation's airwaves with the formula, as well as a handful of other equally rigid radio formats. They also turned talk radio into a nationwide monolith, making (mostly conservative) big names like Rush Limbaugh ... bigger and more ever-present than before. Simultaneously, the company reduced resources devoted to local news coverage....
>
> Anyone who complains that there's nothing to listen to on the radio anymore could certainly lay most of the blame on Clear Channel. Since the late 1990s, Clear Channel has been the biggest radio company in the country, in ... revenue and the number of stations it owns. Clear Channel dramatically increased its advertising revenues, even as it alienated scores of radio listeners who had grown weary of ... unimaginative programming....
>
> ...Since Clear Channel became the nation's dominant popular-music promoter in 2000, ticket prices for shows have gone through the roof.... Many fans have found themselves priced out of attending....
>
> But the real trouble started when Clear Channel tried to create synergies between its radio and its concert division.... It alienated a whole generation of concertgoers by turning arenas and amphitheaters into cross-promotional billboards for captive audiences.... Artists complained that they were being bullied into playing Clear Channel-controlled venues or ... risk being banned from the company's radio stations....
>
> ...Clear Channel ... was making loads of money while producing the dullest radio programming in the history of the medium, and doing so in quantities hard to ignore. The concerts it produced were overpriced and poorly managed. Its billboards littered the landscape. And the company made it known ... it did not care, since it regarded advertisers — not consumers — as its customers.[10]

Another sage, citing Clear Channel's "ugly hardball tactics" which it applied in "destroying media diversity in the United States," confirms some of the above while offering a few supplementary insights:

> Several cities, including Denver and Cincinnati, have charged radio station managers with threatening to withdraw certain music from rotation if the artists do not perform at a Clear Channel venue. The tactic, known as "negative synergy,"

has allegedly been used to pressure record companies into buying radio-advertising spots in cities where they want to book concert venues.

...As a result, Clear Channel now owns, operates, or exclusively books the vast majority of amphitheaters, arenas, and clubs in the country. It also controls the most powerful promoters....

...

Far from fostering a diversity of voices, Clear Channel's monopolistic practices are accelerating the homogenization of our airwaves. The company ... shuts out independent artists who can't afford to go through high-priced middlemen, and is responsible for taking the practice of voice tracking to new heights (or depths, depending on your perspective).

Voice tracking is the practice of creating brief, computer-assisted voice segments that attempt to fool the listener into thinking that a program is locally produced, when in fact the same content is being broadcast to upwards of 75 stations nationwide from a central site. So you have one overworked "radio personality" recording the phrases, "Hello Topeka!" "Hi Springfield!" "How you feeling Oakland?" all day long.

...

Traditionally, the segments were recorded a day earlier, and then seamlessly added into an automated broadcast, eliminating the need for human presence.[11]

Following its rapid growth spurt, Clear Channel Communications was in control of roughly 1,233 U.S. radio outlets.[12] Until ratification of the Telecommunications Act of 1996, the total would have exceeded the legal limit permissible by more than 30 times. (Ownership of 40 stations had been authorized until then.) A substantial 27 percent of the nation's radio listeners were tuned to Clear Channel stations, then deriving 27.5 percent of America's radio revenues. In the meantime, Clear Channel's nearest rival, Cumulus Media, possessed slightly more than 200 stations, more than a thousand behind the indisputable leader of the pack.

Among the numerous dispiritingly destructive behaviors exploited following the ownership changes were these, breaking with longstanding customs at various stations:

> Suddenly differently formatted Clear Channel stations in the same market were sharing newspeople, "which we never used to do." Traditionally, each station wanted its own unique sound and approach, a virtual impossibility under the new corporate structure. The same commercials would show up on all the stations in the market, thanks to one production director shared by all the stations.
>
> The Clear Channel argument ... was that listeners don't really care. But [some] ... felt that such repetition watered down the brand of each station.
>
> Then the overnight disc jockeys were replaced by voice-tracked talent from other markets — soon the rule was no live DJs were allowed on the overnight shift.
>
> ...
>
> What was most jarring was the level of deception employed to give listeners the impression they were hearing a local broadcast. Since there were no DJs, the

station hired a student ... to make public appearances around town, posing as a DJ on behalf of the station. When people called in to the station, they often got a busy signal, purposely programmed to avoid revealing the fact that the personalities on the radio weren't in the studio.[13]

Can you truly not fool all of the people all of the time? A better question might be: Did you ever think radio could (or would) be reduced to this level? Most listeners probably didn't. But the medium may have finally reached its lowest ebb (or common denominator) in this century.

Postscript: On September 25, 2007, Clear Channel Communications shareholders approved a merger pact that joined it with Bain Capital and Thomas H. Lee Partners altogether. By then Clear Channel had sold many of its radio properties in smaller markets along with its television holdings in sum.

> In the years since Clear Channel had pioneered its vision of content, popular culture as a whole had shifted its center. The rise of the Internet had primed consumers to expect limitless variety rather than the short list of "hits" that had motivated previous generations to buy product. The expansive cross-promotional marketing campaigns that once provided the conglomerates with their raison d'être were now rendered increasingly ineffective as consumers rebelled against product-driven media juggernauts.
> ...
> The very notion of an intimidating Clear Channel seemed, for perhaps the first time, absurd.[14]

Still another prominent contributor in the burgeoning U.S. satellite radio arena is Sirius XM, the subscriber-paid, commercial-free distribution service. The venture began as competing rival firms in the 1990s. Following Federal Communications Commission (FCC) approval in 2008, however, XM (with more than 170 channels) and Sirius (with more than 130) merged their separate operations into a single enterprise.[15] Sirius XM runs its business as dual independent units with each proffering a smorgasbord of programming options that include comedy, music, politics, sports, and a great deal more. (In early 2013, subscribers could pick from more than 160 channels in premium packages at about $18 per month plus the cost of receivers that typically average from $50 to $210.) In the United States, satellite radio is distinguished by its sovereignty from FCC censorship, by its comparative absence of advertising, and by its capacity for providing a conduit for travelers to pick up the same stations wherever they are as they cross the country.[16]

An active broadcaster on Sirius XM wryly explained: "All revenues raised from listener subscriptions go to overhead — or to pay Howard Stern."[17] Early in its history Sirius XM signed the outrageous shock jock Stern for an obscene sum that allows him to spew his vulgarities freely and uncensored over the airwaves, a privilege that other ethereal platforms and the FCC had denied him.

There are many more "stars" featured by the satellite distributor, of course, who are not considered offensive to mainstream American listeners.

> Being heard on Sirius XM is great for "branding" and for attracting new listeners. Sirius XM claims it is unable to determine how many listeners are tuned into any one of its channels at any hour of the day. Still, it is probably safe to assume that, with their combined 18.5 million subscribers, there are more people listening to progressive talk radio [as one format example] at any time on satellite radio than on all progressive [left-leaning] talk stations combined.[18]

(Note: Among its myriad selections, Sirius XM provides its listeners with both conservative and progressive talk channels. For a frank discussion of the political overtones in contemporary radio, see Chapter 8.)

In addition to traditional radio receivers, Sirius XM radio content is available by subscription over the Internet, on Apple iPhone and Apple iPod Touch devices, on certain 3G enables RIM BlackBerry smartphones, and mobile devices using the Android operating system.

In the last half-century, automation and satellite services have made extraordinarily commanding changes in the way we listen to radio. As technological breakthroughs continue to sweep onto the horizon, many more transformations may be anticipated. On numerous occasions throughout our lives we've been advised by well-meaning mystics that "the best is yet to be." That certainly may be true. Our experience in distancing ourselves farther and farther from the sources we relied upon in the not-too-distant past for generating the enlightenment and entertainment we routinely hear on radio may possibly leave that prospect in a little doubt, however. It would appear, quite frankly, that for every promising gift we receive, there is a caveat of sorts associated with it. Are we better off now than we were 40 years ago? In many ways very definitely the answer is *yes*. But we have relinquished a whole lot that we loved in getting there, too.

11

Pillaging the Public Airwaves

Congress, which sometimes misses the point altogether while ostensibly attempting to assist rather than impede the progress of the sovereign nation, performed a good day's service for the masses in its time by ratifying the Communications Act of 1934. That milestone, among its multifaceted provisos, makes it unconditionally clear that all Americans are authentic stakeholders in the broadcasting enterprise: indeed, *the ether belongs to all of us*. As a consequence, the national interests are well served on our behalf by the empowerment of an oversight order charged with the answerable task of responsibly safekeeping the airwaves for our benefit. The federal troupe is duly entrusted for our expressed benefit with the protection of what we hear and what we see. One of the aims in its creation was to shield us from content that could be considered inflammatory or offensive to our senses.

> The first principle, established by the Congress, was that *the people own title to the wave lengths of the air*. Private persons and commercial companies may use them as lessees for a limited period, but they have no title to them. Every owner of a radio station, before receiving a temporary license to operate, signs a waiver to any permanent claim.
>
> The second principle follows naturally from the first: the people's property must be protected. And the people must be safeguarded not only from any permanent sequestration of their property, but also from immediate abuse of it by those to whom it is temporarily ceded in trust. One hundred and thirty million people cannot take personal responsibility for the day-to-day management of their affairs.... It is the function of government to do this, for government alone is answerable to the people. Hence in 1934 Congress established the Federal Communications Commission as our guardian.
>
> The terms of guardianship are clear. They define the nature of our rights as owners of property. They define also ... the limits of the powers of the Federal Communications Commission.[1]

The FCC merged the administrative responsibilities for regulating broadcasting and wired communications under the rubric of one agency. The new operation was given broad authority to establish "a rapid, efficient, Nation-wide, and world-wide wire and radio communication service." On July 11, 1934, seven commissioners and 233 federal employees began the task of merging rules and procedures from the Federal Radio Commission, the Interstate Commerce Commission and the Postmaster General into one agency subdivided into a trio of sectors: broadcast, telegraph, and telephone. That unit today has expanded duties commanding a workforce of 2,000 individuals with oversight for newer communications technologies like satellite, microwave and private radio transmission.[2]

In 1960, John F. Kennedy was elected U.S. president and, not long afterwards, attorney Newton N. Minow (1926–) was named his new chairman of the Federal Communications Commission.[3] Minow had no media experience yet, nevertheless, instigated pandemonium in the television industry when he urged significant programming overhaul. His reference to the tube as "a vast wasteland" was, so it seems, indelibly etched on the screens of the public's mind, becoming one of the most enduring metaphors in TV's history.[4] Minow served the FCC only a couple of years before returning to private law practice. Nevertheless, while he was at his federal post,

> Minow brought fear into the hearts of broadcasters, demanding that stations embrace the principles of public service, giving indications that he would attempt to circumvent the First Amendment. Broadcasters were concerned that Minow's policies would censor programming, yet he seemed to favor radio more than television.
> Minow stated that "while TV is a vast wasteland, radio is America's roommate; radio is America's traveling companion. It travels with us like a welcome shadow. We also know that more people depend on radio for news as it happens, and for news of community affairs, than they do any other means of communication."[5]

The landscape of which he spoke was of course prevalent then. It has since been frequently altered due to changes in people's interests and habits — in *how* (by what devices or means) and *where* and *when* they tune in to radio, and *how often* they do so — as well as in technological achievements and other factors that have emerged to impact the listening habits. But when Minow spoke his words they were true of the ubiquitous environment in which radio was operating at the time. And the FCC he headed had an unalterable responsibility for fostering the highest standards possible — for the benefit of all the citizens it represented.

Somehow, in the intervening period notwithstanding, something appears to have gotten lost. The ideals of that generation of broadcasters and the works of more recent practitioners are certainly a stretch. In many ways today's operations are a far cry from what the "founding fathers" of Congressional action would seem to have intended. While a proper examination of the revolutionary changes occurring would require more space than is probably practical here — particularly because not all of the actions were as earth-shattering as some —

a few that have taken their toll on American aural broadcasting will be cited. They begin with deregulation in the 1980s.

> Almost from the moment President Ronald Reagan took office in 1981, a great wind of change swept through the Federal government. While President Jimmy Carter had deregulated a few sectors of the economy, most notably the airline industry, Reagan's appointees to the regulatory agencies, and especially to the FCC, the Department of Justice, and the Securities and Exchange Commission (SEC), embraced deregulation almost as a religion.
> ...
> The FCC also changed the so-called 7–7–7 formula. This limited any entity, including networks, to ownership of not more than seven AM radio stations, seven FM radio stations, and seven television stations, only five of which could be VHF. Under the new rules, starting in January 1985, one could own up to twelve stations in each category, as long as the stations collectively reached no more than 25 percent of the total United States population.
> At the same time, other Reagan appointees in the Department of Justice were signaling their intentions to allow virtually any merger or takeover. Many of the considerations that for decades had guided the Antitrust Division's scrutiny went out the window.[6]

In the sweeping changes that occurred during that pivotal epoch, the industry saw license-renewal requirements to determine the needs of community groups abolished. Mandates to apportion 6 to 8 percent of broadcast time for radio news or public service programming also went by the wayside, as did commercial time limits of 18 minutes per hour, and performance summaries from licensees. Applications for station licenses were condensed to postcard size. Then came easing the station ownership limits as well as abolishing a rule that licenses be held for at least three years. Competitive bids for stations also disappeared.[7] It was an altogether new way of doing business for the public trust.

"A gold rush followed," assessed one reporter. In the years 1982–88, sales of radio stations leaped from $602 million to $3.4 billion. Fifteen hundred U.S. outlets changed hands in 1985 alone as the quartet of enduring transcontinental chains (ABC, CBS, MBS, and NBC) became prime takeover targets. "Has the FCC Gone Too Far?" blared a *Business Week* headline.[8]

> An immediate casualty was "localism." Under public interest licensing, on-air access for community groups, local events coverage, and jobs for young talent had been "givens".... Freed from public interest mandates, hordes of stations simply were automated for satellite-relayed music and news/weather headlines.
> An almost complete absence of local on-air staff became the norm. Without specific disclosures to listeners, satellite-relayed "voice-tracking" enabled centrally based announcers, disc jockeys, or newsreaders to serve multiple outlets. By 2000 one-third of U.S. radio outlets had no news personnel. Of the two-thirds which did, 12,000 jobs were part time.[9]

A veteran broadcaster who has closely observed the rise and fall of the tide in radio policies postulates with derision the outcome of deregulation and implementation of new directives on the trade in the last two decades of the 20th century.

> I would argue that, far more damaging to diversity in talk radio than effective abolition of the Fairness Doctrine in 1987 was passage of the Telecommunications Act of 1996.... That legislation hurt in two ways. It both erased the limit on the number of radio stations any one company could own nationwide and increased the limit any one company could own in the same market, from two to eight. Previously, companies were restricted to owning 28 stations nationwide and two stations in any one market. Today, those regulations have been greatly relaxed. As a result, Clear Channel, for example, was able to expand rapidly from its 40 stations to over 1,200. On the national level, allowing one company to own an unlimited number of stations gives a huge advantage to nationally syndicated programming....
>
> ...
>
> For the big companies, it's even sweeter when they own multiple stations in the same market: usually, that means one big 50,000-watt signal, and several smaller, 3–5,000-watt signals. Having shut out any competition in the same market, they are then free to make whatever corporate decisions serve their own purposes, and always do.[10]

"Clear Channel Communications became the obvious poster child of what can happen under a changing regulatory climate," a couple of media researchers, Christopher Sterling and Michael Keith, pontificated.[11] And in the intervening years — as a result — it has been the public itself, without the protections of earlier years, that has unmistakably gotten the shaft.

With the proliferation of stations possible for a single operator to acquire, bad tidings were among whatever shouts of joy may have arisen.

But the dismantling wasn't over even then. In 2003, once more without any public hearings, Bush-appointed chairman Michael Powell led the FCC to legitimize an even greater concentration of station ownership. By a party-line vote of 3–2, the right-leaning FCC raised nationwide audience caps to 45 percent per owner. For print-radio-TV combos the caps were raised to almost half the population (49 percent).

The previous year (2002), 25 such radio broadcasting chains in the United States owned a fourth of all the nation's commercial radio properties with just 15 chains pulling in a third of the trade's advertising revenues. And the four once-powerful national chains (dating back to the 1920s, 1930s, and 1940s) became, at the turn of the century, concentrated in the hands of just two mammoth corporate owners — Viacom Inc. and Walt Disney Company — for whom those broadcasting linkages would be ever-decreasing slices of their operational pies.[12]

The ten largest media concerns in the U.S. in 2011— several of them controlling vast numbers of television and radio networks as well as numerous local outlets — are regularly updated on the Internet. Such information is revised to reflect new acquisitions and innovations (properties, brands, chains, publications, websites, etc.) that have been introduced as well as divestitures. All of it ascertains that what we hear, see, read, and interact with by way of media jurisdiction is placed solidly in the hands of a few tycoons that run those iconic firms. "In many cases," attests a modern watchdog, "these companies are vertically integrated, controlling everything from initial production to final distribution."[13] The source further signifies:

> Broadcasters make billions in profits while using the public airwaves for free. In return, they are supposed to provide programming that fulfills community needs. Instead, lobbyists have successfully fought to make it easier for broadcast companies to gobble up even more free airspace while doing less to serve the public....
>
> Access to high-speed Internet service — also known as broadband — has become a basic public necessity, just like water or electricity. Yet despite its importance, broadband access in the United States is far from universal. Millions of Americans still stand on the wrong side of the "digital divide," unable to tap into the political, economic and social resources of the Web. Meanwhile, cable and phone companies — which hold virtual monopolies over the infrastructure of the Internet — often refuse to build out high-speed broadband to regions that need it most, and actively seek to block communities from seeking their own broadband solutions....
>
> Consolidation has contributed to tough times for the newspaper industry. When the industry was swimming in profits in the 1990s, big media companies used 14–27 percent profit margins to buy up other properties rather than invest in the quality of their existing products or innovate for the future. Now they want to make it possible for a given company to own a newspaper and a broadcast station in the same market....
>
> Giant companies like Apple, Facebook and Google are slowly reconstituting the Internet's walled gardens of old. As these companies try to steer us to their increasingly closed versions of the Internet — and to marketers who benefit from mining our personal information — we must fight for policies that protect our rights as Internet users.

In 2011, the top 10 media behemoths in America and their revenues that year included (alphabetically):

- Bain Capital/Thomas H. Lee Partners (Clear Channel) — $6.2 billion
- CBS Corporation — $14.2 billion
- Comcast Corporation — $55.8 billion
- Gannett Company — $5.2 billion
- News Corporation — $33.4 billion
- Time Warner, Inc. — $29 billion
- Tribune Company — $3.2 billion
- Viacom — $14.9 billion

- Walt Disney Company — $40.1 billion
- Washington Post Company — $4.2 billion
- *Grand total for top 10 in one year* — $206.2 billion

That's not a shabby haul for 10 outfits in a single year that so heavily influence the sources we depend on for our everyday education and entertainment.

A review of America's radio stations in 2007 conducted by the Center for American Progress/Free Press revealed that the largest concentration of the nation's news-talk radio outlets was in the hands of just five powerful media conglomerates that plainly dominated that industry. Although the five acted independently of each other, they provided listeners across the country with an enveloping load of the very same syndicated programming. As a result those five titanic-proportioned operators determined much of what Americans could tune in to on their radios.

That handful of owners directed a significant percentage of the powerful 50,000-watt superchannel outlets available. (As an aside, of the 257 stations with news-talk formats owned by those five megapowers, 229 — 89.2 percent, or nine out of ten — were exclusively airing conservative-oriented programming while the remaining 28 favored progressives.[14] The political slant, according to one partisan, is because "that's what conservative owners demand," a hypothesis that has been difficult to refute.[15]) It's a disclosure concerning the radio resources that the U.S. relies upon for its information. (As *Dragnet's* Jack Webb used to say, "Just the facts," and that's what these are.) At the time of the study referenced, the five mega *mediarites* included:

- Clear Channel — 145 stations
- Cumulus — 31 stations
- CBS — 30 stations
- Salem — 28 stations
- Citadel[16] — 23 stations

Another of the debilitating outcomes of federal deregulation experienced by the public is the effect that has occurred — and progressively worsened — in regard to the lifting of controls over broadcast advertising policies. Parenthetically, there were more than 1500 U.S. stations running without direct advertising revenues in 2010.[17] They relied on a diverse number of sources for support embracing foundations, fund-raisers, small individual gift-givers, organizational and public treasuries, volunteers, wealthy donors, and so forth.

Most of the remaining stations, however — a preponderance of all U.S. radio outlets — run in traditional businesslike fashion, almost wholly dependent upon time sales to commercial enterprises for their operating income. In 1981, the FCC allowed them to dramatically adjust the way they perform that task, departing from their longstanding traditions. A few years ago, while researching another tome, this author condemned the turn of events that has allowed radio advertising to distance itself so far from its roots.[18]

> The next time you tune in a talk show or golden oldies showcase on your automated format radio station, punctuated by four to six commercial interruptions every hour, each typically extending three to six minutes, think about the advertising during radio's heyday. The greed of unmitigated excess so pervasive now would have been unimaginable then. Traditionally, the golden age commercials occupied about 12 minutes of network air per hour before evening arrived, and only six minutes during the primetime hours....
> "And now, a word from our sponsor" all those years ago meant essentially that. By comparison, that would be welcome relief today. Those staunch detractors of radio commercials from the 1920s to the 1950s, if alive now would think they had been dabbling in mere child's play.

In the late 1920s and early 1930s, a tide of opposition toward radio advertising began to dissipate and turn toward an attitude of acceptance. The Federal Radio Commission (FRC), established in 1927, was at the forefront of this movement. It had considered a small handful of options available to the U.S. broadcasting industry for underwriting its bills. As a result, the FRC had concluded that advertising proffered the most practical and redeeming qualities.[19]

Today, however, advertising's incessant intrusion into programming time (impacting several recent decades) has left commercialization of the airwaves vulnerable to some public criticism and even disdain. Millions of citizens are disgusted by the lengthy commercial breaks that frequently and interminably intrude into entertainment. In addition to switching to other radio or television fare, audience members may turn off their sets, leave a set's location until the commercial break has ended, or pursue scores of competing activities in the interim that are vying for their attention — e.g., verbal exchanges, child care, pet care, cooking, vacuuming, telephoning, check writing, reading, etc.

"Many people feel that the decline in radio listening in the United States is due in large part to 'commercial clutter,'" protests a contemporary website. "Some radio stations devote almost half of their broadcast time to commercials and infomercials."[20] The latter group consists of "programming inserts" that are fostered onto (sometimes unsuspecting) audiences of radio and TV productions as if they are amusement and information. In reality, they are merely longer advertising plugs and usually for a single underwriter.

Sponsors spend millions of dollars appealing to whatever part of the audience remains for their sales pitches. Of course, by the time a dozen or more advertising pitches have been delivered back-to-back, most listeners or viewers couldn't identify as many as three that they've just been exposed to. While enough merchandise is being moved to satisfy most sponsors, couldn't better recognition occur and translate into greater sales volume if a commercial stood alone? (That's the way it used to be.) Perhaps we would pay better attention to the ads we're exposed to if that was the case. (Note: In Chapter 7 the author offers a practical tip for at least partially stemming the barrage of protracted radio commercial breaks bombarding the airwaves.)

Today radio is raking in billions of dollars annually, about 7 percent of all resources spent on advertising in this country. While radio's share of the advertising pie was cut sharply following the inception of TV, it's attracting still more dollars now than it did during the Golden Age. In 1948, during the aural medium's halcyon days, about 35 percent of radio's income was derived by local spot sales. The current percentage doubles that.[21]

The situation was perceived as so untenable to one journalist that he obsessed over it in this manner in a 2004 discourse:[22]

> A rock station in Sydney, Australia, has drawn worldwide attention for its promise never to play more than two commercials in a row. A locally owned country station in Lisbon, N.D., made a similar pledge....
> Result: The Sydney station rocketed to the top of the ratings and the North Dakota station won immediate and strong praise from listeners.
> But in most of the radio industry, such breaks from the rule of eight-, 10- and even 15-minute marathons of commercials are viewed as an aberration.
> Defenders of the standard American "stop set"—the industry term for what happens when the music stops and a station plays one ad after another—say that only stations facing little competition can afford to cut their commercial load. Most stations face competition in which the other guy offers advertisers discounted rates, which means you have to lower your price for air time, which in turn requires you to sell more time to make the same money—thus, ad clutter.
> Not long ago, the standard radio ad break was perhaps 90 seconds or two minutes. But the meaning of "We'll be right back" has changed dramatically in recent years. Federal regulators once set a cap of 18 minutes of commercials per hour, but all government guidelines for programming were erased in the 1981 radio deregulation.
> Now some FM stations' ad packs are approaching the interminable—up to the 15-minute breaks heard on talk shows such as Howard Stern's morning raunch-fest. Ad breaks on the Stern show have been clocked at as long as 18 minutes 48 seconds, with as many as 30 separate spots jammed together.
> With commercial loads of 25 minutes per hour increasingly common on the radio, does anyone stick around until the next segment of the program?
> Stations sell ad time based on research showing that the fewer times programs break each hour, the happier and more loyal listeners will be. Thus evolved the two-per-hour stop set.
> What should stations do? The trade magazine Radio World recently urged stations to reinvent how they present commercials, with fewer and shorter spots that might well prove more effective for advertisers, who aren't exactly thrilled about having their message run as No. 17 in a clump of 25 consecutive ads.
> As for listeners, they continue to flee to Internet radio and satellite radio, both of which are largely commercial-free.

On yet another expedition down that same track, one of the many profilers of newsman Edward R. Murrow — biographer Bob Edwards, who identified Murrow as the "patron saint" of the profession — lamented that the networks, just like the stations under remote thumbs today, paid a heavy price under their new ownership. Edwards offered one example:[23]

> It's difficult to imagine Murrow lasting very long in broadcast journalism today because his programs would be required to make money. Nonbroadcasters acquired the networks in the 1980s when the FCC no longer mandated public service programming. The new owners, principally concerned with profits and share prices, ordered the network news divisions to be profitable. They saw no reason why the news division should not be a profit center, just like the movie studio, publishing house, or other properties they owned. When news has to make money, the substance, character, and look of the news changes. In the public service era, the networks produced documentaries. In the profit era, documentaries have been replaced by magazine programs heavy on crime, items about celebrities, feel-good features, and the latest trendy disease. These programs have to compete with entertainment programs in prime time. The only way a news program can compete in prime time is to become an entertainment program.

Have you seen a pattern here? The wealth and influence of a few owners is plainly visible, concentrated in the hands of monumental conglomerates of insane immensity. And the interests of the American public, quite disappointingly, have been sold out many times in getting to the bottom line.

12

Multicolored Radio

The question of ethnicity in radio broadcasting and its multidimensional impact on a pervasive industry is expressively fascinating and grows with time. We'll examine the trend's profound and sundry inferences in some detail in the inquiry just ahead. But first a few facts and figures are in order to indicate where we are and where we are headed prior to a review of where we have been in aural broadcasting — and thus, how we arrived at where we are now.

The significant rise in racial and cultural diversity in America in the last half century has produced teeming implications for the country as a whole. Research conducted in 2010 confirms just how far the nation has come.[1] The U.S. Census that year revealed that 44 percent of America's suburban residents live in what the federal agency terms "a diverse community." That is classified as a place in which no fewer than 20 and no more than 60 percent of residents are nonwhite, mounting from 38 percent a decade earlier. Booming Hispanic and Asian populations are driving the current demographic transformation.

With 50.5 million Hispanics living in the U.S.A. in 2010, that segment represented one in six Americans and constituted the largest minority group in the nation at 16.4 percent. Hispanics surpassed African Americans in the mid–1990s to claim the title of the nation's largest nonwhite body. The black population of America in 2010 was 42 million or 14 percent of the total. Asians — consisting of 18.2 million of America's denizens in 2010 — accounted for 6 percent of its inhabitants. Another 5.2 million were classified in the joint American Indian and Alaska Native contingent with 1.7 percent of the total. Together these four ethnic groups encompass 115.9 million of 308.7 million Americans (at that time) or about 37.7 percent of the nation's populace.

By one estimate, in the first half of the 21st century (the year 2050), the U.S. is expected to be made up of a population that is 23 percent Hispanic, 16 percent black, and 10 percent Asian-Pacific Islander for a total nonwhite habitation of 49 percent.[2] *Broadcasting-Cable Yearbook 1996* found a score of ethnic audience segments on which American and Canadian radio was focused near the close of the 20th century. Included were American Indian, Arabic, black, Chinese, Eskimo, ethnic, Filipino, French, Greek, Italian, Japanese, Korean, Polish, Portuguese, Reggae (Jamaican), Russian, Serbian, Spanish, Tejano (bicultural including Spanish), and Vietnamese. The preponderance of the stations was Spanish (447) followed by black (172).[3] Quite interestingly and maybe somewhat astonishingly, in one investigation it was reported that Asian-Americans residing in this nation tune in to fewer hours of radio programming than most other leading nonwhite racial and cultural groups. That research disclosed further that African-Americans and Hispanics listen to more hours of radio daily on average than do their Caucasian peers.[4]

From findings gathered in late 2012 by Arbitron, the gargantuan U.S.-based media research firm, several surprising factors emerged regarding the radio-listening habits of minorities in this country.[5] The black audience composed of those aged 12 and above, for instance, increased its reliance on radio by more than 920,000 listeners in a single year (December 2011–December 2012). Arbitron affirmed that radio reaches 92.4 percent of all U.S. African-Americans in that age cluster.

With the same age cohorts among Hispanics, however, the allure of radio is even more remarkable. Listenership in that cultural sect grew during the same one-year period (December 2011–December 2012) by almost 2.5 million, accessing nearly 95 percent of Spanish-speaking and Spanish-descendant residents in the U.S. For those in the 25–54 age range, one most appealing to advertisers, the boost was an impressive 1.8 million weekly listeners.

During what many people consider to have been the medium's heyday, radio was nevertheless branded as a "vast wasteland" for people of color. There is no better evidence to support it than radio's treatment of (and some would say, disregard for) the American black population. Writing in 1954, one observer considered radio "the worst offender of the Negro entertainer."[6] That year, William Worthy, a correspondent for the *Baltimore Afro-American*, may have become the first black American to report for a network program. Speaking by shortwave for CBS from Moscow, he did so as a freelancer, not as a CBS staff member. Nevertheless, Worthy repeated that historic triumph with a similar event in 1956, speaking then from Beijing. At the time he was a Neiman Fellow at Harvard and once again not a CBS staffer.[7]

The first national chain to engage a black reporter on a permanent basis was ABC. It happened when the net picked Mal Goode from a field of about 30 applicants, eight of whom were selected for auditioning on August 9–10, 1962. Goode told *Newsweek* he became a candidate because, "What the hell, I'm 54 years old. What can I lose?"[8] For 14 years he had reported for a black newspaper, the *Pittsburgh Courier*, while delivering news for ABC's Pittsburgh radio affiliate KQV. The experience with the microphone was clearly to his credit when the choice was made.[9]

CBS was next in line among the coast-to-coast chains to hire a black newsman. From 1963–65, Ben Holman — a college-educated reporter for the *Chicago Daily News* (1954–63), who added commentary in 1962 at the Windy City's CBS owned-and-operated WBBM-TV to his resume — was selected for an assignment editor post at CBS News in New York. He pursued stories sporadically. Holman rose to media relations with the U.S. Justice Department, was an NBC producer, and directed community relations in the Justice Department — the highest ranking black in the agency. Named to the latter post by President Richard M. Nixon, Holman served through both Nixon and Ford administrations.[10]

And although Holman initially reported for CBS, he was never dubbed a correspondent there. Hal Walker became the first black reporter elevated by CBS to that title. Paradoxically, having lost an audition to Holman six years before, Walker — a native South Carolinian who was reared in New York City and educated at a trio of universities — was promoted in 1969 from assignment reporter with CBS's Washington bureau to correspondent. He covered foreign and domestic proceedings including the inaugurals of three presidents. Walker joined ABC as a foreign correspondent in 1980.[11]

In March 1963, NBC News hired its initial black correspondent, Bob Teague, who had reported for the *New York Times* before writing for Big Apple radio and TV stations. "Like [ABC's Mal] Goode and other black reporters in a predominantly white society, Teague was constantly reminded of his blackness," wrote Ed Bliss, broadcast news documentarian.[12] Goode told the *New York Times Magazine* that he had made "a getaway of sorts from the ghetto."[13] Nevertheless, NBC president Robert Kintner labeled Teague "the first black ever to go on camera as a network correspondent covering a story" after the reporter contributed to a multiple-hour TV documentary, *The American Revolution of '63*, screened on Labor Day that year.[14]

> In the mid–1960s, the Goodes, Holmans, and Teagues were a rarity. The major stations in New York City, with the largest black population of any city in America, had almost no black reporters. Then came the riots, first in the Watts section of Los Angeles, then in Newark and Detroit, then in the nation's capital with helmeted troops in the streets. How did the violence begin? Why had it taken so many by surprise?
>
> The Kerner Commission, headed by Governor Otto Kerner of Illinois, said it was due, in large part, to the distorted picture newspapers and radio and television had presented of black America. "The ills of the ghetto, the difficulties of life there, the Negro's burning sense of grievance," it said, "are seldom conveyed." It urged that more black reporters be hired.
>
> Broadcasters scrambled for black faces, not solely because of the commission's finding and fear of FCC action; they needed black reporters to cover stories white reporters could not get or covered at their peril. Radio station WLIB in Harlem lost five of its black newsmen to New York outlets overnight.[15]

Pittsburgh's KDKA, believed by many old-time radio buffs to be "the" pioneer radio station for its having aired the national election returns in 1920, was typical of the lagging broadcast business for blacks: in July 1964, as it approached its 44th birthday, the outlet hired an initial Negro performer.[16] The impression some have harbored that the South dragged its heels in progressive race relations, while absolutely on target many times, doesn't distinguish Dixie's practices from those of sundry geographical zones. The tensions prevailed between the races almost everywhere then and weren't germane to a specific region to the exclusion of all the others.

> Despite its tremendous need for personnel, however, the industry in its so-called Golden Age offered only limited opportunities for black men and women to develop. In fact, of all the popular arts, commercial radio possessed one of the more effective policies of discrimination along racial lines. It was manifested in the failure to employ black technical operators or actors, and it was evident in the strident stereotyping of black characters in actual broadcasts. That radio was a medium unfriendly to black talent was obvious to Carleton Moss, a black writer, who told an interviewer in 1950 that prejudice in broadcasting was only a reflection of its existence in the general society.[17]

Of course the disparity between black and white citizens (and thus radio listeners) was borne out with several more ethnic cultures beyond African-Americans. Most notably are large groups of Asian-Americans, Hispanics, and Native Americans. Programming for minority audiences is generated in major metropolitan centers with large populations of any of these racial groups today. But it wasn't always so.

From its start, the broadcasting industry in America matured without giving much of its thought or power to minorities. The large, capital-intensive conglomerates often found at the forefront of the media movement saw little recompense for themselves by sharing their opportunities with people of color. Early on, when minority groups took a crack at gaining some influence in radio, they were mostly rebuffed by a trade focused on mass audiences and other ideas that virtually ignored their concerns. NBC expressed its racial feelings through early policies shared with staff.

> In 1938, the network reiterated its internal guidelines, distributing a general memorandum to its employees concerning racial language and bigoted discourse, particularly in popular songs: "Please let this serve as a reminder that songs containing the words 'nigger,' 'darky,' and 'coon,' etc. in the title and lyrics should not be programmed. These always bring complaining letters from negro listeners and if this can be explained to sponsors or program builders they surely will see the wisdom of not including anything on programs which may be offensive to any people." As the rationale for content monitoring indicates, however, it was not the commitment to respectful representation of blacks that motivated the network's policy but the desire to protect sponsors' interests by avoiding inappro-

priate content that might taint their corporate or product image. This perspective dominated at NBC through the 1940s and into the 1950s.
...
Through the 1940s and into the early 1950s, however, NBC's record of employing blacks was abysmal, and although critics from black civil rights organizations assailed NBC for lagging behind its competitor CBS in its racial policies, it was probably not much worse than many other corporations of similar scale. In 1950, of an estimated two thousand NBC employees at the network's New York headquarters, only thirty-five were black, and of these only one (a recording technician named Ray Hall) was a trained professional; the rest were primarily clerical or custodial hires.[18]

The employment record seemed to be indicative of the discriminatory issues that found their way into programming content. What was transpiring at NBC, of course, would have been similar to the attitudes and actions occurring at hundreds of radio stations across the United States during those decades. Not until the Kerner Commission disclosed broadcasting's culpability for perpetuating racism in 1967 was there radical change. With that revelation, officials in the medium's leadership began to genuinely examine policies that perpetually shunned ethnics in employment, for instance, and their inclusion in most programming features in any favorable light.

Commercial AM radio outlets in the 1970s sustained a mean average 86 percent Caucasian employment and 14 percent minorities.[19] At commercial FM stations the percentage rose to 16 percent minorities; and to 18 percent for the same full-time occupational segment at public radio stations. As minimal as these percentages are, by the mid 1990s, just 15 percent of U.S. radio stations employed *any* minorities; 85 percent of all outlets had no individual of color on its full time staff in any post. The presumptive strides forward weren't yet all that evident.

Just ahead of the federal government's belatedly growing occupancy with the country's racial practices in the 1950s — including desegregation of the public schools at mid-decade — and culminating in the landmark legislation of the Civil Rights Act of 1964, broadcasters were starting to take genuine notice of the American black. In many quarters, for the very first time, the potential that people of color offered to the ethereal trade rose to paramount levels. Ironically, this shifting of opinions may have its roots deeply embedded in the Second World War which had a "salutary effect" on the impression and rank of blacks in American broadcasting. One wag, Fred MacDonald, waxed eloquently in regard to the situation:

> The war galvanized in many black actors and white sympathizers the decision to speak forthrightly against racism and its restrictive grip on the American popular arts. The Nazi enemy, moreover, presented Americans with an insidious picture of the implications of bigotry. Thus, there arose in many people an awareness of the paradox of fighting against a racist enemy abroad, while practicing segrega-

tion and exclusion at home. Out of such conditions developed the most important re-evaluation of the role of Afro-Americans in American society since the Civil War.[20]

At least one historiographer, Ryan Ellett, identified a "golden age of African American radio" in which Negroes offered "broadcasts of diversity and variety" unmatched until a resurgence appeared some years hence. *That* Golden Age included the succinct span between 1927 and 1933. "African Americans could find nearly as wide a mix of radio content geared to them as could their white counterparts, if not in as much quantity," said Ellett.[21]

The liberating lessons of the Second World War weren't lost on network radio. Prejudice, left unchecked throughout America's brief history, became especially tested through numerous exclusive broadcasts that featured some leading Caucasian citizens appealing for tolerance and brotherhood.[22] Out of this and other inducements the narrow, polarized thinking that had been so widely and prominently evidenced across the ages slowly began to dissipate. Deep-seated convictions softened. And in time broadcasting was to be one of the influential media that was affected by the shifts in individual judgments. The National Broadcasting Company was one of the leading architects of this attitudinal modification as indicated by a new code of standards and practices which the network adopted in mid–1951:

> All program materials present with dignity and objectivity the varying aspects of race, creed, color, and national origin. The history, institutions and citizens of all nations are fairly represented.... Defamatory statements or derogatory references expressed or implied, toward an individual, nationality, race, group, trade, profession, industry, or institution are not permitted.[23]

"By 1960, the potential for a balance between integrated and all-black programming, free from the open bigotry of the past, had been achieved in radio," Fred MacDonald claimed.[24] Portraying the African-American as an exclusively shiftless, menial, stereotypically lazy, dispossessed fellow or black mammy figure — virtually an indentured servant in many cases — was suddenly out of vogue on the transcontinental chains. America's level of intolerance for distorted persuasions had simply grown weary and radio was in step with the widespread restlessness of opinions on the status quo.

> Amid intimations of death, radio began to interest itself in the Negro. Magazines like *Ebony* were attracting advertising because they were found to reach a buying public not touched by "white" media. The years 1948–52 saw an eruption of "Negro radio stations" aiming at the same "market," mainly through "rhythm and blues" music. Most of these stations, while using Negro talent and seeking a Negro audience, were white-owned; but there were exceptions.... In some communities the Negro-oriented stations were not so well received.[25]

Reporter Sonja Williams gives a fairly intimate glimpse of how all this transpired in Memphis, Tennessee, in black radio's earliest days.

In 1947, WDIA owners Bert Ferguson and John Pepper fought bankruptcy by trying many different types of programming formats before they settled on the previously untapped creative and commercial "Negro" market. During the latter part of 1948, a WDIA black music program hosted by Nat D. Williams, known as the "Mid-South's First Black DJ," became so popular among Memphis' nearly 40 percent black population that Ferguson and Pepper experimented with expanding the show. Their gamble paid off, and they eventually transformed WDIA into a "black-appeal" station, the nation's first radio station programmed entirely by and for African Americans. WDIA's programming mainstay was the popular rhythm and blues (R&B) and gospel music of the day, hosted by a personable DJ staff that included Nat D., Riley B. King (blues great B.B. King), R&B singer Rufus Thomas, and Martha Jean "The Queen" Steinberg. WDIA's commercial spots were often hilarious and attention grabbing, and white advertisers, who were initially reluctant to deal with an all-black station, soon saw the lucrative economic potential of the African-American consumer. Eventually, WDIA became the first Memphis station to earn a million dollars from advertising, and the station jumped to the top of the city's popularity charts.[26]

While the first two black-owned radio stations in America went on the air in 1949, little happened that was to substantially augment those numbers in the dual decades that were to follow.[27] Just 16 of the nation's 8,000 aural outlets were black owned by 1970, some .002 percent. (Seven of those 16 had some white investors as well.) Yet 310 U.S. radio broadcasters aimed their full time programming at the African-American population. Caucasian ownership overshadowed these black-appeal operations and represented the bulk of their advertising billings, mounting to $35 million in 1969. White station managers were predominantly favored by white owners: in 1970, only one black-oriented, white-owned station had a black manager. (It may also be observed that, while in 1943 just four stations in the U.S. were offering *any* black-oriented programs, the total grew to 260 outlets by 1953 — in just one decade. They were also drawing local and national sponsors to their black-slanted shows.[28])

There were some notable exceptions, nevertheless, providing rare opportunities for blacks to excel in radio as a profession. And as it turned out, some were instrumental in creating a communal cohesiveness that transcended to larger opportunities for racial evolution as a whole. "Throughout the 1950s and 1960s, the powerful presence and influence of African American on-air personalities dominated black radio," affirmed one Web report. "Working from an extensive African American oral tradition, black disc jockeys shaped black (and often white) musical tastes and created a social grapevine that contributed largely to the empowerment of the growing civil rights movement. Southern black stations in particular became clearinghouses for information and forums for discussion among black communities cut off from each other by segregation and geography. Black radio personalities ... drew praise from ... African American leaders for their contributions to civil rights efforts."[29]

There were some major criticisms leveled at many of the seemingly black-focused operations in certain quarters.[30] One was that a spate of African-American DJs who had emerged in the 1950s suddenly lost control over the musical contents of their own shows. Their input was effectively squelched in the 1960s when the stations for which they worked adopted a new Top 40 soul music format. This programming breed netted the further outcome of marginalizing, at best, and eliminating, at worst, the local news and public-affairs features that had been a unique attribute of black-appeal radio in the past.

In spots around the country, groups of protesters surfaced, operating fairly independently and in somewhat subdued tones at first. Eventually, however, they grew into a rather raucous and organized crescendo of demonstrators. In general they disputed perceived or actual evidence of unfavorable practices at black-appeal stations toward African-Americans. Their objections included limited station ownership, management, and on-air personalities among people of color as well as the programming itself. A 1970 newspaper assessment was typical, criticizing the Top 40 soul format over Newark's WNJR which was controlled by Rollins, Incorporated. Rollins was one of a handful of U.S. white-owned, soul music radio chains.

> Stations like this feed our communities and our children monotonous music, skimpy news, and very little relevant programming. The only thing our children can aspire to are songs about drugs, getting high, and abnormal love affairs, with nothing about what's going on and what needs to be done to better our community. We are protesting ... against the pattern of paternalistic, mediocre broadcasting that has set in at the so-called soul stations around the country. Are the Black and Puerto Rican communities to be continually insulted by programming that imagines all we can do is wiggle our backsides and chug-a-lug brew?[31]

Although the growing interest in black ownership of America's radio stations witnessed a boom of 600 percent in the 1970s, the ratio still yielded a dismal outcome of less than 2 percent of the nation's total.[32] "The problem is that you don't own anything," some activists at a members' conclave disparaged. "Unless you own something, you can't change it.... Rather than talking about conditions for the disc jockeys and for radio announcers, own the station."[33]

> The 1970s marked a period of dramatic change in African American radio. Some of this change occurred as a result of industry-wide trends: standardized programming formats de-emphasized the news and public affairs programming that had become a staple of black radio; the emergence of FM radio, with its "more music, less talk" philosophy, exacerbated the trend away from news and discussion shows that targeted African American audiences. Yet the most significant change in black radio took place off the air, as the socioeconomic empowerment of African Americans in the 1960s produced a dramatic increase in the number of black-owned radio stations in the 1970s. During this decade the number of black-owned stations grew from sixteen to eighty-eight, closing somewhat the

wide gap between the number of black-owned stations and the number of stations broadcasting black-oriented programming.[34]

One factor augmenting the improvement of black ownership of radio stations occurred in the late 1970s by way of a new federal mandate. President Jimmy Carter signed into law the Minority Ownership Policy of 1978 that was passed by Congress. Its policies are credited with significant gains in expanding the control of radio outlets to people of color.[35]

Only a couple of years earlier, in 1976, the National Association of Black Owned Broadcasters (NABOB) formed.[36] The trade society symbolized the concerns of African-American owners of American radio-TV facilities. Through extensive lobbying, NABOB kept Congress and the FCC aware of members' legislative and regulatory issues. Pressure on the FCC from NABOB and the Black Media Coalition to address and remedy media-ownership inequalities was influential in prompting the 1978 federal legislation. NABOB maintains lobbying today to ensure that African-American broadcasting owners aren't forced to sell nor prevented from buying in markets where small outlets increasingly compete with media behemoths with manifold broadcasting properties.

An inaugural conference on minority ownership was held in 1973, spearheaded by the National Association of Broadcasters. And as an anonymous thinker hypothesized: From humble beginnings come great things. A major breakthrough in the ownership struggle occurred in that decade as a pair of black-owned radio networks was launched. On May 1, 1972, MBS inaugurated the Mutual Black Network based in New York City. It was sold a short while later to the Sheridan Broadcasting Company of Pittsburgh to form the Sheridan Broadcasting Network (SBN). In 1973, the National Black Network (NBN) premiered in New York City. (Two decades before in 1954, a black-oriented National Negro Network had debuted, operating with about 50 subscribing outlets — presumably with most of those owned by Caucasians. Yet it failed within a year for lack of capital.) NBN, however, arriving at the behest of instigators representing the parent Unity Broadcasting Corporation, told a different story.

> The idea for a National Black Network was conceived by former ABC Radio and Mutual Broadcasting Network President Robert Pauley in 1969 as a way to utilize Mutual's contracted but unused network lines for the benefit of African-Americans. The goal was to tie together the 117 black-oriented radio stations in the country. Pauley, a white American, was unable to organize the niche African American oriented news business and therefore turned to Eugene D. Jackson, an African American electrical engineer working as a consultant raising capital for black business investments. Sydney L. Small, a former employee of ABC Radio Network was recruited to join the group. Mr. Pauley finally became frustrated with the difficult task of raising the $1,000,000 in capital needed to start the

operation and abandoned the effort. Jackson and Small along with Del Raycee of Mutual Broadcasting Network persevered and finally launched the National Black Network on July 2, 1972 in New York City with 25 affiliates.[37]

NBN was to be the nation's earliest prevailing African-American radio chain. At its inception it offered affiliates a largely black-oriented news service: five-minute on-the-hour newscasts, and a nightly sportscast, business report, and news commentary, all in separate doses. Although NBN provided scintillating on-air personalities who were well-versed in their specific genres, the hookup thrashed about during its first few years. While it had little difficulty signing new affiliates, advertisers were nevertheless reluctant to be as receptive, at least until NBN had become an established commodity. With an operating shortfall of $2 million by 1976, things were looking bleak for NBN. Just then, the tide began to turn. The outfit had finally passed muster and become a proven venture to potential clients. It raked $2.5 million into its coffers that year.[38]

With 17 million listeners, 82 affiliates, 50 full-time employees (two-thirds of them in the news division), and 200 part-time black reporters canvassing the nation, all of a sudden the trade was viewing NBN with admiration rather than skepticism. Program offerings swelled to embrace more public-affairs features, educational series, and cultural diversions ranging from storytelling and poetry to music and drama. By the close of the 1970s, the chain was grossing in excess of $10 million annually.

It included 94 affiliates and covered 20 million black listeners.[39] Consumer-oriented, black entertainers, women's, and call-in talk shows were added to the lineup. After buying a couple of Philadelphia radio outlets in 1980 and a New York cable franchise shortly thereafter, Unity Broadcasting (NBN's parent firm) appeared to be readying to become America's first black media conglomerate. If that was the case, however, those plans were due for a revision early in the 1990s.

The other leading African-American radio hookup, SBN, realized an even speedier ascent, in some measure possibly due to the spectacular trail of growth and acceptance blazed by NBN. SBN was formed in 1979. That year the outstanding shares of the independent Mutual Black Network (MBN)—a derivative of the Golden Age's Mutual Broadcasting System (MBS, 1934–1999)—were purchased by the Sheridan Broadcasting Corporation (SBC). Both MBN and SBC had been established in 1972.[40] Combined, they represented 91 affiliates and grossed $3 million annually, giving SBN a slight edge over its principal competitor, NBN, then with 80 outlets and $2.5 million in revenues. By the end of the 1980s, however, SBN had escalated to 150 affiliates and almost $15 million in annual revenues.[41]

The Sheridan parent firm was the innovation of Philadelphia native Ronald R. Davenport Sr. (1936–), the dean of the law school at Duquesne University in Pittsburgh. Davenport had already taken it on himself to seek opportunities to boost the ownership levels of commercial and cultural institutions among African-Americans. He was convinced the spoils of the civil rights movement could be upheld only if economic growth among blacks was intensified. When a quartet of radio stations was put up for sale in 1971, Davenport and his wife, Judith, sought a few black investors to provide the capital to buy them. Within a few months they had raised $2 million, the purchase price, and named their enterprise after the street where Davenports lived.

In its early years, the SBN hookup's programming offered *Straight Up*, a daily news commentary; *Minority Business Report*, a weekly survey on commerce of interest to African-Americans; *To Your Health*, a daily wellness feature; a weekly focus on environmental conditions; sports coverage of black college gridiron matches; and *The Black College Sports Review*, a weekly insert. SBN later added *White House Report*, a weekly half-hour public affairs program; a series of brief features including *Money Smarts*, a 90-second daily financial round-up, and *Coming Soon*, a one-minute movie review; and a trio of sports features with in-depth coverage of professional athletic teams and players: *Major League Baseball Notebook*, *NBA Report*, and *NFL Playbook*.

In late 1991, Sheridan Broadcasting Corporation completed the largest transaction in black radio's history: that year it purchased NBN, merged it into SBN, and established American Urban Radio Networks (AURN), headquartered in Pittsburgh. Late in the 20th century, AURN boasted more than 250 affiliates and was positioned to touch the lives of 90 percent of African-Americans living in the United States. In 2012, the company reported it was then generating more than 200 weekly programs for in excess of 300 affiliated stations.[42] Claiming "the broadest reach of the African-American marketplace of any media," AURN maintained a presence available to 94 percent of the nation's black population at the time. In 2006, perhaps astoundingly, it announced that its morning drive-time audience included more 18-to-49-year-olds — the age group most frequently targeted by advertisers — than the combined number of viewers of *The Early Show*, *Good Morning America*, and *Today*, according to Mediamark Research, Inc.

A historiographer of black broadcasting assessed: "Ron Davenport's American Urban Radio Networks is one of black radio's most important success stories.... AURN has been a major source of black radio's syndicated programming — in the process, becoming indispensable to its growth and prosperity. But perhaps even more impressive, Davenport's ... radio network conglomerate is competitive with its white corporate counterparts on a national level."[43]

At this writing the only African-American chain radio company in the U.S., AURN contends it is the largest capable of being heard by the most Americans residing in metropolitan areas: "Through three programming networks and our marketing division, American Urban Radio Networks reaches more African-Americans than any other medium in America and produces more urban programming than all other broadcasting companies combined."[44] It's also the only African-American broadcaster currently with bureaus in the White House, Atlanta, Chicago, Detroit, Los Angeles, New York, Pittsburgh, and Washington, D.C.

Sheridan established a 24/7 Sheridan Gospel Network with its own corporate division which it hurled under the banner *The Light* in 1997. At the start of 2013, *The Light* was heard over outlets in 50 American radio markets.[45] Hype from the hookup's website vindicated its efforts:

> The music of "The Light" includes the hits of today's inspirational music world, the crossover, as well as the classic sounds of gospel and the favorites from the grass roots legends. It's a combination that blends the excitement of new talent with the tradition of the legends of gospel music.
> "The Light" is the new Urban Adult format for the new millennium. This special blend of traditional classics and contemporary hits combined with specialized programming elements and strategic promotions allows SGN to inspire, uplift and encourage listeners of all ages.[46]

Women between the ages of 25 and 54 are *The Light's* target audience.[47] To retain and gain faithful listeners, the chain pursues a blend of promotional strategies including concerts, guest interviews, conferences, sweepstakes, prizes, etc. Sheridan also pursues synergies with a handful of religious-oriented music publishers resulting in rewards for the network and the periodicals promoting it.[48]

Deregulation of radio ownership that transpired in two waves in 1992 and 1996, previously referenced, had a mainly negative impact on the African-American broadcasting community. A justification for the policy shift was to guarantee variety in radio ownership and programming. On the contrary, nonetheless — as witnessed during the previous decade with the Reagan Administration steering the ship — the Federal Communications Commission prioritized deregulation over diversity and the latter was lost in the resulting shuffle. The impetus applied to combining radio outlets in the milestone Telecommunications Act of 1996 dealt a crushing blow to black broadcasters.

> Ownership consolidation is having an adverse effect on the prosperity and proliferation of black-owned stations. The decline in revenue and numbers is taking place because a majority of these stations are individually owned and operated, putting them at a big disadvantage when competing with the new duopolies and superduopolies for advertising dollars. Advertisers are much more likely to buy spots on a cluster of stations than on a single station in the same market, since the cluster gives them access to a larger pool of consumers.[49]

Today black radio faces some other dispiriting pressures. The industry's embrace of digital technology favors Caucasian-owned media giants that are better equipped to make costly investments in new equipment and training than less prestigious, poorer-financed black-owned stations. Beyond that, as many African-Americans have risen to greater levels of prosperity they have relocated to suburban districts, leaving a preponderance of their brothers and sisters behind in decaying ghettos of the inner-cities. This has contributed to age-group differences where they live, too, as more and more young people depart the only environment they have known. Black radio, as a result, has frequently abandoned the all-purpose, community-focused outlets to concentrate on format segmentation generated by economic and age levels.

Thus digital technology and demographic fragmentation are regularly reconfiguring the playing field for African-Americans in the radio trade. "But to their credit," affirmed academic William Barlow, "black radio broadcasters have weathered many crises in their long struggle for racial equality, freedom of expression, and self-sufficiency. Against great odds, they have made radio a centerpiece of African American life. This resilience in the face of adversity offers some hope that black radio will remain an independent and progressive voice."[50] There are episodes stemming from black radio that make it all worthwhile.

> Throughout urban America there are stations ... airing talk programs designed to cater to the black audience.... Most of these shows make it clear that they do not expect nonblacks to be listening. Shows often are structured to suggest that there is a common black radio audience united by the black experience. "What are we going to do about this?" a host on a black station will ask the audience about a problem, and the inference is clear: What are we as blacks going to do about the problem? Callers may well refer to previous callers with language for the most part confined to the black community, such as, "I agree with the sister who just called."
>
> After listening to black talk shows in Detroit for the *Detroit Free Press*, reporter Constance Prater came up with a long list of subject matter unlikely to appear on the city's white-oriented radio stations.... "Topics included," she wrote, "how to buy *kinte* cloth, and healthier eating habits for African Americans. Only on black radio," said Prater, "would you hear a host tell young listeners on a snowy morning that school will be open and to get up and 'get yourself some grits and eggs and go to school.'"[51]

Little gems like these not only make radio worthwhile but a veritable treasure.

In an America that has, within the past two decades, seen the African-American community surpassed by the Hispanic community to form the nation's largest number of people of color, U.S. citizens have realized that we are definitely a multiracial country, and forever will be.[52] Indeed, just before the turn of the century, immigrants from 22 Spanish-speaking nations comprised a radio audience in America that also made it the world's fifth largest homeland for Hispanics. Mexicans encompassed 64.2 per cent of that total; 15 percent hailed from Central and South American nations; another 11 percent were Puerto Rican; and 5 percent were from Cuba.

By 2025, a governmental projection indicates that the United States will be the permanent address of more Hispanics than any other country on the planet.[53] In the last half of the 20th century, our nation's Hispanic inhabitants swelled by more than 600 percent. Nine out of 10 Hispanics lived in just 10 American states by 1997, including California, Texas, New York, Florida, Illinois, Arizona, New Jersey, New Mexico, Colorado, and Massachusetts.

The age factor makes a tremendous impact on all of these figures. The mean age of the Hispanic population in the United States approaching the turn of the century was 28.6 years, with the largest proportion (25 percent) being from birth through 11 years of age. Men from 25 to 49 years of age (19.9 percent) and women in the same age span (18.4 percent) made up the second and third largest contingents of the U.S. Hispanic inhabitants, prime targets for radio advertisers. The mean household income among these residents was $37,500 with Cubans leading that realm at $45,200.

An estimated 63 percent of the U.S. Hispanic population in the late 20th century lived in ten metropolitan districts, from greatest to least: Los Angeles, New York, Miami, San Francisco, Chicago, Houston, San Antonio, McAllen-Brownsville, Dallas-Fort Worth, and El Paso. At that same time, Arbitron disclosed that 96 percent of *all* Hispanics in America (not merely those aged 12 and above) tuned in to Spanish-language radio stations, with older people relying on those stations more than younger ones. In *daily* listening time, these stations reached more women above age 55 than any other segment. But the same outlets drew 96.6 percent of men ages 18 to 34 for a *weekly* audience high.[54]

America's first Spanish-language broadcaster, San Antonio's KCOR Radio, took to the ether in 1947.[55] By 2013, nearly 800 such stations (AM and/or FM) were on the air in the U.S.A., many of them serving some of the nation's largest metropolitan areas.[56] Among some of America's larger cities with prominent Spanish-language communities currently are Albuquerque, Chicago, Houston, Los Angeles, Miami, New York, Phoenix, Sacramento, San Antonio, San Diego, San Francisco, and Tampa.

> The number of commercial FM stations programming in a foreign language, either part- or full-time, also increased in the early 2000s, reflecting increased immigration in major markets. Spanish-language stations led in this category and, in fact, were rated number one in several cities. Indeed, as the nation's Hispanic population grew into the largest minority early in the new century, so did the number of stations programming Hispanic music and talk. The first Hispanic station to achieve a number-one ranking among the largest markets was KLVE in Los Angeles, which reached that point in 1995 and grew even bigger in the months to follow. Among the most popular radio stations in New York City by the early 2000s were no less than four FM outlets programming exclusively to a Hispanic audience. No other FM format, with the exception of sports talk, showed as much growth potential as did Hispanic music and talk.[57]

According to an Asian-American website, just 15 percent of U.S. minorities tuned in Asian-language radio in a recent year.[58] There is but a handful of these terrestrial outlets operating within the United States. Among their most loyal adherents are commuters, store owners, and older individuals. With this racial and cultural grouping another factor appears to have taken hold. Asians were among the first segments of society to gain access to the Internet and are more likely to swell its ranks than any other nonwhite demographic breed. Yet a study conducted by Los Angeles's KSCI-TV in 2009 concluded that "the U.S.-based Asian media have failed to accumulate a solid audience online." The station's findings suggested, "Part of the issue seems to be that Asian Internet users tend to go to overseas sites when looking for Asian content." Does that also translate to radio fare?

Despite it, several members of the handful of radio outlets in America currently broadcasting in Asian dialects are streaming their programming online, making those stations readily available to the large percentage of Asian-Americans owning or having access to computers. Technology, after all, can be considered almost part of the DNA of a majority of Asians, whether they were born overseas or here. It's plainly identified with their heritage. In 2007, according to the U.S. Census Bureau, Asian-Americans slightly outpaced native-born Caucasians in access to computers at home: 67.8 percent Asian to 66.9 percent white non–Hispanics. Black households were third at 45.3 percent.

Among the leading Asian-speaking radio broadcasters that Asian-Americans tune into regularly are these:

- **KBS World Radio**, geared to exploring Korean culture, politics, and society. Its news and feature programs are presently available in 11 languages (including English since 1953). The "Voice of Korea" carries programming on both North and South Korea. It may be accessed through a variety of methods: shortwave, Internet, KBS KONG and Radio Tune, satellite, and overseas through local FM and AM bandwidths.[59]
- **Little Saigon Radio**, based in Westminster and San Jose, California, is linked to outlets in myriad Golden State cities. Each day it carries broadcasts of international Vietnamese programming from the British Broadcasting Corporation, Radio France Internationale, and Radio Free Asia. It also offers online webcasts of its features.[60]
- **Saigon Radio**, with local station operations in Los Angeles and San Jose, California, and Houston, Texas, plugs its "rich traditions of the Vietnamese language and culture." It focuses on international, national, and local events while proffering advice, entertainment, and interactive features. It can be accessed on the Internet.[61]
- **Sing Tao Chinese Radio** leases time from KVTO-AM in Berkeley,

California. It began broadcasting in Cantonese on KEST-AM in 1996 and KVTO the following year. Mandarin language programming was added. By 2010, KSQQ carried Sing Tao's programming to the Mandarin-speaking population in the South Bay district. KEST Cantonese broadcasts were eliminated in 2005, but are still heard today over KVTO. Sing Tao is accessible on the Web.[62]

In contrast to these stations, a smattering of largely FM outlets situated mostly in the far West (including Alaska) and Midwest were programmed exclusively for this country's most enduring residents, its Native Americans.[63] By the 1990s, a score of stations focused almost exclusively on Indian cultural heritage. Tribal dialect, aboriginal music, and time-honored storytelling were pervasively scheduled. Drum beats, powwow melody, and Native American news accounts were characteristic of the stations' offerings. Although most of their features were originated by each local outlet, these operations partnered with multiple suppliers to enhance their programming. In addition to distribution channels like National Public Radio and Public Radio International, the tribal-owned outlets drew on the resources of the National Federation of Community Broadcasters and the American Indian Radio on Satellite. The latter enterprise, established in the mid 1990s, was created with federal funding and help from the Native American Public Broadcasting Consortium.

From their inception, the Native American radio outlets became a fundamental dynamic in safeguarding Indian life. Michael Keith, a researcher who turned a media spotlight on minority groups in the United States, reported on the Indian radio stations, acknowledging: "[They are] free to express the values of their own unique cultures in both their Native language and in English. They are free to provide public service announcements and other information important to their listeners. In short, they can be a liberating and creative force in their mission to get the 'word' out to their communities."[64]

> The stations are able to break down barriers which exist between the reservations and the off-reservation community. They are a strong vehicle for educating non–Indians about the history, culture, conditions, and activities of reservation population.... By broadcasting in Native languages and focusing on local customs and practices, they reinforce the value of tribal cultures and the identity of Indian people ... they can counter many of the negative racist stereotypes held by non–Indians. The stations also broadcast news, information, and other programming relating directly to the needs and concerns of reservation populations. This gives legitimacy to these concerns ... especially when they are not addressed by other media.... The reservation-based public radio stations are special in the public radio arena, because they represent a particularly unique and little understood segment of ethnic culture.[65]

Native American radio stations, for the most part broadcasting their signals directly from the reservations, premiered in the early 1970s. At the time their languages and cultures were threatened with obliteration from the Indians' sweeping absorption into Anglo-Saxon mainstream society. As part of the civil rights movement of the 1960s, Native Americans began to look askance at their manipulation by the dominant culture. "This resulted in greater Indian activism and creation of groups, such as the American Indian Movement (AIM), whose objectives include calling attention to human rights violations against indigenous peoples, ensuring that solidarity among Native Americans," said broadcasting historian Keith. "Developing reservation broadcast outlets was perceived as one very important means of accomplishing these objectives."[66]

Most of the Native American stations are operated without commercials and rely heavily upon federal or tribal governmental assistance. The Corporation for Public Broadcasting (CPB) has supplied only limited funds due to its being subject to the whims of Congress which has often made deep cuts in CPB allocations. Programming at the Native American radio stations is "very diverse and often eclectic," Keith reports. Music is the key component on most agendas including country, folk, jazz, rock, and many of the genres that are popular with Caucasian and Black Americans. Most stations air traditional tribal music and language features. Some do so almost exclusively.

U.S. Native American radio outlets are currently in their fifth decade since harnessing the ether. Employing satellite sophistication, they beam programs that exhibit their culture, customs, and language to the indigenous outlets on the reservation, across the country, and around the globe.

While we may not be speaking the same language with most of the diverse cultural subsets currently occupying American turf—as some impressive figures have borne out already—radio-listening habits remain a pervasive force in Americans' lives, whatever their racial birthright. The fact that the medium itself has broadened into so many exciting new technological platforms is a fairly good barometer that radio will continue to be a reliable and influential force in the lives of millions of Americans for the foreseeable future—no matter what their ethnic legacy. And our ability to readily access broadcasters of various stripes wherever we are seems to say a great deal about these *united* states in which we share a common bequest.

13

An Acoustical Smorgasbord

The radio that you have known and loved, possibly for years and maybe even for decades, may be — as one reporter discloses it — destined for the relic pile (e.g., closet shelf, attic, basement, or garage storage space, or — heaven forbid!— the dumpster) in the not-too-distant future:

> Industry experts predict that it won't be long before the radio as such becomes an unnecessary appliance. People will still listen to the radio, mind you. They just won't listen to the radio on their radio; they'll listen to the radio on their phone, either at home or in the car. In fact, it's already happening. The iPhone has a radio application, by which listeners can connect to any radio station carrying their favorite show and listen live. Plus most ... radio shows today ... post a podcast, a commercial-free version of their program, on iTunes, enabling fans to download the show to their iPhone and listen to it anytime, anywhere they want. Even over and over again. The popularity of podcasts as the most convenient way to listen to favorite radio shows is growing rapidly. Michael Harrison, publisher of *Talkers* magazine, predicts that the podcast and the exclusive content provided on podcasts represents the future..., and that radio appliances, as we now know them, will soon be obsolete.[1]

Think it can't happen? Remember the audiocassette, the mimeograph machine, the rotary telephone, the telephone booth, and the typewriter? It might be time to think again.

The last couple of decades of the 20th century and the early years of the 21st witnessed numerous alterations in American radio and in our preconceived notions of the form it must take. The introduction of new platforms was pivotal among them. But that was only part of the tweaking of radio's proud heritage. Virtually all of the changes that have transpired in the last third of a century would have been completely unknown and unrecognizable to the broadcasters of the Golden Age. The same is true of most of their successors in the first couple of decades (1960s, 1970s) beyond that salient watershed.

About the only variation that most of the ancestral group would have been familiar with, in fact — and not universally so at that — were the AM and FM bands as well as monophonic and stereophonic sound. That is, unless the myriad effects that were prompted by ushering in portable transistors and a profusion of radio-equipped vehicles are counted. The audience's increasing mobility emanating from those sources radically reordered America's audio listening habits. Furthermore, there were the powerful effects of refocusing broadcasting on limited segments of the mass audience instead of trying to appeal to everybody within range of a transmitter.

Taken together, these were some of the principal innovations that most widely impacted the medium prior to about 1980. Several also had the net effect of revamping much of the programming that was available on the air.

In more recent times a portion of the nation's media landscape has been identified in a diverse nomenclature mixture.[2] Included is at least a quintet of monikers (and there may be more): *Free Radio*, *Low Power FM*, *Micro Radio*, *Micropower Radio*, and *Pirate Radio*. These are low-powered community-based aural broadcasting endeavors that may or may not be certified as airworthy by officialdom. An active *Microradio Movement* purports to revolutionize current radio licensing laws, giving greater accessibility to the airwaves to more candidates desiring to use it in undersized geographical territories.

As the decades have rolled by, the commonly employed "pirate radio" emerged in pockets across the nation, gaining some relevance and threatening mayhem to the formally sanctioned order. Pirate radio's clandestine operators, generally typified as youthful, rebellious, and daring, performed their quests under shadowy cover, shrouded in mysterious movements, and unlicensed to broadcast by anybody. They competed for precious restricted space on the continuum just as those who had paid hefty fees had done.

Most were in business with less than 100 watts, some with as little as 0.1 watt.[3] And without excusing any unseemly pursuits, a motive cited for this growing predisposition in the 1980s and 1990s (which had been gradually gaining ground since the 1960s) was attributed to a system some abhorred: media conglomerates grabbing most FM stations in the nation in the 1980s and 1990s, spurring roguish opportunists to seize openings to fill gaps in the resulting erosion of local service and programming diversity.[4]

The outcome in some quarters was utter chaos, creating disturbing interference with authentic (legitimate) signals. The Federal Communications Commission went after the offenders, not always consistently but at times with an unflagging vengeance. (The FCC is tasked with the regulation of every radio and TV station, phone company, satellite broadcaster, antenna tower, cell phone and pager service, and everything else that emits a broadcast signal down to microwave ovens — check the label on the back of yours if you're in doubt.)

The beginnings of pirate radio in America can be traced to 1933. That year a Panama-licensed operator with a supercharged transmitter able to overrun stations in every North American nation was temporarily removed from the air by the FCC. Unwilling to give up, however, it retaliated by sending a signal to the mainland from a ship docked off the California coastline. Only a couple of additional unauthorized attempts would succeed by beaming their fare briefly from U.S. offshore locations, and not until 1973 was that even repeated.[5]

In the late 1960s, a handful of intrepid amateur hobbyists were predisposed to carry their ambitions from imagination to a more engrossing level. (Recall that in radio's earliest days there were hams or wireless operators fascinated by the sound-wave experiments they were conducting. In many ways those innovators laid the foundation for the bona fide stations that appeared in the 1920s.) By the 1960s and 1970s, the amateurs then fooling around in audio were steeped in several decades of history, experience, and technological advancement. If independently they couldn't figure out how to make something work there were probably books and pamphlets with simple diagrams, photographs, and text that revealed it. There were also manufacturers supplying parts for just about anything they could hope to need.

In that regard those broadcasting entrepreneurs had it far better than their ancestors of a half-century earlier who pretty much had to figure out everything and often did so working all alone. In the absence of costly factory-made receiving sets or kits, for instance, which many of those industrious experimenters couldn't afford, they sometimes fashioned homemade receivers by winding copper wires around oatmeal canisters.[6] Nevertheless as the 1920s wore on, they bought more and more ready-made radio receivers. (Parenthetically, the 1922 retail purchase price of these sets averaged $50 each. By 1929, as demand increased and fabrication methods improved, radios soared beyond $135. In the brief span between 1922 and 1925, 4.1 million sets were commercially produced in the U.S.[7])

In an irreverent autobiography published in recent years, free-spirited journalist Sue Carpenter revealed her double-life odyssey as a newspaper reporter in the daylight hours and a rebellious nonconformist in the dark. Through her exposé, readers gained clear reflections from the interior to antiestablishment "criminal" broadcasting activity. The effort focused on a surge in maverick pursuits that occurred in the latter years of the 20th century and was heightened on the West Coast, although not exclusively limited to that geographical territory. Carpenter turned a second "career" running an illegal low-power DJ-oriented transmitting outlet into three years of hide-and-seek.

Dubbing herself "an FM radio Robin Hood," she divulged how (under the alias Paige Jarrett) she and a few co-conspirators managed to covertly place a transmitter alongside those of legit broadcasters atop the roof of a tower structure at the crossroads of Hollywood's celebrated Sunset and Vine thoroughfares. The Feds, in hot pursuit, finally caught up with her and shut her little enterprise down, taking the $500 transmitter with them.

Disclosing what attracted her to pursue her errant notion originally, Carpenter confessed: "The fear part is the draw. I'm attracted to pirate radio for the same reason I ride motorcycles: It terrifies me.... I like the idea of doing something illegal and getting away with it. I've been playing by the rules for too long, and it hasn't gotten me anywhere.... I like the idea of creating something unique and totally my own."[8]

The cat-and-mouse conspirator could have been fined $10,000 had she successfully re-grouped and returned to the airwaves in an unlawful manner. She maintained, "Many of the illegal stations that were on the air at the same time ... are still operating, even those that were caught by the FCC."[9] The consequences, if arrested, hardly seem worth the risks to some poorly-funded operators, no matter how much they aspire to nabbing a piece of the ether.

In that regard, not long after Carpenter was busted late in the 20th century, the FCC began exploring a promising strategy for allowing community-based organizations to begin transmitting within a reach of about 3.5 miles with up to 100 watts of power.[10] It's all part of a design labeled LPFM (low-power FM radio). The FCC even allowed radio's ex-pirates to apply for that privilege if they remained off the air once they were discovered. The competition for the coveted sanctions was rightly anticipated as crushing and stupefying. (About 13,000 initially applied out of 30,000 "expressions of interest."[11]) With the airwaves already saturated in metropolitan centers, contenders there were skeptical that few if any permits would be granted.

The Radio Broadcasting Preservation Act of 2000 gained congressional approval but stringently limited the LPFMs. "Stations" had to be sited on fourth-adjacent frequencies — four clicks from the next closest station on the radio dial. That dispelled four-fifths of the applicants even before they became serious contenders, ex-pirate Carpenter contended. "The only place where there's enough room for fourth adjacencies is in minuscule towns that really are forty watts from nowhere, so the approval of LPFM was a bittersweet victory," she argued.[12] (The four-clicks were reduced to three.) Neither did LPFM do anything to supply ethereal access to moderate-sized cities, let alone to behomothic municipalities like Atlanta, Boston, Chicago, Houston, Los Angeles, New York, Philadelphia, Phoenix, and San Antonio.

Nevertheless, by May 2004, more than 600 construction permits had been issued for LPFMs with some 275 already on the air. Within a year those figures doubled with 770 low-power outlets broadcasting by early 2007. The first, second, and third number of licenses were issued, in descending order, to religious-based, community-based, and either educational- or municipal-based operators.[13]

In sweeping modifications, Congress subsequently passed the Local Community Radio Act of 2010 which altered FCC regulations, eliminating most third-adjacent minimum distance separation stipulations. This applied to (1) low-power FM stations and (2) full-service FM stations, FM translator stations, and FM booster stations. On its passage Julius Genachowski, FCC chairman, attested: "Low power FM stations are small, but they make a giant contribution to local community programming. This important law eliminates the unnecessary restrictions that kept these local stations off the air in cities and towns across the country."[14]

As is so often the case, the Internet provides a forum for batting the pros and cons of various sides of the issues related to LPFM. At one contemporary site, arguments are made for and against perceived reasons why LPFM has fallen short of the promise envisioned for it upon its creation. The problem is stated in a nutshell:

> Using traditional FCC station spacing rules, over 100,000 LPFM stations potentially could be broadcasting in the United States. Yet, despite the FCC's hopes of "thousands of new voices" on the airwaves, today the number of LPFM stations is less than 1,000. To this day, there's only one LPFM station located in a top 50 media market, where most radio audiences live. Why, more than a decade after these stations were first allowed, are so few in existence?[15]

Here's one side of that equation:

> When faced with the regulatory restrictions imposed on LPFM stations it's clear why there is so much untapped potential. Power limits aside, LPFM stations are subject to onerous ownership and advertising rules.... LPFM stations can be licensed only to local entities, and those entities cannot own more than one station.
>
> Further — and most limiting — stations must be noncommercial. Despite their hyperlocal appeal, LPFM stations are prohibited from running advertisements from local restaurants, churches, retail stores, and car dealers. Constrained to relying mostly on donations and volunteer staff, few stations ever get on the air.
> ...
> ...The activists will blame Big Radio for limiting LPFM in Big Radio's markets, but the blame belongs equally to the noncommercial mandates.
> ...After a decade of filings, notices, and rule changes, the FCC and the activists ... have LPFM ... right back where it started — small, isolated, and rare.[16]

Here's another side of that equation:

> Nearly all of the 800+ LPFM stations on the air today are in rural and suburban markets. That's not because of the noncommercial mandate or ownership limits, it's because Congress set spacing restrictions (demanded by incumbent broadcasters) that have kept community radio out of big cities....
> ...
> The Local Community Radio Act is the repeal the FCC was waiting for. It won't give LPFM flexibility as other stations, but the law will pave the way to double or triple the number of LPFM stations on the air. Most importantly, it

will allow new stations within the city limits of most of the top 50 markets in the U.S.

...

...Commercial advertising isn't what most stations are asking for. Most often, we hear that stations need more power, specifically an increase from 100 to 250 watts. In rural areas, the 3.5-mile radius of an LPFM signal just isn't enough. More power means reaching more local businesses to purchase underwriting, more volunteers to staff the station, and more listeners to donate.

But in urban areas, even a 100-watt LPFM station can reach hundreds or thousands of listeners — many times more than the population most rural LPFM stations are reaching.

...

We'll soon see LPFM stations in the largest markets in the country. For the first time, LPFM will have a fair shot at developing the community support needed to thrive — with or without commercials.[17]

And there's still more about the possibility of commercializing these outlets:

It's entirely plausible, especially in higher-density areas that businesses with mostly local patrons — the neighborhood Chinese takeout, the local moving company, a maid service — would be interested in very cheap ads targeted at the local 3.5-mile populace. These establishments are not advertising on full-power stations and ... local businesses would develop their own estimates for "ears reached." In any case, it would not be an expensive ad experiment.[18]

There are other questions that none of the previous comments have addressed. An overriding issue pertains to the program matter itself that is being transmitted and essentially, the rationale behind an LPFM's existence in the first place. "The microstations," authors Robert Hilliard and Michael Keith maintain, "although operating with very low power and reaching only a limited area — from a few miles to a 10- or possibly 20-mile radius — offer a free and unfettered opportunity for those with even the most outrageous messages and exhortations to reach the public."[19] It's a concern for some that has never gone away.

Many advocates of LPFM accordingly have become relatively apprehensive following the micro-medium's invasion and — to a degree in some quarters — subsequent capture by a protracted and determined sector of fundamentalist-conservative religious promulgators. The faction has scooped up as many noncommercial frequencies — primary and secondary — and translators as well, as many as it possibly can to diffuse its gospel.[20]

Does it hold such an intimidating and imbalanced share of the public airwaves that the possibility of real competition from other aspirants with different messages can be jeopardized or maybe even silenced altogether? Can the power of this valuable public resource be potentially concentrated in too few hands? We probably have only to examine the fleeting history of broadcasting in this country since the deregulatory measures of 1996 went into effect to correctly answer those questions.

The Internet has pumped renewed life into some of these start-up ventures while some pirate endeavors continue to run without the intervention of the FCC by maintaining less than a watt of power.[21] Those living in modern America have burgeoning options to select from in obtaining electronic enjoyment and explication. As LPFM continues to evolve, it bears watching (and hearing!) for there are budding implications that it may eventually impact more Americans, possibly in greatly increased numbers, who live and work in confined territories. One of LPFM's chief intents is to return local interest to the audience. In some places LPFM could be about all that is provided in localized programming by radio broadcasters for their limited constituencies.

Stay tuned.

Returning to the topic of the Internet, introduced already, this has potential for radio broadcasters perhaps like nothing else. Some of its many offshoots have been furnishing alternative applications to standard transistor, table model, floor model, vehicle, public address system, and headphone sets for years. Writing in 2009, Brian Jennings, a broadcasting veteran, observed:

> Soon when you get into your car you will be able to tune in to media that gives you complete access to the product of free speech — unedited, frank, maybe off-color, unfiltered, but free. You will have access to everything from advice on personal relationships to outdoor wilderness survival. You'll be able to hear commentary from every left-wing group and every right-wing group.... You'll also be able to access previously unknown counterculture audio stations offering any and every point of view conceivable to mankind.[22]

If you haven't visited a new car dealer's showrooms in recent years, stop by. They'll be glad to let you see for yourself how much of this has come to pass already and is now standard equipment in some makes and models. As one Ford executive remarked in late 2012, the technology in communications devices available in vehicles is developing so quickly that "obsolescence is one of our greatest concerns."

"The availability of Wi-Fi has expanded beyond coffee shops, businesses, and residential homes to previously disconnected transportation options such as trains, automobiles, even airplanes," claimed Jennings, a skilled technician for a radio station, just a few years ago. "The Web-enabled car is possible now, and will only become more practical in the coming months."[23] You can now add buses to that list.[24]

Internet radio entails streaming media, offering listeners an unremitting audio flow that can't be paused or replayed, much like mainstream broadcast media. That separates it from on-demand file serving. Internet radio is further distinguished from podcasting, a process requiring downloading instead of streaming. Many Internet radio services are tied to a parallel conventional (or terrestrial) radio station or radio network. Those services are normally within reach anywhere on the planet. This adds to their regard among expatriates and those whose interests remain unmet by local radio outlets. Internet-only radio stations are free of these links. Music, news, sports, talk, and other elements demonstrated by conventional radio are among typical Internet radio programming components.

In streaming, audio data is serially dispatched incessantly (streamed) over the local network or Internet in TCP (Transmission Control Protocol) or UDP (User Datagram Protocol) packets. (The packets are a basic unit of information in network transmission.) Before being played a second or two later, it's all reassembled at the receiver. Streaming, in the meantime, has been around for only a couple of decades. After tests were conducted in the summer of 1994, a couple of terrestrial radio stations in Atlanta (WREK-FM) and Chapel Hill, North Carolina (WXYC-FM), were the first to broadcast on the Internet. Both did so the same day, November 7, 1994.[25] Other experimenters followed that trail as soon as practical.

After Microsoft, Nullsoft, and similar manufacturers released streaming audio players as free downloads, and when software audio players were available, many Web-based radio stations sprang up. As bandwidth became more economical, after the turn of the century, most Internet radio stations increased stream quality. Most stations currently stream between 64 kbit/s and 128 kbit/s with near CD-quality audio.[26]

In the meantime, as far as terrestrial radio stations go, within the last couple of decades they have harvested both good and not-so-good responses to the Internet's sweeping expansion into peoples' daily lives in America. On the plus side, stations have often been able to effectively turn the Web into both a conduit for valuable audience research as well as applying it to distinguish themselves with clever marketing strategies. Still more benefits for the radio broadcaster have accrued from the Internet's prolific and powerful authority.

Almost all radio stations maintain their own websites now. While this is a great promotional opportunity, the sites have become cyber-extensions of outlets' on-air signals. This allows those sitting before computers or hand-held gadgets at home, work, or while routinely traveling to easily receive a favorite station's current programming. Broadcasters maintaining websites, meanwhile, provide a visual link to themselves. This component offers greater exhibition for a once sightless medium, while the outlet concurrently streams its audio services. One wag explained: "Websites compliment all terrestrial broadcast systems, supplementing and expanding content. They give stations reach they never had before — locally, nationally, and globally."[27] That's absolutely true.

At the same time, there is a downside to all this euphoria over the Internet's entrenchment into our lives from a radio station's point of view. The Web's profusion casts a pall of gloom over local broadcasters because it has provided still more means for serious competition (divvying up the audio pie with radio's terrestrial share being cut into still thinner slices). By offering free musical services such as Pandora, Slacker, and other suppliers as well as streaming hundreds of additional radio stations online, the opportunities to "turn the dial" ("click onto something else") are begging everywhere.

Beyond that, now anyone with the proper computer and compatible software can convert himself into a broadcaster or cybercaster; an Internet encoder will allow the home user to transmit his voice (and shows) to listeners at home and abroad. None of this portends optimistic good fortune for the local radio station owner who may be ultimately forced into fighting for his very existence, if he isn't doing so already. The insider's point-of-view is one we may not often consider. For all its promising fortune, the Internet nevertheless doesn't come without challenges.

Yet another dimension of audio transmission that will profoundly affect what we hear and how we hear it in the near future (if not so already) is on the horizon. Digital Audio Broadcasting (DAB) has been branded a "murky issue." In a treatise appearing in 2010, media historiographer Michael Keith ruminated: "It's coming, but we don't really have a fix on when and in what form. Will it create even more outlets?"[28] Considerations like this one prompt unanswered questions that are presently left to speculation.

Developed out of a European research project in the 1980s, DAB's first channel (NRK Klassisk) went into service June 1, 1995, under the auspices of the Norwegian Broadcasting Corporation. Three months later, the British Broadcasting Corporation aired its first digital radio features. European broadcasters have been swiftly moving into the realms of digital since, with more than 20 nations transmitting in DAB.[29] A quartet of digital wireless radio systems certified by the International Telecommunications Union was operational globally in 2012. They included a couple in Europe — DAB and DRM (Digital Radio Mondiale) — plus one each in Japan (ISDB-T) and the United States (HD-Radio/IBOC).[30]

Digital signaling portends a more sophisticated age in radio broadcasting. Traditionally, America has been viewed as a nation of audiophiles who expect nothing less than high-quality resonance. The marvel of interference-free reception and improved frequency sensation that digital signals generate puts analog broadcasting at such a clear disadvantage that — once a user is exposed to digital sound — analog transmission is hardly competitive any more, rendered vulnerable and sterile by many who compare them.

The high regard Americans hold for home and portable digital music gadgets like CDs, MP3s, and iPods has prompted broadcasters to convert their signals from an analog AM-FM mode to DAB in order to stay competitive. How soon the buying public will shift its collective allegiance to digitized terrestrial radio (called HD Radio) is one of the questions on which the jury is still out, although an overwhelmingly positive verdict is probably anticipated. Robust confidence is out there evidenced by consumers' voracious appetites for experimentation as well as for new and improved sound, two attributes for which there appears to be little sign of any retrenchment surfacing at the moment.

> Early in the twenty-first century, the FCC authorized U.S. analog radio broadcasters — both AM and FM — to transmit in-band, on-channel (IBOC) digital services, which is based on technology developed by iBiquity Digital Corporation (their brand for this technology is HD radio). Since other countries are planning to implement digital radio using other technologies, it is likely that digital radio systems will be incompatible across national borders, while current analog systems are readily transportable.... Both the AM- and FM-band IBOC systems provide other data-carrying options, including the display of the station's call letters, program or song titles, artist or guest names, or even news and weather on a receiver.[31]

Note: According to iBiquity, *HD Radio* is the firm's trade name for its proprietary digital radio system. The nomenclature isn't a substitute for either *high definition* or *hybrid digital*, designations often mistakenly applied to iBiquity's schematic.[32] One informant advances the hypothesis that a key rationale for HD radio technology is "to offer some limited digital radio services while preserving the relative 'stick values' of the stations involved and to insure that new programming services will be controlled by existing licensees."[33]

Digital radio's capacity to do still more things is viewed as another significant positive. iBiquity developed a technology allowing outlets that broadcast digitally to diffuse data to portable digital services such as cell phones. The ability to multicast (offer side-channel communications) is a bonus for HD Radio. HD2, as it is known, permits the medium to supply two to eight channels of added program streams.

In 2005, radio manufacturers began producing HD radio receivers, allowing stations to offer multiple programs on solitary frequencies. HD Radio let conventional stations furnish increased programming selections while counterbalancing the menace posed by satellite. Digital radio's introduction required listeners to purchase new receivers initially retailing at about $300. Digital radios weren't available overnight in most new vehicles; however, earlier in the millennium manufacturers BMW, Ford, Hyundai, Jaguar, Lincoln, Mercedes, MINI, Mercury, Scion, and Volvo offered factory-installed digital options with more carmakers since joining their ranks.[34] Analysts believe wireless broadband access will be available in most new automobile models in time, significantly improving HD Radio's survivability.

HD's inception marked the first time since the arrival of FM that traditional radio had begun to intently expand its fare. The digital capabilities are allowing outlets to imitate the almost boundless smorgasbord of features that can be found on satellite radio which its ascendancy is threatening.

Before leaving the subject of DAB and other taxonomy now being applied, let us take note that not all observers of aural broadcasting on the planet are convinced that digital radio proffers a listening plus. United Kingdom newspaper columnist Matthew Bell is one. At the end of 2010, he shared some of his concerns with readers of the *Independent*.[35] Bell cited a few pitfalls and urged restraint instead of automatically embracing the new technology. While some of it is relevant to the UK, just the same he surfaced some potentially troubling matters for all potential digital users.

> Since January 2009, when Lord Carter's report said that the future of radio was digital, scare stories have hinted that FM will one day be switched off.... This year's Digital Economy Act said that Britain must prepare for a switchover, and 2015 has been pencilled [sic] in ... though this has now been put back to 2017.
> But the assumption that a switchover is inevitable is wrong; like ID cards, it could simply never happen. A Department of Media, Culture and Sport (DCMS) spokeswoman said it would be dropped if it failed to attract enough support. "We're not going to force DAB on to an unwilling public," she said....
> Although the coalition has committed itself to proposals set out by the previous government, it points out that they remain conditional on two points. First, that at least 50 per cent of listeners are using digital radio by 2013; second, that geographical coverage of DAB matches that of FM. Neither criteria are near being met.
> ...Many listeners say DAB radios are not as good as they are cracked up to be: the sound quality is worse, not better, they say; they use more battery power; they are more expensive; cars do not yet have them; they don't work well on the move; pirate radios can't broadcast via them; and the scrapping of perfectly good analogue radios is ecologically unsound.
> The main complaint, however, is that the DAB signal remains poor in many areas. Thus a catch-22 situation: a switchover cannot take place until digital audiences grow, but while coverage remains poor, there is no incentive to switch....
> ...
> Indeed, the enthusiasm of successive governments for the switchover has prompted some to question their motive. One suggestion is that, once obsolete, the FM bandwidth could be sold to mobile phone companies.
> The DCMS spokeswoman said there were no plans for a sell-off "at the moment," but did not rule it out. "We may come to a situation where a proportion of bandwidth is no longer required, and will consider possible other uses for it." However, she added that it was intended that FM be made available to community radio stations.
> In the meantime, the future of radio remains in the hands of the listeners. If the public chooses not to invest in digital radios..., DAB will go the way of ID cards.

Could those issues hold merit in America? Many questions are unanswered as we stand on the precipice of digital's more pervasive implementation. A commercial outfit attempting to sell digital apparatus offers a wide panorama of digital's upside at http://www.crutchfield.com/S-AjHnf00UnIf/learn/learning-center/car/hdradio.html.

Meanwhile, you've heard the expression, "Everything that was old is new again," haven't you? It has implications for radio today. Reaching way, way back to a method of diffusion that was available prior to the Golden Age, we (the uninitiated, or not-well-versed) are finding that shortwave radio never went completely out of style. There are organizations and individuals that are still applying it every day in contemporary times. Dating back well before the first real radio station (as we think of them) went on the air in 1920, the experimental operators (sometimes labeled "hams") behind shortwave's early use were busy communicating with one another not long after the turn of the century. Shortwave filled a gap, particularly in the wilderness of remote sections, by providing a method of reaching help in emergency and safety situations. Furthermore, it developed as a pastime for two or more parties interacting with one another, applied domestically and internationally.

Shortwave receivers generally cost more than standard AM-FM radios ($40–$200 is about the going rate). Shortwave runs on frequencies that can't be accessed by the AM-FM set. Shortwave's stations also must be licensed by the FCC just like the others. Despite its dubbing as "low-tech," shortwave radio nevertheless functions admirably for a large contingent of private networks now. This results in "a sort of unfiltered, as-it-happens sense of events" much like the Internet, Court TV, C-Span, and similar alternative sources to the slicker, packaged offerings of the broadcast TV chains. Meanwhile, a century after the advent of ham radio, it's obvious that what's old is looking new to some modern practitioners.

> Many shortwave radio stations are operated by individuals as well as by groups. The cost of building and operating a shortwave radio station can be as low as a few thousand dollars, using second-hand equipment and requiring no staff. Many shortwave stations, including some that have developed national and worldwide exposure for their content and for their on-air personalities, operate out of a spare room in individual homes or apartments.[36]

A word to the wise: Never throw out anything. It may come around again.

Compounding the frenetic competition for hearing audiences, of course, are the cable companies that offer in-home and in-business music services for the bulk of their clients. Comcast cable users, one example of the many, received in excess of 50 music channels in a recent year.[37] Some of these are niche-specific, playing to subscribers' own preferences and tastes. Such commercially-liberated lines of assorted musical persuasion with simultaneous on-screen data revealing what and who is being heard and perhaps even more detail with it are bonuses to paying consumers.

But for traditional radio, the bottom line is clearly that another mode of diluting the crowd which used to be wholly dependent on the radio set is prospering. The original juke box within radio has proliferated into numerous formats and platforms that apparently will know no end.

14

Tune in Again Tomorrow

Are you into statistics?

Here are some that will tell you something about where radio stands in the United States in this contemporary age.[1]

- 90 percent of Americans over the age of six hear the radio every week.
- 96 percent of all U.S. automobiles are equipped with radios (about 140 million compared to a daily newspaper subscription aggregate of 50 million in this country).
- 80 percent of American adults listen to radio in their vehicles every week.
- 99 percent of U.S. households are reached by more than 13,500 radio stations in this nation.
- With almost a billion working radios in America, less than 1 percent of all residences have fewer than five radio sets, and most have at least eight. There were just 325 million receivers in the nation as recently as 1970, further substantiating a continual, pervasive, and fascinatingly compelling reliance upon the medium.
- 94 percent of Americans age 12 and older listen to radio 18 hours weekly.
- 95 percent of African Americans and Hispanics are reached by radio every week.
- Two-thirds of all full-time working women in the U.S. gain their first news every morning from radio. Only 16 percent of adult Americans rely upon newspapers as their first source of news for the day.
- The airwaves prevail in introducing new music to most people. Some 43 percent say radio is their prime source for hearing new songs; 13 percent say tips from other people is their key informant; and 8 percent get endorsements from YouTube. The data deflates some notions about our craving for blogs and social networking sites.
- More than 95 percent of adults age 25 to 54 with college degrees and household incomes of $75,000 or more tune in to radio on a weekly

basis—almost 26 million in this demographic. Nearly 70 million adults age 18 to 49 (94 percent) with household incomes of $75,000 or more tune to radio on a weekly basis.

Impressive? You bet! Those numbers would be hard for any naysayers to refute.

With a half-century in broadcasting to his credit at stations in Houston, New York, Miami, Dallas, Chicago, and Los Angeles, plus further stints with the National Association of Broadcasters and the Radio Advertising Bureau, retired executive Lynn Allan Christian (1932–) pondered the status of the industry in the modern environment not so long ago.

> Today's broadcast radio has lost several of its former major components. First, the introduction of new popular music is being overtaken by the Internet and other personal electronic media choices. Large segments of the radio audience no longer go to the radio to discover a new recording artist, a new release or experimental alternative bands or singers. This is a big loss for program directors and on-air talent. Second, local news is still important to radio listeners, but national news has been moving away from both radio and television networks for the last 10 years. Cable and satellite networks are now, combined, the major source for both National and International news programming. Only NPR News seems to be growing. Third, talk radio remains very important to the media, especially on the AM dial, but it's being marginalized by the services of the half-dozen 24-hour news, sports, financial, and weather cable networks and by the general national opinion that most talk radio is controlled by conservative or right-wing commentators and networks. Talk radio is becoming stagnant.... Christian radio on FM and AM is also diluting much of AM's talk radio audience, too. [These are] troublesome times for radio in the midst of an economic recession, yet challenging for those entrepreneurial professionals who believe radio's problems ... are bottoming out.[2]

To be sure there are observers who wax nostalgically for the days of yore. Those days are still genuinely grieved in the passing of the Golden Age, albeit now more than a half-century later. Sadly for them, radio today offers very little to stir the imagination and create the excitement it presented then. One naysayer, Gerald Nachman, committed his thoughts to paper in the late 1990s. More than a decade-and-a-half later, his words continue to sting: very little has given anyone of his persuasion much optimism during the intervening time.

> Radio in the late 1990s seems as far removed from the radio heyday of the 1930s, 1940s, and early 1950s as did radio's heyday from the prim and primitive radio of the late 1920s. Radio today, oddly and ironically, echoes those first bland and hesitant years, killing airtime with words that make use of only radio's most basic forms of news, music, sports, and talk. Maybe the saddest part is that nobody seems to notice, much less care, primarily because few listeners under fifty-five realize that radio was ever anything more — that it once throbbed with theatrical

life and exploded with laughter. People in their twenties, thirties, and even forties are scarcely aware that radio flourished with as much variety and vitality as TV does now, throwing its wide net over the full spectrum of human experience, knowledge, and entertainment.

Radio today, stuck on a relentless treadmill of news-music-sports, interrupted for warmed-over weather, commute, and stock updates every ten minutes, has once again shrunk the medium to a single-cell, one-dimensional organism. Hapless stations employ their listeners to entertain themselves with a babble of opinion, most of it mindless and mean-spirited, whipped on by shrill talk-show hosts.... While all of this goes on, as radio is reduced to a wisp of its once robust self, the Federal Communications Commission applauds with apparent satisfaction the idea that radio is serving the public.[3]

Many other scholars take a wary view of radio's present circumstances and offer dire predictions for its future. Some have been among the medium's most fervent advocates. Randy Michaels, ex-CEO of Clear Channel Communications, is one of those who sees clouds gathering, and who seems to want to paint a grim picture for terrestrial radio. "There is no question that today's radio model is a leaky bucket," said he. "The way people get their entertainment and information is changing, and radio had better adapt to the changing ways and look at what's happening."[4] He may be on to something. Results of a 2005 investigation revealed that radio was popularly viewed as "a mere utility, lacking any ability to raise audience passion. Usage tends to be narrowing to the car."[5] Not much enthusiasm there; thank goodness for auto radios. That's a subject we'll encounter again momentarily.

From another province not long ago, Michael C. Keith, a lifelong researcher of mass media in this country, offered some intrinsic valuation to those within the audio broadcasting trade. Calling for radio to shelve the "mass appeal" representation that has prevailed throughout its history, Keith believes those efforts should be redirected elsewhere: to a focused, personal means for reaching individuals older than 25 in specified markets of working consumers. "The radio industry knows too little about its own customers; fixing this will require a commitment to identify, target, and develop a relationship with radio's core listeners to enable it to be more responsive, useable, and relatable," Keith maintains. Even in the face of mounting technological breakthroughs that portend further diminishment, he's not yet ready to write a final chapter for traditional terrestrial radio. With visionary leadership for the future, radio "will still be there to inform, stimulate, and entertain in more ways than ever before," he purports.[6]

To attempt to be fair and objective here, you've been exposed to radical viewpoints on radio from two conflicting sides of the coin — the disparagement that exists in spades and the more optimistic take on what's transpiring. Out of that pair of thought processes perhaps you can draw some conclusions about where you think radio may be headed: depressingly demoralized, stimulatingly upbeat, or maybe something in between? Of course, time will reveal the outcome.

The options seem to suggest, however, that radio won't be allowed to drift and become (remain?) stagnant endlessly. It could, of course, disappear from the scene altogether. But a more logical scenario may be that it continues to evolve into something practical and useful, and possibly so in form and content and transmission structures that we can't begin to fathom right now. The appalling predictions of its finish — its demise — hardly seem viable in the foreseeable future given the flourishing technology that has never approached any outer limits. When or if that happens, radio could be doomed, along with a whole lot of unrelated additional ventures.

Nevertheless...

> Satellite radio, Internet radio, iPods, and whatever new technologies are created in the next few years are all competition for the world's ears. The economic viability is still a question mark, but there's no shortage of compelling sound being created by nontraditional audio providers.
>
> Radio needs to mobilize its benefits: theater of the mind production; immediate and credible information; the bible of music, old, new, and of all genres; voices that you become addicted to; and the list goes on. But if you listen to many stations today, that edge is being lost. Production using tired old-school voices with *Star Wars* sound effects, stale news presentations, limited playlists that are behind the curve and generic voices with little character. Radio needs to accept these facts ... and aggressively attack them ... and write the new playbook for the twenty-first century.[7]

Stop for a moment and consider a real-life paradigm and the potential outcome for that scenario, had the skills, the expertise, and the tools we're accustomed to now just been in place. Media journalism historian Ed Bliss records a poignant tale that occurred during the final days of the Second World War with an ending that modern technology would have thwarted altogether had those methods been available then. President Harry S. Truman was still at sea, crossing the Atlantic on his way back to Washington in the summer of 1945 after attending the Potsdam Conference in Germany following that nation's surrender.

> Truman had already left for Potsdam to confer with Churchill and Stalin when the first atom bomb was successfully tested in the New Mexico desert on July 16. This epochal news was withheld until after the Hiroshima raid, although the President had confided in reporters traveling with him to Potsdam. But one correspondent, Morgan Beatty of NBC, claimed special knowledge. According to Beatty, it came to him during a poker game. They were aboard the cruiser *Augusta* on their way home. Truman was enjoying the game when an aide brought him a radio message. The President then asked for a map, and Beatty, facing Truman at the table, watched closely as the aide pointed with a pencil at a Japanese city. A bright light behind Truman made the map almost transparent.

Beatty could see the name of the city. It was Hiroshima, and Beatty guessed it would be the world's first atomic target. There was no way to get the story out, even if he had wanted to. And, after all, it was only a guess.[8]

What Beatty could have done with an Android, BlackBerry Playbook, cell phone, iPad, laptop, PDA, or some other communicative gadget at that moment! (Even press access to AT&T, teletype, UPS, and Western Union would have worked had they been available!)

Despite whatever concerns that may exist over the future of radio, in the minds of a more optimistic contingent there's little room for disparagement or discouragement. Experts within the industry suggest that the exodus of a few talk-radio figures to satellite systems, for instance, haven't left local radio outlets bereft of the ability to cope by any stretch of the imagination. Collectively, a number of media scholars predict that the informational format "remains terrestrial radio's best bet."[9] Even in the face of superlative technological innovations, one of their number, optimistic radio consultant Holland Cooke, was quoted a few years ago as saying: "News/talk/sports is radio's last bastion.... The traffic tangle, up ahead, the quickly changing weather forecast, the Red Sox game, and other content too perishable to store, will continue to compel users to exit new-tech for AM/FM radio."[10]

Carving out their conclusions in 1980, a pair of journalists reminded readers that radio is "the most ubiquitous of the mass media."[11] How we receive the audio medium has been dramatically altered in the intervening time. Yet it's a safe bet that legions are still tuning in — and turning on — to what they hear daily pouring forth from the sources that derive radio. We may not be paying full attention to what is being delivered to us but, notwithstanding that, many of us out here in Radioland are still humming along with the music (and perhaps singing some of it too); we're catching bits and pieces of local, national, and international happenings along the way; and we're being energized animatedly, emotionally, and possibly even vocally by the sports competitions and call-in conversations we're privileged to eavesdrop on that so utterly hook us at times. We become some kind of semi-permanent adherents thereby — even if it's processed by way of vicarious participation.

In mid–2008, some readers of the *Inquisitr* were startled to read a wordsmith's essay that counseled that television's value to the denizens of planet Earth had about reached its zenith. TV would no longer be much of a persuasive factor in our lives within a decade (2018), the sage assured. Radio, too, is on the way out, the soothsayer projected, although not quite as quickly as television, to wit:

> The move away from traditional or mainstream media is currently accelerating as more and more people switch to the Internet for their information and entertainment. Sales of newspapers are declining, radio advertising is down, and television viewers are switching off [sets] in record numbers.

...

The television switch off is real. In the United States, 2.5 million viewers switched off in the spring of 2008.... Statistically this is only a small percentage of the overall viewing audience, but among those still watching television, the amount of television they watch each day is declining.

The decline in television viewing is stronger among younger statistical groups.... The television switch off in the United States among younger people has seen the average age of a TV viewer increase to 50.

...

In stark contrast to the television industry, the newspaper industry is best suited to last well into the foreseeable future. That newspapers are in decline is a fact, but what is often ignored is another important statistic: readership to newspapers online is increasing, and ... has resulted in a net increase in newspaper readership....

The switch to online newspapers is not even across all newspaper sites, so we will still see the sector shrink greatly in size from where it is today, however ... significant numbers of newspapers will remain, perhaps in 10 or 20 years time as online services only, without a print edition.

...Put simply, newspapers are changing with the times.

The death of radio has long been predicted, even way back when television first launched, but it still goes on. Radio has two distinct advantages in lasting longer than television: mass consolidation has already taken place resulting in a low cost base, and car radio.

Consolidation of radio in the United States led by Clear Channel is well known.... This consolidation of ownership and content delivers a positive: of all traditional forms of media, radio is best suited to lasting over the short to medium turn due to its economies of scale. Whereas television is seeing a downward spiral, radio has already gone through much of the cost cutting other forms of traditional media are experiencing relative to their decline in audience.

Radio also has one advantage in consumption: the car. Depending on which figures you consider, consumption of radio is anywhere from 50–80% in a car. Like television, there is no immediate replacement to radio.... Many do play CDs or iPods, consumption is shifting, but people still listen to radio in their cars. The car advantage however is on borrowed time. More and more cars now come with iPod docking as standard, making it easier for people to play their own choice of content. Chrysler in introducing Internet access to their cars, delivering all the possibilities access provides but on the road. In 10–20 years' time, the notion of tuning into a radio station, as many do today, will be considered old-fashioned, and ... commercial radio will cease to be.

...

...I am not suggesting that the experience of sitting around a large screen TV watching sport or other content is going to fall. It never will, but content delivery via broadcast television (i.e., television networks, or collectively the television media) will fall. There will always be a place for a television set in many lounge rooms, but that set in the future will be a conduit for digitally delivered, on-demand or custom mixed content, delivered over the Internet, from many different providers.[12]

Along those lines yet another journalist, Michelle Goldberg, disclosed how easily the Internet can be adapted to more or less craft one's very own radio station — conveniently and yet possibly alarmingly so. As more and more options surface, isn't one more nail being driven in the coffin of traditional terrestrial radio?

> As I write this, it's bleak and rainy outside, putting me in the mood for languorous, lugubrious songs. I open Radio Mongo at MongoMusic and request ultraslow, medium-heavy indie rock songs, and the moody Tortoise track that opens my set perfectly suits my melancholy. More dolorous tracks follow. Later, wanting to cheer up a bit, I make the weight one point lighter and the tempo one point faster. A delicious track by the gritty-girlie pop-punk band Clare Quilty comes on.... After 15 minutes of playing around on MongoMusic, I've created a station that surprises and delights me with the songs it plays. The music may be speaking right to me, but it's alienating, being a niche market of one.[13]

The concept of creating community through radio works so well that thousands and perhaps millions of citizens now use their computers to defy the established (and long accepted) form of radio. They're making their own radio shows (termed *podcasts*) and sending them to the Web for free availability to anybody who cares to download them. Whoever cares to may play their music back on iPods or other digital devices vying to replace CDs and conventional radio. With lightning momentum following that technology's launch in 2003, thousands who couldn't tune in the music they loved on the radio reinvented themselves as podcasters.

> Just as an earlier generation used the latest technology to make cassette tapes of their favorite tunes and pass them around to friends, podcasters rely on word of mouth and search engine to bring them an audience....
> Podcasting ... combines the garage band ease of Internet radio with the go-anywhere convenience of an iPod.... Soon hundreds of thousands of podcasts vied for an audience. The first popular programs were talk shows, especially about technology and media; diaries of relationships, essentially aural blogs; and music programs.... With unprecedented speed, the major media companies grabbed hold ... within a year of the technology's launch [2004], more than a third of the most popular podcasts were programs regularly heard on National Public Radio or the BBC, and the big commercial broadcasters ... as well. Listeners seemed most interested in using podcasting as a tool to time-shift their favorite radio shows, listening when they chose to rather than when their local station told them to.
> But music lovers and people with stories to tell were undeterred. They loaded their podcasts onto the Web, waiting to see who might listen. Podcasts proved once more the human passion to share culture through sound. In an atomized society in which personalized media technologies seem to narrow the possibility of a mass shared experience, people of all ages still gravitate toward the corners of the media landscape that offer serendipity and community.[14]

Customized radio won't presage the end of conventional broadcasting. It will signify adjustments, nonetheless, for contemporary radio's research-driven technique. With access to the Net being inexpensive, readily available, user-friendly, and transportable, online services are causing long-established stations to be seriously challenged in attracting and retaining listeners. This is particularly true when direct-satellite radio and micro broadcasting are thrown into the competitive mix vying for listeners' time.

"Traditional radio stations will be able to do one thing ... that an automated, Web-based system can't," insists one scholar, Jesse Walker. "They can [still] hire skilled hosts who know their music and understand how to put disparate songs together in creative sets that no scheduling engine could conceive. Then," he adds, "program directors could stop playing super–DJ and take on the larger visionary role of shaping their stations' personalities, of figuring out the boundaries of what they will play and finding the right staff to play it."[15] And if the established stations don't respond satisfactorily, there will very likely be some Internet sites and micro outlets that will do this in a heartbeat.

Appendix: A Half-Century of Radio Evolution

1960

• Radio's Golden Age unofficially ends as the last major chain (CBS) with tangible remnants of its enduring schedule removes the final soap operas and a few lingering dramas, variety, and music series (November 25–27). The agenda is reordered to stress news and a handful of five-minute features, with a couple of weekend dramas on life support. Departing: *The Amos 'n' Andy Music Hall*; *Best Seller*; *The Couple Next Door*; *Have Gun, Will Travel*; *Ma Perkins*; *The Second Mrs. Burton*; *The Second Mrs. Burton*; *Whispering Streets*; *Young Doctor Malone*. Historiographers signify their departure as "Black Friday," dubbing November 25 "the day radio drama died."

• The epicenter of radio in the U.S. transitions from the networks to the local stations as the decades overshadowed by the transcontinental chains comes to a close.

• Radio listeners are spending 1 hour 40 minutes with their radios per day while TVs in the 87 percent of U.S. homes so equipped are running more than five hours daily.

• The 1,621 AM radio stations that had existed in America in 1948 burgeon to 3,558 outlets — more than double that figure — in a dozen years, signifying the physical hardware to increase listenership is available.

• Nearly 750 commercial FM stations air in the U.S., an increase of 41 percent over 530 outlets in 1957, and the first sign that FM can move beyond also-ran status.

• More than a million FM receivers sold in America in 1958 and 1959 nearly double in 1960 sales with one out of every five being German or Japanese imports.

• Ben Hoberman, manager of Los Angeles's KABC, is cited as "the father of talk radio," an imposing label with lasting implications for the industry. Hoberman, however, will later claim that talk radio didn't gain a serious edge at KABC until 1974.

• San Francisco's KFAX Radio shifts to an all-news focus; sans sufficient advertising and $250,000 in arrears after four months, it reverts to typical formats. Its attempt inspires several copycats to try what will soon become a trade trend however.

• A fourth owner in three years buys MBS — Minnesota Mining and Manufacturing Co. (3M). It will run the radio broadcaster a half-dozen years.

1961

• CBS cancels long-running western *Gunsmoke* (June 18), leaving just two dramas still airing that extend from the Golden Age.

- Transistor radios sell for less than $10 in the U.S., having been $50-$90 since going on the market in 1954. Nine million Americans buy in 1961; by mid-decade 12 million will be buying transistors in the U.S. every year.
- A trio of the year's five bestselling LP albums (*Camelot* and *The Sound of Music* Broadway soundtracks plus the same from celluloid's *Never on Sunday*) turn up often on FM stations. The fare underscores the classical and "beautiful music" attracting listeners to FM, creating a gratifying niche for legions.
- XETRA Radio, Tijuana, Mexico, uses its 50,000 watts to reach San Diego and Los Angeles as it becomes the first booming broadcaster with all-news formatting.
- President John F. Kennedy names lawyer Newton Minow to head the FCC. Minow is in hot water with the industry by calling for a major overhaul of TV, branding it "a vast wasteland," a metaphor still in vogue. "He seemed to favor radio more than television" says one critic who recalls Minow's positive assessment of radio.
- CBS's annual report (1961) starts with its amplified news accent. CBS News supplied 55 percent of CBS Radio's schedule and beyond 17 percent of CBS-TV's. This is a 40 percent increase in regularly scheduled information programming.

1962

- CBS's pithy slate of few remaining evening music and drama features is scrubbed (September 28–30). Departing: *The Big Crosby-Rosemary Clooney Show*; *Suspense*; *Yours Truly, Johnny Dollar*.
- The FCC reports that 983 FM stations are operating in the United States.
- America's first communications satellite, Telstar I, is boosted into orbit (July). While it has instant implications for global TV, it won't affect radio profoundly for a couple of decades, at which time it will transform much of how everything is sent.
- From a field of about 30 applicants, newspaper journalist Mal Goode is hired by ABC, the first radio net to pick a full time black reporter. Goode's experience doubling as a newsman over ABC's Pittsburgh outlet pays off at his audition.

1963

- Some 62 percent of new cars rolling off U.S. assembly lines this year bear factory-installed radios, adding momentum to listeners' demand for radio wherever they go.
- U.S. carmakers are busily engaged in adding FM to products just two years after the FCC approved stereo broadcasting on FM.
- CBS is the second net hiring a black newsman as Chicago journalist and TV reporter Ben Holman is tapped for duty in New York. Holman's star continues rising as he moves to NBC and the U.S. Justice Deptartment later. His post at the Justice Department under a Nixon appointment makes him the highest ranking black in two administrations.
- NBC News hires its first black reporter, New York newspaperman Bob Teague, who has also written for Gotham radio and television outlets.

1964

- The FCC rules AM stations owning FM outlets in large markets must — by 1967 — provide separate programming on FM 50 percent of the time. This extends to smaller burgs in the next decade securing FM's drift into explicit formatting such as AM.
- Total net revenues taken in by U.S. FM radio stations reach $19.7 million.
- Herb Jepko debuts *The Other Side of the Day* as the first overnight talk feature on Salt Lake City's KSL. It will go national in a decade.
- Sports trivia whiz "The A-Maz-In" Bill Mazer of Buffalo introduces radio listeners to sports talk as a new species by instituting it over New York's WNBC-AM.

• Pittsburgh's KDKA, which many radio buffs revere as "the daddy of radio," hires its first black performer (July). The station is approaching its 44th birthday (November).

1965

• A revolution occurs when the four transcontinental radio chains emerge from deficit balances and announce profits for the first time in 11 years.
• The six million FM radio receivers in use in the U.S. in 1960 soar to 30 million.
• A trio of radio operators switches to all-news formatting — the first on U.S. soil — setting a pace for others: WNUS, Chicago; WINS, New York; KYW, Philadelphia.

1966

• NBC Radio launches *Second Sunday*, a monthly 55-minute documentary destined to win multiple iconic awards before fading from the air following a 16-year run.
• In a September article, *Business Week* reveals how one announcer can operate a radio station by himself all day with the automation tools which are emerging this decade. The innovation portends lots more expansion in the future.
• A partnership headed by businessman John P. Fraim purchases MBS from 3M Co. Fraim and associates will run the radio network for 11 years, giving it stability.

1967

• U.S. carmakers equip 85 percent of new vehicles with radios while tape-players are added to 2 percent in their first year on the market.
• An FCC "non-duplication rule" mandates that FM outlets in large markets may not simply repeat all the programming of sister AM stations.
• Nonprofit American Public Media forms in Minnesota. It's to become the largest owner-operator of public radio stations in America and a foremost producer-distributor of public radio programming.
• President Lyndon B. Johnson signs the Public Broadcasting Act of 1967, paving the way for the birth of the Corporation for Public Broadcasting which will launch NPR.
• After being milady's companion on weekdays for almost 23 years, Art Linkletter's *House Party* departs the ether (October 13). Since 1952, it had been simulcast on CBS-TV.
• After 22 years as spokesman for NBC's prestigious *News of the World* nightly quarter-hour, retiring Morgan Beatty relinquishes those reins (September 27) to Bill Ryan.
• After the Kerner Commission (named for its chairman, Ohio Gov. Otto Kerner) cites the distortion in races among U.S. broadcasters and newspapers, a mad scramble follows to hire more blacks. Perpetuating racism is out; policies shunning ethnics in employment, on the air, and as professionals are examined and altered.

1968

• ABC Radio announces it is reordering most of its schedule to expand into a quartet of continental networks. It will expand into six chains under its corporate umbrella later and inspire rivals to divide as well.
• The first sale of an FM radio outlet for a million dollars is completed.
• Los Angeles's KFWB and San Francisco's KCBS transition to all-news radio formatting. A virtual floodgate is opening in that realm.
• Don McNeill's *Breakfast Club* hits the end of the line (December 27) as ABC pulls the plug on the longest running daytime show in network radio at 35.5 years.

1969

• At midyear, NBC Radio scrubs the longplaying *News of the World* (since 1940) from

its deck, removing that final quarter-hour evening newscast/commentary, focusing then on top-of-the-hour bulletins and not a whole lot more.
- Hal Walker is elevated from assignment reporter to correspondent at CBS's Washington bureau, the first black to become a reporter for the net. (Ben Holman, CBS's first black journalist, had duties other than reporting when named in 1963.)
- CBS president Frank Stanton, at the Radio-TV News Directors Assn. (September 24), warns of a "deeply troubling trend toward government curbs on broadcast journalism." The Nixon White House's attempts to control the press in 1969 and 1970 are defied by CBS and NBC. After Stanton's remarks, U.S. Information Agency staffer Frank Shakespeare, Nixon appointee and ex-CBS man, charged that many prominent broadcast journalists possess a disturbingly "strong and visible liberal bias."

1970

- *Music Till Dawn*, airing six hours nightly on CBS owned-and-operated stations in a handful of big cities, ends a run launched in 1953. That hookup gives impetus to a growing pattern of local stations linked with others sharing programming.
- Americans tune to FM on 93 million sets. A decade earlier, six million FM receivers were active. There's little doubt now about where listening habits are widely lodged.
- WCBS, New York, flagship station of CBS, adopts an all-news configuration.
- National Public Radio is organized in Washington, D.C.
- Only 16 of the nation's 8,000 radio stations (.002 percent) are black-owned while seven of those have some white investors. A total of 310 outlets aim their full-time programming at African-Americans.
- Americans own 325 million working radio sets; by 2010, that figure will rise to almost a billion, hinting that an addiction to the medium isn't ebbing.
- Seasonal *Monday Night Football* broadcasts begin on MBS and continue through 1977.

1971

- NPR's *All Things Considered* debuts as a late afternoon newsfeature, judged by many contemporary listeners as the foremost feature of its type at that time of day.
- CBS pulls the plug (December 18) on the last of its remote broadcasts from hotel bandstands featuring aggregates headlined by some of the biggest names in popular music, a radio institution extending back to the 1930s.
- Ronald and Judith Davenport head a unit of investors buying four radio stations which will eventually play a pivotal role in helping to launch a successful black chain (Sheridan).
- David Sarnoff dies (December 12) at 80, broadcasting mogul who made NBC a powerhouse. He served parent firm RCA 1919–70 as its president (1930) and chairman (1947). Though he ran the parent, he never took hands off the child; NBC was "his baby."

1972

- A staggering 95 percent of households in Boston and Chicago have at least one FM receiver, a symbol that will soar in many more of the nation's large cities in the future.
- The FCC acknowledges that there are 2,328 FM stations in operation in America, up 137 percent from 983 a decade earlier.
- Edward F. McLaughlin becomes president of ABC Radio networks. It's a stepping-stone to a high watermark when he will impact the design of talk radio for decades.
- *Arthur Godfrey Time* leaves CBS Radio for the final time (April 30). The broadcasting icon who commanded power and prestige tarnished his image at the peak of his popularity, losing much of his following, and never recovering during a 27-year run.

- Mutual Black Network is inaugurated by MBS (May 1). It's soon sold to Sheridan Broadcasting Co. to form Sheridan Broadcasting Network, also a black operation.

1973

- CBS becomes the first coast-to-coast chain (April 2) to air hourly newscasts 24/7.
- The nation's classic music FM stations is reduced by half of what it was a decade ago.
- Racy, indecent, and profane language is toned down on the ether after the FCC thwarts an Oak Park., Illinois outlet for abusing the airwaves.
- Mutual Progressive Network, an MBS news service tied to rock-centered outlets and going head-to-head with a similarly-themed ABC chain, premiers.
- New York's WRVR airs a new play under *X Minus One* (January 17) branding from 15 years before. The exposure stirs imaginations not only of listeners but of a sleeping giant that sees even greater possibilities during a nostalgia-heightened epoch.
- NBC launches a monthly trial (June 24) of repeats of sci-fi anthology *X Minus One* transcriptions from the 1950s. Regrettably, NBC doesn't set a regular time and day, leaving potential fans frustrated, seldom knowing when their show will air.
- Before a 13-week run of the syndicated weeknight drama *The Zero Hour* (debuting September 10) is complete, MBS acquires rights to air it nationally (starting October 15). MBS will repeat it beginning April 29, 1974.
- National Association of Broadcasters holds its first symposium on black ownership of broadcasting outlets. It marks the start of more inclusiveness in the trade.
- Unity Broadcasting Corp. launches National Black Network, competition for Sheridan.
- Pirate radio gains momentum after a couple of tries beaming unauthorized programs from U.S. offshore locations are victorious — their first known success in 40 years. This will inspire other daring, equally ambitious malcontents, stimulating a fad.

1974

- NBC joins CBS in airing hourly newscasts 24/7 (January 1).
- More than 85 percent of cars on U.S. roads have radios mounted inside, with about one-fourth proffering FM reception.
- In the last decade, the revenues of American FM radio stations combined has increased 12.6 times, to $248.2 million.
- *The Herb Jepko Nightcap Show* on MBS becomes the first nationwide nocturnal talk feature, soon drawing 10 million insomniacs and nighttime workers.
- *The CBS Radio Mystery Theater* premiers (January 6), gaining a ringing endorsement from vintage radio buffs. It will persist nine years on weeknights with mostly new tales of chilling suspense, veteran actors, writers, directors, and narrated by movie legend E.G. Marshall. It's an awesome find for the true disciples of radio drama.

1975

- NBC Radio introduces a News and Information Service netting national/international news 47 minutes per hour 14/7. Aggressive wire service rivalry, few affiliates signing up, and a staff of 500 makes it an albatross. It won't survive two years.
- NBC cancels *X Minus One* repeats (March 22); inconsistent scheduling is a major cause.
- FCC chairman Richard A. Wiley leads the panel in a 5–2 vote permitting broadcasters to cover presidential debates as "bona fide news events" exempt from the Equal Time statute. This enables airing debates in 1976 and in subsequent years.

1976

- FCC says some 3,700 FM stations are broadcasting in this country, up 59 percent in four years, up 276 percent in 14 years.
- Two out of five U.S. radio listeners tune in to FM, which earns a fifth of radio revenues.
- National Association of Black Owned Broadcasters forms to facilitate the issues of African-American owners of radio-TV facilities. Its efforts will widen black ownership.
- When things look bleakest at $2 million in arrears, National Black Network sells $2.5 million in advertising, putting it in the (ahem) black. It will soon bill $10 million annually, vastly increasing its esteem industry-wide. It will also soon have 94 affiliates, draw 20 million black listeners, and expand programming and staff.

1977

- Within one year, FM revenues climb 30 percent to $543.1 million.
- NBC's News and Information Service (debuting 1975) is shut down after 23 months.
- Long John Nebel and spouse Candy Jones supplant Herb Jepko on Mutual's overnight talkathon during a transitory period.
- President Jimmy Carter revives FDR's Fireside Chats in a modern style when he begins taking phone calls from average Americans on a feature aired intermittently on CBS Radio. He draws far more listeners at nine million than any other talk show.
- *The General Mills Radio Adventure Theater* debuts on weekends (February 5) on CBS under producer-director Himan Brown. When its run ends in six months, it's re-titled *The CBS Radio Adventure Theater* (August 6) and the episodes are repeated.
- Seasonal *Monday Night Football* broadcasts end on MBS, having begun in 1970.
- Amway Corp. buys MBS from a partnership and will run it for eight years.

1978

- *Advertising Age* notes that stations are instituting "tight format control" to reach a given "target audience," signaling more curtailment of "mass audience" focuses.
- Larry King of Miami's WIOD launches a nightly nationwide interview-and-talk series on MBS that is to project him to CNN TV in a similar gig with international acclaim.
- *The CBS Radio Adventure Theater* departs after airing its full run twice (January 29).
- The Minority Ownership Policy of 1978, signed into law by President Jimmy Carter, greatly expands access to people of color for control of radio stations.

1979

- More than half the stations on the top 10 lists in the nation's top 50 radio markets are on the FM continuum. It's a clear indication where radio listeners' ears are focused.
- *Broadcasting* reports that — for the first time — FM has exceeded AM in total listenership.
- Arbitron reveals that "beautiful music" is radio's most popular format. When emphasis shifts to satisfying baby-boomers in the next decade, "beautiful music" starts to drop; in less than a fortnight it's favored by just 1 percent of the audience.
- NPR's *Morning Edition* debuts as an A.M. drive-time newsfeature considered by many contemporary listeners to be the premier show of its type at that time of day.
- *The Sears Radio Theater* bows five nights weekly on CBS (February 5) produced by Elliott Lewis. When its six-month run ends, the dramas are repeated (August 6).
- NBC tests a taped Willie Nelson concert (February 9) after ABC draws a large youth crowd with live-on-tape music specials. A strong response prompts NBC to launch *The*

Source, a youth-oriented audio hookup (May 28). Beyond sporadic concerts, it covers topics of interest to youth in hourly two-minute presentations.

1980

• *The Sears Radio Theater* ends a second run on CBS (February 11). Its dramas are repeated more times on MBS as *The Mutual Radio Theater* (February 14–December 19 inclusive).

1981

• *Nighttalk* nocturnal call-in series debuts on NBC offering a model for verbal exchanges with gurus in sundry disciplines. It leads to replicas while also boosting the careers of Dean Edell, Sally Jessy Raphael, Harvey Ruben, and Bruce Williams.

• Enterprise Radio, the nation's first all-sports broadcaster, doesn't fare well and is gone in eight months.

• Satellite Music Network is launched. It provides a renaissance for AM stations with live 24-hour music programming under myriad formats and big name talent. A station needs little more than a computer and satellite hookup to get the signal.

• The FCC rewrites the rulebook on broadcast advertising, allowing a veritable boatload of commercials to come cascading down on listeners every hour, expanding from six minutes per hour nighttime and 12 minutes per hour daytime in the past to nearly double the highest rates any time. It's a shock to many.

• NBC proudly announces it is airing "the first live network radio drama in a quarter of a century" by broadcasting "A Halloween Story" (October 31) on a solo *All Star Radio Theater* performance. One shot doesn't bring drama back to radio, however.

• As newsman Walter Cronkite retires from CBS, his daily *Walter Cronkite Reporting* segments on current issues exit CBS Radio, replaced by *Dan Rather Reporting*. Rather is Cronkite's heir as anchor of *The CBS Evening News* on television.

• A 90-minute live call-in show, *Rockline*, originates over ABC's KLOS-FM in Los Angeles (May 4) and aired on a hookup of 17 stations scattered over the U.S.A. Pointed at teens and twentysomethings, veteran deejay B. Mitchell Reed hosts.

1982

• NBC Radio ends the year by scrubbing virtually all its daily, weekly, and monthly features, leaving only hourly newscasts, two-minute *Comment on the News* inserts, and a recorded *Meet the Press* from NBC-TV still running. To listeners, the chimes chain appears mortally wounded. Disappearing: *Ask Dr. Brothers* with psychologist Joyce Brothers; *Here and Now* with newsman Roger Mudd; *The Jensen Report* with financier Mike Jensen; *Man about Anything* with entertainment reporter Gene Shalit; *Willard's Weather* with weatherman Willard Scott; and the award-winning documentary *Second Sunday*.

• ABC launches *Talkradio* to try to stem the tide of NBC's *Nighttalk*. ABC's answer offers live interviews and interactive phone calling with hosts Ray Briem and Ira Fistell.

• CBS premiers *RadioRadio* with pithy news summaries, music, features, lifestyle trends, and health updates pitched to an advertiser's dream — the young adult crowd.

• CNN Radio kicks off symptoms of a 24/7 news service, initially airing audio of TV's CNN Headline News. By mid–1983, it will bloom into long-form news.

• *Byline Magazine*, a package of news features syndicated by CBS Radio, bows.

• *Newsmark*, a CBS Radio documentary series, takes to the airwaves late in the year.

• *The CBS Radio Mystery Theater* grinds to a halt (December 31) after diminishing outlets and advertisers make the project unprofitable. Inspired innovator Himan Brown never concurs with the trade that radio and drama can't be sustained together.

- In the next six years, as a result of new deregulation rules, the sale of U.S. radio stations rises from $602 million to $3.4 billion, mostly to outfits growing their holdings.

1983
- An estimated 1.6 million U.S.-built cars (26 percent of sales) are equipped with AM-FM stereo units with cassette players.

1984
- Congress passes legislation to let broadcasters increase their holdings from seven AM, seven FM, and seven TV stations to a dozen of each in 1985 if no more than 25 percent of the U.S. population is affected. It's just the tip of the iceberg as much more deregulatory action will soon allow much higher ownership of properties.

1985
- An early sign the Fairness Doctrine is in trouble occurs when the FCC asserts that the dogma deprives the public, defying free speech assured by the First Amendment.
- Approximately 1,500 U.S. radio stations change hands in one year, mostly to burgeoning leviathans amassing as many stations as possible in the wake of relaxed regulatory policies.
- MBS is sold by Amway Corp. to its final owner, Westwood One, for $30 million. In the late 1950s, MBS went for $2 million with almost no programming now.

1986
- AM-FM stereo systems are installed in 46 percent of U.S.-manufactured autos while only 5 percent sport AM-only factory-installed units.
- FM draws 70 percent of the nation's radio audience and a similar percentage of radio's revenues, up from 40 percent of listeners and 20 percent of income in a decade.
- *Meet the Press* is canceled on radio by NBC (July 27); it debuted on MBS in 1946. Simulcast over NBC-TV since 1952, it persists in the video incarnation.
- Radio Corporation of America, parent of NBC, is taken over by General Electric. At its start, NBC was fostered by RCA, GE, and Westinghouse. The first two fabricated the radio gear while the latter retailed it even before there was a network.
- Capital Cities Communication engineers a takeover of an earlier maneuver producing a blend of United Paramount Theaters and ABC, buying out the outfit to net Capital Cities/ABC, Inc., which will stand for nine years.

1987
- The FCC revokes the Fairness Doctrine, a statute it enacted in 1949. While a couple of provisions will remain in force to 2000, the repeal will have epic repercussions on radio programming almost instantly and ostensibly for the future.
- Edward F. McLaughlin, ex-ABC Radio networks' president, establishes EFM Radio which is to have a profound bearing on the future of all talk radio.

1988
- WNBC, New York, flagship outlet of the National Broadcasting Co., vanishes from the ether (October 7); its spot on the dial is taken by WFAN, an all-sports station. The action sends the ominous message that the glory days of NBC are well in the past.
- EFM Radio engages brassy, unabashed Sacramento talk show host Rush Limbaugh, turning him loose on a national hookup that draws a cult-like following, zooming to first place on radio, a spot he still holds in 2013. An outspoken conservative, Limbaugh eventually reaches 20 million listeners to 600-plus stations weekdays.

1989

- AM stations are struggling to regain listeners lost to FM as they try format changes, promotions, new personalities, and whatever else might work. All-talk formatting appears to be a clear choice of many, especially in larger markets.

1990

- CBS Spectrum Radio Network merges the CBS Radio network and *RadioRadio*.
- William S. Paley dies (October 26) at 89; he was an early innovator of network broadcasting, and a tycoon running CBS as corporate president-chairman from 1928–90. Seen as a "radio man," at times Paley withstood TV's encroachment to protect his first love.

1991

- NPR's first conversational dialogue series, *Talk of the Nation*, bows. Recognizing that people wish to discuss current issues on public radio, soon NPR introduces a news-talk format, an effect of the Gulf War.
- Sheridan Broadcasting Corp. negotiates the biggest deal in black radio, buying National Black Network, joining it with Sheridan Broadcasting Network to open American Urban Radio Networks based in Pittsburgh. Before the century turns, AURN will have more than 250 affiliates and reach 90 percent of U.S. African-Americans.

1992

- Nearly 75 percent of all U.S. radio listeners are tuned to FM, its highest saturation level ever.

1993

- U.S.-built cars equipped with AM-FM stereo units with cassette players, on the rise since 1983, hit 5.2 million this year, 76 percent of all new vehicles. Other sophisticated systems appear this year: AM stereo, compact-disc players, amplifiers, equalizers, and specially designed speakers.
- A bid by some left-leaning politicians fails to reinstate broadcasting's Fairness Doctrine.
- The introduction of NPR Worldwide lets the supplier send features beyond U.S. borders for the first time while allowing incredible expansion of what it has to offer.
- Three of the four original radio chains (CBS, MBS, NBC) — staunch rivals for most of their existences — are swept under one operating umbrella when corporate maneuvers merge them via acquisitions, along with Fox News and CNN Radio. Only ABC persists independently. That blueprint continues two decades afterward.

1994

- After conducting tests in the summer, two FM stations are first to stream their programming over the Internet, on the same day (November 7): WREK, Atlanta; WXYC, Chapel Hill, North Carolina. Others are poised to follow in this new method of dispatching radio.

1995

- Los Angeles's KLVE becomes the first Hispanic radio station in a major American city to achieve first-place status with listeners in its market. It will grow even more.
- Digital Audio Broadcasting's initial channel, NRK Klassisk, debuts (June 1) under the auspices of the Norwegian Broadcasting Corp. Three months hence the BBC follows suit. These actions portend new dimensions for the industry's future.

- CBS, Inc. is sold for $5.4 billion to Westinghouse Electric Corp., ending the net's 68-year history as an independent enterprise. In six months (June 1996), Westinghouse and Infinity Broadcasting Corp. will announce plans to merge.
- Walt Disney Co. buys Capital Cities/ABC, Inc. for $19 billion. Soon, the head of the joint venture, Robert Iger, who ran ABC, will exhibit profound disdain for radio.

1996

- The Telecommunications Act of 1996 ups the national broadcast holdings of an owner while increasing properties in single markets to eight from two. Clear Channel Communications expands inventory from 40 to 1,200 stations. Single black-owned outlets lose big, unable to compete with the behemoths for ad buys.
- Disney CEO Robert Iger decides to unload ABC Radio, "a non-core asset." How quickly Johnny-come-latelys forget. Radio was the broadcasting empire's start-up unit!

1997

- *The Light* is created by Sheridan Gospel Network, a division of Sheridan Broadcasting.
- Nine out of ten Hispanics in the U.S. live in ten states, a fact with huge implications on radio's future in these top states: California, Texas, New York, Florida, Illinois, Arizona, New Jersey, New Mexico, Colorado, and Massachusetts.
- Westinghouse Electric Corp. alters its name to CBS Corp. (December 1). CBS unites CBS, Westinghouse, Infinity, TDI, and Gaylord Entertainment. Westinghouse taxonomy persists in the marketplace, affixed to consumer goods, business and industrial products, the result of selling or leasing the name to manufacturers that rely on recognition and purchaser confidence in that nomenclature.

1999

- MBS officially breathes its last as its owners pull the plug (April 17) on the national chain that was inaugurated in 1934.
- NBC's owners pare the radio operation to a mere hint of its broadcasting excellence, with nothing but a few hourly news bulletins daily. Dubbed "the 17-minute network," it proffers 17 scattered minutes of original material on a typical weekday, in sharp contrast to its scores of hours of fresh programming each week during its heyday.

2000

- A couple of minor provisos of the Fairness Doctrine still in force past the FCC's repeal of the canon in 1987 expire, reducing still further any limitations on programming.
- The Radio Broadcasting Preservation Act of 2000 is bittersweet to low-power FM advocates, its rules preventing 80 percent hoping to open a station from doing so.
- Viacom completes a $39.8 billion merger with CBS Corp. The name Viacom, Inc. will be applied for five years after which it will all revert to CBS Corp. once more.

2002

- One fourth of the country's commercial radio properties are owned by 25 U.S. radio broadcasters, and 15 draw a third of the trade's ad revenues.

2003

- On a party-line vote, the FCC ok's raising station ownership to serve 45 percent of U.S. residents per owner with print-radio-TV caps upped to 49 percent per owner.
- Podcasting lets one create his own radio shows, send them to the Web for free down-

loading, and bypass conventional radio for just the music one loves. This is seen by many in the trade as a threat to the future of terrestrial radio.

2004
- By May, 600-plus construction permits are issued for low-power FM stations with 275 already airing, attributable to the Radio Broadcasting Preservation Act of 2000.

2005
- Broadcast radio advertising expenses rise a trifling 0.3 percent as the radio audience falls 0.8 percent to a sparse 27.4 million listeners in a recent report.
- A new attempt by Congress to reinstate broadcasting's Fairness Doctrine goes nowhere.
- Manufacturers begin making HD radio receivers which allows stations to offer multiple programming on singular frequencies.
- The results of one study of modern radio brands the medium "a mere utility, lacking any ability to raise audience passion. Usage tends to be narrowing to the car."
- The identification of Viacom, Inc. is replaced with CBS Corporation.

2006
- MediaMark Research, Inc. reports American Urban Radio Networks reaches more 18- to-49-year-olds than ABC, CBS, and NBC early morning TV shows combined.
- Disney announces the sale (February 6) of all remaining ABC Radio property to Citadel Broadcasting Co. except Radio Disney and ESPN Radio. The FCC approves moving ABC's 24-outlet radio unit to Citadel for $2.6 billion. In three months, Citadel removes ABC News & Talk Radio from its satellite. ABC News, an ABC-TV unit, still generates ABC News Radio. Citadel will dispense it for a decade, likely to 2017.

2007
- With streaming of radio via the Internet growing, U.S. Census data just released reflects home computer use. Asian-Americans outpace native Caucasians in computer access 67.8 percent to 66.9 percent. Black households are third at 45.3 percent.
- Some 770 low-power FM stations are broadcasting in the U.S. very early in the year.

2008
- Some conservatives are convinced that the election of a Democrat to the White House will mean instant reinstatement of the Fairness Doctrine in broadcasting. After a Democrat is elected to that post, there is no serious effort to reinstate the canon.
- Arbitron reports there are presently 1,500 U.S. radio stations with talk-oriented formats. More than 100 of these are squarely focused on sports.

2010
- No income is earned by 1,500 U.S. radio stations from paid advertising. Support arrives from foundations, fund-raisers, individuals, organizational and public treasuries, volunteers, philanthropists, etc.
- Booming Hispanic and Asian immigrants net what the Census Bureau labels "diverse communities" in 44 percent of suburban America, up from 38 percent in 2000. One in six Americans, 50.5 million Hispanics, comprises 16.4 percent the nation, its largest minority. Other minorities: 42 million blacks (44 percent); 18.2 million Asians (6 percent); 5.2 million Indian/Alaskan natives (1.7 percent). This growing diversity has strong implications for the airwaves of the future.

- The Local Community Radio Act of 2010 removes most third-adjacent minimum distance separation rules applied to all FM stations, translators, and boosters.

2011

- *Talkers* magazine identifies six (and possibly seven) of the top ten radio talk-show hosts as right-wingers in a group based on audience size.
- With $55.8B in assets, Comcast has more than any other U.S. media firm controlling what we hear, see, read, and interact to. Runner-ups: Walt Disney, $40.1B; News Corp., $33.4B; Time Warner, $29B; Viacom, $14.9B; CBS, $14.2B. Assets of the highly influential broadcast-newspaper-Internet giants total $187.4B.

2012

- NBC Radio takes a few strides to make a tenuous comeback even though it remains a microscopic figment of its former robust self.
- Arbitron discloses that 94.2 percent of African-Americans tune to radio every week. In December, nearly a million more were listening over the previous December.
- Hispanic listeners reach almost 95 percent, up 2.5 million in the same timeframe.
- American Urban Radio Networks, aimed at black audiences, reports it is delivering more than 200 weekly programs to more than 300 affiliates and reaching 94 percent of the U.S. black population. No competitor is able to top its figures.
- Four digital wireless radio systems certified by the International Telecommunications Union are functioning globally: Europe, 2; Japan, 1; HD-Radio/IBOC in the U.S.

2013

- Nearly 100 U.S. radio stations exhibit the freeform programming style; the vast majority is situated on college and university campuses.
- Major syndicators of U.S. sports talk radio now include ESPN Radio, Fox Sports Radio, Sports Byline USA, and Yahoo Sports Radio.
- More than 50 U.S. radio markets are on *The Light*, a Sheridan gospel music network.
- Almost 800 U.S. Spanish-language radio stations are on the air, often set in key metro centers like Albuquerque, Chicago, Houston, Los Angeles, Miami, New York, Phoenix, Sacramento, San Antonio, San Diego, San Francisco, and Tampa.
- The *CBS World News Roundup*, the most durable of its type with news pickups from around the globe, hits its 75th birthday (March 13). It began in 1938 with venerated newsmen Edward R. Murrow and Robert Trout at its helm and brought others to the forefront, making their names household words in the pre–TV epoch.

Notes

Preface

1. Alec Foege, *Right of the Dial: The Rise of Clear Channel and the Fall of Commercial Radio* (New York: Faber and Faber, 2008), pp. 9–10.
2. Susan J. Douglas, *Listening In: Radio and the American Imagination, from Amos 'n' Andy and Edward R. Murrow to Wolfman Jack and Howard Stern.* (New York: Times Books, 1999), p. 9.
3. http://www-958.ibm.com/software/data/cognos/manyeyes/datasets/total-number-of-daily-newspapers-in-/versions/1; http://benton.org/node/65435; Brian Jennings, *Censorship—The Threat to Silence Talk Radio: The "New" Fairness Doctrine Exposed* (New York: Threshold Editions, 2009), p. 152.
4. Quoted in Michael C. Keith, *The Radio Station: Broadcast, Satellite & Internet*, 8th ed. (Burlington, MA: Focal Press, 2010), p. 28.
5. Joe Abrams, "Foreword to the Eighth Edition," in Keith, *The Radio Station*, p. xiii.
6. Keith, p. 1.
7. Bill Press, *Toxic Talk: How the Radical Right Has Poisoned America's Airwaves* (New York: Thomas Dunne Books, 2010), p. 236.
8. Ibid.
9. Radio Advertising Bureau figures.
10. Charles Kuralt, *Charles Kuralt's America* (New York: G. P. Putnam's Sons, 1995), p. xv.

Chapter 1

1. Alfred Balk, *The Rise of Radio, from Marconi through the Golden Age* (Jefferson, NC: McFarland, 2006), p. 13.
2. Ibid., p. 139.
3. Gerard J. Holzmann and Bjorn Pehrson, "The First Data Networks," *Scientific American*, January 1994.
4. One analysis professes that "the first actual scratchy 'broadcast' occurred on Christmas Eve, 1906" when Reginald Fessenden, using his invention of a "high-frequency alternator" spoke over the airwaves and played a violin. The following year, 1907, Lee de Forest, by applying the "audion" tube he developed, transmitted a yachting race 14 miles. Those instances and more purport that radio, albeit in primitive fashion, was in place and being perfected long before most subsequent users realized. (Gerald Nachman, *Raised on Radio: In Quest of The Lone Ranger, Jack Benny, Amos 'n' Andy, The Shadow, Mary Noble, The Great Gildersleeve, Fibber McGee and Molly, Bill Stern, Our Miss Brooks, Henry Aldrich, The Quiz Kids, Mr. First Nighter, Fred Allen, Vic and Sade, The Cisco Kid, Jack Armstrong, Arthur Godfrey, Bob and Ray, The Barbour Family, Henry Morgan, Joe Friday, and Other Lost Heroes from Radio's Heyday* (New York: Pantheon Books, 1998), p. 15.
5. Samuel F. B. Morse (1791–1872) is credited with developing the first practical, commercially successful telegraph system. His memorable four-word line, "What hath God wrought?" dispatched by "Morse Code" from Washington, D.C., to Baltimore, MD, on May 24, 1844, confirmed his theory. Non-electric telegraphy had existed since 1794, with limited success. All rapid, long-distance communication depended on the telegraph afterward to 1877. That year, Alexander Graham Bell (1847–1922)—hoping to enhance the telegraph—formed the Bell Telephone Co. He had transmitted his voice through an electric connection to a cohort in an adjacent room on March 10, 1876, speaking the lingering command: "Mr. Watson, come here. I want you!" Improvements by Bell and others guaranteed the telephone's feasibility, eventually supplanting the telegraph in increasing communications situations.
6. Nachman, p. 18.
7. Norman H. Finkelstein, *Sounds in the Air: The Golden Age of Radio* (New York: Charles Scribner's Sons, 1993), p. 117.
8. Alan Havig, *Fred Allen's Radio Comedy*

(Philadelphia: Temple University Press, 1990), pp. 19–20.

9. Movie theaters emptied out on the nights *Pot o' Gold* (1939–41) aired because patrons didn't want to miss the prospect of a phone call from the show that could result in financial gain. Some cinema owners went on the offensive, staging ostentatious "bank nights" that offered moviegoers $1,000 if they missed calls from *Pot o' Gold*. A decade hence, *Stop the Music!* plus contemporary series reprised the sleazy "bank nights" in theaters. Filmgoers were indulged with bargain tableware and cheap dishes disbursed from movie stages between double bills — results of concerted efforts by picture-show operators to draw people from TVs. Jim Cox, *The Great Radio Audience Participation Shows: Seventeen Programs from the 1940s and 1950s* (Jefferson, NC: McFarland, 2001), p. 142.

10. Volney B. Palmer (1799–1864) of Philadelphia, PA, is recognized for opening America's initial advertising agency in 1843. Jim Cox, *Sold on Radio: Advertisers in the Golden Age of Broadcasting* (Jefferson, NC: McFarland, 2007), pp. 11, 32.

11. Figures in this section are adapted from *Sold on Radio*, p. 34.

12. With figures like those it's easy to guess how the national chains could reach into deep pockets a few years hence to finance the steep outlay for TV's start-up phase. After radio underwrote it, the new kid repaid its older brother by kicking radio under the bus.

13. http://www.museum.tv.htm.

14. Leonard Maltin, *The Great American Broadcast: A Celebration of Radio's Golden Age* (New York: Penguin Putnam, 1997), p. 154.

15. For a lively and delightfully charming introspective into how actors handled all of the constant travel under tight time pressures, read Mary Jane Higby, *Tune in Tomorrow: Or How I Found The Right to Happiness with Our Gal Sunday, Stella Dallas, John's Other Wife, and Other Sudsy Radio Serials* (New York: Cowles Education Corporation, 1968), pp. 168–183.

16. Nachman, p. 471.

17. Jim Ramsburg, *Network Radio Ratings, 1932–1953: A History of Prime Time Programs through the Ratings of Nielsen, Crossley and Hooper* (Jefferson, NC: McFarland, 2012), pp. 163, 207, 218.

18. Although *Lux Radio Theater* premiered on October 14, 1934, it presented adaptations of Broadway plays in its first two seasons, moving from New York to Hollywood in 1936, by then refocused on films.

19. Although the first programs under the revised plan did not air until 1947, Paley began charting his approach for recovering the programming from the ad agencies a year earlier. Christopher H. Sterling and John M. Kittross, *Stay Tuned: A Concise History of American Broadcasting*, 2nd ed. (Belmont, CA: Wadsworth Publishing, 1990), p. 269.

20. Historian Alfred Balk refers to this windfall as being akin to "a Klondike strike" for the ad agencies. Using an hourly broadcast time charge of $10,000 as typical, Balk cites the fact that an agency would garner $1,500 in production commission plus, he suggests, another $900 from a potential $6,000 in talent fees, or $2,400 for an hour on the air. (Balk, p. 127.) At 2010 levels (the most recent year for which figures by The Inflation Calculator are available), the $2,400 turns into $37,938 an hour or, for a 39-week radio season in 1932, a tidy $1,479,582 for the agency. A gold rush, indeed.

21. Peter Baida, "A Legendary Chairman." *American Heritage Magazine*, July-August 1987; http://www.americanheritage.com/content/legendary-chairman.

22. Sylvester L. Weaver and Thomas M. Coffey, *The Best Seat in the House: The Golden Years of Radio and Television* (New York: Alfred A. Knopf, 1994), p. 4. Weaver depicts how he initially discovered that the ad agencies were "in charge" of programming at the chains (see pp. 43–44). Throughout his memoir he hastens to underscore that he is entitled for reversing an industry system in the early 1950s that had been in place for two decades — except we *know* that Paley had been pursuing the tactic at CBS since 1946.

23. Maltin, p. 165.

24. Nachman, p. 477.

Chapter 2

1. Sylvester L. Weaver and Thomas M. Coffey, *The Best Seat in the House: The Golden Years of Radio and Television* (New York: Alfred A. Knopf, 1994), p. 21.

2. Norman H. Finkelstein, *Sounds in the Air: The Golden Age of Radio* (New York: Charles Scribner's Sons, 1993), p. 112.

3. Alfred Balk, *The Rise of Radio: From Marconi, through the Golden Age* (Jefferson, NC: McFarland, 2006), p. 266.

4. Ibid., p. 274.

5. Estimates based on calculations from table of U.S. Households, Families, and Married Couples, 1890–2007, http://www.infoplease.com/ipa/A0005055.html.

6. Balk, p. 266.

7. September 13, 1925.

8. Craig Havinghurst, *Air Castle of the South: WSM and the Making of Music City* (Urbana, IL: University of Illinois Press, 2007), p. 159.

9. Eugene Lyons, *David Sarnoff: A Biography — The Extraordinary Story of an Immigrant Boy Who Became an Industrial Giant* (New York: Harper & Row, 1966), pp. 205–206.

10. Weaver and Coffey, pp. 20–21.

11. Jim Ramsburg, *Network Radio Ratings,*

1932–1953: A History of Prime Time Programs through the Ratings of Nielsen, Crossley and Hooper (Jefferson, NC: McFarland, 2012), p. 101.

12. Ibid., p. 143.

13. Leonard Maltin, *The Great American Broadcast: A Celebration of Radio's Golden Age* (New York: Penguin Putnam, 1997), p. 292.

14. Ramsburg, p. 161.

15. David Halberstam, *The Fifties* (New York: Villard Books, 1993), p. 185.

16. F. Leslie Smith, *Perspectives on Radio and Television: An Introduction to Broadcasting in the United States* (New York: Harper & Row, 1979), p. 69.

17. *Variety*, July 28, 1948, p. 41.

18. Balk, p. 275.

19. John Dunning, *On the Air: The Encyclopedia of Old-Time Radio* (New York: Oxford University Press, 1998), p. 86.

20. In the interest of full disclosure, radio provided listeners with at least one more significantly impressive series, NBC's *Monitor*. On weekends for two decades (1955–75) it informed, educated, and amused listeners from coast to coast. While *Monitor* was a phenomenal feat, it was never staged before a live studio audience. Instead, it let its home/traveling fans "eavesdrop" on action taking place around the globe, often as it was occurring. *Monitor* was the last imposing show premiered during radio's Golden Age.

21. Balk, p. 277.

22. Susan J. Douglas, *Listening In: Radio and the American Imagination, from Amos 'n' Andy and Edward R. Murrow to Wolfman Jack and Howard Stern* (New York: Times Books, 1999), p. 219.

23. Philip H. Ennis, *The Seventh Stream: The Emergence of Rocknroll in American Popular Music* (Hanover, NH: Wesleyan University Press, 1992), p. 132.

24. Christopher H. Sterling and John M. Kittross, *Stay Tuned: A Concise History of American Broadcasting*, 2nd ed. (Belmont, CA: Wadsworth Publishing, 1990), p. 275.

25. Ibid., p. 277.

26. Balk, p. 267.

27. Ibid.

28. Seminar: "Network News in the Age of Cable," Center for the Study of Popular Television, Syracuse University, 1994.

29. Jim Cox, *Radio Speakers: Narrators, News Junkies, Sports Jockeys, Tattletales, Tipsters, Toastmasters and Coffee Klatch Couples Who Verbalized the Jargon of the Aural Ether from the 1920s to the 1980s — A Biographical Dictionary* (Jefferson, NC: McFarland, 2007), p. 88. "[Walter] Cronkite and all the other TV anchormen who have come along since are the direct descendants of Douglas Edwards." Gary Paul Gates, *Air Time: The Inside Story of CBS News* (New York: Harper & Row, 1978.)

30. Joseph E. Persico, *Edward R. Murrow: An American Original* (New York: Dell Publishing, 1988), pp. 497–498.

31. Sterling and Kittross, p. 271.

32. Ibid.

33. The facts presented here and subsequently are adapted from Sterling and Kittross, p. 271.

34. David Halberstam, *The Powers That Be: Within the Kingdom of the Media: How Luce's Time, Paley's CBS, the Grahams' Washington Post and the Chandlers' Los Angeles Times Became Rich and Powerful and Changed Forever the Shape of American Politics and Society* (New York: Alfred A. Knopf, 1979), p. 127.

35. Ibid.

36. 2010 figure from The Inflation Calculator.

37. Balk, p. 267.

38. Ibid., p. 275.

39. Ibid., p. 267.

40. Sterling and Kittross, p. 263.

41. Ibid., pp. 269–270.

42. Douglas, p. 19.

43. Finkelstein, p. 116.

44. Brock Brower, "A Lament for Old-time Radio," in Irving Settel's *A Pictorial History of Radio: The Complete Story of Radio Broadcasting in America from Crystal Sets to Transistors with All the Stars, All the Great Shows of Radio's Golden Age* (New York: Grosset & Dunlap, 1967), pp. 9–10.

45. Jim Cox, *This Day in Network Radio: A Daily Calendar of Births, Deaths, Debuts, Cancellations and Other Events in Broadcasting History* (Jefferson, NC: McFarland, 2008), p. 1.

46. Charles A. Siepmann, *Radio, Television and Society* (New York: Oxford University Press, 1950), pp. 328–329.

47. Adapted from Balk, pp. 279–280, and http://www.infoplease.com/ipa/A0005055.html.

48. Halberstam, 1979, p. 130.

49. Douglas, p. 220.

50. Dan Rather, with Digby Diehl, *Rather Outspoken: My Life in the News* (New York: Grand Central, 2012), p. 115.

51. The metaphor's origin has been variously attributed to several Asian lands without settling that. In the U.S., its popular use stems from the line, "One look is worth a thousand words," coined by advertising executive Fred R. Barnard in 1921. He altered the supposed Oriental proverb, as have many successors likewise. http://dictionary.reference.com/browse/picture+is+worth+a+thousand+words,+one.

52. The figures herewith are adapted from Michele Hilmes's chapter, "NBC and the Network Idea: Defining the 'American System,'" in Michele Hilmes, ed., *NBC: America's Network* (Berkeley, CA: University of California Press, 2007), p. 16.

53. Jim Cox, *American Radio Networks: A History* (Jefferson, NC: McFarland, 2009), p. 26.

54. Ibid.

55. Hilmes, p. 17.

56. Jim Cox, *Say Goodnight, Gracie: The Last*

Years of Network Radio (Jefferson, NC: McFarland, 2002), p. 17.
   57. Sterling and Kittross, p. 158.
   58. Some details presented here and in subsequent paragraphs are adapted from Cox, 2002, pp. 17–18.
   59. Cox, 2009, p. 65.
   60. "Pick up your marbles and go home": To suddenly leave an activity you have been involved in with other people, because you do not like what is happening. (*Cambridge Idioms Dictionary*, 2nd ed. (New York: Cambridge University Press, 2006).
   61. *Suspense* returned to the CBS airwaves seven months later when another durable drama, *Gunsmoke*, was dropped. *Suspense*, plus *Yours Truly, Johnny Dollar* and *The Bing Crosby and Rosemary Clooney Show* continued to air through the weekend of September 28–30, 1962. Art Linkletter's *House Party* remained on radio through October 13, 1967, while *Arthur Godfrey Time* appeared through April 30, 1972. In the meantime, *Gunsmoke* and *House Party* had long been seen in TV incarnations.
   62. Edward Bliss, Jr., *Now the News: The Story of Broadcast Journalism* (New York: Columbia University Press, 1991), p. 467.
   63. Peter Fornatale and Joshua E. Mills, *Radio in the Television Age* (Woodstock, NY: Overlook Press, 1980), p. xv.

Chapter 3

   1. Erik Barnouw, *The Golden Web: A History of Broadcasting in the United States*, Vol. II —1933 to 1953 (New York: Oxford University Press, 1968), pp. 216–217.
   2. Erik Barnouw, *A Tower in Babel: A History of Broadcasting in the United States*, Vol. I — to 1933 (New York: Oxford University Press, 1966), p. 20.
   3. Alvin F. Harlow, *Old Wires and New Waves: The History of the Telegraph, Telephone and Wireless* (New York: Appleton-Century, 1936), p. 455.
   4. An exposition from this millennium on contemporary DJs purports that the unidentified singer on Fessenden's recording was likely English concert artist Dame Clara Ellen Butt (Rumford) (1872–1936). The contralto debuted professionally in London in 1892 and was widely recognized for performances of ballads and oratorios. She was an early recording vocalist, fueling speculation of partaking in Fessenden's historic broadcast. Sir Thomas Beecham jokingly said of her booming voice: "On a clear day, you could have heard her across the English Channel." And the audience of the first broadcast may have heard her for thousands of miles over the Atlantic, too, by the magic of recording. Bill Brewster and Frank Broughton, *Last Night a DJ Saved My Life: The History of the Disc Jockey* (New York: Grove Press, 2000); www.nytimes.com/books/first/b/brewster-dj.html; http://en.wikipedia.org/wiki/Clara_Butt; http://www.britannica.com/EBchecked/topic/86593/Dame-Clara-Butt; http://www.marstonrecords.com/butt/butt_liner.htm.)
   5. Thomas A. DeLong, *The Mighty Music Box: The Golden Age of Musical Radio* (Los Angeles: Amber Crest Books, 1980), p. 7.
   6. Helen M. Fessenden, *Fessenden: Builder of Tomorrows* (New York: Coward-McCann, 1940), p. 153.
   7. De Forest is one of a small handful of scientists who invented radio, and the initial use of the term *radio* is ascribed to him by some sources. He is credited with originating space telegraphy, the triode amplifier, and the audion tube. In the early 1900s, he designed an efficient, delicate detector of electromagnetic radiation. That made amplifying a radio frequency signal possible — one picked up by an antenna before it was sent to the receiver detector. Weaker signals could be heard than was possible earlier. De Forest's efforts culminated in the amplitude-modulated (AM) system, permitting a multiplicity of radio stations. His work retired outdated spark-gap transmitting. http://inventors.about.com/od/rstartinventions/a/radio.htm.
   8. Bill Jaker, Frank Sulek, and Peter Kanze, *The Airwaves of New York: Illustrated Histories of 156 AM Stations in the Metropolitan Area, 1921–1996* (Jefferson, NC: McFarland, 1998), p. 1.
   9. Two decades prior to Hertz's discovery, in 1864, a Scot, James Clerk Maxwell (1831–79), worked out the theory of the transmission of electromagnetic waves — vibrations moving through space without physical support. Pierre Miquel, *Histoire de la radio et de la télévision* (Paris: Perrin, 1984).
   10. Tom Carpenter, *Wireless#: Certification Official Study Guide* (New York: McGraw-Hill, 2006), p. 5.
   11. Also credible in arriving at Marconi's ultimate achievements are the experiments of Michael Faraday (b. 1845), Maxwell (1864–73), Hertz (b. 1887), Edouard-Eugène Branly (b. 1890), and Aleksandr Stepanovich Popov (b. 1896). Henri-Jean Martin, *The History and Power of Writing* (Chicago: University of Chicago Press, 1994), p. 473.
   12. Edward Bliss, Jr., *Now the News: The Story of Broadcast Journalism* (New York: Columbia University Press, 1991), p. 2.
   13. This data is from Michael Jay's *The History of Communications: Advances That Have Changed the World* (New York: Thomson Learning, 1995), pp. 20–21.
   14. Martin, p. 474.
   15. Josh Pahigian and Kevin O'Connell, *The Ultimate Baseball Road Trip: A Fan's Guide to Major League Stadiums*, 2nd ed. (Guilford, CT: Lyons Press, 2012), p. 1.

16. Major limitations of the crystal set — in widespread use for decades and still used by hobbyists — were the nuisance in finding the right setting with the cat's whisker. It was solved by affixing the whisker at the factory and sealing the crystal in a case. Also, there was a deficiency in the simple receiver's ability to amplify weak incoming signals. Christopher H. Sterling and John M. Kittross, *Stay Tuned: A Concise History of American Broadcasting*, 2nd ed. (Belmont, CA: Wadsworth Publishing, 1990), p. 33.

17. John Rayburn, *Cat Whiskers and Talking Furniture: A Memoir of Radio and Television Broadcasting* (Jefferson, NC: McFarland, 2008), p. 2.

18. Sterling and Kittross, p. 79.

19. Michael Emery, Edwin Emery, and Nancy L. Roberts, *The Press and America: An Interpretive History of the Mass Media*, 9th ed. (Boston: Allyn and Bacon, 2000), pp. 267–268.

20. Anthony Rudel, *Hello, Everybody! The Dawn of American Radio* (Orlando, FL: Harcourt, Inc., 2008), pp. 15–16, 17.

21. Sterling and Kittross, pp. 79–80, 81.

22. It took 240 salesclerks to dispense 5,300 Freed-Eisemann Neutrodyne five-tube receivers at a May 1925 sale at New York's Gimbel's dry goods store. Units sold for $98.75 — several months of a workingman's wages — but Gimbel's accepted $15 down and terms (Ibid., p. 81.)

23. Susan J. Douglas, *Listening In: Radio and the American Imagination, from Amos 'n' Andy and Edward R. Murrow to Wolfman Jack and Howard Stern* (New York: Times Books, 1999), p. 17.

24. While boasting more than 26,000 patents and inventions by the close of the 20th century, "Bell Labs is probably best known for the development of the transistor, which ushered in the solid-state communications and computer era." Fritz Messere, "Bell Laboratories," in Donald G. Godfrey and Frederic A. Leigh, eds., *Historical Dictionary of American Radio* (Westport, CN: Greenwood Press, 1998), pp. 37, 38.

25. Douglas, pp. 225, 226.

26. Peter Fornatale and Joshua E. Mills, *Radio in the Television Age* (Woodstock, NY: Overlook Press, 1980), p. 18.

27. J. Fred MacDonald, *Don't Touch That Dial! Radio Programming in American Life from 1920 to 1960* (Chicago: Nelson-Hall, 1991), p. 86.

28. http://www.radiomuseum.org/forum/first_car_radios_history_and_development_of_early_car_radios.html.

29. Barnouw, 1966, p. 210. Exactly when the commercial introduction of radios fitted for cars occurred is debated; some sources claim it didn't occur before 1930. Galvin Manufacturing Corp., named for owner-operator siblings Joseph E. and Paul V. Galvin, is credited with originating the mode with their Motorola model 5171, sold at a pricey $130 in 1930. (That year, a Ford Model A deluxe coupe — *sans* radio — sold at $540.) The Galvins' early success led them to revise their firm's name to Motorola Corp. http://en.wikipedia.org/wiki/Vehicle_audio. Citing the Galvins, *Car and Driver* affirms that the first in-car radio appeared in 1930; the first FM radio, in 1952. http://www.caranddriver.com/features/the-history-of-car-radios. Yet Delco Radio Corp. fabricated tubes for car radios by 1929, hinting that radios very likely existed before 1930, as Erik Barnouw affirms. Other major car radio manufacturers in 1929 were Midwest Radio Co. and Silver-Marshall Manufacturing Co. In 1930, Philco acquired Automobile Radio Corp., allegedly for its car radio line. Philco produced car radios for ARC under the Philco brand. http://www.radiomuseum.org/forum/first_car_radios_history_and_development_of_early_car_radios.html.

30. Charles F. Aust, "Automobile Radio," in Godfrey and Leigh, p. 29.

31. Jim Cox, *Say Goodnight, Gracie: The Last Years of Network Radio* (Jefferson, NC: McFarland, 2004), p. 101.

32. Aust, pp. 29–30.

33. Figures herewith adapted from Aust, p. 30.

34. Adapted from Alex Russo's unpublished manuscript, *No Particular Place to Go*, and from Simon Frith, *Sound Effects: Youth, Leisure, and the Politics of Rock 'n' Roll* (New York: Pantheon, 1981), p. 216.

35. A couple of rival networks, observing what *Monitor* did for NBC, made half-hearted attempts to join the magazine bandwagon. MBS debuted *Companionate Radio* in July 1955; ABC premiered *New Sounds* on weeknights in November 1955. Both experiments fizzled quickly, finding less than enthusiastic audiences.

36. Pat Weaver with Thomas M. Coffey, *The Best Seat in the House: The Golden Years of Radio and Television* (New York: Alfred A. Knopf, 1994), p. 225.

37. "The DJ was a postwar phenomenon, as transforming of 1950s radio as the transistor and the automobile, and a critical money-saving and marketing device." (Douglas, p. 229.)

38. Ibid., p. 353.

39. Stephen C. Runyon, "Transistors," in Godfrey and Leigh, p. 396.

Chapter 4

1. http://www.ehow.com/about_7548648_average-radio-dj-salaries.html.

2. Arnold Passman, *The Deejays* (New York: Macmillan, 1971), p. 7.

3. Thomas A. DeLong, *The Mighty Music Box: The Golden Age of Musical Radio* (Los Angeles: Amber Crest Books, 1980), p. 2.

4. Gerald Nachman, *Raised on Radio: In Quest of The Lone Ranger, Jack Benny, Amos 'n' Andy, The Shadow, Mary Noble, The Great Gildersleeve, Fibber

McGee and Molly, Bill Stern, Our Miss Brooks, Henry Aldrich, The Quiz Kids, Mr. First Nighter, Fred Allen, Vic and Sade, Jack Armstrong, Arthur Godfrey, Bob and Ray, The Barbour Family, Henry Morgan, Our Gal Sunday, Joe Friday, and Other Lost Heroes from Radio's Heyday (New York: Pantheon Books, 1998), p. 155.

5. Ibid., p. 179.

6. Philip A. Lieberman, *Radio's Morning Show Personalities: Early Hour Broadcasters and Deejays from the 1920s to the 1990s* (Jefferson, NC: McFarland, 2009), p. 25.

7. All the classified advertisements were published in *Broadcasting* in 1954 or 1955.

8. Kathleen M. O'Malley, "Freeform Radio," in Donald G. Godfrey and Frederic A. Leigh, eds., *Historical Dictionary of American Radio* (Westport, CT: Greenwood Press, 1998), p. 172; Steve Post, *Playing in the FM Band: A Personal Account of Free Radio* (New York: Viking Press, 1974); http://www.wfmu.org.

9. http://en.wikipedia.org/wiki/WBAI.

10. Ibid.

11. John McMillian, *Smoking Typewriters: The Sixties Underground Press and the Rise of Alternative Media in America* (New York: Oxford University Press, 2011), p. 123. See also: Marc Fisher, "Voice of the Cabal: Bob Fass and the Slow Fade of Countercultural Radio," *New Yorker*, December 4, 2006, pp. 58–65.

12. http://en.wikipedia.org/wiki/Empire_State_Building; http://en.wikipedia.org/wiki/WBAI.

13. http://en.wikipedia.org/wiki/Freeform_(radio_format).

14. The DJ also currently remains an unadorned, underappreciated staff member at many outlets. For 2010, the U.S. Bureau of Labor Statistics reported the typical radio-TV announcer — many playing music on the air — commanded a median salary (some higher, some lower) of $26,850 annually, or $12.99 hourly. With 61,900 staffing these jobs, the feds predicted a "slower than average" rise in the trade of 4,100 jobs over the ensuing decade, up 7 percent. http://www.bls.gov/ooh/media-and-communication/announcers.htm.

15. Jim Cox, *American Radio Networks: A History* (Jefferson, NC: McFarland, 2009), pp. 182–183.

16. Alfred Balk, *The Rise of Radio: From Marconi through the Golden Age* (Jefferson, NC: McFarland, 2006), pp. 282–283.

17. *Variety*, July 21, 1941.

18. http://inventors.about.com/od/gstartinventions/a/gramophone.htm; http://www.invent.org/hall_of_fame/13.html.

19. Passman, p. 21.

20. More types: Club DJs select and play music in bars, nightclubs, and discothèques, or at parties, raves, or stadiums. Hip hop disc jockeys select and play music on assorted turntables, often to back up one or more emcees. They may also do turntable scratching to create percussive sounds. In reggae, the DJ is a vocalist who raps, toasts, or chats over prerecorded rhythm tracks; a person choosing and playing them is dubbed a *selector*. Mobile DJs tour with portable sound systems and play recorded music at a myriad of events.

21. Bill Brewster and Frank Broughton, *Last Night a DJ Saved My Life: The History of the Disc Jockey* (New York: Grove Press, 2000).

22. Passman, p. 26; www.nytimes.com/books/first/b/brewster-dj.html.

23. "Dr. Frank Conrad, Radio Pioneer, Dies," *New York Times*, December 12, 1941.

24. Although a Detroit experimental outfit aired returns from the same election, that outlet wasn't yet licensed by the feds. The delay gave rise to the widely accepted claim of Pittsburgh's authenticity.

25. Jim Cox, *Sold on Radio: Advertisers in the Golden Age of Broadcasting* (Jefferson, NC: McFarland, 2008), p. 20.

26. Passman, p. 23.

27. From their modest efforts, San Jose radio station KQW emerged in 1921; two decades hence, it was relocated to San Francisco. In 1949, KQW was rebranded KCBS, by then recognized as the Bay Area affiliate of CBS, and still operating in that capacity in the modern epoch. It was what occurred in those pioneer days in San Jose that grabs our attention for the present discourse.

28. Passman, p. 23.

29. This is the basis for KCBS's present claim as the nation's first broadcast station. To be first, one would have to be on the air earlier than others on a regular schedule and be "broadcasting" in the truest sense. Almost all prior radio communication had been point to point, with a specific person as receiver. Herrold, his wife, and students transmitted to whomever. Later, he said he was the first in radio for "broadcasting." Jim Cox, *Radio Journalism in America* (Jefferson, NC: McFarland, 2013).

30. http://en.wikipedia.org/wiki/Disc_jockey.

31. Newby's appearance on *I've Got a Secret* occurred on September 27, 1965, and was rebroadcast by the Game Show Network on May 22, 2008. His secret was: "I was the world's first radio disc jockey." That doesn't really take into account Reginald Fessenden's or Lee de Forest's exploits, nor does it answer the question, "At what point was Charles Herrold himself playing records on the air as he says he was — before or after his students?" It leads to speculation, but nothing more.

32. Passman, p. 23.

33. 8MK, incidentally, had also aired the Harding-Cox election returns in 1920. It had not become commercially licensed to operate by the U.S. Department of Commerce, so Pittsburgh's KDKA — which *was* licensed — gained the edge, and with it, bragging rights as the nation's first radio station.

34. Passman, p. 23; http://tenwatts.blogspot.com/2008/09/dr-elman-b-meyers.html. There is an inconsistency between these dual accounts. Passman is correct in stating that Charles Herrold's first wife, Sybil M. True (her remarried name), was an early (if not the very first) female DJ. The Internet source inaccurately states she is the wife of Elman B. Myers.

35. Passman, p. 25.

36. Ibid.

37. DeLong, 1980, p. 263. Some other sources claim the year was 1922.

38. The succeeding Federal Communications Commission clearly favored live music, giving accelerated license consent to stations pledging not to use recordings in their first three years of operation. Many recording artists, meanwhile, attempted to keep their works off the air by having their discs labeled as illegal for airplay. A 1940 federal court order determined that a recording artist had no legal power over a record after it was sold. Marc Fisher, *Something in the Air: Radio, Rock, and the Revolution That Shaped a Generation* (New York: Random House, 2007), p. 13.

39. DeLong, 1980, p. 276.

40. Peter Fornatale and Joshua E. Mills, *Radio in the Television Age* (Woodstock, NY: Overlook Press, 1980), p. 13.

41. DeLong, 1980, p. 271.

42. Adapted from Brewster and Broughton. See also: www.nytimes.com/books/first/b/brewster-dj.html.

43. "Race music" was the industry term for black artists' pop-tinged tunes with a heavy beat and lyrics packed with sexual innuendo that displaced jazz tunes as the musical passion of blacks in some areas (Fisher, p. 31).

44. Cox, 2009, pp. 181–182.

45. http://radio-locator.com/cgi-bin/finder?format=old&count=20&s=R&sr=1&is_lic=Y&is_cp=Y&is_unl=Y&is_ful=Y&is_lp=Y&scope=all&prev=20.

46. Leo Walker, *The Wonderful Era of the Great Dance Bands* (New York: Da Capo Press, 1990), p. 155.

47. Bill Jaker, Frank Sulek, and Peter Kanze, *The Airwaves of New York: Illustrated Histories of 156 AM Stations in the Metropolitan Area, 1921–1996* (Jefferson, NC: McFarland, 1998), p. 16.

48. B. Eric Rhoads, *Blast from the Past: A Pictorial History of Radio's First 75 Years* (West Palm Beach, Fla.: Streamline Publishing, 1996), p. 302.

49. Ibid., pp. 302–303.

50. http://www.wolframalpha.com/widgets/gallery/view.jsp?id=fd272fe04b7d4e68effd01bddcc6bb34.

51. Walker, p. 157.

52. Freed's difficulties with the TV station weren't payola-related as such; instead, they pertained to his not paying union-scale wages to featured artists. However, WNEW-TV would have been aware of his well-publicized dismissal by WABC two days earlier, which may have influenced the TV outcome. Subsequently, at Los Angeles's KDAY Radio, Freed — on the air with a daytime show — was arrested on May 20, 1960, on commercial bribery charges, along with a half-dozen other staffers. He was specifically indicted for plugging the discs of six recording firms and receiving $30,650. He pled guilty in 1962 to some of those charges while at Miami's WQAM, receiving a suspended six-month sentence and a $300 fine. Not long before his death, Freed was again indicted, this time for income-tax evasion, totaling $47,920. He hadn't reported income from payola receipts between 1957 and 1959. Freed's final gig was at Los Angeles's KNOB, although he had intended to return to New York (Passman, p. 238).

53. Jaker, Sulek, and Kanze, p. 16.

54. Cox, 2009, p. 213; Jim Cox, *This Day in Network Radio: A Daily Calendar of Births, Deaths, Debuts, Cancellations and Other Events in Broadcasting History* (Jefferson, NC: McFarland, 2008), pp. 162, 226.

55. Rhoads, p. 304.

56. Passman, pp. 238–239.

57. Adapted from Brewster and Broughton. See also: www.nytimes.com/books/first/b/brewster-dj.html.

58. J. Fred MacDonald, *Don't Touch That Dial! Radio Programming in American Life from 1920 to 1950* (Chicago: Nelson-Hall, 1991), pp. 367–368, 369.

59. www.nytimes.com/books/first/b/brewster-dj.html.

60. Fisher, 9.

61. Ibid., p. 16.

62. Ibid., pp. 16–17.

63. James Miller, *Flowers in the Dustbin: The Rise of Rock and Roll, 1947–1977* (Lady Lake, FL.: Fireside Publications, 2000).

64. McLendon operated under the philosophy, "There are only two things that radio can do either as well as or better than television — music and news." Philip K. Eberly, *Music in the Air: America's Changing Tastes in Popular Music, 1920–1980* (New York: Hastings House, 1982).

65. The Top 40 sensation didn't last forever. With nearly 50 radio stations in the late 1960s, the New York nighttime Top 40 audience diminished from nearly 50 percent to 15 percent (Passman, p. 19).

66. Adapted from Brewster and Broughton. See also: www.nytimes.com/books/first/b/brewster-dj.html.

67. Fisher, p. 84.

68. Lieberman, pp. 1–2.

69. Ibid.

70. Nachman, p. 180.

71. http://www.ehow.com/about_7548648_average-radio-dj-salaries.html.

72. Jesse Walker, *Rebels on the Air: An Alter-*

native History of Radio in America (New York: New York University Press, 2001), pp. 279–280.
73. Cox, 2009, p. 183.

Chapter 5

1. Christopher H. Sterling and John M. Kittross, *Stay Tuned: A Concise History of American Broadcasting*, 2nd ed. (Belmont, CA: Wadsworth Publishing, 1990), p. 328.
2. Louisa Fletcher, "The Land of Beginning Again," in *The Land of Beginning Again* (Cambridge, MA: Small, Maynard and Co., 1921), 3–4.
3. Sterling and Kittross, p. 328.
4. J. Fred MacDonald, *Don't Touch That Dial!: Radio Programming in American Life from 1920 to 1960* (Chicago: Nelson-Hall, Inc., 1991), p. 88.
5. Marc Fisher, *Something in the Air: Radio, Rock, and the Revolution That Shaped a Generation* (New York: Random House, 2007), p. 132.
6. For a comprehensive delineation of the history of news on the hour, see: Jim Cox, *Radio Journalism in America: Telling the News in the Golden Age and Beyond* (Jefferson, NC: McFarland, 2013), Chapter 8.
7. Sterling and Kittross, p. 338.
8. Rick Sklar, *Rocking America, An Insider's Story: How the All-Hit Radio Stations Took Over* (New York: St. Martin's Press, 1984), p. 89.
9. Ibid., pp. 140–141.
10. Jim Cox, "Whatever Happened to NBC Radio? The One-Minute Chain Ups the Ante," *SPERDVAC* (The Society to Preserve and Encourage Radio Drama, Variety and Comedy), *Radiogram*, September 2012, p. 9.
11. Ibid., pp. 10, 12. A fuller discussion of NBC's current status and future potential is presented.
12. Jim Cox, *American Radio Networks: A History* (Jefferson, NC: McFarland, 2009), p. 87.

Chapter 6

1. Christopher H. Sterling and Michael C. Keith, *Sounds of Change: A History of FM Broadcasting in America* (Chapel Hill, NC: University of North Carolina Press, 2008), pp. 2, 12.
2. Charles A. Siepmann, *Radio's Second Chance* (Boston: Little, Brown and Co., 1947), p. 240.
3. Even then, however, the concept for it goes back nearly a half-century further, when Danish inventor Valdemar Poulsen patented an arc generator in 1902 (popularly dubbed the "Poulsen Arc") that was applied in experiments for two decades. Testing ended in the early 1920s when radio engineers believed FM's sound distortion was too great to overcome. Details: Christopher H. Sterling and John M. Kittross, *Stay Tuned: A Concise History of American Broadcasting*, 2nd ed. (Belmont, CA: Wadsworth Publishing, 1990), pp. 30, 142.
4. Susan J. Douglas, *Listening In: Radio and the American Imagination, from Amos 'n' Andy and Edward R. Murrow to Wolfman Jack and Howard Stern* (New York: Times Books, 1999), p. 257.
5. Robert Jourdain, *Music, the Brain, and Ecstasy: How Music Captures Our Imagination* (New York: William Morrow, 1997), p. 260.
6. See Chapter 4 of this text.
7. www.cybercollege.com/frtv/frtv020.htm.
8. www.madehow.com/inventories/12/Edwin-Howard-Armstrong.html.
9. Lee de Forest titled his autobiography *Father of Radio*, proclaiming for himself that sole distinction.
10. www.madehow.com/inventories/12/Edwin-Howard-Armstrong.html.
11. Lawrence Lessing, *Man of High Fidelity: Edwin Howard Armstrong* (Philadelphia: J. B. Lippincott, 1956), pp. 234–252.
12. Mary E. Beadle, "Edwin Armstrong," in Donald G. Godfrey and Frederic A. Leigh, *Historical Dictionary of American Radio* (Westport, CT: Greenwood Press, 1998), p. 23.
13. Sterling and Kittross, p. 142.
14. Tom Lewis, *Empire of the Air: The Men Who Made Radio* (New York: HarperCollins, 1991), p. 254.
15. *Merriam-Webster's Collegiate Dictionary*, 10th ed., 2001, defines *ionosphere* thusly: "The part of the earth's atmosphere in which ionization of atmospheric gases affects the propagation of radio waves, which extends from about 30 miles to the exosphere, which is divided into regions of one or more layers whose altitudes and degrees of ionization vary with time of day, season, and solar cycle, and which is contiguous with the upper portion of the mesosphere and the thermosphere."
16. In 1949, 85 percent of U.S. FM stations were owned by AM licensees. The FM outlet was usually viewed by owners as insurance against the potential demise of AM, which seemed a very real threat in the late 1940s, and/or as protection against independent rivals (Sterling and Kittross, p. 255).
17. Sterling and Kittross, p. 145.
18. Experimental TV and the feds received added space in other parts of the spectrum. Sometimes dubbed the *electromagnetic spectrum* or the *radio spectrum*, spectrum refers to frequencies used in transmitting signals from one point to another. Its abstract concept was introduced in 1822 by Jean-Baptiste Fourier. Decades hence, James C. Maxwell wrote an article in which he advocated that a signal could be dispatched electromagnetically via the spectrum. In 1888, Heinrich Hertz physically tested and proved Fourier's and Maxwell's hypotheses. In 1895, Guglielmo Marconi experimented in wireless; it led to using the spectrum for ship-to-shore telegraph and eventually "radiotelephony"—sending voice messages by wireless (Dom Caristi, "Spectrum," in Godfrey and Leigh, p. 367).

19. Craig Havinghurst, *Air Castle of the South: WSM and the Making of Music City* (Urbana, IL: University of Illinois Press, 2007), p. 99.
20. Sterling and Kittross, p. 212.
21. William Barlow, *Voice Over: The Making of Black Radio* (Philadelphia: Temple University Press, 1999), p. 226.
22. Jesse Walker, *Rebels on the Air: An Alternative History of Radio in America* (New York: New York University, 2001), p. 46.
23. Erik Barnouw, *The Golden Web: A History of Broadcasting in the United States*, Vol. II, 1933–1953 (New York: Oxford University Press, 1968), pp. 242, 243.
24. www.cybercollege.com/frtv/frtv020.htm.
25. Sterling and Kittross, pp. 144–145.
26. Ibid., pp. 262, 329.
27. Ibid., p. 255.
28. Sterling and Kittross, p. 323.
29. Barnouw, 1968, p. 284. D.H.V. Erickson in *Armstrong's Fight for FM Broadcasting: One Man vs. Big Business and Bureaucracy* (Tuscaloosa, AL: University of Alabama Press, 1973) hints that Armstrong's suicide may have been a consequence of action/inaction by David Sarnoff's business enterprise (RCA). This is similarly referenced by Sterling and Keith, p. 217.
30. Sterling and Kittross, p. 142; Sterling and Keith, p. 19.
31. A longstanding lawsuit against RCA, possibly the largest of the claims, was settled for $1 million, more than 11 months after Armstrong's demise (*Broadcasting-Telecasting*, January 10, 1955, p. 84).
32. Sterling and Keith, p. 323.
33. www.cybercollege.com/frtv/frtv020.htm.
34. Barlow, p. 227.
35. Sterling and Kittross, p. 324.
36. Ibid., p. 352.
37. Ibid., pp. 289–290.
38. http://www.wolframalpha.com/widgets/gallery/view.jsp?id=68c86f3f9a4eefdc31...
39. Sterling and Kittross, p. 353; http://www.wolframalpha.com/widgets/gallery/view.jsp?id=68c86f3f9a4eefdc31...
40. Marc Fisher, *Something in the Air: Radio, Rock, and the Revolution That Shaped a Generation* (New York: Random House, 2007), pp. 134, 135.
41. Steven C. Runyon and David Spiceland, "Multiplexing," in Godfrey and Leigh, p. 268. AM, as well as FM, broadcasters may multiplex services on the same carrier. Subcarrier transmissions are dubbed SCS (Subsidiary Communications Service). In the early 1980s, the FCC relaxed stipulations on subcarrier transmission and let data services, as well as audio services, be diffused. Simultaneously, noncommercial outlets were allowed to offer services on their subcarriers for profit. Beyond stereo, broadcasters can use multiplex services for background music for offices and stores, reading services for the visually impaired, distributing audio networks, data transmission, paging services, and regulating appliances in peak electrical demand periods.
42. Fisher, p. 133.
43. Douglas, p. 265.
44. Ibid., p. 258.
45. FCC commissioners Kenneth Cox and Robert E. Lee successfully contended that frequencies were so scarce, and demand so great, that duplication was "a luxury we can't afford." The answer to overcrowding of the AM spectrum was insistently utilizing FM, the feds proclaimed.
46. In cities with 100,000-plus inhabitants, AM-FM outlets couldn't duplicate more than half their programming on dual bands concurrently. While this affected just 337 of 1,560 commercial FM stations then operating — and 137 were already programming independently — it urged more enterprising efforts. From 1964 to 1967, 500 added commercial and 50 more educational FM broadcasters went on the air ("FM: It Has Arrived," *Broadcasting*, March 29, 1965, p. 88; "FM Gets a Shake-up," *Newsweek*, November 28, 1966; Sterling and Kittross, p. 633).
47. Sterling and Kittross, p. 397.
48. Hadley Cantril and Gordon Allport, *The Psychology of Radio* (North Stratford, NH: Ayer Company, 1986), p. 11, reprint of Harper & Brothers 1935 edition.
49. The figures given are distilled from a composite of sources: "The FM Boom," *Newsweek*, May 22, 1972, p. 57; "The Rites of Passage Are All Over for FM Radio; It's Out on Its Own," *Broadcasting*, September 24, 1973, p. 31; "Cox Says It's Nowhere but Up for FM Medium," *Broadcasting*, September 13, 1976, p. 50; Sterling and Kittross, p. 379.
50. Ibid., p. 381.
51. Adapted from Douglas, p. 259. Criticisms of mass culture are delineated in Bernard Rosenberg and David Manning White, eds., *Mass Culture: The Popular Arts in America* (New York: Free Press, 1957). The counterculture is explored by Charles Reich, *The Greening of America* (New York: Random House, 1970); and by Todd Gitlin, *The Sixties* (New York: Bantam Books, 1987). A classic intellectual critique of popular music is Theodor Adorno's "On Popular Music," *SPSS* 9, 1941; "A Social Critique of Radio Music," Kenyon Review 7, Spring 1945; and Simon Frith, *Sound Effects: Youth, Leisure, and the Politics of Rock'n'Roll* (New York: Pantheon Press, 1981).
52. Douglas, p. 259.
53. "Cox Says It's Nowhere but Up for FM Medium," *Broadcasting*, September 13, 1976, p. 50; "The Upbeat Tempo of FM 1974," *Broadcasting*, October 7, 1974, pp. 41–42.
54. "Bach vs. Rock," *Newsweek*, March 19, 1973, p. 83.
55. "FM Rockers Are Taming Their Free Formats," *Broadcasting*, November 25, 1974, pp. 47–49.

56. Douglas, pp. 279–280.
57. *Advertising Age*, May 29, 1978, pp. R1, R26; Peter Fornatale and Joshua E. Mills, *Radio in the Television Age* (New York: Overlook Press, 1983), p. 142.
58. Sterling and Kittross, p. 487.
59. Douglas, p. 280.
60. Ibid., p. 281.
61. "Monitor," *Broadcasting*, May 28, 1979, p. 64.
62. Sterling and Keith, p. 155.
63. The subject of formatting in radio is explored in depth in the following chapter.
64. Sterling and Keith, pp. 162–163.
65. Walker, p. 10.
66. Ibid.
67. Sterling and Keith, p. 12.
68. Ibid., p. 223.

Chapter 7

1. www.museum.tv/eotvsection.php?entrycode=narrowcasting.
2. www.webopedia.com/TERM/N/narrowcast.html.
3. http://www.google.com/#hl=en&q=narrowcast&tbs=dfn:1&tbo=u&sa=X&ei=DjWUUKvFGsrm2QWQm4CgAg&sqi=2&ved=0CCUQkQ4&bav=on.2,or.r_gc.r_pw.r_qf.&fp=32142d4a7aa176f8&bpcl=37189454&biw=1440&bih=799
4. www.wisegeek.com/what-is-narrowcasting.htm
5. www.narrowcasting.com/6/narrowcasting-information/#more-6.
6. Christopher H. Sterling and John M. Kittross, *Stay Tuned: A Concise History of American Broadcasting*, 2nd ed. (Belmont, CA: Wadsworth Publishing Co., 1990), pp. 42, 43.
7. Sally Bedell Smith, *In All His Glory: The Life of William S. Paley, the Legendary Tycoon and His Brilliant Circle* (New York: Simon & Schuster, 1990), p. 155.
8. Art Weinstein, *Market Segmentation: Using Demographics, Psychographics and Other Niche Marketing Techniques to Predict Customer Behavior*, rev. ed. (Chicago: Richard D. Irwin, 1994), p. 2.
9. Frederic A. Leigh and Donald G. Godfrey, "Introduction: A Brief History of 'The Whispering Gallery of the Skies,'" in Godfrey and Leigh, eds., *Historical Dictionary of American Radio* (Westport, CT: Greenwood Press, 1998), pp. xviii, xix.
10. Weinstein, p. 3.
11. B. Eric Rhoads, *Blast from the Past: A Pictorial History of Radio's First 75 Years* (West Palm Beach, FL: Streamline Press, 1996), pp. 348–349.
12. Bruce Mims, "Beautiful Music," in Godfrey and Leigh, p. 36; Margot Hardenbergh, "Easy-Listening Format," in Godfrey and Leigh, p. 133; Susan Tyler Eastman and Douglas A. Ferguson, *Broadcast/Cable Programming Strategies and Practices*, 5th ed. (Belmont, CA: Wadsworth Publishing, 1996); Joseph Lanza, *Elevator Music: A Surreal History of Muzak, Easy-Listening and Other Moodsong* (New York: St. Martin's Press, 1994).
13. The "zoo format" is an archetype of top-40 radio. Primarily applied in morning drive time, the zoo includes co-hosts, sidekicks, telephone calls, sound effects, sarcasm, malcontents, and an abundance of behavior not unlike "a bunch of wild animals." A radio academician explained: "Juvenile by design and appeal, the zoo format throws put-ons, celebrity interviews, pop culture references, contests, rim shots, talk-ups, hot hits, and pimple cream spots up in the air to form a tightly structured, timing-intensive, playlist-driven ... spontaneous, live entertainment program, characterized by a cacophonous, yet euphonious, on-air environment." (Joseph R. Piasek, "Zoo Format," in Godfrey and Leigh, pp. 429–430.)
14. J. R. Rush, "Good-Music Format," in Godfrey and Leigh, p. 185; Robert L. Hilliard, *Radio Broadcasting: An Introduction to the Sound Medium*, 3rd ed. (New York: Longman, 1985); Michael C. Keith, *Radio Programming: Consultancy and Formatics* (Boston: Focal Press, 1987); J. T. Lull, L.M. Johnson and C. E. Sweeney, "Audiences for Contemporary Radio Formats," *Journal of Broadcasting*, Fall 1978, p. 439.
15. http://en.wikipedia.org/wiki/Radio_format.
16. Michael C. Keith, *The Radio Station: Broadcast, Satellite & Internet*, 8th ed. (Burlington, MA: Focal Press, 2010), p. 75.
17. Robert G. Finney, "Format Radio," in Godfrey and Leigh, p. 168.
18. See Sterling and Kittross, pp. 396–398, for a succinct overview of "Radio Specialization."
19. http://xroads.virginia.edu/~ugoo/30n1/radioshow/1920radio.htm.
20. www.cybercollege.com/frtv/frtv022b.htm.
21. Peter Fornatale and Joshua E. Mills, *Radio in the Television Age* (Woodstock, NY: Overlook Press, 1980), pp. 192–193.
22. Keith, 2010, pp. 25–26.
23. Ibid., p. 98.
24. Michael C. Keith, "Underground, Commercial Radio," in Godfrey and Leigh, p. 399. See also: Michael C. Keith, *Voices in the Purple Haze: Underground Radio in the Sixties* (Westport, CT: Praeger, 1997); Jim Ladd, *Radio Waves: Life and Revolution on the FM Dial* (New York: St. Martin's Press, 1991); Steve Post, *Playing in the FM Band: A Personal Account of Free Radio* (New York: Viking Press, 1974).

Chapter 8

1. B. Eric Rhoads, *Blast from the Past: A Pictorial History of Radio's First 75 Years* (West Palm Beach, FL: Streamline Press, 1996), p. 349.
2. Bruce Boliek, "FCC finally kills off fairness

doctrine," http://www.politico.com/news/stories/0811/61851.html.
3. www.en.wikipedia.org/wiki/Fairness_Doctrine.
4. Steve Randall, "The Fairness Doctrine: How we Lost it, and Why We Need it Back," http://www.commondreams.org/views05/0212-03.htm.
5. www.en.wikipedia.org/wiki/Fairness_Doctrine.
6. FCC video, *NBCUniversal*, 1987; Robert D. Hershey, Jr., "F. C. C. Votes Down Fairness Doctrine in a 4–0 Decision," *New York Times*, August 5, 1987.
7. www.en.wikipedia.org/wiki/Fairness_Doctrine.
8. Christopher H. Sterling and John M. Kittross, *Stay Tuned: A Concise History of American Broadcasting*, 2nd ed. (Belmont, CA: Wadsworth Publishing, 1990), p. 487.
9. Robert K. Avery, "All-Talk Format," in Donald G. Godfrey and Frederic A. Leigh, eds., *Historical Dictionary of American Radio* (Westport, CT: Greenwood Press, 1998), p. 14; Robert K. Avery, "Talk Radio: The Private-Public Catharsis," in Gary Gumpert and Sandra L. Fish, eds., *Talking to Strangers: Mediated Therapeutic Communication* (Norwood, NJ: Ablex Publishing, 1990), pp. 87–97; Robert K. Avery, Donald G. Ellis and Thomas W. Glover, "Patterns of Communication on Talk Radio," *Journal of Broadcasting* (Winter 1978): pp. 5–17.
10. For a fuller discussion of the telephone's pivotal role in the radio quiz genre, see: Jim Cox, *The Great Radio Audience Participation Shows: Seventeen Programs from the 1940s and 1950s* (Jefferson, NC: McFarland, 2001), pp. 134–135.
11. Leonard H. Goldenson and Marvin J. Wolf, *Beating the Odds: The Untold Story Behind the Rise of ABC: The Stars, Struggles, and Egos That Transformed Network Television By the Man Who Made It Happen* (New York: Charles Scribner's Sons, 1991), pp. 303, 304.
12. http://en.wikipedia.org/wiko/Talk_radio.
13. In late 2011, new KGO owner Cumulus Media dumped most of its broadcast issues-oriented features; it revamped the station's format toward hard news in an effort to reverse a sharp ratings decline that saw KGO fall from first to seventh place in its market.
14. Limbaugh had a colorful career before becoming a national celebrity. At 16, he worked for a hometown radio station in Cape Girardeau, MO. At 20, he joined an ABC-owned outlet in Pittsburgh. After tiring of broadcasting, at 28 he became a sales staffer for the Kansas City Royals baseball team. But at 32, his interest in radio was rekindled: he joined Kansas City's KBMC as a political commentator. The following year (1984) he hosted a daytime talk show at Sacramento's KFBK, a slot that opened up after Martin Downey, Jr.'s "failure" there. Limbaugh's national platform from New York followed in 1988. Annie M. Brewer, *Talk Shows and Hosts on Radio: A Directory Including Show Titles and Formats, Biographical Information on Hosts, and Topic/Subject Index*, 3rd ed. (Dearborn, MI: Whitefoord Press, 1995), pp. 182–183; Peter Laufer, *Inside Talk Radio: America's Voice or Just Hot Air?* (New York: Birch Lane Press, 1995), p. 122.
15. www.radiohof.org/executive/edwardmclaughlin.html.
16. "Jacor Sets Its Sights on Syndication," *Broadcasting and Cable*, June 9, 1997, p. 28.
17. www.examiner.com/article/best-conservative-talk-radio-hosts.
18. Brian Jennings, *Censorship—The Threat to Silence Talk Radio: The "New" Fairness Doctrine Exposed* (New York: Threshold Editions, 2009), p. 47.
19. Fred V. Lucas, *The Right Frequency: The Talk Radio Giants Who Shook Up the Political and Media Establishment* (Palisades, NY: History Publishing, 2012), p. 11.
20. Rhoads, p. 377.
21. Robert L. Hilliard and Michael C. Keith, *Waves of Rancor: Tuning in the Radical Right* (Armonk, NY: M. E. Sharpe, 1999), p. 146.
22. Dick Morris and Eileen McGann, *Fleeced: How Barack Obama, Media Mockery of Terrorist Threats, Liberals Who Want to Kill Talk Radio, the Do-Nothing Congress, Companies That Help Iran, and Washington Lobbyists for Foreign Governments Are Scamming Us ... And What to Do About It* (New York: HarperCollins, 2008), p. 86.
23. Ibid., pp. 4, 79, 1.
24. Ibid., p. 13.
25. Jennings, p. 81.
26. Glenn Garvin, "Talk Radio Industry Fears Fairness Law Could Silence Them; Some Talk Radio Fans Fear Democrats Are Ready to Reimpose the Fairness Doctrine, Which Mandates Ideological Balance," *Miami Herald*, December 21, 2008.
27. Michael Graham, *That's No Angry Mob, That's My Mom: Team Obama's Assault on Tea-Party, Talk-Radio Americans* (Washington, D.C.: Regnery Publishing, 2010), p. 99.
28. Lucas, p. 146.
29. Brian C. Anderson, *South Park Conservatives: The Revolt Against Liberal Media Bias* (Washington, D.C.: Regnery Publishing, 2005), p. 50.
30. Bill Press, *Toxic Talk: How the Radical Right Has Poisoned America's Airwaves* (New York: Thomas Dunne Books, 2010), p. 13.
31. "2011 Talkers Heavy Hundred," *Talkers*, February 25, 2011.
32. Press, p. 12.
33. Michael Rust, "Tuning to America," *Washington Times*, July 17, 1995, p. 11.
34. Jim Simmon, "Echo Chamber," *Houston Press*, June 29–July 5, 1995, p. 6.
35. Tim Madigan, "Are Media Talkers Stirring

Up a Hornet's Nest?" McClatchy Newspapers, October 18, 2009.
 36. Lucas, p. 245.
 37. Press, p. 175.
 38. Tom Taylor, "National Public Radio Says Listening Is Up," *Inside Radio*, March 29, 2005.
 39. Brewer, p. vii.
 40. Morris and McGann, pp. 79–80.
 41. Laufer, p. 208.
 42. Hilliard and Keith, p. xv.
 43. Press, p. 7.
 44. Ibid., p. 178.
 45. Graham, p. 93.
 46. Ibid. This is an abridgment of remarks by newsman Randall Bloomquist.
 47. Michael C. Keith, *The Radio Station: Broadcast, Satellite and Internet*, 8th ed. (Burlington, MA: Focal Press, 2010), p. 82.
 48. Rhoads, pp. 351–352.
 49. Robert K. Oermann, *Behind the Grand Ole Opry Curtain: Tales of Romance and Tragedy* (New York: Center Street, 2008), p. 167.
 50. Gerald Nachman, *Raised on Radio: In Quest of The Lone Ranger, Jack Benny, Amos 'n' Andy, The Shadow, Mary Noble, The Great Gildersleeve, Fibber McGee and Molly, Bill Stern, Our Miss Brooks, Henry Aldrich, The Quiz Kids, Mr. First Nighter, Fred Allen, Vic and Sade, The Cisco Kid, Jack Armstrong, Arthur Godfrey, Bob and Ray, The Barbour Family, Henry Morgan, Joe Friday, and Other Lost Heroes from Radio's Heyday* (New York: Pantheon Books, 1998), p. 499.
 51. Brewer, p. vii.
 52. http://thedianerehmshow.org.
 53. Hilliard and Keith, p. 133.
 54. Donella H. Meadow, "Talk Shows Don't Make Democracy," *Houston Chronicle*, February 21, 1993, pp. 1F, 4F.
 55. Laufer, p. 18.
 56. Ibid.
 57. Jim Cox, *Say Goodnight, Gracie: The Last Years of Network Radio* (Jefferson, NC: McFarland, 2002), p. 155.
 58. Robert K. Avery, "All-Talk Format," in Godfrey and Leigh, p. 14.
 59. Jim Cox, *American Radio Networks: A History* (Jefferson, NC: McFarland, 2009), p. 186; Cox, 2002, p. 162; Edward Bliss, Jr., *Now the News: The Story of Broadcast Journalism* (New York: Columbia University Press, 1991), pp. 193, 194–195.
 60. Brewer, pp. 211–269.
 61. Ibid., p. viii.
 62. Laufer, p. 28.
 63. Graham, p. 21.
 64. Walter Sabo, "My FM Talk Diary," *Talkers*, April 2007, p. 10.
 65. Michael Harrison, "Talk Media on the Front Lines of Reality," *Talkers*, January 2005, p. 8.
 66. Kevin Casey, "The Coming Rise of FM Talk," *Talkers*, November 2005, p. 6.
 67. Christopher H. Sterling and Michael C. Keith, *Sounds of Change: A History of FM Broadcasting in America* (Chapel Hill, NC: University of North Carolina Press, 2008), p. 190.
 68. Bliss, pp. 190–191.
 69. Joshua Mills, "Development and Refinement of All-News Programming at Radio Stations and Networks," paper presented at the annual meeting of the Association for Education in Journalism, Boston, MA, August 1980, p. 3.
 70. Lewis J. Paper, *Empire: William S. Paley and the Making of CBS* (New York: St. Martin's Press, 1987), p. 286.
 71. Press, pp. 10–11. There was plenty of disparity in the political verbiage at the 257 stations. An estimated 91 percent of the total weekday talk radio programming was conservative, with the remaining 9 percent progressive. On weekdays, the 257 broadcast 2,570 hours and 15 minutes of conservative talk to 254 hours of progressive, the latter 10 percent of the former. In the country's top 10 radio markets, 76 percent of the news-talk outlets aired conservative talk to 24 percent progressive. Figures are from 2007.
 72. Keith, 2010, p. 161.
 73. Jim Cox, *Radio Journalism in America: Telling the News in the Golden Age and Beyond* (Jefferson, NC: McFarland, 2013), Chapter 14.
 74. Sterling and Keith, p. 190.
 75. Laufer, p. 99.
 76. http://www.findagrave.com/cgi-bin/fg.cgi?page=gr&GRid=6953556.
 77. Ibid.
 78. Cox, 2002, p. 174.
 79. Peter Fornatale and Joshua E. Mills, *Radio in the Television Age* (Woodstock, NY: Overlook Press, 1980), p. 85.
 80. Not long ago, a sports-talk outlet in Detroit (WXYT-FM) became the highest-rated station in its market, the only place that happened, according to Personal People Meter. That led its owner, CBS Radio, to convert affiliates in a half-dozen cities to sports-oriented formats on the FM dial, including Baltimore, Boston, Cleveland, Dallas, Pittsburgh, and Washington, D.C. www.en.wikipedia.org/wiki/Sports_radio.
 81. Keith, 2010, p. 82.
 82. Ibid.
 83. ElDean Bennett, "Sports Radio Format," in Godfrey and Leigh, p. 369. See also: Laurence Bergreen, *Look Now, Pay Later: The Rise of Network Broadcasting* (Garden City, NY: Doubleday, 1980).
 84. http://www/mewsdau.com/sports/columnists/neil-best/first-time-long-time-for-bill-mazer-1.2962262.
 85. Cox, 2009, pp. 42–43.
 86. Bill Jaker, Frank Sulek, and Peter Kanze, *The Airwaves of New York: Illustrated Histories of 156 AM Stations in the Metropolitan Area, 1921–1996* (Jefferson, NC: McFarland, 1998), pp. 133–134.
 87. Cox, 2009, p. 43; www.oldradio.com/archives/prog/nbc.htm.

88. Data in the APM paragraphs is drawn from Cox, 2009, p. 186, and several related websites: http://americanpublicmedia.publicradio.org/; http://americanpublicmedia.publicradio.org/programs/; http://americanpublicmedia.publicradio.org/services/; http://americanpublicmedia.publicradio.org/support/.

89. Translators are low-power unattended repeater stations boosting weak broadcast signals, amplifying them, and rebroadcasting them on different frequencies via transmitters. A translator lets a signal be picked up on a sensitive receiver and rebroadcast to reach an audience in remote areas that can't get the signal because of physical barriers (mountains, structures, etc.). For supreme coverage, translators are situated at the highest elevations. Bruce W. Russell, "Translators," in Godfrey and Leigh, p. 396.

90. Data in the NPR paragraphs is drawn from: Cox, 2009, pp. 186–187; Alan G. Stavitsky, "National Public Radio (NPR)," in Godfrey and Leigh, pp. 278–279; William E. Buzenberg, "Growing NPR," in Edward C. Pease and Everette E. Dennis, eds., *Radio: The Forgotten Medium* (New Brunswick, NJ: Transaction Publishers, 1995), pp. 185–192; Thomas Looker, *The Sound and the Story: NPR and the Art of Radio* (Boston: Houghton Mifflin, 1995); Alan G. Stavitsky, "The Changing Conception of Localism in U.S. Public Radio," *Journal of Broadcasting & Electronic Media* (Winter 1994): pp. 19–33; Alan G. Stavitsky and Timothy W. Gleason, "Alternative Things Considered: A Comparison of National Public Radio and Pacifica Radio News Coverage," *Journalism Quarterly* (Winter 1994): pp. 775–786; and related websites: http://www.npr.org/; http://www.npr.org/sections/news/; http://www.npr.org/sections/arts/; http://www.npr.org/music/; www.npr.org/about/aboutnpr/history.html; http://en.wikipedia.org/wiki/NPR.

91. Several college-sponsored noncommercial radio stations appeared in the early 1920s. One dates its start to 1909 when the University of Wisconsin, Madison, physics department conducted audio testing. WHA Radio was established about 1915; voice transmission began in 1917, then licensed as 9XM. It was pressed into service by the U.S. Navy in the First World War to reach ships of the Great Lakes Training Center. Much later, WHA became the nucleus of an FM chain extending university programming across Wisconsin. Lawrence W. Lichty, "WHA," in Godfrey and Leigh, pp. 416–417. See also: R. Franklin Smith, "Oldest Station in the Nation?" *Journal of Broadcasting* (Winter 1959–1960): pp. 40–55).

92. Charles Osgood, *See You on the Radio* (New York: G. P. Putnam's Sons, 1999).

Chapter 9

1. The holdover series mentioned in these paragraphs were researched in the following texts: Edward Bliss, Jr., *Now the News: The Story of Broadcast Journalism* (New York: Columbia University Press, 1991); Mitchell V. Charnley, *News by Radio* (New York: Macmillan, 1948); Jim Cox, *American Radio Networks: A History* (Jefferson, NC: McFarland, 2009); Jim Cox, *The Great Radio Audience Participation Shows: Seventeen Programs from the 1940s and 1950s* (Jefferson, NC: McFarland, 2001); Jim Cox, *Music Radio: The Great Performers and Programs of the 1920s through Early 1960s* (Jefferson, NC: McFarland, 2005); Jim Cox, *Musicmakers of Network Radio: 24 Entertainers, 1926–1962* (Jefferson, NC: McFarland, 2012); Jim Cox, *Radio Journalism in America: Telling the News in the Golden Age and Beyond* (Jefferson, NC: McFarland, 2013); Jim Cox, *Radio Speakers: Narrators, News Junkies, Sports Jockeys, Tattletales, Tipsters, Toastmasters and Coffee Klatch Couples Who Verbalized the Jargon of the Aural Ether from the 1920s to the 1980s—A Biographical Dictionary* (Jefferson, NC: McFarland, 2007); Jim Cox, *Say Goodnight, Gracie: The Last Years of Network Radio* (Jefferson, NC: McFarland, 2002); Jim Cox, *This Day in Network Radio: A Daily Calendar of Births, Deaths, Debuts, Cancellations and Other Events in Broadcasting History* (Jefferson, NC: McFarland, 2008); Irving E. Fang, *Those Radio Commentators!* (Ames, IA: Iowa State University Press, 1977); Michele Hilmes, ed., *NBC: America's Network* (Berkeley, CA: University of California Press, 2007); Roger Mudd, *The Place to Be: Washington, CBS, and the Glory Days of Television News* (New York: Public Affairs, 2008); Roger C. Paulson, *Archives of the Airwaves*, Vol. 1 (Boalsburg, PA: BearManor Media, 2005).

2. NBC inaugurated daily network news after hiring swashbuckling newspaper correspondent Floyd Gibbons (1887–1939) as *The Headline Hunter* in 1929, attracting an instant following and a sponsor, GE. By 1930, Gibbons was airing a daily quarter-hour under the banner *The Literary Digest* (Bliss, p. 27.)

3. Kaltenborn had maintained his regular job as an editor at the *Brooklyn Eagle* to 1930, seemingly unsure if "this radio thing" would fly. Not until CBS signed him did he resign his day post. The weeknight work was steady; moving to NBC in 1940, he stayed to retirement in 1955. One of radio's most enduring, influential, and fascinating commentators, Kaltenborn's life and career are extensively profiled in Cox's *Radio Journalism in America*.

4. Bill Ryan had a descriptive skill and vocabulary reminiscent of CBS's famed Edward R. Murrow. "No one could fail to admire it," suggested one source. "Bill Ryan and his colleagues seemed more knowledgeable with a bigger bag of words than the hair-sprayed elite of today could hope to possess." www.imdb.com/name/nm0752434/bio; http://educationforum.ipbhost.com/index.php?showtopic=14915; http://radiodiscussions.com/smf/index.php?topic=74553.0; http://articles.chicago

tribune.com/1988-10-26/features/8802100758_1_bill-ryan-coverage-chet-huntley; www.findagrave.com/cgi?page=gr&GRid=44165052; http://en.wikipedia.org/wiki/Bill_Ryan_(journalist).

5. Aside from hourly newscasts, national observances, sports events, seasonal specials, and a few pithy features still airing on national hookups, in the early 1970s there was *Meet the Press, Monitor,* and *Music and the Spoken Word from the Crossroads of the West.* From 1960, *The Metropolitan Opera* was carried over a special hookup not sanctioned by the four transcontinental chains. The *Grand Ole Opry,* the oldest continuous ex-network feature (since 1925), is even now aired by Nashville's WSM. CBS trimmed its *Face the Nation* simulcast to TV-only in 1970, ending another radio legend. *Monitor* left the airwaves January 26, 1975. Network-headlining newscasters still on the job were Lowell Thomas, to May 14, 1976, and Paul Harvey, to late February 2009. *The Osgood File,* begun by CBS resident poet, philosopher, and news commentator Charles Osgood in 1971, was still running several times daily in 2013. Also airing were the CBS *World News Roundup* (mornings since March 13, 1938) and the CBS *World News Roundup Late Edition* (a nighttime roundup titled *The World Tonight* for years). McFarland volumes by Jim Cox: *American Radio Networks,* 2009; *Radio Journalism in America,* 2013; *Radio Speakers,* 2007; *Say Goodnight, Gracie,* 2002; *This Day in Network Radio,* 2008.

6. http://my.safaribooksonline.com/book/audio/9780240811864/production/ch09lev1sec13.

7. Michael C. Keith, *The Radio Station: Broadcast, Satellite and Internet,* 8th ed. (Burlington, MA: Focal Press, 2010), p. 91.

8. Some of the material appearing here and in several ensuing pages is adapted and expanded from Cox, *Say Goodnight, Gracie,* 2002, pp. 32–34, 100, 168–170.

9. http://en.wikipedia.org/wiki/List_of_science-fiction_films_of_the_1950s.

10. Leonard Maltin, *The Great American Broadcast: A Celebration of Radio's Golden Age* (New York: Penguin Putnam, 1997), p. 302.

11. Jay Hickerson, *The 3rd Revised Ultimate History of Network Radio Programming and Guide to All Circulating Shows* (Hamden, CT: Presto Print II, 2005), p. 489.

12. John Dunning, *On the Air: The Encyclopedia of Old-Time Radio* (New York: Oxford University Press, 1998), pp. 199–200.

13. Merriam-Webster defines the theremin as "a purely melodic electronic musical instrument typically played by moving a hand between two projecting electrodes."

14. Maltin, p. 58. Maltin's reference to radio drama writing becoming "more adult" in the 1950s would have acknowledged the genres of western and city police force dramas, both of which significantly improved with age. They focused on adults with comprehensive skills and played in settings that appeared realistic. Thus, in the 1950s you had western-themed adventures like *Gunsmoke, Have Gun—Will Travel, Luke Slaughter of Tombstone,* and *The Six Shooter;* and police dramas like *Broadway Is My Beat, Dragnet, The Line Up,* and *Twenty-First Precinct,* all of which seemed light years ahead of the amateurish, juvenile predecessors that had previously dominated the airwaves.

15. Martin Grams, Jr., *Radio Drama: American Programs, 1932–1962* (Jefferson, NC: McFarland, 2000), pp. 134–135.

16. Ibid.

17. Dunning, 1998, pp. 729, 730.

18. John Dunning, *Tune in Yesterday: The Ultimate Encyclopedia of Old-Time Radio, 1925–1976* (Englewood Cliffs, NJ: Prentice-Hall, 1976), p. 653.

19. Grams, pp. 524–528.

20. Ibid.; Dunning, 1976, p. 654.

21. These dramas would be gone in 1959. Jim Cox, *The Great Radio Soap Operas.* (Jefferson, NC: McFarland, 1999), pp. 133–144, 157–169; Jim Cox, *Historical Dictionary of American Radio Soap Opera: Historical Dictionaries of Literature and the Arts,* no. 3 (Lanham, MD: Scarecrow Press, 2005), pp. 161–163, 175–176, 247–248.

22. http://archive.org/details/galaxymagazine.

23. At the time of this writing (2013), WRVR-FM is a continuous soft rock station in Memphis, TN.

24. Personal correspondence from Jim Widner, January 14, 2013. Used by permission. Meade Frierson III and Jim Widner are coauthors of *Science Fiction on Radio: A Revised Look at 1950–1975* (Birmingham, AL: Alabama Fictioneers and Booksmyths, 1996).

25. Cox, 2002, p. 168.

26. Ibid., p. 169; Hickerson, p. 531. Personal correspondence from Martin Grams, Jr., January 14, 2013. Used by permission.

27. Gerald Nachman, *Raised on Radio: In Quest of The Lone Ranger, Jack Benny, Amos 'n' Andy, The Shadow, Mary Noble, The Great Gildersleeve, Fibber McGee and Molly, Bill Stern, Our Miss Brooks, Henry Aldrich, The Quiz Kids, Mr. First Nighter, Fred Allen, Vic and Sade, The Cisco Kid, Jack Armstrong, Arthur Godfrey, Bob and Ray, The Barbour Family, Henry Morgan, Joe Friday, and Other Lost Heroes from Radio's Heyday* (New York: Pantheon Books, 1998), p. 318.

28. Joseph Berger, "Himan Brown, Developer of Radio Dramas, Dies at 99." *New York Times,* June 6, 2010.

29. Emma Brown, "Himan Brown, producer of radio dramas including 'Dick Tracy,' dies at age 99." *Washington Post,* June 8, 2010.

30. Nachman, p. 317.

31. Ibid., p. 319.

32. Berger.

33. Ibid. When *Inner Sanctum* became a syn-

dicated TV show, it didn't weather well in the medium. Once characters were visible, the viewers became disenchanted. "The creaky door had lost its spell," assessed obit writer Berger. (www.nytimes.com/2010/06/07/arts/07brown.html?_r=0.)
  34. Dunning, 1998, p. 143.
  35. Nachman, p. 318.
  36. Ibid., p. 500.
  37. Ibid.

Chapter 10

  1. Peter Fornatale and Joshua E. Mills, *Radio in the Television Age* (Woodstock, NY: Overlook Press, 1980), pp. 143–144.
  2. Christopher H. Sterling and Michael C. Keith, *Sounds of Change: A History of FM Broadcasting in America* (Chapel Hill, NC: University of North Carolina Press, 2008), p. 137.
  3. Erik Barnouw, *The Image Empire: A History of Broadcasting in the United States*, Vol. III—from 1953 (New York: Oxford University Press, 1970), p. 208.
  4. www.cybercollege.com/frtv/frtv022b.htm.
  5. Sterling and Keith, p. 175.
  6. Ibid.
  7. Michael C. Keith, *The Radio Station: Broadcast, Satellite and Internet*, 8th ed. (Burlington, MA: Focal Press, 2010), p. 26.
  8. http://www.bonneville.com/?nid=67.
  9. Alec Foege, *Right of the Dial: The Rise of Clear Channel and the Fall of Commercial Radio* (New York: Faber and Faber, 2008), p. xvi.
  10. Ibid., pp. xii, xiii.
  11. Jeff Perlstein, "Clear Channel: the Media Mammoth that Stole the Airwaves," www.daveyd.com/articlesclearchannelbyjeffpearlstein.html; Foege, p. 158.
  12. "Radio Deregulation: Has It Served Listeners and Musicians?" Report released by Future of Music Coalition, November 18, 2002.
  13. Foege, pp. 157–158, 159.
  14. Ibid., p. 257.
  15. Both companies were losing money before the merger and were rumored to be facing bankruptcy. The combined outfit explained that merger was a way to avoid bankruptcy as that outcome would result in diminished competition for existing terrestrial radio and streaming services like Pandora. www.en.wikipedia.org/wiki/Sirius_XM_Radio.
  16. http://en.wikipedia.org/wiki/Digital_radio.
  17. Bill Press, *Toxic Talk: How the Radical Right Has Poisoned America's Airwaves* (New York: Thomas Dunne Books, 2010), p. 276.
  18. Ibid.

Chapter 11

  1. Charles A. Siepmann, *Radio's Second Chance* (Boston: Little, Brown and Co., 1947), pp. 6–7.

  2. Jim Cox, *American Radio Networks: A History* (Jefferson, NC: McFarland, 2009), p. 120.
  3. Minow succeeded John C. Doerfer as chairman of the FCC. Doerfer resigned due to alleged improprieties, accepting vacations on the Storer Broadcasting yacht and submitting double and triple billings on travel expense vouchers. B. Eric Rhoads, *Blast from the Past: A Pictorial History of Radio's First 75 Years* (West Palm Beach, FL: Streamline Publishing, 1996), p. 305.
  4. www.museum.tv/eotvsection.php?entrycode=minownewton.
  5. Rhoads, p. 305.
  6. Leonard H. Goldenson and Marvin J. Wolf, *Beating the Odds: The Untold Story Behind the Rise of ABC: The Stars, Struggles, and Egos That Transformed Network Television By the Man Who Made It Happen* (New York: Charles Scribner's Sons, 1991), pp. 450–451.
  7. Christopher H. Sterling and John M. Kittross, *Stay Tuned: A Concise History of American Broadcasting*, 2nd ed. (Belmont, CA: Wadsworth Publishing, 1990), pp. 517–518, 523–526; Robert Britt Horwitz, *The Irony of Regulatory Reform: The Deregulation of American Telecommunications* (New York: Oxford University Press, 1989), pp. 245, 259–260; Vincent M. Ditingo, *The Remaking of Radio (Broadcasting & Cable Series)* (Boston: Focal Press, 1995), pp. 2–4; David K. Dunaway, "Save Our Stations," *New York Times*, May 23, 1992.
  8. "Forty Years of Station Transactions," *Bdc/Cable Yearbook* 1995, p. A-97; "Has the FCC Gone Too Far?" *Business Week*, August 5, 1985, pp. 48–54.
  9. Alfred Balk, *The Rise of Radio: From Marconi through the Golden Age* (Jefferson, NC: McFarland, 2006), p. 284.
  10. Bill Press, *Toxic Talk: How the Radical Right Has Poisoned America's Airwaves* (New York: Thomas Dunne Books, 2010), pp. 244, 245.
  11. Christopher H. Sterling and Michael C. Keith, *Sounds of Change: A History of FM Broadcasting in America* (Chapel Hill, NC: University of North Carolina Press, 2008), p. 182.
  12. Benjamin N. Compaine and Douglas Gomery, *Who Owns the Media?: Competition and Concentration in the Mass Media Industry*, 3rd ed. (Mahwah, NJ: Erlbaum Publishing, 2000), pp. 399–402; Robert W. McChesney, *Rich Media, Poor Democracy: Communication Politics in Dubious Times* (Urbana, IL: University of Illinois Press, 1999), pp. 74–75; Lydia Polgreen, "The Death of Local Radio," *Washington Monthly*, April 1999; Margot Hornblower, "Radio Free America," *Time*, April 20, 1998; William Safire, "Broadcast Lobby Triumphs," *New York Times*, July 23, 1997; Eben Shapiro, "A Wave of Buyouts Has Radio Industry Beaming with Success," *Wall Street Journal*, September 18, 1997; Balk, p. 285.
  13. www.freepress.net/ownership/chart.
  14. Press, p. 243.
  15. Ibid., p. 141.

16. Subsequently, Citadel bought the Disney-owned stations (which, in the process, added impressive conservative talk outlets in Chicago, Los Angeles, New York, and San Francisco to Citadel's holdings).
17. Michael C. Keith, *The Radio Station: Broadcast, Satellite and Internet*, 8th ed. (Burlington, MA: Focal Press, 2010), p. 11.
18. Jim Cox, *Sold on Radio: Advertisers in the Golden Age of Broadcasting* (Jefferson, NC: McFarland, 2008), p. 31.
19. Ibid., p. 19.
20. www.cybercollege.com/frtv/frtv022b.htm.
21. Keith, 2010, p. 15.
22. Marc Fisher, "Radio's latest 'innovation': 30 commercials in a row, 'We'll be right back' is starting to mean 'See you in 15 minutes or so,'" *Los Angeles Times*, July 19, 2004.
23. Bob Edwards, *Edward R. Murrow: And the Birth of Broadcast Journalism* (Hoboken, NJ: John Wiley & Sons, 2004, pp. 161–162.

Chapter 12

1. Figures for 2010 are reported by the U.S. Census Bureau, from a U.S. 2010 Project conducted by Brown University, Providence, Rhode Island, and from *Facts and Trends* (Winter 2013).
2. Fran R. Matera, "Ethnic Issues, Ethnic Music," in Donald G. Godfrey and Frederic A. Leigh, eds., *Historical Dictionary of American Radio* (Westport CT: Greenwood Press, 1998), p. 145.
3. Ibid., p. 146.
4. Gilbert A. Williams, "Racial Issues," in Godfrey and Leigh, p. 329.
5. 2012 figures and comparisons are from http://arbitron.mediaroom.com/index.php?s=43&item=849.
6. Estelle Edmerson, "A Descriptive Study of the American Negro in United States Professional Radio, 1922–1953," Master's thesis at the University of California at Los Angeles, 1954, p. 100.
7. Edward Bliss, Jr., *Now the News: The Story of Broadcast Journalism* (New York: Columbia University Press, 1991), pp. 327–328. When William Worthy returned to America, his passport was lifted by the State Department, which had banned travel to Communist China. Worthy knew of the ban but chose to go behind the Iron Curtain anyway. He was supported by CBS's news director Edward R. Murrow and the American Civil Liberties Union after he filed suit in federal court to reclaim his passport. Worthy argued that citizens had the right to free movement, barring any wartime conditions. The court sided with the State Department, however.
8. *Newsweek*, December 4, 1967.
9. James C. Hagerty, the longest-serving U.S. presidential press secretary in the nation's history (serving two full terms as Dwight D. Eisenhower's press agent, 1953–61), was VP in charge of news at ABC earlier and made the decision to employ Mal Goode. Upon hiring Goode, Hagerty sent him to the United Nations. One of his duties was to deliver lectures to minority groups, including the NAACP. His premise was: "I did it; so can you." (Bliss, p. 328.)
10. Ibid.
11. Ibid., pp. 328–329.
12. Bliss, p. 329; *Harper's*, June 1965.
13. *New York Times Magazine*, September 15, 1968.
14. Bliss, p. 329.
15. Ibid.
16. *Variety*, July 8, 1964.
17. J. Fred MacDonald, *Don't Touch That Dial! Radio Programming in American Life, 1920–1960* (Chicago: Nelson-Hall, 1991), p. 327.
18. Murray Forman, "Employment and Blue Pencils: NBC, Race, and Representation, 1926–55," in Michele Hilmes, ed., *NBC: America's Network* (Berkeley, CA: University of California Press, 2007), pp. 119–120.
19. The figures presented here plus some of this material is adapted from: Gilbert A. Williams, "Minority Programming and Employment," in Godfrey and Leigh, p. 260; Janette L. Dates and William Barlow, eds., *Split Image: African Americans in the Mass Media*, 2nd ed. (Washington, D.C.: Howard University Press, 1993); Marilyn D. Fife, "Regulatory Processes in Broadcasting," Ph.D. dissertation, Stanford University, 1983; Katherine McAdams, "Minorities," in Erwin K. Thomas and Brown H. Carpenter, eds., *The Handbook on Mass Media in the United States* (Westport, CT: Greenwood Press, 1994), pp. 191–206.
20. MacDonald, p. 346.
21. Ryan Ellett, *Encyclopedia of Black Radio in the United States, 1921–1955* (Jefferson, NC: McFarland, 2012), p. 6.
22. MacDonald, pp. 351, 352.
23. *Variety*, July 18, 1951, p. 1.
24. MacDonald, p. 370.
25. Erik Barnouw, *The Golden Web: A History of Broadcasting in the United States*, Vol. II —1933 to 1953 (New York: Oxford University Press, 1968), p. 289.
26. Sonja Williams, "Black Formats," in Godfrey and Leigh, p. 48. See also: Louis Cantor, *Wheeling on Beale: How WDIA-Memphis Became the Nation's First All-Black Radio Station and Created the Sound that Changed America* (New York: Pharos Press, 1992).
27. The figures here and immediately following are adapted from Fred Ferrentti, "The White Captivity of Black Radio," *Columbia Journalism Review* (Summer 1970): pp. 35–39. The first two black-owned stations referenced were WERD-AM, Atlanta, and KPRS-AM, Kansas City, MO.
28. MacDonald, p. 366.
29. http://mburchet.hypermart.net/century12.htm.

30. William Barlow, *Voice Over: The Making of Black Radio* (Philadelphia: Temple University Press, 1999), pp. 245–246.
31. "Station WNJR Brings out Realities of Community Control," *African World*, October 28, 1970, p. 10.
32. Barlow, 1999, p. 249.
33. Del Shields, interview by Sonja Williams, September 1995, New York City, for *Black Radio: Telling It Like It Was* (Washington, D.C.: Smithsonian Institution, 1996), p. 35.
34. http://mburchet.hypermart.net/century12.htm.
35. Williams, p. 260.
36. Sonja Williams, "National Association of Black Owned Broadcasters," in Godfrey and Leigh, p. 274; F. Leslie Smith, Milan Meeske, and John W. Wright II, *Electronic Media and Government: The Regulation of Wireless and Wired Mass Communication in the United States* (White Plains, NY: Longman Press, 1995); http://www.fcc.gov/.
37. http://en.wikipedia.org/wiki/National_Black_Network.
38. Figures herewith adapted from Hal Bennet [sic] and Lew Roberts, "National Black Network: Black Radio's Big Brother," *Black Enterprise*, June 1977, pp. 141–142.
39. Ibid., pp. 143–146.
40. Louis Calta, "Mutual to Begin News for Blacks," *New York Times*, April 29, 1972, p. D63; William H. Jones, "Black Group Buys Rest of Mutual Network." *Washington Post*, September 7, 1979, pp. E1–2
41. Barlow, 1999, p. 257.
42. http://www.aurn.com/affiliates/aurnhistory.php.
43. Barlow, pp. 258–259.
44. http://www.aurn.com/affiliates/aurnoverview.php.
45. http://www.sgnthelight.com/article.asp?id=205772.
46. Ibid.
47. Bob Lochte, *Christian Radio: The Growth of a Mainstream Broadcasting Force* (Jefferson, NC: McFarland, 2006), p. 157.
48. Ibid., p. 156.
49. Barlow, 1999, p. 261.
50. Ibid., p. 298.
51. Peter Laufer, *Inside Talk Radio: America's Voice or Just Hot Air?* (New York: Birch Lane Press, 1995), p. 218.
52. Christopher H. Sterling and Michael C. Keith, *Sounds of Change: A History of FM Broadcasting in America* (Chapel Hill, NC: University of North Carolina Press, 2008), p. 191.
53. Fran R. Matera, "Hispanic Listeners and Radio Markets," in Godfrey and Leigh, pp. 198–199; Jennifer Cheeseman Day, *Population Projections of the United States, by Age, Sex and Hispanic Origin: 1993–2050* (Washington, D.C.: U.S. Department of Commerce, Economics and Statistics, Bureau of the Census, 1993); *The Latin American Market Planning Report* (Miami: Strategy Research Corporation, 1996); *The U.S. Hispanic Market* (Miami: Strategy Research Corporation, 1996); *The U.S. Hispanic Population Book* (Miami: Strategy Research Corporation, 1997); Ana Veciana-Suarez, *Hispanic Media, USA* (Washington, D.C.: Media Institute, 1987).
54. Ibid.
55. Peter Fornatale and Joshua E. Mills, *Radio in the Television Age* (Woodstock, NY: Overlook Press, 1980), p. 72.
56. http://radio-locator.com/cgi-bin/finder?format=spa&sr=Y&s=R.
57. Sterling and Keith, p. 191.
58. http://stateofthemedia.org/2010/ethnic-summary-essay/asian-american/.
59. http://world.kbs.co.kr/english/about/about_program.htm; http://world.kbs.co.kr/english/about/.
60. http://streema.com/radios/Little_Saigon_Radio; www.yelp.com/biz/little-saigon-radio-westminster.
61. www.saigonradio.com; http://radiosaigonhouston.net.
62. www.tunein.com/radio/Singtao-Chinese-Radio-p355064/; http://en.wikipedia.org/wiki/Sing_Tao_Chinese_Radio; http://en.wikipedia.org/wiki/KVTO.
63. Ibid., p. 170.
64. Michael C. Keith, *Signals in the Air: Native Broadcasting in America* (Westport, CT: Praeger Publishing, 1995), p. 98.
65. Nan Rubin, *Final Report on the Native American Training Project* (Washington, D.C.: Native American Public Broadcasting Consortium, 1987), p. 104.
66. Michael C. Keith, "Native-American Radio," in Godfrey and Leigh, pp. 282–283. See also Vine Deloria, Jr., *Custer Died for Your Sins* (Norman, OK: University of Oklahoma Press, 1969).

Chapter 13

1. Bill Press, *Toxic Talk: How the Radical Right Has Poisoned America's Airwaves* (New York: Thomas Dunne Books, 2010), p. 277.
2. www.c-journal.org/journal/vol3/Iss3/rogue4/highspeed.html.
3. www.en.wikipedia.org/wiki/Micropower_radio.
4. Christopher H. Sterling and Michael C. Keith, *Sounds of Change: A History of FM Broadcasting in America* (Chapel Hill, NC: University of North Carolina Press, 2008), p. 12.
5. Jesse Walker, *Rebels on the Air: An Alternative History of Radio in America* (New York: New York University Press, 2001), pp. 174, 197–198.
6. John Rayburn, *Cat Whiskers and Talking Furniture: A Memoir of Radio and Television Broad-*

casting (Jefferson, NC: McFarland, 2008), pp. 2, 4–5.

7. Christopher H. Sterling and John M. Kittross, *Stay Tuned: A Concise History of American Broadcasting*, 2nd ed. (Belmont, CA: Wadsworth Publishing, 1990), p. 66. The public soon realized that inexpensive sets were no bargain due to their lack of quality and performance, and the average price per set climbed well above $100. (p. 80).

8. Sue Carpenter, *40 Watts from Nowhere: A Journey into Pirate Radio* (New York: Scribner, 2004), pp. 8, 9.

9. Ibid., p. 219.

10. Depending on local conditions, a few low-power stations would be granted permission to broadcast at up to 1,000 watts of signal clout. (Sterling and Keith, 2008, p. 194.)

11. Marc Fisher, *Something in the Air: Radio, Rock, and the Revolution That Shaped a Generation* (New York: Random House, 2007), p. 309.

12. Carpenter, p. 218.

13. Sterling and Keith, 2008, p. 195.

14. A summary of the pros and cons of LPFM broadcasting appeared online recently at www.en.wikipedia.org/wiki/Low-power_broadcasting.

15. http://techliberation.com/2012/11/01/lpfm-will-likely-fail-again/.

16. Ibid.

17. Ibid.

18. Ibid.

19. Robert L. Hilliard and Michael C. Keith, *Waves of Rancor: Tuning in the Radical Right* (Armonk, NY: M.E. Sharpe, 1999), p. 102.

20. Michael C. Keith, *The Radio Station: Broadcast, Satellite and Internet*, 8th ed. (Burlington, MA: Focal Press, 2010), p. 29.

21. "Activists Have Big Plans for Tiny Station," *Boston Globe*, March 9, 2000.

22. Brian Jennings, *Censorship—The Threat to Silence Talk Radio: The "New" Fairness Doctrine Exposed* (New York: Threshold Editions, 2009), p. 157.

23. Ibid., pp. 152–153.

24. Greyhound, the interstate long-distance carrier, reports: "Our buses are equipped with Wi-Fi hot spots. This technology is new, and there are spots on the trip where the service may be unavailable. We also do not advise downloading large files, as the speed will be relatively slow. The Wi-Fi service is free of charge." http://www.greyhound.com/express/FAQs.aspx.

25. http://en.wikipedia.org/wiki/Internet_radio.

26. Ibid.

27. Darryl Pomicter of Ressen Design, quoted in Keith, 2010, p. 102.

28. Keith, 2010, p. 18.

29. http://en.wikipedia.org/wiki/Digital_Audio_Broadcasting.

30. http://en.wikipedia.org/wiki/Digital_radio.

31. Sterling and Keith, 2008, p. 231.

32. http://en.wikipedia.org/wiki/Digital_radio.

33. Ibid.

34. Ibid.

35. http://www.independent.co.uk/news/media/tv-radio/so-who-thinks-dab-is-the-future-not-enough-of-us-to-make-it-so-2151512.html.

36. Jean Marbella, "Paranoid Flock of Conspiracy Hunters Turns Short-wave Radio Far to the Right," *Baltimore Sun*, July 21, 1995, p. 1D.

37. Keith, 2010, p. 26.

Chapter 14

1. Figures adapted from: Michael C. Keith, *The Radio Station: Broadcast, Satellite and Internet*, 8th ed. (Burlington, MA: Focal Press, 2010), pp. 1–2, 161; Edna Gundersen, "Friends' tips, radio still propel musical choices," *USA Today*, August 6, 2012, p. B1; http://arbitron.mediaroom.com/index.php?s=43&item=849.

2. Quoted in Keith, 2010, p. 38.

3. Gerald Nachman, *Raised on Radio: In Quest of The Lone Ranger, Jack Benny, Amos 'n' Andy, The Shadow, Mary Noble, The Great Gildersleeve, Fibber McGee and Molly, Bill Stern, Our Miss Brooks, Henry Aldrich, The Quiz Kids, Mr. First Nighter, Fred Allen, Vic and Sade, The Cisco Kid, Jack Armstrong, Arthur Godfrey, Bob and Ray, The Barbour Family, Henry Morgan, Joe Friday, and Other Lost Heroes from Radio's Heyday*. New York: Pantheon Books, 1998, pp. 497–498.

4. "Love of Radio Endures for Randy Michaels," http://radioandrecords.com//Newsroom/2005_03_14/loveof.asp.

5. *Inside Radio*, May 13, 2005, p. 2.

6. Keith, 2010, p. 330.

7. Joe Abrams, "Foreword to the Eighth Edition," Keith, 2010, p. xiv.

8. Edward Bliss, Jr., *Now the News: The Story of Broadcast Journalism* (New York: Columbia University Press, 1991), p. 173.

9. Christopher H. Sterling and Michael C. Keith, *Sounds of Change: A History of FM Broadcasting in America* (Chapel Hill, NC: University of North Carolina Press, 2008), p. 190.

10. "Consultant Pins Radio's Hopes vs. Satellite on News/Talk," *RAIN: Radio and Internet Newsletter*, http://www.kurthanson/archive/news/031405/index.asp.

11. Peter Fornatale and Joshua E. Mills, *Radio in the Television Age* (Woodstock, NY: Overlook Press, 1980), p. ix.

12. http://www.inquisitr.com/1917/television-will-fall/.

13. Michelle Goldberg, "Mood Radio," *Noise*, November 2000.

14. Marc Fisher, *Something in the Air: Radio, Rock, and the Revolution That Shaped a Generation* (New York: Random House, 2007), pp. 315–317.

15. Jesse Walker, *Rebels on the Air: An Alternative History of Radio in America* (New York: New York University Press, 2001), p. 281.

Bibliography

Books

Abrams, Joe. "Foreword to the Eighth Edition." In *The Radio Station: Broadcast, Satellite & Internet*, by Michael C. Keith. 8th ed. Burlington, MA: Focal Press, 2010.

Anderson, Brian C. *South Park Conservatives: The Revolt Against Liberal Media Bias.* Washington, D.C.: Regnery Publishing, 2005.

Aust, Charles F. "Automobile Radio." In *Historical Dictionary of American Radio*, edited by Donald G. Godfrey and Frederic A. Leigh. Westport, CT: Greenwood Press, 1998.

Avery, Robert K. "All-Talk Format." In *Historical Dictionary of American Radio*, edited by Donald G. Godfrey and Frederic A. Leigh. Westport, CT: Greenwood Press, 1998.

_____. "Talk Radio: The Private-Public Catharsis." In *Talking to Strangers: Mediated Therapeutic Communication*, edited by Gary and Sandra L. Fish. Norwood, NJ: Ablex Publishing, 1990.

Balk, Alfred. *The Rise of Radio, from Marconi through the Golden Age.* Jefferson, NC: McFarland, 2006.

Barlow, William. *Voice Over: The Making of Black Radio.* Philadelphia: Temple University Press, 1999.

Barnouw, Erik. *The Golden Web: A History of Broadcasting in the United States.* Vol. II — 1933 to 1953. New York: Oxford University Press, 1968.

_____. *The Image Empire: A History of Broadcasting in the United States.* Vol. III — from 1953. New York: Oxford University Press, 1970.

_____. *A Tower of Babel: A History of Broadcasting in the United States.* Vol. I — to 1933. New York: Oxford University Press, 1966.

Beadle, Mary E. "Edwin Armstrong." In *Historical Dictionary of American Radio*, edited by Donald G. Godfrey and Frederic A. Leigh. Westport, CT: Greenwood Press, 1998.

Bennett, ElDean. "Sports Radio Format." in *Historical Dictionary of American Radio*, edited by Donald G. Godfrey and Frederic A. Leigh. Westport, CT: Greenwood Press, 1998.

Berard, Jeanette M., and Klaudia Englund, eds. *Radio Series Scripts, 1930–2001: A Catalog of the American Radio Archives Collection.* Jefferson, NC: McFarland, 2006.

Bergreen, Laurence. *Look Now, Pay Later: The Rise of Network Broadcasting.* Garden City, NY: Doubleday, 1980.

Bliss, Edward, Jr. *Now the News: The Story of Broadcast Journalism.* New York: Columbia University Press, 1991.

Bower, Brock. "A Lament for Old-time Radio." In *A Pictorial History of Radio: The Complete Story of Radio Broadcasting in America from Crystal Sets to Transistors with All the Stars, All the Great Shows of Radio's Golden Age*, by Irving Settel. New York: Grosset & Dunlap, 1967.

Brewer, Annie M., *Talk Shows and Hosts on Radio: A Directory Including Show Titles and Formats, Biographical Information on Hosts, and Topic/Subject Index.* 3d ed. Dearborn, MI: Whitefoord Press, 1995.

Brewster, Bill, and Frank Broughton. *Last Night a DJ Saved My Life: The History of the Disc Jockey.* New York: Grove Press, 2000.

Buzenberg, William E. "Growing NPR." In *Radio: The Forgotten Medium*, edited by Edward C. Pease and Everette E. Dennis. New

Brunswick, NJ: Transaction Publishers, 1995.
Cambridge Idioms Dictionary. 2d ed. New York: Cambridge University Press, 2006.
Cantor, Louis. *Wheeling on Beale: How WDIA-Memphis Became the Nation's First All-Black Radio Station and Created the Sound that Changed America*. New York: Pharos Press, 1992.
Cantril, Hadley, and Gordon Allport. *The Psychology of Radio*. North Stratford, NH: Ayer Co., 1986; reprint of same title issued by: New York: Harper & Brothers, 1935.
Caristi, Dom. "Spectrum." In *Historical Dictionary of American Radio*, edited by Donald G. Godfrey and Frederic A. Leigh. Westport, CT: Greenwood Press, 1998.
Carpenter, Sue. *40 Watts from Nowhere: A Journey into Pirate Radio*. New York: Scribner, 2004.
Carpenter, Tom. *Wireless#: Certification Official Study Guide*. New York: McGraw-Hill, 2006.
Charnley, Mitchell V. *News by Radio*. New York: Macmillan, 1948.
Compaine, Benjamin N., and Douglas Gomery. *Who Owns the Media?: Competition and Concentration in the Mass Media Industry*. 3d ed. Mahwah, NJ: Erlbaum Publishing, 2000.
Cox, Jim. *American Radio Networks: A History*. Jefferson, NC: McFarland, 2009.
_____. *The Great Radio Audience Participation Shows: Seventeen Programs from the 1940 and 1950s*. Jefferson, NC: McFarland, 2001.
_____. *The Great Radio Soap Operas*. Jefferson, NC: McFarland, 1999.
_____. *Historical Dictionary of American Radio Soap Opera: Historical Dictionaries of Literature and the Arts*. No. 3. Lanham, MD: Scarecrow Press, 2005.
_____. *Music Radio: The Great Performers and Programs of the 1920s through Early 1960s*. Jefferson, NC: McFarland, 2005.
_____. *Musicmakers of Network Radio: 24 Entertainers, 1926–1962*. Jefferson, NC: McFarland, 2012.
_____. *Radio Journalism in America: Telling the News in the Golden Age and Beyond*. Jefferson, NC: McFarland, 2013.
_____. *Radio Speakers: Narrators, News Junkies, Sports Jockeys, Tattletales, Tipsters, Toastmasters and Coffee Klatch Couples Who Verbalized the Jargon of the Aural Ether from the 1920s to the 1980s—A Biographical Dictionary*. Jefferson, NC: McFarland, 2007.
_____. *Say Goodnight, Gracie: The Last Years of Network Radio*. Jefferson, NC: McFarland, 2002.
_____. *Sold on Radio: Advertisers in the Golden Age of Broadcasting*. Jefferson, NC: McFarland, 2007.
_____. *This Day in Network Radio: A Daily Calendar of Births, Deaths, Debuts, Cancellations and Other Events in Broadcasting History*. Jefferson, NC: McFarland, 2008.
Dates, Janette L., and William Barlow, eds. *Split Image: African Americans in the Mass Media*. 2d ed. Washington, D.C.: Howard University Press, 1993.
Day, Jennifer Cheeseman. *Population Projections of the United States, by Age, Sex and Hispanic Origin: 1993–2050*. Washington, D.C.: U.S. Department of Commerce, Economics and Statistics, Bureau of the Census, 1993.
De Forest, Lee. *Father of Radio: The Autobiography of Lee de Forest*. Chicago: Wilcox and Follett, 1950.
DeLong, Thomas A. *The Mighty Music Box: The Golden Age of Musical Radio*. Los Angeles: Amber Crest Books, 1980.
_____. *Radio Stars: An Illustrated Biographical Dictionary of 953 Performers, 1920 through 1960*. Jefferson, NC: McFarland, 1996.
Deloria, Vine, Jr. *Custer Died for Your Sins*. Norman, OK: University of Oklahoma Press, 1969.
Ditingo, Vincent M. *The Remaking of Radio (Broadcasting & Cable Series)*. Boston: Focal Press, 1995.
Doolittle, John. *Don McNeill and His Breakfast Club*. Notre Dame, IN: University of Notre Dame Press, 2001.
Dunham, Corydon B. *Fighting for the First Amendment: Stanton of CBS vs. Congress and the Nixon White House*. Westport, CT: Praeger, 1997.
Dunning, John. *On the Air: The Encyclopedia of Old-Time Radio*. New York: Oxford University Press, 1998.
_____. *Tune in Yesterday: The Ultimate Encyclopedia of Old-Time Radio, 1925–1976*. Englewood Cliffs, NJ: Prentice-Hall, 1976.
Douglas, Susan J. *Listening In: Radio and the American Imagination, from Amos 'n' Andy and Edward R. Murrow to Wolfman Jack and Howard Stern*. New York: Times Books, 1999.
Eastman, Susan Tyler, and Douglas A. Ferguson. *Broadcast/Cable Programming Strategies and Practices*. 5th ed. Belmont, CA: Wadsworth Publishing, 1996.
Eberly, Philip K. *Music in the Air: America's Changing Tastes in Popular Music, 1920–1980*. New York: Hastings House, 1982.
Edwards, Bob. *Edward R. Murrow, and the*

Birth of Broadcast Journalism. Hoboken, NJ: John Wiley & Sons, 2004.

Ellett, Ryan. *Encyclopedia of Black Radio in the United States, 1921–1955*. Jefferson, NC: McFarland, 2012.

Emery, Michael, Edwin Emery, and Nancy L. Roberts. *The Press and America: An Interpretive History of the Mass Media*. 9th ed. Boston: Allyn and Bacon, 2000.

Ennis, Philip H. *The Seventh Stream: The Emergence of Rocknroll in American Popular Music*. Hanover, NH: Wesleyan University Press, 1992.

Erickson, D. H. V. *Armstrong's Fight for FM Broadcasting: One Man vs. Big Business and Bureaucracy*. Tuscaloosa, AL: University of Alabama Press, 1973.

Fang, Irving E. *Those Radio Commentators!* Ames, IA: Iowa State University Press, 1977.

Fessenden, Helen M. *Fessenden: Builder of Tomorrows*. New York: Coward-McCann, 1940.

Finkelstein, Norman H. *Sounds in the Air: The Golden Age of Radio*. New York: Charles Scribner's Sons, 1993.

Finney, Robert G. "Format Radio." In *Historical Dictionary of American Radio*, edited by Donald G. Godfrey and Frederic A. Leigh. Westport, CT: Greenwood Press, 1998.

Fisher, Marc. *Something in the Air: Radio, Rock, and the Revolution That Shaped a Generation*. New York: Random House, 2007.

Foege, Alec. *Right of the Dial: The Rise of Clear Channel and the Fall of Commercial Radio*. New York: Faber and Faber, 2008.

Forman, Murray. "Employment and Blue Pencils: NBC, Race, and Representation, 1926–55." In *NBC: America's Network*, edited by Michele Hilmes. Berkeley: University of California Press, 2007.

Fornatale, Peter, and Joshua E. Mills. *Radio in the Television Age*. Woodstock, NY: Overlook Press, 1980.

Frierson, III, Meade, and Jim Widner. *Science Fiction on Radio: A Revised Look at 1950–1975*. Birmingham: Alabama Fictioneers and Booksmyths, 1996.

Frith, Simon. *Sound Effects: Youth, Leisure, and the Politics of Rock 'n' Roll*. New York: Pantheon Books, 1981.

Gitlin, Todd. *The Sixties*. New York: Bantam Books, 1987.

Godfrey, Donald G., and Frederic A. Leigh, eds. "Introduction: A Brief History of 'The Whispering Gallery of the Skies.'" *Historical Dictionary of American Radio*. Westport, CT: Greenwood Press, 1998.

Goldenson, Leonard H., and Marvin J. Wolf. *Beating the Odds: The Untold Story Behind the Rise of ABC: The Stars, Struggles, and Egos That Transformed Network Television By the Man Who Made It Happen*. New York: Charles Scribner's Sons, 1991.

Graham, Michael. *That's No Angry Mob, That's My Mom: Team Obama's Assault on Tea-Party, Talk-Radio Americans*. Washington, D.C.: Regnery Publishing, 2010.

Grams, Martin, Jr. *Radio Drama: American Programs, 1932–1962*. Jefferson, NC: McFarland, 2000.

Gumpert, Gary, and Sandra L. Fish, eds. *Talking to Strangers: Mediated Therapeutic Communication*. Norwood, NJ: Ablex Publishing, 1990.

Halberstam, David. *The Fifties*. New York: Villard Books, 1993.

———. *The Powers That Be: Within the Kingdom of the Media: How Luce's Time, Paley's CBS, the Grahams' Washington Post and the Chandlers' Los Angeles Times Became Rich and Powerful and Changed Forever the Shape of American Politics and Society*. New York: Alfred A. Knopf, 1979.

Hardenbergh, Margot. "Easy-Listening Format." In *Historical Dictionary of American Radio*, edited by Donald G. Godfrey and Frederic A. Leigh. Westport, CT: Greenwood Press, 1998.

Harlow, Alvin F. *Old Wires and New Waves: The History of the Telegraph, Telephone and Wireless*. New York: Appleton-Century, 1936.

Hart, Dennis. *Monitor (Take 2): The Revised, Expanded Inside Story of Network Radio's Greatest Program*. New York: iUniverse, Inc., 2003.

Harvey, Rita Morley. *Those Wonderful, Terrible Years: George Heller and the American Federation of Television and Radio Artists*. Carbondale, IL: Southern Illinois University Press, 1996.

Havig, Alan. *Fred Allen's Radio Comedy*. Philadelphia: Temple University Press, 1990.

Havinghurst, Craig. *Air Castle of the South: WSM and the Making of Music City*. Urbana, IL: University of Illinois Press, 2007.

Hickerson, Jay. *The 3rd Revised Ultimate History of Network Radio Programming and Guide to All Circulating Shows*. Hamden, CT: Presto Print II, 2005.

Higby, Mary Jane. *Tune in Tomorrow: Or How I Found The Right to Happiness with Our Gal Sunday, Stella Dallas, John's Other Wife, and Other Sudsy Radio Serials*. New York: Cowles Education Corp., 1968.

Hilliard, Robert L. *Radio Broadcasting: An In-*

troduction to the Sound Medium. 3d ed. New York: Longman, 1985.

Hilliard, Robert L., and Michael C. Keith. Waves of Rancor: Tuning in the Radical Right. Armonk, NY: M. E. Sharpe, 1999.

Hilmes, Michele. "NBC and the Network Idea: Defining the 'American System.'" In NBC: America's Network, edited by Michele Hilmes. Berkeley: University of California Press, 2007.

Horwitz, Robert Britt. The Irony of Regulatory Reform: The Deregulation of American Telecommunications. New York: Oxford University Press, 1989.

Jaker, Bill, Frank Sulek, and Peter Kanze. The Airwaves of New York: Illustrated Histories of 156 AM Stations in the Metropolitan Area, 1921–1996. Jefferson, NC: McFarland, 1998.

Jay, Michael. The History of Communications: Advances That Have Changed the World. New York: Thomson Learning, 1995.

Jennings, Brian. Censorship—The Threat to Silence Talk Radio: The "New" Fairness Doctrine Exposed. New York: Threshold Editions, 2009.

Jourdain, Robert. Music, the Brain, and Ecstasy: How Music Captures Our Imagination. New York: William Morrow, 1997.

Keith, Michael C. "Native-American Radio." In Historical Dictionary of American Radio, edited by Donald G. Godfrey and Frederic A. Leigh. Westport, CT: Greenwood Press, 1998.

_____. Radio Programming: Consultancy and Formatics. Boston: Focal Press, 1987.

_____. The Radio Station: Broadcast, Satellite & Internet. 8th ed. Burlington, MA: Focal Press, 2010.

_____. Signals in the Air: Native Broadcasting in America. Westport, CT: Praeger, 1995.

_____. "Underground, Commercial Radio." In Historical Dictionary of American Radio, edited by Donald G. Godfrey and Frederic A. Leigh. Westport, CT: Greenwood Press, 1998.

_____. Voices in the Purple Haze: Underground Radio in the Sixties. Westport, CT: Praeger, 1997.

Kuralt, Charles. Charles Kuralt's America. New York: G. P. Putnam's Sons, 1995.

Ladd, Jim. Radio Waves: Life and Revolution on the FM Dial. New York: St. Martin's Press, 1991.

Lanza, Joseph. Elevator Music: A Surreal History of Muzak, Easy-Listening and Other Moodsong. New York: St. Martin's Press, 1994.

The Latin American Market Planning Report. Miami: Strategy Research Corp., 1996.

Laufer, Peter. Inside Talk Radio: America's Voice or Just Hot Air? New York: Birch Lane Press, 1995.

Lessing, Lawrence. Man of High Fidelity: Edwin Howard Armstrong. Philadelphia: J.B. Lippincott, 1956.

Lewis, Tom. Empire of the Air: The Men Who Made Radio. New York: HarperCollins, 1991.

Lichty, Lawrence W. "WHA." In Historical Dictionary of American Radio, edited by Donald G. Godfrey and Frederic A. Leigh. Westport, CT: Greenwood Press, 1998.

Lieberman, Philip A. Radio's Morning Show Personalities: Early Hour Broadcasters and Deejays from the 1920s to the 1990s. Jefferson, NC: McFarland, 2009.

Lochte, Bob. Christian Radio: The Growth of a Mainstream Broadcasting Force. Jefferson, NC: McFarland, 2006.

Looker, Thomas. The Sound and the Story: NPR and the Art of Radio. Boston: Houghton Mifflin, 1995.

Lucas, Fred V. The Right Frequency: The Talk Radio Giants Who Shook Up the Political and Media Establishment. Palisades, NY: History Publishing, 2012.

Lyons, Eugene. David Sarnoff: A Biography—The Extraordinary Story of an Immigrant Boy Who Became an Industrial Giant. New York: Harper & Row, 1966.

MacDonald, J. Fred. Don't Touch That Dial!: Radio Programming in American Life from 1920 to 1960. Chicago: Nelson-Hall, 1991.

Maltin, Leonard. The Great American Broadcast: A Celebration of Radio's Golden Age. New York: Penguin Putnam, 1997.

Martin, Henri-Jean. The History and Power of Writing. Chicago: University of Chicago Press, 1994.

Matera, Fran R. "Ethnic Issues, Ethnic Music." In Historical Dictionary of American Radio, edited by Donald G. Godfrey and Frederic A. Leigh. Westport, CT: Greenwood Press, 1998.

_____. "Hispanic Listeners and Radio Markets." In Historical Dictionary of American Radio, edited by Donald G. Godfrey and Frederic A. Leigh. Westport, CT: Greenwood Press, 1998.

McAdams, Katherine. "Minorities." In The Handbook on Mass Media in the United States, edited by Erwin K. Thomas and Brown H. Carpenter. Westport, CT: Greenwood Press, 1994.

McChesney, Robert W. Rich Media, Poor Democracy: Communication Politics in Dubious Times. Urbana, IL: University of Illinois Press, 1999.

McMillian, John. *Smoking Typewriters: The Sixties Underground Press and the Rise of Alternative Media in America.* New York: Oxford University Press, 2011.

Messere, Fritz. "Bell Laboratories." In *Historical Dictionary of American Radio*, edited by Donald G. Godfrey and Frederic A. Leigh. Westport, CT: Greenwood Press, 1998.

Miller, James. *Flowers in the Dustbin: The Rise of Rock and Roll, 1947–1977.* Lady Lake, FL: Fireside Publications, 2000.

Mims, Bruce. "Beautiful Music." In *Historical Dictionary of American Radio*, edited by Donald G. Godfrey and Frederic A. Leigh. Westport, CT: Greenwood Press, 1998.

Miquel, Pierre. *Historie de la radio et de la télévision.* Paris: Perrin, 1984.

Mish, Frederick C., ed. *Merriam-Webster's Collegiate Dictionary: The Words You Need Today.* 10th ed. Springfield, MA: Merriam-Webster, Inc., 2001.

Morris, Dick, and Eileen McGann. *Fleeced: How Barack Obama, Media Mockery of Terrorist Threats, Liberals Who Want to Kill Talk Radio, the Do-Nothing Congress, Companies That Help Iran, and Washington Lobbyists for Foreign Governments Are Scamming Us ... And What to Do About It.* New York: HarperCollins, 2008.

Mudd, Roger. *The Place to Be: Washington, CBS, and the Glory Days of Television News.* New York: Public Affairs, 2008.

Nachman, Gerald. *Raised on Radio: In Quest of The Lone Ranger, Jack Benny, Amos 'n' Andy, The Shadow, Mary Noble, The Great Gildersleeve, Fibber McGee and Molly, Bill Stern, Our Miss Brooks, Henry Aldrich, The Quiz Kids, Mr. First Nighter, Fred Allen, Vic and Sade, The Cisco Kid, Jack Armstrong, Arthur Godfrey, Bob and Ray, The Barbour Family, Henry Morgan, Joe Friday, and Other Lost Heroes from Radio's Heyday.* New York: Pantheon Books, 1998.

Oermann, Robert K. *Behind the Grand Ole Opry Curtain: Tales of Romance and Tragedy.* New York: Center Street, 2008.

O'Malley, Kathleen. "Freeform Radio." In *Historical Dictionary of American Radio*, edited by Donald G. Godfrey and Frederic A. Leigh. Westport, CT: Greenwood Press, 1998.

Osgood, Charles. *See You on the Radio.* New York: G. P. Putnam's Sons, 1999.

Pahigian, Josh, and Kevin O'Donnell. *The Ultimate Baseball Road Trip: A Fan's Guide to Major League Stadiums*, 2nd ed. Guilford, CT: Lyons Press, 2012.

Paper, Lewis J. *Empire: William S. Paley and the Making of CBS.* New York: St. Martin's Press, 1987.

Passman, Arnold. *The Deejays.* New York: Macmillan, 1971.

Paulson, Roger C. *Archives of the Airwaves*, Vol. 1. Boalsburg, PA: BearManor Media, 2005.

Pease, Edward C., and Everette E. Dennis, eds. *Radio: The Forgotten Medium.* New Brunswick, NJ: Transaction Publishers, 1995.

Persico, Joseph E. *Edward R. Murrow: An American Original.* New York: Dell Publishing, 1988.

Piasek, Joseph R. "Zoo Format." In *Historical Dictionary of American Radio*, edited by Donald G. Godfrey and Frederic A. Leigh. Westport, CT: Greenwood Press, 1998.

Post, Steve. *Playing in the FM Band: A Personal Account of Free Radio.* New York: Viking Press, 1974.

Press, Bill. *Toxic Talk: How the Radical Right Has Poisoned America's Airwaves.* New York: Thomas Dunne Books, 2010.

Ramsburg, Jim. *Network Radio Ratings, 1932–1953: A History of Prime Time Programs through the Ratings of Nielsen, Crossley and Hooper.* Jefferson, NC: McFarland, 2012.

Rather, Dan, with Digby Diehl. *Rather Outspoken: My Life in the News.* New York: Grand Central, 2012.

Rayburn, John. *Cat Whiskers and Talking Furniture: A Memoir of Radio and Television Broadcasting.* Jefferson, NC: McFarland, 2008.

Reich, Charles. *The Greening of America.* New York: Random House, 1970.

Rhoads, B. Eric. *Blast from the Past: A Pictorial History of Radio's First 75 Years.* West Palm Beach, FL: Streamline Publishing, 1996.

Rosenberg, Bernard, and David Manning White, eds. *Mass Culture: The Popular Arts in America.* New York: Free Press, 1957.

Rudel, Anthony, *Hello, Everybody!: The Dawn of American Radio.* Orlando, FL: Harcourt, Inc., 2008.

Runyon, Steven C. "Transistors." In *Historical Dictionary of American Radio*, edited by Donald G. Godfrey and Frederic A. Leigh. Westport, CT: Greenwood Press, 1998.

Runyon, Steven C., and David Spiceland. "Multiplexing." In *Historical Dictionary of American Radio*, edited by Donald G. Godfrey and Frederic A. Leigh. Westport, CT: Greenwood Press, 1998.

Rush, J. R. "Good-Music Format." In *Historical Dictionary of American Radio*, edited by Donald G. Godfrey and Frederic A. Leigh. Westport, CT: Greenwood Press, 1998.

Russell, Bruce W. "Translators." In *Historical Dictionary of American Radio*, edited by Donald G. Godfrey and Frederic A. Leigh. Westport, CT: Greenwood Press, 1998.

Settel, Irving. *A Pictorial History of Radio: The Complete Story of Radio Broadcasting in America from Crystal Sets to Transistors with All the Stars, All the Great Shows of Radio's Golden Age*. New York: Grosset & Dunlap, 1967.

Siepmann, Charles A. *Radio, Television and Society*. New York: Oxford University Press, 1950.

_____. *Radio's Second Chance*. Boston: Little, Brown and Co., 1947.

Silverman, Francine. *Talk Radio Wants You: An Intimate Guide to 700 Shows and How to Get Invited*. Jefferson, NC: McFarland, 2009.

Singer, Arthur J. *Arthur Godfrey: The Adventures of an American Broadcaster*. Jefferson, NC: McFarland, 2000.

Sklar, Rick. *Rocking America, An Insider's Story: How the All-Hit Radio Stations Took Over*. New York: St. Martin's Press, 1984.

Smith, F. Leslie. *Perspectives on Radio and Television: An Introduction to Broadcasting in the United States*. New York: Harper & Row, 1979.

Smith, F. Leslie, Milan Meeske, and John W. Wright II. *Electronic Media and Government: The Regulation of Wireless and Wired Mass Communication in the United States*. White Plains, NY: Longman Press, 1995.

Smith, Sally Bedell. *In All His Glory: The Life of William S. Paley, the Legendary Tycoon and His Brilliant Circle*. New York: Simon & Schuster, 1990.

Stavitsky, Alan G. "National Public Radio (NPR)." In *Historical Dictionary of American Radio*, edited by Donald G. Godfrey and Frederic A. Leigh. Westport, CT: Greenwood Press, 1998.

Sterling, Christopher H., and Michael C. Keith. *Sounds of Change: A History of FM Broadcasting in America*. Chapel Hill, NC: University of North Carolina Press, 2008.

Sterling, Christopher H., and John M. Kittross. *Stay Tuned: A Concise History of American Broadcasting*, 2nd ed. Belmont, CA: Wadsworth Publishing, 1990.

Terrace, Vincent. *Radio Programs, 1924–1984: A Catalog of Over 1800 Shows*. Jefferson, NC: McFarland, 1999.

Thomas, Erwin K., and Brown H. Carpenter, eds. *The Handbook on Mass Media in the United States*. Westport, CT: Greenwood Press, 1994.

The U.S. Hispanic Market. Miami: Strategy Research Corp., 1996.

The U.S. Hispanic Population Book. Miami: Strategy Research Corp., 1997.

Veciana-Suarez, Ana. *Hispanic Media, USA*. Washington, DC: Media Institute, 1987.

Walker, Jesse. *Rebels on the Air: An Alternative History of Radio in America*. New York: New York University Press, 2001.

Walker, Leo. *The Wonderful Era of the Great Dance Bands*. New York: Da Capo Press, 1990.

Weaver, Sylvester L., and Thomas M. Coffey. *The Best Seat in the House: The Golden Years of Radio and Television*. New York: Alfred A. Knopf, 1994.

Weinstein, Art. *Market Segmentation: Using Demographics, Psychographics and Other Niche Marketing Techniques to Predict Customer Behavior*. Rev. ed. Chicago: Richard D. Irwin, 1994.

Williams, Gilbert A. "Minority Programming and Employment." In *Historical Dictionary of American Radio*, edited by Donald G. Godfrey and Frederic A. Leigh. Westport, CT: Greenwood Press, 1998.

_____. "Racial Issues." In *Historical Dictionary of American Radio*, edited by Donald G. Godfrey and Frederic A. Leigh. Westport, CT: Greenwood Press, 1998.

Williams, Sonja. "Black Formats." In *Historical Dictionary of American Radio*, edited by Donald G. Godfrey and Frederic A. Leigh. Westport, CT: Greenwood Press, 1998.

_____. *Black Radio: Telling It Like It Was*. Washington, DC: Smithsonian Institution, 1996.

_____. "National Association of Black Owned Broadcasters." In *Historical Dictionary of American Radio*, edited by Donald G. Godfrey and Frederic A. Leigh. Westport, CT: Greenwood Press, 1998.

Periodicals

"Activists Have Big Plans for Tiny Station." *Boston Globe*, March 9, 2000.

Adorno, Theodor, "On Popular Music." *SPSS* (September 1941).

Advertising Age, May 29, 1978.

Avery, Robert K., Donald G. Ellis, and Thomas W. Glover. "Patterns of Communication on Talk Radio." *Journal of Broadcasting* (Winter 1978).

"Bach vs. Rock." *Newsweek*, March 19, 1973.

Baida, Peter. "A Legendary Chairman." *American Heritage Magazine* (July–August 1987).

Bennet, Hal, and Lew Roberts. "National Black Network: Black Radio's Big Brother." *Black Enterprise* (June 1977).

Berger, Joseph. "Himan Brown, Developer of Radio Dramas, Dies at 99." *New York Times*, June 6, 2010.

Broadcasting, varied issues, 1954, 1955.

Broadcasting-Telecasting, January 10, 1955.

Brown, Emma. "Himan Brown, Producer of Radio Dramas Including 'Dick Tracy,' Dies at Age 99." *Washington Post*, June 8, 2010.

Calta, Louis. "Mutual to Begin News for Blacks." *New York Times*, April 29, 1972.

Casey, Kevin. "The Coming Rise of FM Talk." *Talkers*, November 2005.

Cox, Jim. "Whatever Happened to NBC Radio? The One-Minute Chain Ups the Ante." *SPERDVAC* (The Society to Preserve and Encourage Radio Drama, Variety and Comedy) *Radiogram* (September 2012).

"Cox Says It's Nowhere but Up for FM Medium." *Broadcasting*, September 13, 1976.

"Dr. Frank Conrad, Radio Pioneer, Dies." *New York Times*, December 12, 1941.

Dunaway, David K. "Save Our Stations." *New York Times*, May 23, 1992.

Facts and Trends (Winter 2013).

Ferrentti, Fred. "The White Captivity of Black Radio." *Columbia Journalism Review* (Summer 1970).

Fisher, Marc. "Radio's Latest 'Innovation': 30 Commercials in a Row, 'We'll Be Right Back' Is Starting to Mean 'See You in 15 Minutes or So.'" *Los Angeles Times*, July 19, 2004.

———. "Voice of the Cabal: Bob Fass and the Slow Fade of Countercultural Radio." *New Yorker*, December 4, 2006.

"The FM Boom." *Newsweek*, May 22, 1972.

"FM Gets a Shake-up." *Newsweek*, November 28, 1966.

"FM: It Has Arrived." *Broadcasting*, March 29, 1965.

"FM Rockers Are Taming Their Free Formats." *Broadcasting*, November 25, 1974.

"Forty Years of Station Transactions." *Broadcasting/Cable Yearbook 1995*.

Garvin, Glenn. "Talk Radio Industry Fears Fairness Law Could Silence Them; Some Talk Radio Fans Fear Democrats Are Ready to Reimpose the Fairness Doctrine, Which Mandates Ideological Balance." *Miami Herald*, December 21, 2008.

Goldberg, Michelle. "Mood Radio." *Noise* (November 2000).

Gundersen, Edna. "Friends' Tips, Radio Still Propel Musical Choices." *USA Today*, August 6, 2012.

Harper's, June 1965.

Harrison, Michael, "Talk Media on the Front Lines of Reality." *Talkers*, January 2005.

"Has the FCC Gone Too Far?" *Business Week*, August 5, 1985.

Hershey, Robert D., Jr., "F. C. C. Votes Down Fairness Doctrine in a 4–0 Decision." *New York Times*, August 5, 1987.

Holzmann, Gerald J., and Bjorn Pehrson. "The First Data Networks." *Scientific American* (January 1994).

Hornblower, Margot. "Radio Free America." *Time*, April 20, 1998.

"Jacor Sets Its Sights on Syndication." *Broadcasting and Cable*, June 9, 1997.

Jones, William H. "Black Group Buys Rest of Mutual Network." *Washington Post*, September 7, 1979.

Lull, J. T., L.M. Johnson, and C.F. Sweeney. "Audiences for Contemporary Radio Formats." *Journal of Broadcasting* (Fall 1978).

Madigan, Tim. "Are Media Talkers Stirring Up a Hornet's Nest?" McClatchy Newspapers syndicate, October 18, 2009.

Marbella, Jean. "Paranoid Flock of Conspiracy Hunters Turns Short-Wave Radio Far to the Right." *Baltimore Sun*, July 21, 1995.

Meadow, Donella H. "Talk Shows Don't Make Democracy." *Houston Chronicle*, February 21, 1993.

"Monitor." *Broadcasting*, May 28, 1979.

New York Times Magazine, September 15, 1968.

Newsweek, December 4, 1967.

Polgreen, Lydia. "The Death of Local Radio." *Washington Monthly*, April 1999.

"The Rites of Passage Are All Over for FM Radio; It's Out on Its Own." *Broadcasting*, September 24, 1973.

Rust, Michael. "Tuning to America." *Washington Times*, July 17, 1995.

Sabo, Walter. "My FM Talk Diary." *Talkers*, April 2007.

Safire, William. "Broadcast Lobby Triumphs." *New York Times*, July 23, 1997.

Shapiro, Eben. "A Wave of Buyouts Has Radio Industry Beaming with Success." *Wall Street Journal*, September 18, 1997.

Simmon, Jim. "Echo Chamber." *Houston Press*, June 29–July 5, 1995.

Smith, R. Franklin. "Oldest Station in the Nation?" *Journal of Broadcasting* (Winter 1959–1960).

"A Social Critique of Radio Music." *Kenyon Review 7* (Spring 1945).

"Station WNJR Brings Out Realities of Community Control." *African World*, October 28, 1970.

Stavitsky, Alan G. "The Changing Conception

of Localism in U.S. Public Radio." *Journal of Broadcasting & Electronic Media* (Winter 1994).

Stravitsky, Alan G., and Timothy W. Gleason. "Alternative Things Considered: A Comparison of National Public Radio and Pacifica Radio News Coverage." *Journalism Quarterly* (Winter 1994).

Taylor, Tom. "National Public Radio Says Listening Is Up." *Inside Radio*, March 29, 2005.

"2011 Talkers Heavy Hundred." *Talkers*, February 25, 2011.

"The Upbeat Tempo of FM 1974." *Broadcasting*, October 7, 1974.

Variety, July 21, 1941; July 28, 1948; July 18, 1951; July 8, 1964.

Miscellanea

Edmerson, Estelle. "A Descriptive Study of the American Negro in United States Professional Radio, 1922–1953." Master's thesis at the University of California at Los Angeles, 1954.

FCC video, *NBCUniversal*, 1987.

Fife, Marilyn D. "Regulatory Processes in Broadcasting." Ph.D. dissertation, Stanford University, 1983.

I've Got a Secret, originally appearing on CBS-TV on September 27, 1965; repeated on Game Show Network, May 22, 2008.

Mills, Joshua. "Development and Refinement of All-News Programming at Radio Stations and Networks." Paper presented at the annual meeting of the Association for Education in Journalism, Boston, MA, August 1980.

"Radio Deregulation: Has It Served Listeners and Musicians?" Report released by Future of Music Coalition, November 18, 2002.

Rubin, Nan. *Final Report on the Native American Training Project*. Washington, D.C.: Native American Public Broadcasting Consortium, 1987.

Russo, Alex. *No Particular Place to Go*. Unpublished manuscript. Middletown, CT: Wesleyan University, 1996.

Seminar: "Network News in the Age of Cable." Center for the Study of Popular Television, Syracuse (NY) University, 1994.

U.S. Census Bureau figures for 2010, reported from a U.S. 2010 Project conducted by Brown University, Providence, RI.

Websites

In addition to scores of Internet addresses included in the Notes section, hundreds of additional sites were consulted for this volume. The Web is a priceless resource for comprehensive information for a project such as this. Much of this material would have been inaccessible to researchers prior to the technological revolution that created the Internet.

Index

Act to Regulate Radio Communication (1912) 48
advertising agencies 14–15, 18, 19
advertising's dominance of air time 174–176
affiliates vs. networks 36, 37–43
Allen, Fred 12–13
AM (Amplitude Modulation) 2, 5, 54, 87–104, 117
American Indian/Alaska Native demographics 178–179, 193–194
American Public Media (APM) 138–140
American Urban Radio Networks (AURN) 188–189
Armstrong, Edwin Howard 11, 89–95, 97, 98, 102
Asian-American demographics 178–179, 192
automated programming 74, 77, 102, 159–168, 171
Automatic Frequency Control 96
automotive radio 53–54, 67, 98, 196, 209, 212

beautiful music/easy-listening format 109–110, 160
Berliner, Emile 61–62
big band remotes 146–147
black demographics in the U.S.A. 178–179
black station ownership 183–188, 189–190
Block, Martin 68
block programming 107
broadcast journalism's birth 46

cafeteria-style programming 81
The CBS Radio Adventure Theater 157
The CBS Radio Mystery Theater 154–156
Clear Channel Communications 165–167, 172, 209, 212
clock-hour formatting 113–114
Communications Act of 1934 169
Conrad, Frank 11, 63–64, 66

Continental Radio Network 93, 94
counterculture behavior 95, 115, 201

De Forest, Lee 1, 45–46, 49, 63, 64, 89
demise of radio 35, 36
Dickens, Charles 9
Digital Audio Broadcasting (DAB) 203–205
Dimension daytime features (CBS) 80
Dimension X/X Minus One 148–153
DJs 5, 44, 45, 46, 56, 57–75, 85, 89, 95, 98, 101, 102, 113, 128, 160, 162, 163, 166–167, 184, 185, 197, 214
drama makes a comeback 148–157

Emphasis daytime features (NBC) 80
Equal Time Rule 116
ethnic diversity in broadcasting 178–194

Fairness Doctrine 116–117, 119, 120, 121, 124, 172
Federal Communications Commission 91, 93, 98, 99, 103, 116, 117, 119, 121, 124, 129, 163, 167, 169–170, 171, 172, 177, 180, 189, 196, 197, 198, 199, 201, 204, 206, 209
Federal Radio Commission 66, 93, 170, 175
Fessenden, Reginald 11, 44, 45, 46, 49, 62–63, 64, 66, 90
fidelity in sound 88–89
Flair Reports daytime features (ABC) 80
FM (Frequency Modulation) 2, 5, 54, 59, 87–104, 117, 185, 205
Freed, Alan "Moondog" 70–71
Freeform radio 59–60, 101, 196

Godfrey, Arthur 143–144
Golden Age defined 4, 5, 9, 10
Gramophone Company 61

ham (amateur) radio operators 48–49, 106, 197, 206

253

HD radio 104, 203, 204
Herrold, Charles David "Doc" 64, 65, 66
Hertz, Heinrich 11, 46
high fidelity apparatus 98, 99
Hispanic demographics in the U.S.A. 178–179, 190–191
Hispanic radio broadcasting 191

internet radio 77, 104, 176, 192, 201–203, 208, 210, 212, 213, 214
internet usage 173, 199, 211

KDKA, Pittsburgh 48, 63, 180
Kuralt, Charles 6, 7

The Light black gospel network 189
Limbaugh, Rush 119–120, 121, 122, 123, 124, 126, 127, 128, 165
Linkletter, Art 142–143
Local Community Radio Act of 2010 198–199
low power FM (LPFM) stations 103, 104, 196, 198–201

magazines of the aural air 54–56, 109
Marconi, Guglielmo 11, 46–47, 49, 89
Maxwell, James 11
MBS's cessation 84
McLaughlin, Edward F. 118, 120
McLendon, Gordon 72–73, 133
McNeill, Don 143
micro radio 196, 214
microwave relay linkage 97, 170
minorities in broadcasting 178–194
multiple affiliates 82–83
multiplex broadcasting 97
Murrow, Edward R. 31, 78, 177
Music Till Dawn 85
The Mutual Radio Theater 157
narrowcasting 98, 102, 105–115, 196, 209

National Black Network (NBN) 186–187
National Public Radio (NPR) 119, 122, 123, 138, 140–141, 208, 213
Native American demographics 178–179, 193–194
NBC retrenchment 83–84
news formatted stations 133
News of the World (NBC) 144–146
news on the hour 79–80

Obama, Barack 120–121
overnight radio broadcasting 85, 135–136

Paley, William S. 18–19, 31, 42–43, 106, 134
Payola 68–72, 73

pirate radio 104, 196–198, 201
podcasting 213
portability factor 51–56, 67, 108
power shifts to local stations 85–86
progressive FM radio format 95

racial implications 69, 70, 71–72, 178–194
radio audience demographics 207–208
Radio Broadcasting Preservation Act of 2000 198
Radio City 13
radio consultant 101
radio set obsolescence 195
relay broadcasting 94
rhythm and blues (R&B) music 69, 70–72, 183, 184

Sarnoff, David 26, 32, 92, 93, 94, 95
satellite radio 54, 77, 104, 106, 112, 125, 132, 159–168, 170, 171, 172, 176, 193, 194, 204, 208, 210, 211, 214
segmenting the audience 108
Sheridan Broadcasting Network (SBN) 186, 187, 188
shock talk 126, 167
shortwave radio 206
Sirius XM 167–168
sportscasting 136–138
Stanton, Frank 31, 32, 33, 106, 107
stereo broadcasting 97, 98, 99, 159
Storz, Todd 72, 73
streaming radio 201–203
Stubblefield, Nathan 11
syndicated programming 102, 123, 129, 140, 148, 152–153, 174

talk radio 116–141, 208, 209
telecommunications Act of 1996 172, 189
television: financing 32–33, 35, 40, 92; overtakes radio 34–35; predicted 25–28; threatens radio 28–31
Telsa, Nikola 11
terrestrial radio 104
Thomas, Lowell 78–79
top 40 stations 72–73, 108, 160, 185
transistor radio 50–51, 53, 56, 67, 96, 98, 108, 196

underground radio 114–115

Weaver, Sylvester (Pat) 19, 33, 56

Yankee Network 94

The Zero Hour 154

www.ingramcontent.com/pod-product-compliance
Lightning Source LLC
Chambersburg PA
CBHW051215300426
44116CB00006B/587